Bray Marina   Windsor Marina

What makes our Thames marinas so special?

- Superb locations on the River Thames
- Direct access to the river, giving you some great boating opportunities right on your doorstep
- Easily reached by road, so you spend more time on your boat and less time getting to it
- Delightfully tranquil settings
- Sheltered waters providing a safe haven
- Extensive facilities including water and electricity on pontoons, fuel, toilets and showers, CCTV, hard standing, engineering and repair services
- Professional, friendly staff on hand to provide assistance
- Club Outlook membership giving a range of benefits such as visitor berthing at other MDL marinas*

For further information, see pages 41 and 60 in this publication or contact the relevant marina manager quoting ref. RTB.

Bray Marina Tel: 01628 623654 Fax: 01628 773485
Email: bray@mdlmarinas.co.uk

Windsor Marina Tel: 01753 853911 Fax: 01753 868195
Email: windsor@mdlmarinas.co.uk

Penton Hook Marina Tel: 01932 568681 Fax: 01932 567423
Email: pentonhook@mdlmarinas.co.uk

*For annual berth holders, subject to Club Outlook terms and conditions.

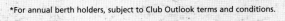

Environment Agency

creating a better place

River Thames
On the freshwater Thames, you are never far from an environment that offers you the space to relax. We manage this famous river and work hard to ensure that it can be enjoyed by the millions who use it every year. For ideas about what to do and where to go, see **www.visitthames.co.uk** and download free publications.

We look after the River Thames for boaters
We use the money from boat registrations to maintain the channels, improve locks, moorings and sanitary stations, help protect the environment and provide angling platforms, camping and picnic areas and other leisure facilities.

Call **0118 953 5650** to register your boat and receive a free copy of 'River Thames a user's guide' including lock opening times, river safety, moorings and boating facilities. You can download an application form at **www.visitthames.co.uk/forms**

Call **0845 988 1188** or see **www.visitthames.co.uk** for details of our winter maintenance programme, lock closures and river conditions.

To find out more about our work nationally, visit
www.environment-agency.gov.uk

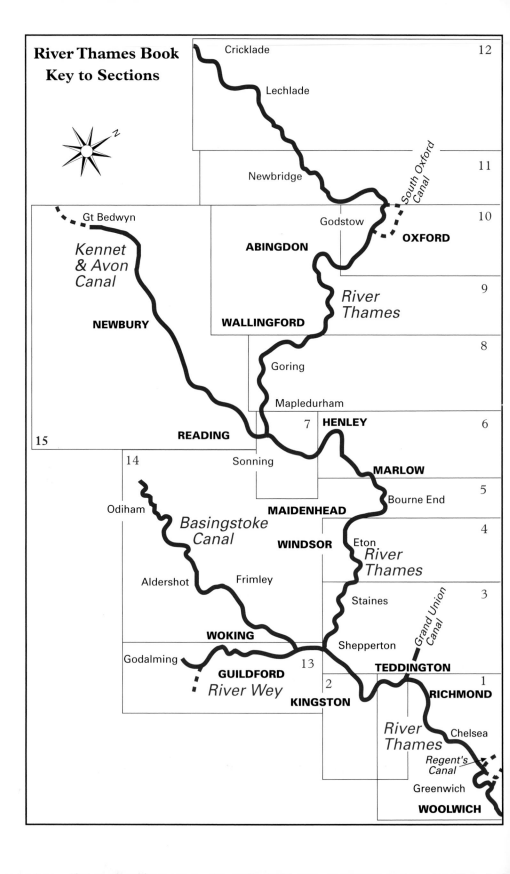

**River Thames Book
Key to Sections**

12 Cricklade
Lechlade

11 Newbridge

South Oxford Canal

10 Godstow OXFORD

Gt Bedwyn

Kennet
& Avon
Canal

ABINGDON

River
Thames

9

NEWBURY

WALLINGFORD

8

Goring

Mapledurham

7 HENLEY 6

READING

15

14

Sonning

MARLOW

5 Bourne End

Odiham

Basingstoke
Canal

MAIDENHEAD

WINDSOR

Eton
River
Thames

4

Aldershot

Frimley

3 Staines

Grand Union Canal

WOKING

Godalming

GUILDFORD
River Wey

13

Shepperton

TEDDINGTON

2

KINGSTON

1 RICHMOND

River
Thames

Chelsea

Regent's
Canal

Greenwich

WOOLWICH

The
River Thames
Book

A guide to the Thames from the Barrier
to Cricklade with the River Wey,
Basingstoke Canal and
Kennet & Avon Canal to Great Bedwyn

CHRIS COVE-SMITH

Imray Laurie Norie & Wilson

Published by
Imray Laurie Norie & Wilson Ltd
Wych House The Broadway, St Ives
Cambridgeshire PE27 5BT England
☎ 01480 462114 *Fax* 01480 496109
Email ilnw@imray.com
www.imray.com
2006

1st edition 1996
2nd edition 1998
3rd edition 2002
4th edition 2006

© Chris Cove-Smith 2006
Chris Cove-Smith asserts the moral right to be
identified as the author of this work.

British Library Cataloguing in Publication Data

A catalogue record for this book is available from
the British Library

ISBN 0 85288 892 9

CAUTION
Whilst every care has been taken to ensure
accuracy, neither the publishers nor the author
will hold themselves responsible for errors,
omissions or alterations in this publication. They
will at all times be grateful to receive information
which tends to the improvement of the work.

Printed in Singapore.

KEY TO SYMBOLS USED ON THE PLANS

A	Anglers' supplies
B	Boatbuilding/sales
A	Chandlery
♈	Repairs
⊤	Boatyard
F	Passenger trip/Ferry services
🚂	Towing Service
H	Hire
DH	Daily hire
PH	Private hire
WH	Weekly hire
⚙	Marine engineer
⚓	Crane
L	Landling stage/pier
⬅	Launching slip
🛟	Mooring
↻	Winding point
⚑	Yacht/sailing club
⚏	Caravan site
⅄	Camping
P	Car park
☏	Telephone
P⛽	Petrol
D⛽	Diesel fuel
⬤	Bottled gas
⚱	Water
wc	Toilet
ⓝ	Sanitary station/pump-out
⛢	Chemical toilet disposal
🗑	Refuse disposal
✉	Post office
✕	Restaurant
⚡	Electric launch recharging
⊠	Waypoints(Tideway)
▲	Drawdocks(Tideway)
△	Public landing points(Tideway)
⏛	Pub
☕	Teashop

Scales

Unless shown otherwise the maps are at the
following scales
Maps 1 to 31   1:25000 or 2½″ to 1 mile
Map 32   1:50000 or 1¼″ to 1 mile
River Wey   1:28000 or 2¼″ to 1 mile
Kennet & Avon and Basingstoke Canals
                1:63360 or 1″ to 1 mile

Contents

Acknowledgements *viii*
The River Thames Society *viii*

River Thames
1. The Tideway to Teddington from the Thames Barrier *2*
2. Richmond to Hampton *14*
   Thames Hire Cruiser Association *28*
3. Sunbury to Staines *30*
4. Runnymede to Maidenhead *47*
5. Maidenhead to Marlow *68*
   Passenger Boat Association *79*
6. Temple to Henley *80*
   River Users' Groups *92*
7. Reading – Wargrave to Mapledurham, including
   the River Kennet from its mouth to High Bridge *93*
8. Whitchurch to Wallingford *111*
9. Wallingford and Abingdon *121*
10. Oxford – Radley to Binsey *131*
11. Binsey to Newbridge *142*
12. Newbridge to Lechlade and Cricklade *151*
    Rowing and canoeing on the Thames *164*
    Environment Agency – Thames region *168*

Connecting waterways
13. River Wey and Godalming Navigations *175*
14. The Basingstoke Canal – Byfleet to Greywell Tunnel *187*
15. The Kennet & Avon Canal – Reading to Great Bedwyn *199*

Appendix *211*
Useful addresses *211*
Thames Boating Trades Association *211*
Association of Thames Yacht Clubs *212*
Index *213*

Acknowledgements

This fourth edition of The River Thames Book appears with the able assistance of all those people who took part in the gestation of the first three. The list has now grown so long for constant republication but i feel obliged to mention those who have joined the 'team' for the first time as well as some of the stalwarts, and I must not forget the staff at the publishers who have put up with my piecemeal corrections supplied from so may different sources. Much information also came from his travels along the river by Owen bryant who organised the advertising.

Remaining regulars were Peter Allen and his brother Nick from the THCA; Anne Chase and Wendy Copeland of Guildford Boat House on the River Wey, Brian Butcher, George Fielder, Ralph Tompkin, Simon Shepherdson, Jim Chapman, Keith Reeve and John Conroy of the Environment Agency Thames Region; David Millet with the help of Dieter Jebens again on the Basingstoke Canal; and John Crevald and Paul Wagstaffe of the TBTA. Newcomers to the fray included Peter Crawford for his advice on the Kennet and Avon Canal section; Alan Rance, now Secretary of the Passenger Boat Association; and Colin Rennie who chairs the Association of Thames Yacht Clubs. Nor should I forget my constant correspondents, David Wood and Ron Bingham of the Inland Waterways Association.

As a spate of two seasons as a District Relief Lock-keeper, which meant that I was able to meet many of the boating fraternity who offered sound advice and carping criticism on a ratio of about 10 : 1, I was pensioned off but invited to skipper 90ft of passenger launch now approaching her 82nd birthday. This had the advantage of allowing me to see much more of the river than hitherto, so I am indebted to Geoff Minister and my fellow skippers and our crews at Salter's Steamers for pointing out more than a few little changes which have crept in since the last edition. If you see me this season in my bigger boat than yours give us a wave!

Chris Cove-Smith
Maidenhead
August 2005

The River Thames Society

The River Thames Society is
a registered charity.

Administrator
Mrs Alix Horne, Side House,
Middle Assendon, Henley-on-Thames,
Oxon RG9 6AP
☎ 01491 571476

Membership Secretary
Susan Day, 23 Brierley Place, Tilehurst,
Reading, RG31 6FX
☎ 0118 961 5444

The River Thames Society was formed in 1962 by a group of people who were concerned about the flotsam and jetsam which littered the tideway. There is no doubt that by focusing attention on the state of the tideway waters and campaigning for its clearance that the river is cleaner today.
The Society became known as 'The Voice of the River', with the following aims:

- To protect the natural beauty of the river, adjacent lands and buildings of historical and architectural interest and to promote nature conservation;

- To support and contribute to the efforts of other organisations;

- To preserve and extend amenities and to encourage the use of the river for all purposes.

Over the past 43 years the Society has influenced and supported a wide variety of projects from the construction of the Thames Barrier to saving Borough Marsh from industrial development for gravel extraction, and was a founder of the Thames Traditional Boat Rally.

The Society represents all those who live, work or come to enjoy the river throughout its length from its source to the sea; members include boat owners, walkers, fishermen as well as those who care about the river's fascinating history, its traditions, architecture and wildlife. The Society is supported by, among other organisations, the Environment Agency and the Countryside Agency.

Run by a central council, much of the Society's work and social activities are organised by six branches. New members automatically become a member of their nearest branch unless they specify otherwise. Each branch has a role to play in helping to run the Society's River Warden Scheme, monitoring riparian planning applications, educational and promotional projects and social programmes including summer events and winter talks.

Planning Supervisory Scheme

The Society's planning officers monitor planning applications affecting the River Thames. The Society is not a preservation body as such, but seeks to ensure a balance between pressures for development and the needs of the environment. The officers work closely with local planning authorities who seek and respect the Society viewpoint.

River Warden Scheme

The Society's volunteer River Wardens monitor the condition of the Thames, its banks, towing paths and installations. They record the condition of the paths, banks vegetation, fences, countryside 'furniture', safety equipment and water pollution. The wardens work closely with the Environment Agency, local authorities and other agencies to safeguard the river and its environment from the head of navigation at Lechlade down to the Thames Barrier.

Promoting Education

The Society plays an active role in education, working closely with teachers, youth workers and other agencies, including the award winning Thames Explorer Trust. The aim is to cultivate an understanding among young people of the river's value and its traditions. The Society has purchased a Thames Watermen's Cutter, not only to compete in the annual Great River Race, but also to encourage youngsters to take up the skill and pleasures of fixed seat rowing.

RTS Trophy and Annual Award

Nominations are invited each year for corporate projects or schemes which enhance the river or its waterfront. The nominations are judged by a panel representing the Port of London Authority, the Countryside Agency, English Heritage, the Civic Trust and the Environment Agency, Thames Landscape Strategy, Thames 21. An individual cup is also awarded annually to the person deemed to have made the most outstanding contribution to the Thames and the society.

RTS Annual Conference

Each year, the Society organises a conference with different themes reflecting the needs of the tideway, non-tidal river or the river as a whole. The conference is not only attended by members of the Society but local government officers and a wide range of voluntary organisations with an interest in the river.

Thames Guardian

The journal of the River Thames Society, supported by Waterview, the riverside property agency and yacht brokerage, and the Thames Boating Trades Association. Published quarterly, the magazine contains news of river events and people, a diary of forthcoming events, feature articles covering boating, the history of the river, wildlife, leisure pursuits, profiles of river users, lock keepers and others. It also includes river walks, pubs to visit and restaurant reviews.

The Society has its own web site www.riverthamessociety.org.uk

1. The Tideway to Teddington from the Thames Barrier

Distance

27.17 miles (Thames Barrier to Teddington Locks)

For maximum dimensions of craft see panel on page 7.

Navigation authority

The Port of London Authority
Baker's Hall, 7 Harp Lane, London, EC3R 6LB ☎ 020 7743 7900
Fax 020 7743 7998
Chief harbour master
PLA, London River House, Royal Pier Road, Gravesend, Kent, DA12 2BG ☎ 01474 562231
Harbour master (upper)
PLA, Baker's Hall, 7 Harp Lane, London EC3R 6LB 020 7743 7912
Thames Navigation Service duty officer (Woolwich)
PLA, Thames Barrier Navigation Centre (TBNC), Unit 28, 34 Bowater Road, London SE18 5TF ☎ 020 8855 0315
Radio VHF Ch 14[1], 16, 22 London VTS
1. Primary working frequency

River Police

Marine Support Unit, Metropolitan Police
98 Wapping High Street, London, E1 9NE ☎ 020 7275 4421
VHF radio channels Duty launches listen and work on Ch 14.

HM Coastguard (MCA)

Maritime Rescue Sub Centre (MRSC)
Thames Barrier Navigation Centre, Unit 28, 34 Bowater Road, London SE18 5TF
London Coastguard ☎ 020 8312 7380
Emergency communications on VHF Channels 16, 67 or ☎ 999 *London Coastguard*

RNLI

Lifeboats are stationed at Teddington Lock (D class operating above Richmond Lock), Chiswick, Tower Pier and Gravesend (all E class lifeboats). The last three are permanently manned. Rescue co-ordination is conducted by *London Coastguard*.
RNLI Chiswick Boat House
☎ 020 8995 5534
RNLI Tower Pier Boat House
☎ 020 7680 9629

Licensing and registration

Environment Agency (Thames Region)
All launches proceeding above Teddington *must* be registered with the Environment Agency. Details of licensing and registration, for which a charge is payable, may be obtained from the Craft Registration Office. Environment Agency Thames Region, Kings Meadow House, PO Box 214, Reading RG1 8HQ ☎ 0118 953 5650. Details may also be obtained from any lock office. Short period visitor registration is available at entry point locks adjoining connecting waterways.

British Waterways Canals and Rivers
Pleasure Craft Licences are necessary for those craft whose owners wish to take them into the Grand Union Canal system in London. Craft owners wishing only to use the River Lee Navigation via Bow Locks or the Limehouse Cut may pay a reduced, River Registration, charge. Full details are obtainable from the Customer Services Manager, British Waterways, Willow Grange, Church Road, Watford WD1 3QA ☎ 01923 201120, or the Regional Manager's office at British Waterways London, 1 Sheldon Square, Paddington Central, London, W2 6TT ☎ 020 7985 7200. Licences may also be obtained at Brentford and Limehouse during normal business hours 0800–1700, Monday to Friday. British Waterways also control the entrance to the London Docklands area via the West India Dock Entrance. Details of this are given on pages 12 and 13.

Upper Tideway (Port of London)
No licences are required for private pleasure vessels but craft must be navigated in accordance with the *PLA Byelaws* and the current *General Directions for Navigation in the Port of London*, issued by the Port of London Authority and obtainable from the PLA Website www.portoflondon.co.uk or by post from the chief or upper harbour masters at the addresses above.

London River Services Ltd control a number of piers used by tripping and other private charter cruise operators. Details can be obtained from ☎ 020 7222 5600. River Cruise Information from the London Tourist Board is available on ☎ 020 7373 9988.

Lock-working details at points of exit from The Tideway

See charts on pages 4 and 5

Note In calculating opening and closing times of the British Waterways locks leading from the Thames Tideway, bear in mind that HWLB – high water at London Bridge – is always quoted as at Greenwich Mean Time, irrespective of the time of year. British Waterways duty hours are quoted in local time – GMT in winter and BST in summer. Calculations during the period of British Summer Time will therefore have to be made, adding one hour to times of high water at London Bridge in working out your transit arrangements. British Waterways summer duty hours apply from 1 April to 31 October but also include an early Easter and late autumn half-term holiday when outside this period.

A Thames Locks (No. 101), the first tidal locks in Brentford Creek are manned every day including bank holidays, from 2 hours before high water at Brentford until 2 hours after, but only within the period 0800 to 1800 hours in summer (0800–1630 in winter). Times of HW at Brentford are rounded to the nearest quarter of an hour for calculating opening and closing times and are taken as one hour after high water at London Bridge. Passage outside the above manning times is available on a pre-booked basis, but only during the extended period from 0500 hours to 2200 hours (see below). No passage is allowed overnight between 2200 and 0500. A table of the precise daily opening times of these locks and Bow Lock is published every six months and is available free of charge from the chief lock-keeper at Brentford ☎ 020 8568 2779, the lock office at Limehouse or from the London Canals Manager's office at Paddington ☎ 020 7985 7200.

B Brentford Gauging Locks (No. 100), the second pair of locks in from the river are part-tidal and available all day from 0730 to 1830 hours (0730–1700 in winter), and between 0500 and 2200 if pre-booked with Thames Locks. Boaters may work the Gauging Locks themselves but require the BW 'Watermate' key for the control panels. Beware of restricted headroom under Brentford Bridge (between the two pairs of locks) around high water.

C Limehouse Lock (No. 13) is manned daily at the same times as Thames Locks at

Brentford and is worked at most states of the tide within these hours except at low water (springs). As a general guide, when the depth at London Bridge is quoted as less than 3´3˝ (1.0m), craft may have to wait for a short period until the flood gives sufficient depth at the outer cill to allow safe passage. Always advise the lock-keeper of an ETA in either direction on ☎ 020 7308 9930 or on VHF Channel 80 *Limehouse Lock*. Passages required outside the above manning hours are possible between 0500 and 2200 hours if pre-booked as below.

D Bow Lock (Tidal) at the head of Bow Creek leads into the Lee Navigation. Recently reconstructed to maintain a constant level upstream, this lock can be worked from three and a half hours before high water (at London Bridge) until 2 hours after, but only if pre-booked and within the period 0500–2200 hours on ☎ 020 7308 9930. Twenty-four hours notice is required.

E Teddington Locks (EA) are worked daily on a 24-hour rostered-duty basis. However, if you plan to arrive at an unsociable hour, it might be courteous to advise the lock-keeper in advance ☎ 020 8940 8723.

F Richmond Lock (PLA) is operated at all times when the sluices are in position under the three central spans of the footbridge. Hold off close to the lock which is against the Surrey bank and await the lock-keeper's instructions. The sluices are raised for clear passage through the footbridge from 2 hours before to 2 hours after high water except during the winter 'draw-off' period when passage under the sluices is available at all times, subject to the depth in the channel. For advice on timing, ☎ 020 8940 0634.

G The tidal locks at **Brentford Dock Marina, Chiswick Quay, Chelsea Yacht Harbour, St Katharine Haven, South Dock Marina** and **West India Dock Entrance** for Poplar Dock Marina and Blackwall Basin are only workable for specified periods around high water. For details please telephone their respective harbourmasters.

Pre-booking of BW lockings between the Tideway and the London canals system and entry to London Docklands (West India Dock)

Boat owners requiring passage via Limehouse and Thames Locks out of the normal 'core' hours advertised, or Bow Lock which is not normally manned, must pre-book their passages, provided these will take place between the hours of 0500 and 2200 and will also be during an 'open' period when the tide

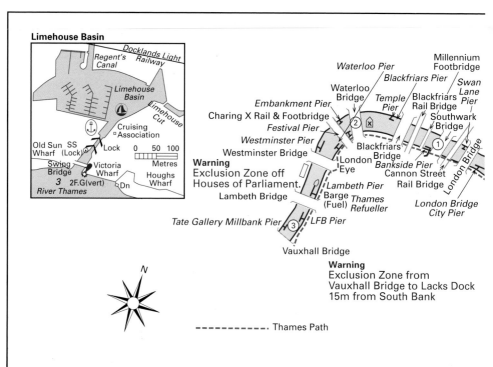

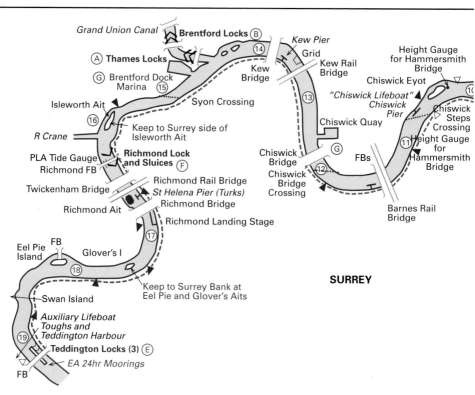

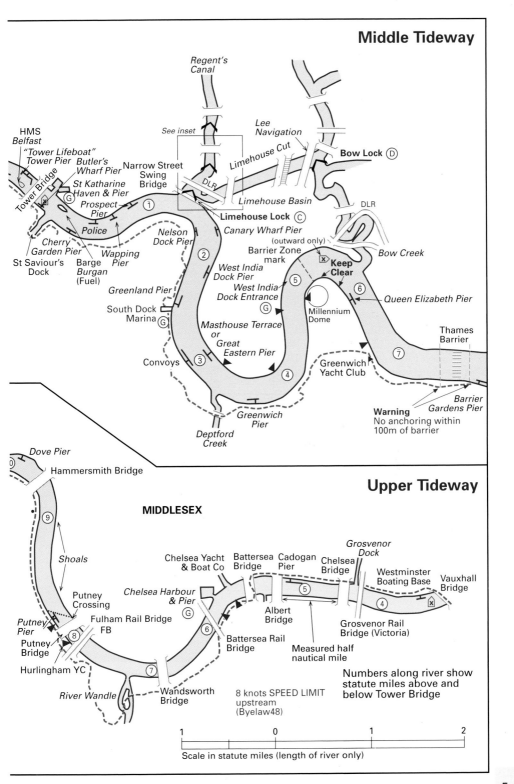

Middle Tideway

Regent's Canal

Lee Navigation

Limehouse Cut

Bow Lock Ⓓ

See inset

HMS *Belfast*
"Tower Lifeboat"
Tower Pier   Butler's
Wharf Pier   Narrow Street
Swing Bridge

St Katharine
Haven & Pier
Prospect Pier

Police

Nelson Dock Pier

Limehouse Basin

Limehouse Lock Ⓒ

Canary Wharf Pier
(outward only)

DLR

Bow Creek

Barrier Zone mark

Ⓧ **Keep Clear**

Cherry Garden Pier
Wapping Pier
St Saviour's Dock   Barge Burgan (Fuel)

West India Dock Pier

West India Dock Entrance Ⓖ

⑤

⑥

Queen Elizabeth Pier

Greenland Pier

Millennium Dome

South Dock Marina Ⓖ

Masthouse Terrace
or
Great Eastern Pier

Thames Barrier

Convoys   ③

④

Greenwich Yacht Club

⑦

Barrier Gardens Pier

Warning
No anchoring within 100m of barrier

Greenwich Pier

Deptford Creek

Dove Pier

Hammersmith Bridge

Upper Tideway

MIDDLESEX

⑨

Shoals

Grosvenor Dock

Chelsea Yacht & Boat Co   Battersea Bridge   Cadogan Pier   Chelsea Bridge

Westminster Boating Base

Vauxhall Bridge

Chelsea Harbour & Pier Ⓖ

Putney Crossing

Fulham Rail Bridge
FB

⑥

Albert Bridge

⑤

Ⓧ

④

Putney Pier
⑧

Putney Bridge

Battersea Rail Bridge

Grosvenor Rail Bridge (Victoria)

Hurlingham YC   ⑦

Measured half nautical mile

River Wandle
Wandsworth Bridge

8 knots SPEED LIMIT
upstream
(Byelaw48)

Numbers along river show statute miles above and below Tower Bridge

1   0   1   2
Scale in statute miles (length of river only)

5

allows, as calculated from the notes on page 3. Bookings should be made no later than noon on the previous day on the following telephone numbers, connected to message recording equipment:

Thames Locks (Brentford)
☎ 020 8568 2779
Limehouse Lock (Regent's)
☎ 020 7308 9930
West India Dock Entrance
(See below)
Bow Lock (River Lee)
☎ 020 7308 9930

No charge is made for this service. Outside normal hours, please use the answerphones on the above numbers, stating clearly:

- your name and phone number for confirmation by the lock office
- the date and time you wish to transit
- details of your passage and transit direction (onto or out of the Thames).

If you cannot make contact on the above numbers, you can leave a message on the London Waterway office number ☎ 020 7985 7200. In an emergency, dial 100 and ask for *Freephone Canals* and the London Duty Officer to be paged. If using a mobile telephone, you may dial 01384 215785. Operational emergencies should be reported to ☎ 0800 47 999 47 stating the name of the waterway, the exact location and the nature of the problem.

Note The initial letters of each paragraph refer to the circled letters on the Tideway charts.

LANDING, MOORING AND FUEL POINTS IN THE TIDEWAY

TELEPHONE NUMBERS

The Boat Shop ☎ 020 8977 9978. Moorings, pump-out, diesel, *Calor Gas*, water, chandlery
Swan Island Harbour ☎ 020 8892 2861. Moorings, diesel, *Calor Gas*, water
W Hammerton & Co ☎ 020 8892 9620. Visitors' and permanent moorings
Richmond Landing Stage[3] ☎ 020 7930 2062. Landing by arrangement
Brentford Dock Marina[1] ☎ 020 8568 0287. All services
Kew Pier[3] ☎ 020 7930 2062. Landing by arrangement
Kew Marina ☎ 020 8940 8364. Water, permanent moorings
Chiswick Yacht & Boat Club
☎ 020 8994 6397. Slipway, landing stage, diesel, *Calor Gas*, refuse disposal, water

Chiswick Quay Marina[1] ☎ 020 8994 8743. Visitors' moorings, slipway, water, refuse disposal
Chiswick Pier[3] ☎ 020 8742 0057. Moorings, pump-out, water
Dove Marina (London Tideway Harbour Company) ☎ 020 8748 2715. Moorings, water
Hurlingham Yacht Club ☎ 020 8788 5547. Landing stage, refuse disposal, permanent moorings
Chelsea Harbour Marina ☎ 020 7225 9100. Visitors' moorings, landing stage, water
Chelsea Yacht and Boat Company Ltd
☎ 020 7352 1427. Moorings
Cadogan Pier[2] ☎ 020 7351 0927 (24 hours notice please). Pontoon, pump-out, water
Barge *Thames Refueller* (Westminster Petroleum) Mobile 07831 110681. Diesel, lubricating oils, dry goods
Festival Pier[2] ☎ 020 7918 4757. Pump-out
St Katharine Haven[1] and Pier
☎ 020 7481 8350 or 020 7264 5312. Moorings, diesel and all usual services in yacht haven
Barge *Freddy* (Westminster Petroleum)
☎ 020 7481 1774. Mooring only
Barge *Burgan* (Westminster Petroleum) Mobile 07747 756125. Diesel, *Calor Gas*, dry goods (operates between Erith and Raven's Ait).
Limehouse Marina ☎ 020 7308 9930. Moorings
South Dock Marina[1] ☎ 020 7252 2244. Visitors' moorings and all usual services
West India Dock Entrance ☎ 020 7987 7260 (Details on page 12)
Poplar Dock Marina ☎ 020 7517 5550
Greenwich Yacht Club ☎ 020 8858 7339. Swinging moorings

It is advisable to plan your passage carefully with the aid of these notes and to arrange landing and mooring in advance by telephone.

1. Only accessible around High Water
2. Riverbus or passenger-boat piers – avoid on weekdays 0700-2000 and summer weekends from 1000 to 1800.
3. Piers available outside trip-boat hours only by arrangement.

Tideway navigation notes

Designed mainly for those who wish to transit the Tideway between the upper, freshwater Thames and the canal system of the Grand Union and the Lee Navigations, this section will also be of help to those who merely wish to potter onto the Tideway and off again by the same route. For convenience, our itinerary starts at the Thames Barrier which is also the commencement of the Thames Path, shown on all Thames maps in this book.

Maximum dimensions of craft (according to tide)

Headroom	12´6˝ (3.80m) Hammersmith Bridge at HWS
Length	Unlimited – unless using Richmond Lock (Lock 250´0˝ 75.2m)
Beam	60´0˝ (18.30m) – unless using Richmond Lock (Lock 26´8˝ 8.1m)
Draught	2´3˝ (0.69m) Chiswick Bridge at LWS
	13´6˝ (4.10m) Richmond Rail Bridge at HWS

Although this section is mainly intended for masters of vessels of less than 40 metres, or of gross tonnage of less than 50 tons, masters of passenger and all other vessels may find the notes useful although they should also acquire a current edition of the *PLA General Directions for Navigation in the Port of London* before entering the Tideway. Details of the Thames Barrier transit arrangements are contained in *PLA Permanent Notices to Mariners*, published from time to time, available at all PLA offices and posted at Teddington, Richmond, Brentford, Bow and Limehouse Locks. Remember also that no vessel may carry more than 12 passengers without a Maritime and Coastguard Agency Certificate under the Merchant Shipping Acts. These statutes also apply on the upper, freshwater Thames controlled by the Environment Agency and also any other inland waterways.

The five transits described are as follows.

1. The navigator coming from the freshwater Thames or the Grand Union Canal (main line), who has to traverse the upper Tideway between Teddington and Brentford in either direction.
2. The navigator coming from the Thames, Grand Union, Regent's Canal or Lee Navigation who wishes to complete the 'London Ring', which can make a rewarding, leisurely week's cruise, although the 'Ring' itself can be completed in 2 or 3 days.
3. The navigator coming from the freshwater Thames above Teddington, or from the Lee Navigation who would like to explore the other's home waters.
4. The navigator who has entered the Thames Estuary from the sea and seeks guidance into the upper Thames or the London canal system; or the navigator outward bound from these areas.
5. Entry to the West India Dock and for moorings in Poplar Dock Marina.

More detailed instructions on navigation for the Tideway to Sea Reach No. 1 Buoy are contained in the publisher's Chart C2 River Thames, Teddington to Southend.

Tides

All tidal calculations are based on the periods after or before the times of high water (HW) at any given point. These times are quoted as 'constants' after or before HW at London Bridge (Tower Pier). The following constants relating to average spring tides will be found useful. At neap tides HW may occur earlier by 2–10 minutes depending on the distance above London Bridge. Later times will apply similarly below London Bridge except at Bow Lock.

Times of HW at given points between Teddington and Bow based on HW London Bridge

Teddington	0115	After HW
Richmond Lock and Weir	0101	After HW
Brentford (Thames Locks)	0055	After HW
Limehouse (Tidal Lock)	0005	Before HW
West India Dock Entrance	0016	Before HW
Thames Barrier	0020	Before HW
Bow Lock (Lee Navigation)	Same time as HW London Bridge	

You can therefore work out the times of HW at any given point by referring to the times of HW for London Bridge (Tower Pier), published daily in *The Times*, or booklets from chandlers' or anglers' shops. A full list of the tides for each year is contained in nautical almanacs from chandlers or in the *PLA Tide Tables*, obtainable from www.portoflondon.co.uk or by post from the Authority. Most good libraries have current nautical almanacs.

In the upper reaches of the Tideway the tide floods (comes in) for from 3½–5 hours and ebbs (goes out) for from 7–8 hours. It therefore rises faster than it falls but the speed of the current is evened out between rise and fall due to flow from the freshwater Thames over Teddington Weir. The tidal stream runs at up to 4 knots and, while it is possible to 'punch' the tide, the passage will take longer and consume more fuel than if one follows the suggestions in these notes. It is not recommended for conventional canal craft to attempt to punch the tide.

The top section of the Tideway above Richmond Lock and sluices is open to the tide for only 2 hours either side of HW at Richmond. Richmond footbridge crosses the lock, the river and a set of boat rollers on the Middlesex side. The three centre spans of this bridge are navigable only when two fixed orange lights are shown in the crown of each arch as on the bridge diagram on page 170, at such times as the patent sluices are raised to allow passage. At all other times when the sluices are lowered into the river, red discs by day or red lights at night in an inverted triangle formation are displayed at each arch and passage is only available through the lock, which is manned on a 24-hour basis. At low tide only shallow draughted boats should attempt to navigate between Richmond and Putney.

Safety first

Before venturing onto the Thames Tideway you must check that you have the right equipment for the trip. Normal equipment for a canal or the upper river may be insufficient for the more hazardous waters you are about to navigate. No boat owner should proceed on tidal waters, especially in an estuary of the nature of the Thames, without the following basic equipment: an anchor; anchor warp; tow rope; tool kit; sharp knife; two lifebuoys and a heaving line. The signal shapes as designated in the *PLA Byelaws* and specified navigation lights should also be carried. Every passenger and each member of the crew should wear a life-jacket, properly inflated or with an auto-inflator in working order.

The weight of your anchor and thickness of chain or nylon anchor warp are related to the displacement tonnage of your vessel, and the length of such warp relates to the depth of water in which you will be navigating and its strength of current. Note that the depth at

around HW springs off Limehouse can be as much as 15m. The recommended length for a chain warp should not be less than three times this figure (and nylon should be five times or more) in order to bed the anchor properly. In strong stream conditions, as when the wind is with the tide or the freshwater Thames is in flood, a chain warp may have to be paid out for up to five times the depth and a nylon warp considerably more.

VHF radio

With the increasing use of VHF radio on the Tideway it is also a distinct advantage to carry on board, and be able to operate, a VHF transmitting and receiving radio set. The set must be able to operate on the International Maritime wavebands and must be of a DTI-approved type. A licence is required for the ship and the radio operator must also possess a VHF *Certificate of Competence*. Details can be obtained from the Royal Yachting Association – full details are given in its publication *G22*.

PLA regulations now require that a VHF transmit/receive set must be carried aboard any craft exceeding 66′6″ (20m) in length, although this does not apply to inland waterways craft in transit above Brentford – these craft, however, must report their transit, before leaving and on arrival, to the duty officer at TBNC ☎ 020 8855 0315.

Emergencies

Engine failure or propeller jammed Remember that if your boat is helpless in a fast-running stream it will be carried quickly along out of control. The set of the tide may well carry it with considerable force to the pier of a bridge or towards moored craft or other obstacles. For this reason you must anchor at once. Make sure that the inboard end of your anchor warp or chain is fastened to its cleat or post at all times while on the Tideway. Don't waste time looking for the cause of the failure while drifting – you can do that as soon as you have anchored, at your comparative leisure.

Man overboard As soon as anyone falls overboard, holler 'Man Overboard!' and swing the stern away from them. Have the lifebuoy thrown towards their position in the water (not attached to a line from the boat) and then manoeuvre alongside the casualty, taking care to face the tide and keep to leeward of them otherwise you will probably run them down. A bowline is the best knot to use at the end of a line to assist a casualty to clamber back on board since it makes a loop which will not slip. It can also be useful if they are unable to help themselves and have to be hauled aboard.

Always insist that life-jackets are worn by your crew and passengers. Set an example – wear one yourself.

Navigation

Commercial traffic Keep clear of all commercial traffic, as many of the larger working vessels have difficulty in manoeuvring and stopping. Keep a careful lookout ahead and astern and take obvious and appropriate action in plenty of time.

Bridges Always use the correct navigation arches of bridges, indicated by the fixed orange lights at the crown of the relevant arch. Diagrams showing which arches should be so lit are given at the back of the *PLA Byelaws* booklet (Appendix IV). Remember that red discs or lights in triangular formation at the crown mean that an arch is closed and no attempt should be made to navigate through it. A bundle of straw (still!) means that headroom is restricted. Steer clear of abutments and note that in the lower reaches of the river a standing wave can occur at some states of the tide, particularly at Lambeth and London Bridges. Small craft approaching a bridge or a bend in the river when going against the tide should give way to vessels approaching with the tide.

The visibility on the bend in the vicinity of Kew Bridge is particularly restricted and passenger boats regularly use Kew Pier. Power-driven vessels are reminded to sound one prolonged blast when approaching the bridge from either direction and when leaving Kew Pier, in accordance with the International Regulations and PLA Byelaws.

Between and including Tower Bridge and Putney Bridge, certain arches of each bridge will display by day and by night, on occasions, a high-intensity isophase white light on the upstream and downstream sides of the bridge. This light will be displayed only when it is activated by an electronic keying device operated by the master of a large vessel or by the Thames Navigation Service (PLA) at Woolwich. The light signifies that one or more large vessels are navigating or about to navigate through the arch displaying the signal. If the white light shows a quick flashing sequence this indicates that two or more large vessels are about to navigate. When the signal light is displayed small craft must keep clear of the arch displaying the signal light and its approaches (*PLA General Directions 2003, (as amended)*).

Note An 'isophase' light is one which is lit and unlit for equal periods. 'Quick flashing' means a series of flashes of light with longer dark periods in between, the flashes occurring between 50 and 60 times a minute.

Passage Keep to the starboard side of the channel. This does not mean, however, that you should approach the right-hand bank too closely. First, you may run aground if you do; second, craft going against the flow of the tide may wish to keep nearer one or other bank where the flow is weaker. Above Wandsworth and in Deptford and Bow Creeks there is a speed limit through the water of 8 knots/9mph (*PLA Byelaw 48*). Note that a large number of rowing clubs above Putney, practise at all states of the tide. Their craft are extremely susceptible to the wash of passing craft and many are noted for their less than perfect record in keeping a good lookout, particularly where they have no coxswain aboard. Slow down and give them a wide berth until you are sure they have seen you. For rowing boats and approved escorting vessels when travelling against the tide special rules have been devised when navigating between Syon Reach and Putney Bridge, in that they may cross to the Surrey shore between Isleworth Ferry Gate and the *Ship Inn* below Chiswick Bridge and to the Middlesex shore as far as Chiswick Pier where they may return to the Surrey shore as far as Putney Pier, irrespective of the normal requirement to keep to the starboard side of the fairway. The crossing points which apply in both directions are shown on the chart on pages 4 and 5.

Wash A tug running free (without a tow of lighters) and some passenger craft will generate considerable wash. Turn into the wash to take the swell squarely on your bow. During the working day passenger craft ply between Westminster, Waterloo Millennium, Embankment, Tower and Greenwich Piers and those sited intermediately and additionally, in summer, between Westminster, Kew, Richmond, Hampton Court and the Thames Barrier at Woolwich. Several commuter services also run in the central section, increasing traffic between 0630 and 0930 and 1630 and 1930 Monday to Friday. Keep a sharp lookout for any highspeed craft of the Riverbus type which may call at these and the intermediate piers shown on the charts on pages 4 and 5. They move faster than the traditional tripping boats and create a larger wash.

Driftwood hazard If you do encounter driftwood, plastic bags, old ropes, etc, you are earnestly requested *not* to re-consign them to the river but to hold them (if possible) for deposit in one of the PLA Driftwood Collection Lighters, sited at Brentford, Putney, Wandsworth, Waterloo, Cherry Garden and Greenwich. Note that these barges are not to be used for domestic refuse, only flotsam.

The Port of London Authority

The Port of London Authority (PLA) is the navigation authority for the Thames from just below Teddington Locks to its seaward limit beyond Southend. There is no requirement for a boat licence or registration for private craft but there are certain directions and byelaws which affect all craft. Details are obtainable from the chief harbour master at PLA, London River House, Royal Pier Road, Gravesend, Kent DA12 2BG ☎ 01474 562200. Other details and information can be obtained from the PLA website, www.portoflondon.co.uk or from PLA Public Relations at Bakers' Hall, 7 Harp Lane, London EC3R 6LB ☎ 020 7743 7900.

The London 'Ring'

The 'Ring' is the affectionate, and probably accurate, name for the complete waterway circuit which is routed via the Thames between Brentford and Bow Creek and via the Lee, Regent's Canal, Paddington Arm and Grand Union Canal between Bow Creek or Limehouse (via the Limehouse Cut or the Regent's Canal to Old Ford) and Brentford. The whole of the 'off-Thames' section of this interesting cruising ground and is controlled by British Waterways whose addresses are given under 'Licensing and registration' on page 2. Note that, for safety, the 'Ring' should only be attempted in a clockwise direction – that is, Limehouse or Bow to Brentford – although it is now easier to cruise anti-clockwise with new arrangements for lock-working at Limehouse.

Transit details – upstream

Brentford to Teddington The times of these transits are dictated by the opening times at Brentford and Thames Locks which are governed by the state of the tide and the working hours. Teddington Locks do not close, so that no prior warning to the lock-keepers is required there. The best time to leave Brentford is as soon as Thames Locks can be worked (about 2 hours before HW at Brentford). You will thus obtain the benefit of the last 2 hours of the flood tide up through Richmond and will not need to make use of Richmond Lock. Use of Richmond lock is now free of charge to leisure craft. A lock-keeper is on duty 24 hours a day.

Distance 5 miles

Average transit time 60 to 70 minutes at a speed of 4mph through the water

Limehouse or Bow to Teddington

Teddington Locks are worked daily on a 24-hour rostered-duty basis. Due to the operation of the sluices at Richmond Footbridge, on certain transits you may be required to use Richmond Lock ☎ 020 8940 0634. Use of Richmond lock is now free of charge to leisure craft. A lock-keeper is on duty 24 hours a day.

When leaving Limehouse try to use an early morning or evening tide to avoid meeting the tripping boats on the river. If you are piloting a narrow boat or cruiser designed for canal working, to maintain usual canal-boat engine speeds leave as soon as the lock is open after low water. To leave later can be hazardous as you will encounter a strong current on the flood in the river.

If you are negotiating the larger 'Ring' by including the circuit of Bow Creek and Greenwich, by leaving the canal system at Bow Lock, you will have to punch the tide down Bow Creek before entering the river to pick up the upstream flood.

From Limehouse

Distance 21 miles (preferred transit)
Average transit times at 4mph through the water:
leaving Limehouse 5 hours before HW, 3½ to 4 hours
[1]leaving Limehouse 3 hours before HW, 5 hours
[1]leaving Limehouse at or after HW, not recommended.

From Bow

Distance 27 miles (slow craft are advised not to use this route)
Average transit times at 4mph through the water:
leaving Bow Lock 4 hours before HW, 5 to 6 hours
[1]leaving Bow Lock 2 hours before HW, 6 to 7 hours
[1]leaving Bow Lock any later is not recommended unless your craft is capable of sustaining a cruising speed of 8mph/7 knots. Passages commencing for about 3 hours after these times are not recommended in view of the adverse tides below Vauxhall.
1. Richmond sluices will be shut. Use Richmond lock. Tide will turn during passage.

Limehouse or Bow to Brentford

Limehouse Lock is worked at most states of the tide during duty hours or as pre-booked with the lock-keeper, except at low water (springs) when the depth on the outer sill will not give sufficient draught. Bow Lock can be worked on all tides for the 5½ hours over high water between 0500 and 2200 hours, but passage must be pre-booked. Thames Locks at Brentford are subject to the more restricted 4 hours, so before leaving either lock at Limehouse or Bow you are advised to contact the lock-keeper at Brentford ☎ 020 8568 2779. Details of the general arrangements for all tidal locks off the Tideway are given on page 3. A seasonal timetable is also available from the keepers at Brentford or from the London Waterway office at Paddington. The best times to leave are:

- from Limehouse, as soon after low water as the tidal lock can be worked

- from Bow, as soon as the lock can be worked, bearing in mind you will have to punch the tide down Bow Creek.

Always consider using the Limehouse Cut into Limehouse Basin if an easier passage is required.

From Limehouse

Distance 16 miles
Average transit times at 4mph through the water:
leaving Limehouse 5 hours before HW, 3 hours
leaving Limehouse 3 hours before HW, 4 hours.

From Bow

Distance 22 miles (slow craft are advised not to use this route)
Average transit times at 4mph through the water:
leaving Bow 4 hours before HW, 4 to 5 hours
[1]leaving Bow 2 hours before HW, 5 to 6 hours.
1. Thames Locks will be shut. Moor at Kew or Richmond. Tide will turn halfway through passage.

Transit details – downstream

Teddington to Brentford

Leave Teddington on or just before HW there, to pass under Richmond sluices and arrive at Brentford (Thames Locks) in a maximum time of 1 hour 50 minutes. Do not leave Teddington much later than about 30 minutes after high water or you may find it difficult to get into Brentford Creek and thus find Thames Locks closed to you. Before leaving Teddington you are advised to check by telephone that the locks at Brentford are being worked ☎ 020 8568 2779. For fuller details of opening hours see the list at the start of this section on page 3.
Distance 5 miles
Average transit time at 4mph through the water: 75 minutes

Teddington to Limehouse or Bow

Limehouse Lock is worked only during the specific duty hours of the keeper, as shown above. You can save fuel by going downstream on the full ebb tide leaving Teddington at, or just before, HW and entering the lock at Limehouse within the opening hours, provided you do not arrive at mean low water springs. Or, second, you can time your passage to arrive on the flood by leaving some 4–5 hours after HW at

Teddington. This latter trip is only advisable for fast-moving craft (over 6mph/5½ knots cruising speed), because you will waste fuel and may meet adverse tides and heavy traffic coming upstream on the flood.

Bow Lock, near the head of Bow Creek, has the same HW times as London Bridge and can only be worked from 3½ hours before to 2 hours after these times. If your craft is capable of punching some of the tide you may be able to complete the trip to Bow Lock in one transit by timing your departure from Teddington about 2½ to 3½ hours after HW there. You will have to use Richmond Lock and you will enter slack water at around Vauxhall Bridge. Maintaining a speed of 6mph through the water should bring you to the tail of Bow Lock at about the time it is due to open on the next flood. In either case, if you do proceed and get into difficulties it may be safer to anchor out of the fairway or moor alongside a pier. Details of landing and mooring points are given separately on page 6.

Note Mooring facilities at the passenger service piers are often only available out of season.

To Limehouse
Distance 21 miles
Average transit times at 6mph through the water: 3½ to 4½ hours; at 4mph through the water: 4½ to 5½ hours, depending on the tide.

Advise estimated time of arrival at Limehouse, particularly if no prior enquiry has been made, ☎ 020 7308 9930.

To Bow Lock
Distance 27 miles
Average transit time at 6mph through the water: 5–6 hours depending on the tide – the last 2 miles up Bow Creek being with the flood (not advisable in one transit at 4mph).
Note Prior notice of arrival at Bow Lock is essential and must be pre-booked, ☎ 020 7308 9930.
Warning Bow Creek dries at low water!

Brentford to Limehouse or Bow
Due to the lock opening hours being restricted with no working after 2200 hours, it may be that, on an afternoon HW, you will have insufficient time to reach Limehouse or Bow and you may have to wait somewhere in the Tideway overnight before entering the East London canal system. Consult the list on page 6 for details of mooring facilities on the Tideway. Prior notice of arrival, even during duty hours, at Limehouse is advisable ☎ 020 7308 9930. Entry at Bow has to be pre-booked on the same number.

To Limehouse
Distance 16 miles
Average transit time at 6mph through the water: 3 hours; at 4mph through the water: 4 hours, assuming a departure from Brentford at HW.

To Bow
Due to lock-working hours and tidal restrictions it may not be possible to complete the transit on one tide. You may therefore have to wait somewhere in the Tideway before you can complete your trip. Do not moor in Bow Creek as it dries out at low water. Prior notice of arrival at Bow Lock is essential ☎ 020 7308 9930.
Distance 22 miles
Average transit time at 4mph through the water: 4½ hours, assuming a departure from Brentford at, or just before, HW and arrival at a suitable mooring such as Greenwich Pier ☎ 020 7918 4757.

West India Dock Entrance

The West India Dock Entrance lock is operated on all states of the tide between the hours of 0700 and 2000 local time except at low water springs when the advertised depth in the river is less than 1m above Chart Datum at London Bridge. However, a charge is made for craft using the lock except for the period of 1 hour before to 1 hour after HW at the entrance, when passage is free to craft with a confirmed berth or pre-booked visitor's mooring. All lockings must be booked 24 hours in advance on ☎ 020 7987 7260. Enquiries for moorings should be made on ☎ 020 7517 5550.

Transits to and from West India Dock Entrance lock from upstream should be calculated on the basis of those for Limehouse Lock, adding approximately 1 hour's cruising at 4mph. From Bow Locks you should allow 45 minutes, leaving Bow just before the turn at HW. Note that you will be punching the tide from the creek entrance from the river so that you should not attempt a transfer later, unless your craft is capable of 6mph or more or you are prepared to arrive outside the free locking period. High water is between 15 and 18 minutes before HW at London Bridge.

HMS Belfast and Tower Bridge

British Waterways

British Waterways (BW) controls the canal system which forms part of the London Ring and craft entering the system at any of the points noted – Brentford, Limehouse or Bow – must be licensed by BW before proceeding.

Vessels will not be permitted to enter BW waters unless they have proof of a valid Boat Safety Certificate and a current insurance cover with a minimum of £1m third party liability.

Details from The Pleasure Craft Licensing Officer, British Waterways Customer Services, Willow Grange, Church Road, Watford WD1 3QA ☎ 01923 201120.

The entrance to Limehouse Basin

Distance

9.11 miles (Richmond to Hampton Ferry)
For maximum dimensions of craft see below.

Navigation authorities

The Port of London Authority

(Richmond to the Teddington Boundary
    Stone)
For details see introduction to Section 1.

Environment Agency – Thames Region

(Teddington Boundary Stone to Cricklade)
Headquarters Kings Meadow House, Kings
    Meadow Road, Reading RG1 8DQ
    ☎ 0118 953 5000
Waterways manager
    ☎ 0118 953 5525
Craft registration PO Box 214, Reading
    RG1 8HQ ☎ 0118 953 5650
Rod and line licences PO Box 215, Reading
    RG1 8HQ ☎ 0118 953 5650
Recorded navigation information service
    ☎ 0845 988 1188 – *Quickdial* 01113

Navigation office and Recreation Offices

Upper Thames Navigation Office
(*Cricklade Bridge to tail of Cleeve Lock*)
    Osney Lock, Bridge Street, Oxford OX2
    0AX ☎ 01865 721271
Middle Thames Navigation Office
(*Tail of Cleeve Lock to tail of Bray Lock*)
    Kings Meadow House, Kings Meadow
    Road, Reading RG1 8DQ ☎ 0118 953
    5533
Lower Thames Navigation Office
(*Tail of Bray Lock to Teddington boundary*)
    Lock Island, Shepperton, Middlesex
    TW17 9LW ☎ 01276 454900
River Police
Metropolitan Police, Marine Support Unit
    All enquiries to HQ at Wapping ☎ 020
    7275 4421
*Thames Valley Police Diving Section (Bell
    Weir to St John's Lock)*
    Police Training Centre, Sulhamsted,
    Reading RG7 4DX ☎ 0118 953 6000

We have already covered some of the more
important suggestions about traversing the
half-tidal section of the river between
Teddington and Richmond Footbridge in the
previous section, but from here we travel
upstream with a commentary about the river,
reach by reach, and with a *Directory* section
at the end of each set of notes.

Craft wishing to enter the freshwater
Thames from the Tideway by negotiating
Teddington Locks) or from the Wey, Kennet
or Oxford Canal must be registered with the
Thames Region of the Environment Agency's
Craft Registration office at PO Box 214,
Reading RG1 8HQ ☎ 0118 953 5650.
There is now no facility for registration in
person at Kings Meadow House at Reading.
Short period registration for visiting craft
may be effected at Teddington Lock or some
other points of entry with the keeper on duty.
There is a fee for registration which covers
short periods for visiting craft or an annual
licence expiring on 31 December each year
for craft permanently based on the Thames.
Payment of the fees includes lock tolls.

Registered craft are subject to inspection
by the Agency's officers to ensure that they
conform to specifications with regard to
construction, fuel, sanitary appliances and
safety requirements. The specifications are
those now agreed by both the Agency and
British Waterways and therefore craft
complying should have no problem in
obtaining the necessary certificates when in
transit between the two authorities'
waterways. Boat Safety Certificates were
required under new regulations and were
phased in from 1 January 1997. Important
points from the *Byelaws* are covered on
pages 168–74. Copies of the *Byelaws* and the
aforementioned specifications are obtainable
from the Waterways Manager, Thames
Region, at Kings Meadow House, Kings
Meadow Road, Reading RG1 8DQ ☎ 0118
953 5525.

For the convenience of boat owners and
hirers entering the freshwater Thames from
the Tideway and for those starting their
cruises in the more popular lower reaches,
we follow the river upstream, contrary to the
usual practice of describing the course in the
downstream direction. It should be noted,
however, that the left bank and right bank
are normally referred to as you face
downstream.

In proceeding upstream, therefore, you must
remember that references to the right bank
will be on your left and those to the left will
be on your right, unless otherwise stated.

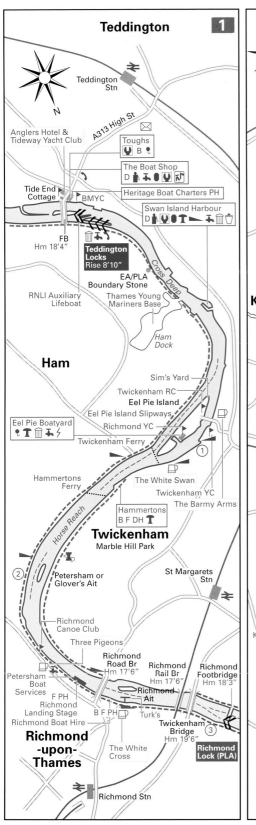

Teddington

1

Teddington Stn

A313 High St

Anglers Hotel &
Tideway Yacht Club

Toughs

The Boat Shop

Heritage Boat Charters PH

Swan Island Harbour

Tide End
Cottage

BMYC

FB
Hm 18'4"

Teddington Locks
Rise 8'10"

EA/PLA
Boundary Stone

Cross Deep

RNLI Auxiliary
Lifeboat

Thames Young
Mariners Base

Ham
Dock

Ham

Sim's Yard

Twickenham RC

Eel Pie Island

Eel Pie Island Slipways

Richmond YC

Eel Pie Boatyard

Twickenham Ferry

Hammertons
Ferry

The White Swan

Twickenham YC

The Barmy Arms

Hammertons
B F DH

Twickenham

Marble Hill Park

St Margarets
Stn

Horse Reach

(2)

Petersham or
Glover's Ait

Richmond
Canoe Club

Three Pigeons

Richmond
Road Br
Hm 17'6"

Richmond
Rail Br
Hm 17'6"

Richmond
Footbridge
Hm 18'3"

Petersham
Boat
Services

F PH
Richmond
Landing Stage

Richmond Boat Hire

B F PH

Richmond
Ait

Turk's

Twickenham
Bridge
Hm 19'6"

(3)

**Richmond
Lock (PLA)**

Richmond
-upon-
Thames

The White
Cross

Richmond Stn

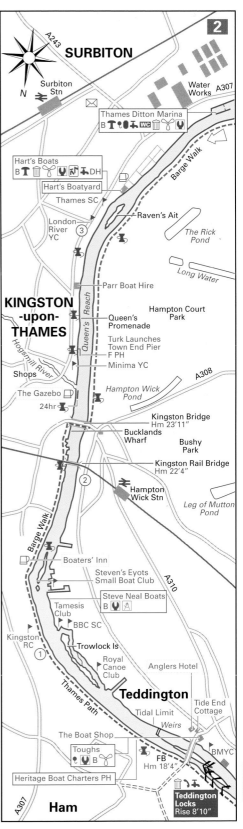

2

A243

SURBITON

Surbiton
Stn

Water
Works   A307

Thames Ditton Marina
B T WC

Hart's Boats
B T DH

Hart's Boatyard

Thames SC

Raven's Ait

Barge Walk

The Rick
Pond

London
River
YC
(3)

Long Water

KINGSTON
-upon-
THAMES

Parr Boat Hire

Hampton Court
Park

Queen's
Promenade

Turk Launches
Town End Pier
F PH

Minima YC

Queen's Reach

Hogsmill River

Shops

The Gazebo

24hr

Hampton Wick
Pond

A308

Kingston Bridge
Hm 23'11"

Bucklands
Wharf

Bushy
Park

Kingston Rail Bridge
Hm 22'4"

(2)

Hampton
Wick Stn

Leg of Mutton
Pond

Barge Walk

Boaters' Inn

Steven's Eyots
Small Boat Club

A310

Steve Neal Boats
B

Tamesis
Club

BBC SC

Kingston
RC

Trowlock Is

Royal Canoe
Club

(1)

Anglers Hotel

Thames Path

Teddington

Tidal Limit

Tide End
Cottage

The Boat Shop

Weirs

Toughs
B

FB
Hm 18'4"

BMYC

Heritage Boat Charters PH

**Teddington
Locks**
Rise 8'10"

A307

Ham

15

Maximum dimensions of craft above Richmond Lock to Sunbury

Headroom	18′4″ (5.58m)	Teddington Footbridge
	17′6″ (5.35m)	Richmond Bridges at HWS
Length	268′4″ (81.78m)	Molesey Lock chamber
Beam	24′9″ (7.54m)	Teddington Barge Lock
Draught	6′6″ (1.98m)	

This section begins at Richmond Lock and Weir which are incorporated below a five-arched footbridge spanning the river. Completed in 1894 to maintain a navigable depth upstream at the instigation of local inhabitants of Richmond, the works were taken over by the Port of London Authority (PLA) on its inception due to the high cost of maintenance of the structure and the reluctance of the riparian boroughs to contribute. Moves to return the lock and sluices to the local authorities have been mooted on several occasions but always resisted since more than one borough was involved until quite recently.

Overhead patent sluices are lowered in the three central spans of Richmond Footbridge to form a weir, from 2 hours after HW to 2 hours before the next HW, thus holding back the river above to give a depth of at least 5′9″ (1.75m) between Richmond and Teddington. When the sluices are in place, thus closing the spans to navigation, three red discs in triangular formation, apex down, are displayed in the arches of each span. Fixed red lights in the same formation are shown at night. While the three central spans are thus closed passage is still possible through the lock which is situated below the fifth span next to the Surrey shore (to port coming upstream). Skiffs and canoes may use the boat rollers which are sited under the first span next to the Middlesex shore (to starboard). A toll for use of the lock, which is manned 24 hours a day by PLA staff, is now payable only by commercial craft. Leisure craft may now use the lock free of charge. Passage beneath the three central spans when open for the four hours over each high tide is also free. When open, each span is so indicated by twin orange lights at the crown of its arch.

Proceeding above Richmond Lock the navigator should bear in mind that, on a rising tide, operating from 2 hours before HW at Richmond, the current will be flowing upstream to some extent, depending on the time of your transit of the footbridge and the amount of upland water coming down from Teddington Weir. It is probably safer and your craft will be more manoeuvrable if you continue your upstream journey just after HW, although your journey time to Teddington will be a little longer.

The first bridge beyond the footbridge is Twickenham Bridge, followed by Richmond Rail Bridge and then Richmond Bridge – the navigation spans of all three being those at the centre, indicated by the twin orange lights at the crown of the relevant arch. Always keep a good lookout for craft coming downstream and give way, especially if you are on a falling tide. Leave the two small aits and Richmond Ait (Corporation Island) between the rail and road bridges and Glover's Island (Petersham Ait) above Richmond Bridge to starboard when navigating upstream. Tripping boats operate from St Helena Pier opposite Richmond Ait (Corporation Island), which should not be used by private craft for landing, and also from the Richmond landing stages above Richmond Bridge. It is possible to land here for a fee, but a prior booking should be made with the lessee on ☎ 020 7930 2062.

Unless visiting any of the yards on Eel Pie Island or mooring for Twickenham, leave the island to starboard (port if coming downstream). At the head of the island the river widens again into Cross Deep reach and Chillingworth Ait, or Swan Island as it is now known, will be seen on the Middlesex side with its marina. A small lock on the Surrey bank about 100 metres above the marina leads into Ham Dock, the former gravel pits of the Earl of Dysart, where the Thames Young Mariners, a youth training project, has its base. In 700m, just past the PLA boundary stone, one reaches the tail of the Teddington Lock Island with the bottom gates of the Barge Lock plainly visible on the left. Teddington Locks are controlled by the Environment Agency, Thames Region, and are manned by keepers 24 hours a day throughout the year. Passage of the locks is not affected by the tides below in view of the operation of the weir sluices at Richmond, as explained above.

Do not enter the Barge Lock just because the bottom gates might be open and are the only sign of a lock you can see as you approach upstream. There are two other locks, both virtually out of sight unless you inadvisedly hugged the Middlesex shore against the moorings there to get a better view of the lock island. The older Launch

Lock, rebuilt in 1858, is more suitable for private and medium sized passenger craft, the Barge Lock having been opened in 1904 for the barge traffic which had been severely hampered by the restricted length of the original 1858 lock. A third lock, (known as the Skiff, or 'Coffin', Lock) sits alongside and at the upstream end of the Launch Lock, but is rarely used. There is also a set of boat-rollers above the Skiff Lock. Opposite the boat-rollers just below the footbridge is a drawdock into Ferry Lane beside The Boat Shop. There is also a tidal grid at Toughs just downstream.

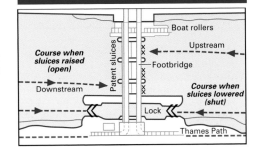

Richmond Lock (PLA) 24-hour service
Towing path, Richmond-upon-Thames, Surrey TW9 1TH ☎ 020 8940 0643
250'0'' (76·20m) long x 26'8'' (8·14m) wide. Maximum rise according to tide 10'0'' (3·05m)
Facilities Boat rollers on Middlesex bank.

Teddington Locks

Lock signals

To assist masters of craft coming upstream to Teddington a signal board has been placed at the downstream end of Teddington Lock Island to the right of the Barge Lock with signal lights indicating to which lock traffic should proceed to gain access to the reach above.

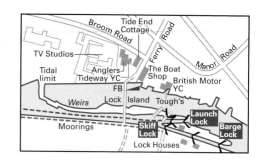

The signal lights indicate the following:

- *central line of red lights* Barge and Launch Locks not ready for upstream traffic.
- *flashing red arrow pointing left* Barge Lock not ready for upstream traffic. When lock is available the red arrow is replaced by a flashing white arrow.
- *flashing red arrow pointing right* Launch Lock not ready for upstream traffic. When lock is available the red arrow is replaced by a flashing white arrow.

Skiff Lock Vessels using the small Skiff Lock are not subject to the above signals and should proceed direct to the tail of this lock and await the directions of the lock staff. Since this lock is rarely used, and may even be closed at certain times, it is as well to telephone in advance to ensure that it is working.

Beyond Teddington Locks there is plenty of mooring space on the Surrey Bank opposite the weir. Overnight and extended daytime mooring is charged for by the Environment Agency, the fee usually being collected by the lock-keeper. Free overnight moorings are available on Steven's Eyot at the opposite end of the main island to the premises of the Small Boat Club but there is no access ashore. There are also a few moorings against the old railway wharf just above the Kingston Rail Bridge on the right bank (left as you go upstream) and provision has recently been made for visiting craft at Kingston at the start of the Queen's Promenade. Finger stages lead ashore to the High Street above Kingston Bridge while, on the Hampton Wick bank, the old wharf now appears to be occupied by long-term craft although it used to be a reasonable alternative.

In seeking moorings in this area in the summer season, bear in mind that a number of passenger-trip boats operate between Richmond, Kingston and Hampton Court. Care should always be taken in the vicinity of trip-boat quays and be aware that to attempt to land at such places is both discourteous and dangerous. St Helena Pier and Richmond landing stage have already

been referred to. Avoid the quays just above and below Kingston Bridge as these are used for various passenger tripping launches. For maintenance services for private craft in this area, the first available boatyard appears to be that at Harts Boats just upstream of Raven's Ait on the Surrey bank although there is now a boat-builder, repairer and chandler at Tamesis Club at Teddington, run by Steve Neal.

Queen's Reach extends to Raven's Ait, an island which houses in part a youth training centre where canoeing and sailing are taught; the other occupant is now a restaurant and conference centre. On the Portsmouth Road side of the island are the London River Yacht Club and the Thames Sailing Club's slipway. Both sides of Raven's Ait are navigable and the rule of the river should be observed. Take care if crossing to visit Harts Boats' yard on the left-hand side as you proceed upstream. Hampton Court Park is on your right and next comes Thames Ditton Marina to the left in what was an old reservoir. Chart 3 takes you past the former home of Maidboats, pioneers in Thames cruiser hire, a site which is being redeveloped for riverside housing, and on to Boyle Farm Island and then Thames Ditton Island, both of which may be passed on either side. However, the Hampton Court Park side, against the towing path, is to be preferred.

You are now entering Albany Reach which runs up to Hampton Court Palace and Hampton Court Bridge. On the left the rivers Mole and Ember enter the Thames and a little higher on the opposite bank below the palace is the Hampton Court landing stage. Casual moorings can be made along the barge walk here which is part of the Thames Path. Above is Whatford's Boat House. Opposite on the Molesey (Surrey) bank is the starting point for Chris Cruises' MV *Lady Christine*, while under the bridge is Martin's skiff hire in the approach to Molesey Lock.

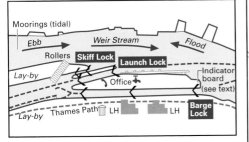

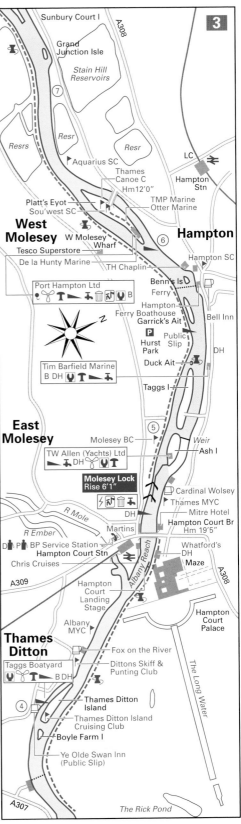

Above Molesey Lock on the starboard hand is Ash Island with the yard of T W Allen & Son (Yachts) Ltd, approachable only by water or by the footpath from the lock and across the weir. Taggs Island, originally Walnut Tree Ait but now named after a previous owner, Tom Tagg, is above Ash Island and Molesey's top weir, and is joined to the Middlesex bank by a new bridge having a headroom of 12'0″ (3.66m). Passage is available to craft on both sides of Taggs, which is famed for its collection of houseboats and also looks onto the former Hucks Boatyard which fronts a genuine Swiss chalet, imported and erected in 1899. The next small island above is Duck Ait, owned by the river authority and available for casual mooring – but only if you are a duck fancier – followed by Garricks Ait which should be left to port proceeding upstream (starboard coming down). Inshore of the tail of Garrick's Ait, is a public launching slip. Keys for the bollards are obtainable from Elmbridge Borough Council ☎ 01372 474474.

Opposite the imposing scene of Hampton Church and the *Bell Inn* where Thames Street almost touches the river, Benn's Island houses Hampton Sailing Club surrounded by the club's moorings, while the former Kenton's boatyard has been superseded by Hampton Ferry Boat House. Above Benn's Island there are moorings for T Harrison Chaplin's workboats. The old established boat building

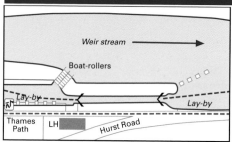

Molesey Lock Daytime only. River Bank, East Molesey, Surrey KT8 9AW
☎ 020 8979 4482
268'4" (81·78m) long x 24'10" (7·56m) wide
Rise (fall) 6'1" (1·85m)
Max. draught 7'11" (2·41m).
Facilities Chemical toilet disposal, pump-out service, refuse bins, toilets, water points for hose and can, electric launch charging point, moorings.
Angling Weir permit holders on overfall.

Weir stream →
Boat-rollers
Lay-by
Lay-by
Thames Path
LH
Hurst Road

and hiring business of Constable's (which stood between the ferry and Chaplin's moorings) has now been closed.

Platt's Eyot looms ahead, home of many notable boating firms in its day, the most famous probably being Thornycroft's, but now the home of Port Hampton, TMP Marine Services Ltd, Otter Marine Services and De la Hunty Marine. The main channel goes to port – left of the island – but the starboard is navigable, the link footbridge having a headroom of some 12'0" (3.66m). This section of the river ends between the many reservoirs which lie below Sunbury.

The Thames Path

The Thames Path continues from below Richmond on the Surrey bank along the boundary of the Old Deer Park, past the lock office, under Twickenham and Richmond Rail bridges, into Cholmondley Walk and Riverside up to Richmond Bridge. Take care above the lock as, on high spring tides around March and October, Cholmondley Walk can be flooded. Beyond Richmond Bridge, the Path remains alongside Petersham Road as far as Buccleuch Gardens where there is a slight detour before it returns to the river at Petersham Meadows. From here the Path continues to follow the river on the Surrey bank right round to Teddington Locks and beyond.

Leaving Teddington Locks, the Thames Path proceeds for about a mile before meeting up with Lower Ham Road which takes it round to Canbury Gardens, followed by a barge walk and under Kingston rail bridge to Thames Side and Bucklands Wharf at Kingston Bridge. Although it is possible to follow the river on the Surrey Bank as far as Ravens Ait along the Queens Promenade, the official path crosses Kingston Bridge and adopts the Middlesex bank, skirting Hampton Court Park along another barge walk as far as Hampton Court Bridge, where it recrosses the river to the Surrey bank to follow past Molesey Lock and on, without straying too far from the river's edge, as far as Weybridge.

Angling

Thames angling is very popular, especially now that the authorities in charge of the river have been able to clean the water and carry out several programmes of restocking and other projects which have been designed to encourage fish to breed. An Environment Agency rod licence is required by all persons aged 12 and over fishing on any water within England and Wales. Rod and line licences are now obtainable from post offices. The locations of post offices close to the river are shown on the charts in this book. All prospective anglers must be in possession of a rod licence, irrespective of whether fishing is free or not. Where fishing is not free, I have tried to indicate whether permission can be obtained (it cannot always be) and from whom; but arrangements change frequently and local advice should be sought from lock-keepers or the staff of tackle shops (also listed) who may be able to help. Fishing for freshwater (coarse) fish and eels, grayling and non-migratory trout is open from mid-June to mid-March. Salmon and migratory trout may be fished from early April to the end of September. These periods do not necessarily apply in other regions.

Above Richmond, fishing is free from a boat or from along the towing path whose route is described above. The local authorities also allow fishing from Terrace Gardens at Richmond and Orleans and Radnor Gardens, below and above Eel Pie Island respectively on the Middlesex bank opposite the towing path. At Teddington, fishing is permitted from the towing path but not in the lock-cut. A good spot may also be found along the barge walk at Canbury Gardens leading into Kingston. There is no fishing permitted between Kingston and Hampton Court Bridges from the south (Surrey) bank. Elsewhere fishing is free.

WEIR PERMITS

At Molesey Lock it is possible to fish off the downstream end of the weir overfall although you will need to obtain an Environment Agency *Lock and Weir Permit* before doing so. Instructions on how to get onto the overfall may be obtained from the lock-keeper, to whom your permit should be shown and whose permission you should obtain before you fish. Your fishing is still subject to the normal *Fishery Byelaws* and close seasons and you are only allowed to fish at sites covered by the *Lock and Weir Permit* during the hours of duty of the lock staff. A table of hours of duty is given on page 172.

Fishing above Molesey, clear of the lock cut, is possible from boats which may be hired locally (see *Directory*) or from the towing path which follows the south (Surrey) bank.

Directory

As far as possible, all firms, clubs and other businesses and features have been listed in their upstream order in each section. Where offices or other contact points are away from the river, the river base or embarkation point for passenger vessels and boat hirers has been the location which has determined the order of listing.

BOATYARDS, MARINAS, CHANDLERIES, TRIPPING AND HIRE

Turk Launches Ltd
St Helena Pier, c/o Turk Launches, Town End Pier, Kingston-upon-Thames, Surrey KT1 1HN ☎ 020 8546 2434. Tripping launches and party hire. (PBA)

Richmond Boat Hire
Mark Edwards, 1, 3 & 4 Bridge Boathouse, Richmond Bridge, Richmond TW9 1TH ☎ 020 8948 8270. Boatbuilder and traditional boat restorer. Repairs, skiff hire.

Richmond Landing Stage
Cambourne Walk, Petersham Road, Richmond TW10 6UJ ☎ 020 7930 2062. Landing stage for tripping and party hire launches.

Colliers Launches Ltd
Cambourne Walk, Petersham Road, Richmond TW10 6UJ ☎ 020 8892 0741 (office: 217 St Margaret's Road,

Twickenham, Middlesex TW1 1LU). Tripping launches and party hire.

Petersham Boat Services
The Boathouse, 85 Petersham Road, Richmond, Surrey TW10 6UT ☎ 020 8940 0173. Working craft moorings, water point.

W Hammerton & Co Ltd
Ferry Boathouse, Marble Hill Park, Twickenham, Middlesex TW1 3BL ☎ 020 8892 9620. Boats and small craft (sales), chandlery, day-boat hire, ferry service, permanent moorings. (TBTA)

Eel Pie Boatyard Ltd
Eel Pie Island, Twickenham, Middlesex TW1 3DY ☎ 020 8892 3626. Permanent and visitors' moorings, hardstanding, 30-ton crane, dry dock, boat repairs, associated industries & engineers on site, refuse disposal, water point, mains electricity.

Eel Pie Island Slipways Ltd
Eel Pie Island, Twickenham, Middlesex TW1 3DY ☎ 020 8891 4481. Visitors' and permanent moorings, boat repairs, slipway.

Lion Moorings Ltd
Eel Pie Island, Twickenham, Middlesex TW1 5DY ☎ 020 8891 1025. Moorings, repairs, slipway.

G S & E A Bell
Ivy Castle, Eel Pie Island, Twickenham, Middlesex TW1 3DY ☎ 020 8892 1308. Residential moorings, mains electricity, repairs, slipway.

Geo. Sims, Racing Boats
Eel Pie Island, Twickenham, Middlesex TW1 3DY ☎ 020 8892 8844. Permanent moorings.

Swan Island Harbour
Swan Island, 1, Strawberry Vale, Twickenham, Middlesex TW1 4RP ☎ 020 8892 2861. Repairs, diesel fuel, *Calor Gas*, permanent and residential moorings, winter storage, landing stage, slipway, water point, showers, mains electricity, refuse and chemical toilet disposal.

F Edwards, Engineers Ltd
Swan Island, 1 Strawberry Vale, Twickenham, Middlesex TW1 4RP ☎ 020 8892 3653. Marine engineers at Swan Island Harbour.

Tough Brothers Ltd
27 Ferry Road, Teddington, Middlesex TW11 9NN ☎ 020 8977 4494. Marine engineers, boat repairs, surveys, brokerage, tidal grid, crane. (TBTA)

Heritage Boat Charters Ltd
27 Berkeley Court, Oatlands Drive, Weybridge, Surrey KT13 9HX (Office) ☎ 01932 224800. Luxury cruises aboard 52ft classic motor yacht *St Joan* for up to 12 guests, above or below Teddington. Special packages for Henley Regatta, etc. (PBA)

The Boat Shop
27 Ferry Road, Teddington, Middlesex TW11 9NN ☎ 020 8977 9978. Boat repairs, *Calor Gas*, chandlery, outboard sales and service, water point, moorings.

Steve Neal Boats
Tamesis Club, Trowlock Way, Teddington, Middlesex TW11 9QY ☎ 020 8977 8886. Boatbuilder, repairs, chandlery.

Turk Launches Ltd
Town End Pier, 68, High Street, Kingston, Surrey KT1 1HN ☎ 020 8546 2434. Party boat charter, public trips, catering aboard, 50-150 passengers. (Richmond – Kingston – Hampton Court.) (PBA)

Parr Boat Hire
Queen's Promenade, Kingston. Office: 48 Victor Road, Teddington, Middlesex TW11 8SR ☎ 020 8977 7570. Passenger boat hire up to 90 people, self-drive day launches, catering afloat, public trips (Kingston – Hampton Court).

Harts Boats
Hart's Boatyard, Portsmouth Road, Surbiton, Surrey KT6 4HJ ☎020 8399 4009. Boat repairs, day-boat hire, permanent moorings, winter storage, water point, pump-out, toilets. (TBTA, THCA)

Thames (Ditton) Marina Ltd
Portsmouth Road, Thames Ditton, Surbiton, Surrey KT6 5QD ☎020 8398 6159/3900. Boat sales, insurance, repairs, marine engineers, diesel fuel, *Calor Gas*, chandlery, permanent moorings, hardstanding, crane, slipway, water point, refuse disposal, chemical toilet, toilets, mains electricity, car parking. (TBTA, ABYA, TYHA)

Tagg's Boatyard Ltd
44, Summer Road, Thames Ditton, Surrey KT7 0QQ ☎ 020 8398 2119. Boat sales, repairs, marine engineers, boat deliveries, consultants. Day-boat hire, moorings, hardstanding, slipway. (TBTA, THCA)

Hampton Court Landing Stage
The Barge Walk, Hampton Court, East Molesey, Surrey KT8. (For service enquiries to Richmond, Kew and Westminster ☎ 020 7930 2062.)

C Whatford and Sons
Palace Boat House, Hampton Court Palace, East Molesey, Surrey KT8 ☎ 020 8977 1567. Day-boat hire.

Chris Cruises Ltd
Downstream side of Hampton Court Bridge off Hampton Court Way, opposite Whatford's. Office: 27 Green Lane, Addlestone, Surrey KT15 2TZ ☎ 01932 855120. Party hire, passenger trips, catering afloat. (PBA)

J Martin & Son
River Bank, Hampton Court Bridge, East Molesey, Surrey KT8 9AJ ☎ 020 8979 5515. Day-boat hire, skiffs, etc.

T W Allen & Son (Yachts) Ltd
Ash Island, East Molesey, Surrey KT8 9AN ☎ 0181 979 1997. Boat builders, repairs, diesel fuel, *Calor Gas*, day-boat hire, party hire, catering afloat, permanent and visitors' moorings, slipway, water, sewage pump-out, toilets. (TBTA)

Tim Barfield Marine
Terrace Garden Boatyard, Hampton
Court Road, Hampton, Middlesex TW12
2EN ☎ 020 8941 2676. Boat sales,
marine engineers, repairs, outboard
service, day-boat hire, permanent
moorings and storage, water point,
slipway.

Hampton Ferry Boat House Ltd
Thames Street, Hampton, Middlesex
TW12 2EW ☎ 020 8979 7471. Dayboat
hire, ferry service.

T Harrison Chaplin
Moorings at Hampton above Benn's
Island (office and works: Meadhurst Park
Nursery, Cadbury Road, Sunbury-on-
Thames, Middlesex TW16 7LZ
☎ 01932 783371). Riparian owner
service, waterside construction, piling,
camp-shedding, etc.

Port Hampton Ltd
Platt's Eyot, Lower Sunbury Road,
Hampton, Middlesex TW12 2HF
☎ 020 8979 8116/8941 6955. Boat
repairs, marine engineers, permanent
moorings, winter storage, hardstanding,
crane, slipway, water point, refuse
disposal, sewage pump-out, mains
electricity, restaurant, car park.

De la Hunty Marine
Platt's Eyot, Lower Sunbury Road,
Hampton, Middlesex TW12 2HF
☎ 020 8979 2121. Boat sales, repairs,
marine engineers, permanent moorings,
hardstandings.

TMP Marine Services Ltd
Unit 2, Platt's Eyot, Lower Sunbury
Road, Hampton, Middlesex TW12 2HF
☎ 020 8979 1568. Boat repairs.

Otter Marine Services
Unit 3, Platt's Eyot, Lower Sunbury
Road, Hampton, Middlesex TW12 2HF
☎ 020 8941 9636. Boatbuilders and
repairers.

EMERGENCY FUEL SUPPLIES

This list does not include suppliers of marine
fuel at marinas and boatyards whose entries
appear in the main *Directory*. As far as I can
ascertain, those listed are the nearest to the
river at any particular location although
some are still a fair distance when
considering the amount of fuel you may wish
to carry.

Note Subject to strict regulations concerning
the specifications and sizes of fuel containers
in which fuel spirit may be supplied, the
following service stations close to the river
may be able to supply the maximum legal
quantities of petroleum spirit to assist boat
owners and hirers. There are also essential
points to consider in the storage of empty
fuel containers on board and the manner in
which engine tanks are filled in close
proximity to the river.

Oak Lane Self Serve
Petrol, diesel
5 Richmond Road, Twickenham,
Middlesex TW1 ☎ 020 8891 1880/5315.
Opposite top of Church Lane, inside Eel
Pie Island.

Albany Park Service Station
Petrol, diesel
215 Richmond Road, Kingston upon
Thames, Surrey KT2 ☎ 020 8541
1817/4537. 500yds from downstream
end of Canbury Gardens, via Ham Road
and Bank Lane.

Total Service Station
Petrol, diesel
122, Portsmouth Road, Thames Ditton,
KT7 ☎ 020 8339 1310.

BP Hampton Court Service Station
Petrol, diesel, groceries
Hampton Court Way, East Molesey,
Surrey KT8 ☎ 020 8783 1762.

ROWING, SAILING AND CRUISING CLUBS AND TUITION

Richmond Canoe Club
Lansdowne Boat House, Petersham
Road, Richmond, Surrey TW10 6TS
☎ 020 8940 9898 (BCU)

Twickenham Rowing Club
Eel Pie Island, Twickenham, Middlesex
TW1 3DY ☎ 020 8892 5291 (ARA)

Richmond Yacht Club
Club House, Eel Pie Island, Twickenham,
Middlesex TW1 3DY
☎ 020 8892 9679 (ATYC)

Twickenham Yacht Club
Riverside, Twickenham, Middlesex TW1
3DN ☎ 020 8892 8487 (RYA)

Thames Young Mariners' Project
Riverside Drive, Ham, Near Richmond,
Surrey TW10 7RX ☎ 020 8940 5550
(RYA, BCU)

British Motor Yacht Club
Ferry Road, Teddington, Middlesex
TW11 9NN ☎ 020 8977 5710 (ATYC,
RYA)

Tideway Yacht Club
c/o Anglers Hotel, 3 Broom Road,
Teddington, Middlesex TW11 9NR

Walbrook & Royal Canoe Club
Royal Canoe Boat House, Trowlock
Island, Teddington, Middlesex TW11
9QY ☎ 020 8977 5269 (ARA, BCU)

Lensbury Motor Cruising Club
Lensbury Club, Broom Road,
Teddington, Middlesex TW11 9QY
☎ 020 8977 8821 (ATYC)

Lensbury Sailing Club
Lensbury Club, Broom Road,
Teddington, Middlesex TW11 9QY
☎ 020 8977 8821 (RYA)

Tamesis (Sailing) Club
Trowlock Way, Broom Road, Teddington,
Middlesex TW11 9QY
☎ 020 8977 3589 (RYA)

BP Yacht Club
Trowlock Way, Teddington, Middlesex
TW11 9QY ☎ 020 8943 1168 or 020
8977 5254/6255 (RYA)

BBC (Ariel) Sailing Club
Trowlock Way, Broom Road, Teddington,
Middlesex TW11 9QY
☎ 020 8977 5834 (RYA)

Skiff Club
The Boathouse, Trowlock Way, Broom
Road, Teddington, Middlesex TW11 9RY
☎ 020 8943 1118 (ARA)

Albany Park Canoe & Sailing Club
Albany Park Canoe & Sail Centre,
Albany Mews, Albany Park Road,
Kingston upon Thames, Surrey KT2 5SL
☎ 020 8549 3066 (BCU)

Kingston Rowing Club
The Boat House, Lower Ham Road, ·
Kingston upon Thames, Surrey KT2 5AU
☎ 020 8546 8592 (ARA)

Small Boat Club
Stevens Ait, Kingston upon Thames,
Surrey KT1 (RYA, ATYC)

Kingston Unit Sea Cadet Corps (TS
Steadfast)
Thames Side, Kingston upon Thames,
Surrey KT1 1PX ☎ 020 8546 6600

Minima Yacht Club
48a, High Street, Kingston upon Thames,
Surrey KT1 1LQ ☎ 020 8546 8241
(RYA)

Raven's Ait Conference & Watersport
Centre
Portsmouth Road, Surbiton, Surrey KT6
4HN ☎ 020 8390 3554

London River Yacht Club
Queens Promenade, Portsmouth Road,
Kingston upon Thames, Surrey KT6 4HL
☎ 020 8546 2072 (ATYC, RYA)

Thames Sailing Club
Portsmouth Road, Surbiton, Surrey KT6
4HH ☎ 020 8399 2164 (RYA)

Thames Ditton Island Cruising Club
c/o 24, The Island, Thames Ditton,
Surrey KT7 0SQ (ATYC)

Ditton Skiff and Punting Club
Albany Cottage, Alexander Road,
Thames Ditton, Surrey KT7 0RS ☎ 020
8398 1642 (ARA)

Albany Motor Yacht Club
Queens Road, Thames Ditton, Surrey
KT7 0QY (ATYC)

British Motor Yacht Club (Sailing Section)
Queens Road, Thames Ditton, Surrey
KT7 0QY (RYA)

Kingston Grammar School Boat Club
Kingston G.S. Boathouse, Aragon
Avenue, Thames Ditton, Surrey KT7
0QZ ☎ 020 8398 5138 (ARA)

Molesey Boat Club
The Barge Walk, East Molesey, Surrey
KT8 9AJ ☎ 020 8979 6583 (ARA)

Thames Motor Yacht Club
The Club House, Hampton Court Road,
East Molesey, Surrey KT8 9BW ☎ 020
8979 2298 (ATYC, RYA)

Hampton Sailing Club
Benn's Island, Hampton, Middlesex
TW12 (RYA)

Sou'West Sailing Club
Platt's Eyot, Lower Sunbury Road,
Hampton, Middlesex TW12 2HF (RYA)

Thames Canoe Club
Platt's Eyot, Lower Sunbury Road,
Hampton, Middlesex TW12 2HF

Aquarius Sailing Club
Lower Sunbury Road, Hampton,
Middlesex TW12 ☎ 020 8979 4720
(RYA)

PUBLIC LAUNCHING SITES

- Water Lane Drawdock, Water Lane,
  Richmond, Surrey
- Richmond Bridge Drawdock, off
  Cambridge Road, Twickenham,
  Middlesex
- Petersham Drawdock, River Lane,
  Petersham Meadow, Richmond, Surrey
- Ham Landing, Ham Riverside, Ham
  Village, Surrey
- Riverside, Twickenham, Middlesex (by the
  White Swan)
- Twickenham Embankment, Church Lane,
  Twickenham, Middlesex
- Ham Dock, Ham Fields, Surrey Towing
  Path
- Teddington Drawdock, Ferry Road,
  Teddington, Middlesex
- Thameside, Kingston upon Thames,
  Surrey

- Ditton Reach, off Portsmouth Road (300yds above Thames Ditton Marina)
- Thames Ditton, next to the *Swan Hotel*, Summer Road, Thames Ditton, Surrey
- Barnes Alley, Hampton (bottom of Church street). Small craft only.
- Hurst Park, West Molesey, Surrey (opposite Garricks Ait). Keys to bollards from council ☎ 01372 474474
- Parish Wharf, Lower Sunbury Road (by car park at Platts Eyot footbridge). Craft must be manhandled.

FISHING TACKLE SHOPS

In this section fishing in the Thames, as specified above, is free – from a boat, the towing path, or where allowed by the riparian owner.

Richmond Angling Centre
360, Richmond Road, Twickenham, Middlesex TW1 2DX ☎ 020 8892 4175

Acton Angling Centre
150, Heath Road, Twickenham, Middlesex TW1 ☎ 020 8892 7660

Guns and Tackle
81, High Street, Whitton, Twickenham, Middlesex TW2 7LD ☎ 020 8898 3129/9040

HOTELS, INNS AND RESTAURANTS

White Swan Inn Old Palace Lane, Richmond. Moor at Water Lane Dock or Cholmondley Walk. Half-tidal. Range 8ft at springs, 4ft at neaps.

White Cross Hotel Water Lane, Richmond. Lunchtime bar meals and restaurant midday and evenings. Moor at Water Lane Dock or Cholmondley Walk. Half-tidal. Range 8ft at springs, 4ft at neaps.

Waterman's Arms Water Lane, Richmond. Moor at Water Lane Dock or Cholmondley Walk. Half-tidal. Range 8ft at springs, 4ft at neaps.

Petersham Hotel Nightingale Lane, Richmond Hill. ☎ 020 8940 7471. Restaurant and accommodation. Moor at Richmond landing stage by prior arrangement (☎ 020 7930 2062).

Barmy Arms Inn The Embankment, Twickenham. Mooring off embankment or draw dock. Half-tidal. Allow 8ft at springs, 4ft at neaps.

The Eel Pie Church Street, Twickenham. Lunchtime bar food. Mooring off embankment or drawdock. Half-tidal. Allow 8ft at springs, 4ft at neaps.

Tide End Cottage Ferry Road, Teddington. Bar food lunch & evenings. Barbecue evenings. Garden. Moor above Teddington Locks and use footbridge.

Anglers Hotel Broom Road, Teddington. Bar meals. Facilities for disabled and children. Garden. Moor above Teddington Locks. Tideway Yacht Club base.

Boaters' Inn Canbury Gardens. Dining Room and bar meals. Children welcome. Jazz on Sunday evenings. Moorings alongside.

TGI Friday's Bentall Centre, Wood Street, Kingston. American style burger/steak bar. Open all day. No booking. Public moorings off High Street upstream, or by rail bridge, downstream.

Philadelphia Exchange Bucklands Wharf, Kingston. Bar and restaurant. Very limited mooring.

Royal Barge Horsefair, Kingston. Hot and cold food 12–3, open 11–11 (excluding Sundays). Mooring as for *Philadelphia Exchange*.

Bishop Out Of Residence Bishops Hall, Thames Street, Kingston. Bar food lunchtimes and evenings. Moorings upstream.

Gazebo Inn Kings Passage, Thames Street, Kingston. Meals. Children's room. Disabled access. Limited moorings outside.

McDonalds Adams Walk, Kingston.

White Hart Hotel High Street, Hampton Wick. Home-cooked lunches every day. Mooring above Hampton Wick wharf.

Swan Bar and Restaurant High Street, Hampton Wick.

Hart's Boatyard Portsmouth Road, Surbiton ☎ 020 8399 7515. Bar meals, dining room. Facilities for disabled. Moorings adjacent.

Ye Olde Swan Summer Road, Thames Ditton. Bar meals, dining and carvery. Moorings and slip adjacent.

The Fox on the River Queens Road, Thames Ditton ☎ 020 8398 7031. Moorings outside hotel.

Carlton Mitre Hotel The Green, Hampton Court Road, East Molesey ☎ 020 8979 9988. Bars and restaurant.

Cardinal Wolsey Hotel The Green, Hampton Court Road, East Molesey ☎ 020 8979 1458. Bar meals.

Bell Inn Thames Street, Hampton. Bar meals and dining.

RAIL STATIONS AND TRAIN SERVICES

London Underground and *South West Trains*. Enquiries ☎ 020 7222 1234 and 08457 484950 respectively

Note Station entries show rail company, location, distance from the river and relevant routes in each direction. Only main stations and those close to the river on the routes are given.

Richmond *South West Trains, North London Line and District Line (London Underground).* The Quadrant, Richmond, Surrey. 900yds from river. *South West Trains:* to Waterloo; to Twickenham and Staines; to Wraysbury, Datchet and Windsor; Ascot and Reading. Trains to Twickenham, Strawberry Hill, Teddington, Hampton Wick and Kingston, then Waterloo. *North London Line:* to Kew Gardens, Willesden Junction, Camden Road, Stratford and North Woolwich. *District Line (underground)* to Kew Gardens, Earl's Court, Victoria, Embankment, Whitechapel and Upminster.

St Margarets (closed on Sundays) *South West Trains* St Margaret's Road, Twickenham. ¾ mile from river. Trains to Twickenham, Strawberry Hill, Teddington, Hampton Wick, Kingston, Waterloo via Wimbledon; or Richmond, Putney and Waterloo. Occasional (peak) service to and from Staines, Windsor, Egham and Reading lines.

Twickenham *South West Trains* London Road, Twickenham. 900yds from river. Trains to Richmond and Waterloo, to Staines, Datchet, Windsor and Reading, also trains to Strawberry Hill, Teddington, Hampton Wick, Kingston and Waterloo. Peak service to Hampton and Shepperton.

Strawberry Hill *South West Trains* Tower Road, Twickenham. 700yds from river. Trains to Twickenham, Richmond and Waterloo; Teddington, Hampton Wick, Kingston and Waterloo via Wimbledon. Peak service only, Monday–Friday pm (to) and am (from) Hampton, Sunbury and Shepperton.

Teddington *South West Trains* Station Rd, off High Street, Teddington. ¾ mile from river. Trains to Twickenham, Richmond and Waterloo; Hampton Wick, Kingston and Waterloo via Wimbledon; Hampton, Sunbury and Shepperton.

Hampton Wick *South West Trains* Station Road, off Seymour Road, Hampton Wick. 750yds from river. Trains to Teddington, Strawberry Hill, Twickenham, Richmond and Waterloo; Teddington, Hampton, Sunbury and Shepperton; and Kingston and Waterloo via Wimbledon.

Kingston *South West Trains* Wood Street, Kingston. 600yds from river. Trains to Hampton Wick, Teddington, Strawberry Hill, Twickenham, Richmond and Waterloo; Hampton Wick, Teddington, Hampton and Shepperton; and Waterloo via Wimbledon.

Surbiton *South West Trains* Victoria Road, Surbiton, Kingston, Surrey. 800yds from river. Trains to Waterloo via Wimbledon; to Woking; to Walton-on-Thames, Weybridge and Woking; to Thames Ditton and Hampton Court; also Guildford via Effingham Junction.

Thames Ditton *South West Trains* Station Road, Thames Ditton, Surrey. 1000yds from river. Trains to Hampton Court; Surbiton and Waterloo via Wimbledon.

Hampton Court *South West Trains* Hampton Court Way, East Molesey, Surrey. 100yds from river. Trains to Thames Ditton, Surbiton and Waterloo via Wimbledon. Change at Surbiton for Guildford and Woking lines and Waterloo lines, and at New Malden for Kingston.

Hampton *South West Trains* Station Road, Hampton, Middlesex. 900yds from river. Trains to Sunbury and Shepperton; Teddington, Hampton Wick, Kingston and Waterloo via Wimbledon. Peak service (Monday–Friday only) to and from Strawberry Hill, Twickenham, Richmond and Waterloo.

BUS AND COACH SERVICES
Richmond to Hampton

Most major towns along the river in this section are connected by regular (at least hourly) bus services. Richmond and Kingston are main starting points and routes run to or through Hampton Court and Staines via Sunbury or Walton, Weybridge, Chertsey and Windsor. Limited stop coach services run through the area between Victoria and Guildford, and Heathrow and Dartford via Hampton and Kingston hourly. There are also night buses from Trafalgar Square to Hampton Court, Richmond, Teddington and Kingston, and Sunbury.

Bus operators:
- London Buslines ☎ 020 8571 2233
- London United ☎ 020 8977 6665
- London General ☎ 020 8646 1747
- Central London routes ☎ 020 7222 1234

Thames Hire Cruiser Association (THCA)

The 124 miles of the river from Lechlade to Teddington, the non-tidal section of the Thames, forms a unique waterway. Beautiful scenery, interesting places to visit, a wide range of tourist attractions and historic towns, such as Windsor and Oxford, all make the Royal River Thames the queen of our English waterways.

HIRING A BOAT

What do I get and how much will it cost?
A five-week period from mid-July is the peak season. Outside those dates you will find the cost of hiring is progressively cheaper back to the beginning and on to the end of the season. Some operators offer a 10 per cent discount for those who wish to hire a boat for a two-week period outside the months of July and August. Typically, costs in 2005 are £850 per week for a recently built boat in mid-May. Hiring the same boat during the peak season would cost about £1200. Work this out on a per person/per night basis and you have approximate figures of £30 and £43 respectively. There are cheaper rates for older but no less reliable nor less comfortable craft. To these you would have to add the cost of food and fuel, but the total will still compare favourably with a hotel-based holiday at home or abroad. There is also the advantage that you have the opportunity to explore the River Thames at your leisure, enjoy the hospitality of its riverside pubs and restaurants, the beautiful landscapes seen from the river, meet other boating holidaymakers . . . all in the comfort and security of your own floating home. In effect you discover a new way of life.

Where to cruise
Look through this book, decide which stretch of the river is for you and recognise that, in cruising for five or six hours per day and allowing for time in passing through locks and sightseeing, you should be able to make the round trip from Reading to Oxford and back (approximately 80 miles) in one week at a leisurely pace. Spend a little longer on the move and you could cover the 120-mile round trip from Hampton Court to Pangbourne and back, which includes the historic towns of Windsor, Marlow and Henley.

The Thames Hire Cruiser Association (THCA) is a group association within the British Marine Federation (BMF), whose members operate hire-boat yards on the Thames and Wey rivers, and on the Basingstoke and Kennet and Avon and South Oxford canals. It works with the appropriate authorities to promote the recreational use of the Thames and its connected waterways. It also concerns itself with the maintenance of high standards in the quality of the boats and services on offer. Information and advice is readily available from the administration office. Enquiries should be made to the Secretary, Peter Allen ☎ 020 8979 1997.

All the members of THCA with whom bookings can be made direct are listed here; alternatively, bookings may be made through the agencies shown against their entries. Full addresses and details are given in the directories at the end of each section and locations shown on the charts. Members' details are shown with the legend (THCA) at the end of their entries.

Thames Ditton
  Harts Boats – day-boats only
  Taggs Boatyard – day-boats only
Guildford (on River Wey)
  Guildford Boat House (*Hoseasons*) –
  punts and skiffs also available
Farncombe (on River Wey)
  Farncombe Boat House (*Hoseasons*) –
  punts and skiffs also available
Odiham (on Basingstoke Canal)
  Galleon Marine
Datchet
  Kris Cruisers (*Blakes*) – day-boats also
  available
Henley-on-Thames
  Hobbs & Sons Ltd – day-boats only
**Padworth, near Reading (on Kennet & Avon
  Canal)**
  Reading Marine Company (*Hoseasons*)
Reading
  Caversham Boat Services (*Blakes*) – skiffs
  also available.
Benson
  Swancraft Boat Services (*Blakes*)
Abingdon
  Kingcraft (Abingdon Boat Centre) – day-
  boats only
Lower Heyford (on Oxford Canal)
  Oxfordshire Narrowboats (*Blakes*)
Lechlade
  Cotswold Boat Hire
Weedon (on Grand Union Canal)
  Canalboat Holidays Ltd.

There is a small number of other hire firms based on the river who, for various reasons, are not members of the THCA but this does not mean that their services may be in any way inferior to those listed. Their details will be found as well as those above in the directories at the end of each section and their locations shown on the charts.

3. Sunbury to Staines

Distance

10.97 miles (Hampton Ferry to Staines Bridge)

Maximum dimensions of craft from Molesey to Staines

Headroom	18′3″ (5.56m) at Walton Bridge 17′0″ (5.18m) if using Desborough Cut
Length	174′5″ (53.16m) at Shepperton Lock
Beam	19′10″ (6.04m) at Shepperton Lock
Draught	6′6″ (1.98m) in main fairway

This section commences upstream of Platt's Eyot with West Molesey and its reservoirs on the right (Surrey) bank – which, please note, is your left if proceeding upstream – and Sunbury Court Island with its many bungalows on your right, off the Middlesex bank. Navigation is possible inside the island but is not recommended as many residents' private craft are moored here. Between the head of Sunbury Court Island and the next, Rivermead Island, is a public slip reached from Lower Hampton road. Public toilets are located in the riverside gardens inside the upstream island, the inner channel not being navigable. Ahead on the right is the village of Sunbury, dominated by its strangely towered 19th-century church and, on the left, the paired Sunbury Locks at the tail of Sunbury Lock Ait where the Middle Thames Yacht Club has its premises.

The former boatyard of Horace Clark & Sons, taken over by R J Turk & Sons is now used for their boat building and repair business although scheduled for redevelopment, like so many of the old riverside boating businesses founded in Victorian and Edwardian times. George Wilson's yard a little further upstream still runs a ferry on request across to the island and provides moorings and slipway facilities close to the *Flower Pot Hotel*. Between Hampton and Sunbury are a number of sailing clubs and dinghy racing is popular, especially in the summer on Saturday afternoons and Sunday mornings. If cruising, give the racers' marker buoys a wide berth and try to interpret which way the dinghy helmsman will want to use the wind. In tree-lined reaches it will often pay you to keep as close to the trees as possible as they create odd air currents and unpredictable eddies for

Sunbury Locks Daytime only. Walton Towing Path, Walton-on-Thames, Surrey KT12 2JD
☎ 01932 782089
Old 154'8" (47·14m) long × 19'3" (5·86m) wide
New 206'0" (62·78m) long × 24'4" (7·41m) wide
Rise (fall) 6'2" (1·87m)
Max. draught, old: 7'5" (2·26m); new: 8'2" (2·48m)
Facilities Toilets, water point for cans, refuse and chemical toilet disposal.

the racing man who doesn't like them and will keep clear!

Sunbury Locks are paired, the larger New Lock on the left as you pass upstream having been constructed and opened in 1927 to handle the barge traffic which frequented this part of the river to go up into the River Wey until the 1960s when that traffic virtually ceased. The Old Lock, dating from 1886 in its present form, is still used from time to time, although it is hand operated in a similar fashion to those above Oxford. Always watch for the lock-keeper's signals and listen out for instructions as to which chamber is in use.

Opposite the *Weir Hotel* is the main weir below which, at the head of Sunburylock Ait, is the boathouse of George Wilson & Sons. Fishermen holding a weir permit may no longer fish from the overfalls opposite the *Weir Hotel* for safety reasons following legal advice given to the Agency. Car parking is available close to the hotel which is reached from Sunbury Lane on the Surrey bank. Beyond the weir comes Wheatley's Ait on your right behind which runs a narrow channel. Ahead lies Walton Reach, where a number of rowing and canoe clubs are located, as well as the exits from Shepperton and Walton Marinas, right and left respectively, just before Walton Bridge. All these may give rise to calls for careful navigation, especially at weekends. There are public launching slips below the *Swan Hotel* at Walton and from the paddock at Cowey Sale, off Walton Lane, about 300 yards above the bridge. There is a public car park and toilets inshore of this latter site. Parking for short periods may be possible in Manor Road at the former.

The navigation channel now divides – the original channel going to the right towards Halliford and Shepperton, and straight ahead, the new Desborough Cut – opened in 1935 by Lord Desborough who was then chairman of the Thames Conservancy, as a bypass to the meander, saving about ¾ mile from your cruise. However, the old river is well worth a visit for its scenery and activity, to say nothing of the various hostelries that lie close to its banks, although care should be taken to keep in the fairway as there can be shallows, particularly on the insides of the bends.

If navigating the straight cut of the Desborough Channel it is advisable to keep a lookout for skiffs and canoes in view of the three clubs who practise here and whose clubhouses are located at the upstream end, close to D'Oyly Carte Island which should be left to port. Part-way up the Desborough Cut two sets of transit marks have been set up so that you may check the speed of your craft by timing your travel between them. If you take less than 60 seconds to cover the distance, then you are exceeding the speed limit of 8kph – just under 5mph. Go to the right of D'Oyly Carte Island proceeding upstream to avoid upsetting moored craft under the footbridge which leads to the premises of Eyot House Ltd. Coming into the basin below Shepperton Lock there is the choice of venturing into the River Wey which comes in from the south to one's left, alongside the weirstream or keeping to the right and entering Shepperton Lock to continue on up the Thames. Details of the Wey and Godalming Navigation which is owned and operated by the National Trust and the Basingstoke Canal which joins the Wey at Byfleet, are contained in separate sections of this book.

Below the lock are two launching slips, one on the Weybridge shore just above Weybridge Marine Ltd, which is free; and the other on the Shepperton shore which is operated by Nauticalia for a fee and accommodates craft of up to about 30ft. The ferry next to the slip, also run by Nauticalia, is the present official crossing point for the Thames Path which, without it, would have to follow a lengthy diversion through

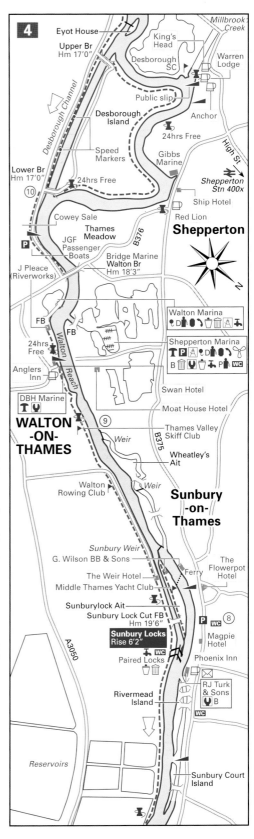

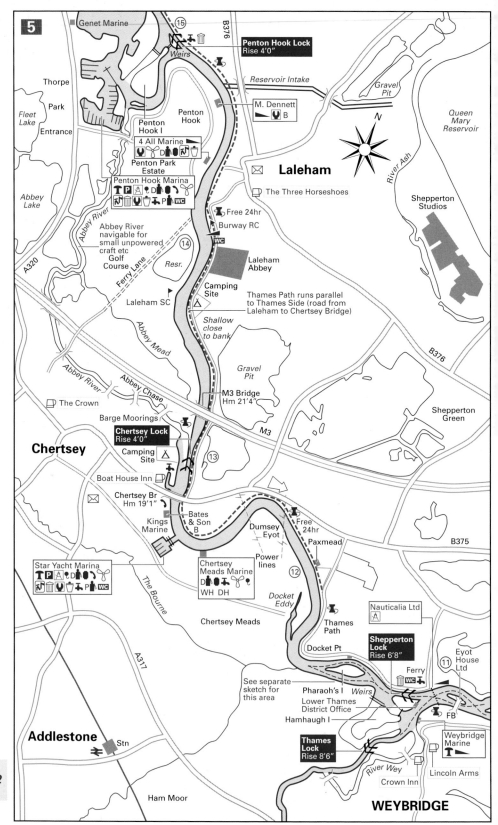

5

Genet Marine

⑮

B376

Thorpe
Park

Fleet
Lake

Park
Entrance

Weirs

Penton Hook Lock
Rise 4'0"

Reservoir Intake

*Gravel
Pit*

Queen
Mary
Reservoir

Penton
Hook

Penton
Hook I

M. Dennett
► ♥ B

Abbey
Lake

4 All Marine
♥ D♥ ☕
Penton Park
Estate

✉ **Laleham**

River Ash

The Three Horseshoes

Shepperton
Studios

Penton Hook Marina
♈ P ♥ D♥ ♫
🔲🗑♥☕⚓ P WC

A320

Abbey River

Abbey River
navigable for
small unpowered
craft etc
Golf
Course

⑭

Ferry Lane

Resr.

Free 24hr
Burway RC

WC

Laleham SC ►

Laleham
Abbey

Camping
Site
△

*Shallow
close
to bank*

Thames Path runs parallel
to Thames Side (road from
Laleham to Chertsey Bridge)

Abbey Mead

*Gravel
Pit*

B376

Shepperton
Green

Abbey River

Abbey Chase

The Crown

M3 Bridge
Hm 21'4"

M3

Barge Moorings

Chertsey Lock
Rise 4'0"

Chertsey

Camping
Site △

⑬

Boat House Inn

Chertsey Br
Hm 19'1"

✉

Bates
& Son
B

Free
24hr

Paxmead

B375

Kings
Marine

Dumsey
Eyot

Power
lines

⑫

Nauticalia Ltd
A

Star Yacht Marina
♈ P △ D♥ ♫
🔲🗑♥☕⚓ P WC

The Bourne

Chertsey
Meads Marine
D♥☕⚓♫
WH DH

*Docket
Eddy*

Thames
Path

**Shepperton
Lock**
Rise 6'8"

Eyot
House
Ltd

A317

Chertsey Meads

Docket Pt

⑪

Ferry

🏛 WC⚓

Pharaoh's I
Weirs

Lower Thames
District Office

Hamhaugh I

FB

Addlestone

See separate
sketch for
this area

■ Stn

Weybridge
Marine
♈▼

**Thames
Lock**
Rise 8'6"

Lincoln Arms

River Wey

Crown Inn

WEYBRIDGE

Ham Moor

Chertsey Lock from one of the arches of Chertsey Bridge

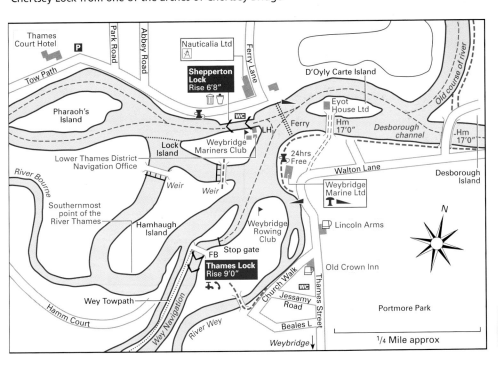

Thames Court Hotel

Park Road

Abbey Road

Tow Path

Nauticalia Ltd

Ferry Lane

D'Oyly Carte Island

Shepperton Lock Rise 6'8"

Pharaoh's Island

Eyot House Ltd

Hm 17'0"

Desborough channel

Hm 17'0"

LH

Ferry

Lower Thames District Navigation Office

Lock Island

Weybridge Mariners Club

24hrs Free

Walton Lane

Desborough Island

River Bourne

Weir

Weir

Weybridge Marine Ltd

Southernmost point of the River Thames

Hamhaugh Island

Weybridge Rowing Club

Lincoln Arms

N

Stop gate

Thames Lock Rise 9'0"

FB

Old Crown Inn

Wey Towpath

Church Walk

Jessamy Road

Thames Street

Portmore Park

Wey Navigation

Hamm Court

River Wey

Beales L

Weybridge ↓

¼ Mile approx

33

Shepperton Lock Daytime only
Towing Path, Shepperton, Middlesex
TW17 9LW ☎ 01932 221840
174'5'' (53·16m) long x 19'10'' (6·04m)
 wide
Rise (fall) 6'8'' (2·03m)
Max. draught 7'5'' (2·26m)
Facilities Shop, toilets, water point for
 cans, chemical toilet and refuse
 disposal.
Angling Weir permit holders from
 walkway on main Shepperton Weir
 and along small section of bank on
 west side of Hamhaugh Island.

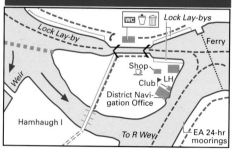

Weybridge which is described under the Thames Path heading at the end of this section.

Close to the Weybridge landing point for the ferry is a free 24-hour mooring site provided by the Environment Agency. On the Shepperton Lock Island is now the Lower Thames District Navigation office. Next door are the premises of the Weybridge Mariners' Club. The channel to the left (south) leads towards the mouth of the River Wey and the tail of Thames Lock which is the lowest on this tributary and the point of entry. Beyond is the weir stream which runs round the back of Hamhaugh Island and into which the Bourne empties after its tortuous journey under the M25 from Virginia Water. This weirstream is of geographical significance as it is the most southerly point of the River Thames.

Above Shepperton Lock, which boasts a small shop where the lock-keeper's wife serves light refreshments, one may pass either side of Pharaoh's Island surrounded by the many bungalows which give the area the atmosphere of a kind of suburban Venice. Moorings can be made on the towing path side close to the *Thames Court Hotel* which has a large car park alongside, or further upstream where Docket Eddy Lane brings the traffic in a one-way direction from the B375 Chertsey Road. Here is the Paxmead

Riverside Base where priority is given to youth groups such as scouts and guides for water-based activities and camping. A free 24-hour mooring is located opposite Dumsey Eyot on the north bank. The river now describes an S-bend around Chertsey Mead and back towards Chertsey Bridge. The yards of Chertsey Meads Marine where there is a slip, and Bates Marina below Bridge Wharf where there is a crane are both on your left-hand side. Shoot Chertsey Bridge through the centre arch but be prepared to give way to traffic coming downstream as the bridge is set within a short distance of Chertsey Lock and weirs. The lock is to your right, against the Middlesex bank and facing you is the weir stream at the top end of which is the mouth of the Abbey Stream, a bypass from the Penton Hook weir stream above and only navigable by small unpowered craft, usually in the downstream direction.

Close by Chertsey Bridge, on the downstream side, is a small car park on the left bank (right as you come upstream), while across it are a telephone and a good-sized service station with shop and fuel. The town of Chertsey is some distance away – about 15 minutes' walk. Below and opposite the weir is the site of the Chertsey Camping Club which boasts a children's play area, shop, and all domestic facilities, with 225 pitches available all year. Details from Chertsey Camping Club, Bridge Road, Chertsey, Surrey KT16 8JX ☎ 01932 562405.

Just above Chertsey Lock comes the sweeping span of the M3 motorway bridge. This might distract the unwary navigator from the pull of Chertsey Weir which can be strong when the flow is above normal. Once

Chertsey Lock Daytime only
Thames Side, Chertsey, Surrey KT16 8LD
☎ 01932 562208
200'8'' (61·16m) long × 21'00'' (6·40m) wide
Rise (fall) 4'0'' (1·22m)
Max. draught 8'1'' (2·46m)
Facilities Water points for cans and tank-
 filling by hose.

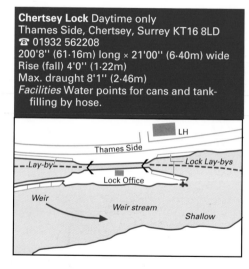

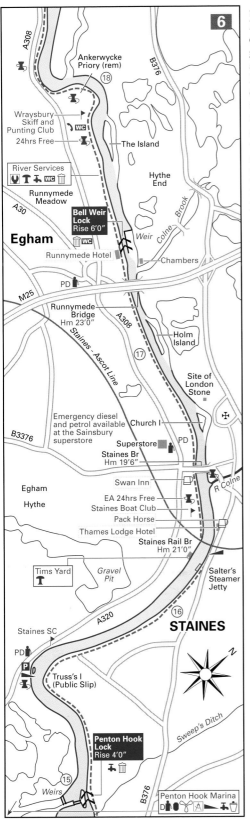

6

Egham

Ankerwycke Priory (rem)
(18)

Wraysbury Skiff and Punting Club
24hrs Free

The Island

Hythe End

River Services

Runnymede Meadow

A30

Bell Weir Lock Rise 6'0"

Weir

Runnymede Hotel

Chambers

Colne Brook

PD

M25

Runnymede Bridge Hm 23'0"

A308

Holm Island

Staines - Ascot Line

(17)

Site of London Stone

Emergency diesel and petrol available at the Sainsbury superstore

B3376

Church I

PD

Superstore

Staines Br Hm 19'6"

Swan Inn

Egham

Hythe

EA 24hrs Free
Staines Boat Club

Pack Horse

R Colne

Thames Lodge Hotel

Staines Rail Br Hm 21'0"

Tims Yard

Gravel Pit

Salter's Steamer Jetty

A320

(16)

STAINES

Staines SC

PD

P

Truss's I (Public Slip)

Sweep's Ditch

Penton Hook Lock Rise 4'0"

(15)

Weirs

B376

Penton Hook Marina

under the bridge, the river meanders up Laleham Reach where rowing, sailing, camping, boat building, picnicking and even golf can be counted among the leisure activities enjoyed. The clubs and services listed in the directories are indicative of the care that may be needed, particularly after the slip and clubhouse of Laleham Sailing Club have been reached. Opposite the sailing club will be seen the Laleham Camping Club where similar facilities to those at Chertsey are available, although only from early April to late September. Details from Laleham Park, Thameside, Laleham, Staines, Middlesex ☎ 01932 564149. One may be tempted to moor to the sylvan-covered left bank (on one's right) but beware, as much of it is shallow and often used by small children in the summer, paddling and splashing, oblivious to the approach of craft whose crew wish to join in! The first suitable mooring for visits to be made ashore to Laleham village is just above the point where the road leaves the towing path where the old Laleham Ferry used to cross. Here there is a 24-hour free mooring point.

Thereafter you will be surrounded by housing on your right and bungalows and boatyards on your left as you approach Penton Hook. Just opposite Mike Dennett's premises on Penton Hook is the reservoir intake to the famous Queen Mary Reservoir, and above are further moorings before the junction of the weir stream on the left which leads to Penton Hook Marina. On your right,

Penton Hook Lock Daytime only
Thameside, Staines, Middlesex TW18 2JA
☎ 01784 452657
266'8" (81·28m) long x 24'10" (7·56m) wide
Rise (fall) 4'0" (1·22m)
Max. draught 8'5" (2·56m)
Facilities Water points for cans and refuse disposal.
Angling Weir permit holders may fish from certain stretches of bank on the two islands which sit in the weir stream circuit. No fishing from the nature reserve or picnic areas.

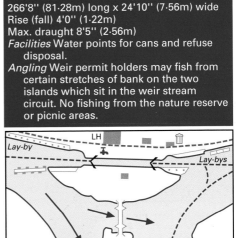

Lay-by

LH

Lay-bys

Marina

Weirs

facing you, is the tail of Penton Hook Lock. **Note** The marina cannot be reached from above the lock. In the approach channel to the marina on your left (port) side you will find some visitors' moorings alongside the yacht club. The harbour master's office is behind the chandlery which lies across the car park at the end of the clubhouse. Penton Hook Marina is a handy stopping-off point for Thorpe Park and mariners are welcome – no prior booking is necessary – but owners or hirers must check with the harbour master's office before leaving their craft on the moorings unattended.

Leaving Penton Hook Lock we approach the conurbation of Staines which, with Ashford and Sunbury, has combined itself into the grandiosely-titled borough of Spelthorne. The river, though, is probably more attractive than hitherto, since thoughtful development has been instigated, especially in the areas between the rail bridge and Runnymede Bridge which carries both the A30 and the M25 across the river below Bell Weir.

Below Staines Bridge (which nominally marks the City of London limit), Runnymede Borough Council, the riparian authority on the Surrey bank has also attended to various improvements, such as the installation of a temporary (max. 4 hours) mooring site at the reclaimed Truss's Island which lies in the crook of the first right-hand bend after Penton Hook. It is worth stopping to read the stone's inscription and the history of this island (which has been saved from neglect and the possibility of unsympathetic development) and to watch the multitude of waterbirds that gather here. There is also a small launching slip for light craft and a reasonable car and trailer park. Across the road is a service station selling petrol and diesel.

Staines is a close and useful stop for provisions. There is a 24-hour mooring below the *Swan* public house on the Surrey bank below Staines Bridge. Under the rail bridge, on the Middlesex bank, is a public launching slip, straight off the B376 Laleham Road.

Sadly, the famous London Stone has been removed from its former home in the park above Church Island, out of reach of vandals, after some 200 years' of uninterrupted, quiet enjoyment – possibly even longer, for parts of it appear to date from 1285. A glass-reinforced plastic replica now sits in its place, while the original can be seen in the Old Town Hall. The former gasworks site

opposite Church Island has been screened by tree-planting and new offices have taken the place of the former temporary structures which used to line the river alongside the Causeway. Leave Holm Island and the tiny Hollyhock Island behind it to starboard as you sail along the boundary into the Royal Borough of Windsor and Maidenhead.

Heading upstream and under the M25 we approach Bell Weir Lock which sits beside the *Runnymede Hotel* and heralds the approach to the Thames' historical associations with Britain's turbulent past, from King John to the Second World War. There is also a memorial to John F Kennedy which, suggests Graham Hayward in his *Stanford's River Thames*, may have been erected a little too soon, perhaps by a millennium!

Above Bell Weir lies a deceptively long reach with a width to trick the unsuspecting into opening the throttle. Remember that, throughout the freshwater Thames, there is a speed limit and cruising speed should never exceed a fast walking pace – no more than just under 5mph. At the head of the reach, on the right bank (left as we proceed upstream), are some free 24-hour moorings just before the Wraysbury Skiff and Punting Club, which

The author as Salter's Steamers skipper

Staines Bridge

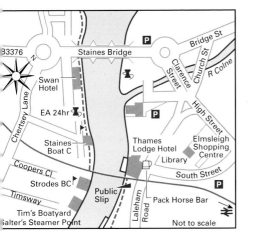

The RAF memorial on Cooper's Hill above Runnymede

precedes Egham Recreation Ground with its car park, café, telephone and toilets towards the main A308 Windsor Road. Around the bend, one passes the remains of Ankerwycke Priory on the left bank and then, on the right bank (left as we proceed upstream), comes Runnymede Meadow with Coopers Hill above it and the Air Forces Memorial nestling in the trees. The meadow is National Trust property but mooring is possible here with care. Avoid trying to moor on the opposite bank or close to Magna Carta Island, which is private. A footpath from the river crosses the meadow and joins Coopers Hill Lane below the entrance to the Memorial, which is worth a visit.

37

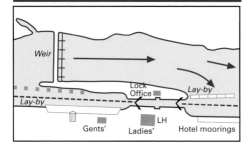

Swans at Truss's Island, Staines

The Thames Path

The Thames Path starts this section on the Surrey bank alongside West Molesey reservoirs and follows uninterrupted through Walton-on-Thames and past three riverside pubs as far as the start of the Desborough Cut, where one has a choice between following the official path along Walton Lane to Weybridge beside a rather narrow and uninteresting stretch of 'cut', or following the river around the old towing path on Desborough Island. This latter course is more interesting for walkers. At present there is a ferry at Weybridge, operated by Nauticalia whose premises are located on the Middlesex bank just below Shepperton Lock. This runs from a point on the Surrey shore just downstream of the free moorings. A bell is provided to summon the ferryman in case he is asleep. If there is no ferry, walkers may wish to cross the river at Walton Bridge, walk through Shepperton village and rejoin the river at the bottom of Ferry Lane just below Shepperton Lock, a distance of about 1½ miles.

One can also elect to avoid the ferry and make a detour into the northern end of Weybridge and cross the Wey beside Thames Lock to follow the towing path of the Wey almost to the A317. From there, a footpath takes you close to Hamm Court Farm, then across the River Bourne from whose bridge keep right across Chertsey Meads and make

for Bates's Marina. From Bridge Wharf, cross Chertsey Bridge and rejoin the official Thames Path which has followed the Middlesex bank from Shepperton Lock and runs up beside the Chertsey Lock to Laleham, Penton Hook and Staines.

At Staines the Thames Path now crosses Staines Bridge, having crossed the entry of the River Colne which bubbles into the Thames between two blocks of apartments and by a curved walkway off the upstream side of the bridge or by steps on the downstream side on the Surrey bank. A short path to Staines Boat Club, which passes the *Swan Hotel* going back downstream from the bridge, is all that is left of the old towing path which ran originally from Tims' Ferry just below the rail bridge. Continuing upstream, the Path stays on the Surrey bank right up to the Berkshire boundary with Surrey at the foot of Priest Hill.

Angling

See notes on pages 20/21

Fishing is free in the river below Staines to holders of a national rod and line licence, either from afloat or from the towing path or accessible banks. Holders of weir permits may be able to fish at sites at Shepperton Weir, Penton Hook (Penton Hook Island) and Bell Weir. Instructions on how to get on to the overfalls or other fishing sites may be obtained from the lock-keeper to whom your permit should be shown and whose permission you should obtain before you fish. Your fishing is still subject to the normal fishery byelaws and close seasons and you are only allowed to fish at sites covered by the Lock and Weir Permit during the hours of duty of the lock staff. A table of hours of duty is given on page 168. More precise details of the type of site are given under individual lock entries.

Directory

BOATYARDS, MARINAS, CHANDLERIES, TRIPPING AND HIRE

R J Turk & Sons
10 Thames Street, Sunbury-on-Thames, Middlesex TW16 5QP ☎ 01932 782028. Boat builders, repairs.

Geo. Wilson & Sons, (Boat Builders) Ltd
Ferry House, Thames Street, Sunbury-on-Thames, Middlesex TW16 6AQ ☎ 01932 782067. Day and hourly launch hire, fishing punt hire, moorings, storage, slipway, water point, ferry to Sunburylock Ait. (TBTA)

DBH Marine
52 Sullivan's Reach, Walton-on-Thames, Surrey KT12 2QB ☎ 01932 226555. Boat repairs, fitting out, moorings. (TBTA)

Shepperton Marina Ltd
Felix Lane, Shepperton, Middlesex TW17 8NS ☎ 01932 243722. Annual and visitors' moorings, diesel fuel, petrol, *Calor Gas,* groceries, restaurant, hardstanding, crane, slipway, electric boat recharging, mains electricity, water point, refuse and sewage disposal, toilets, telephone, car park.

Boat Showrooms Ltd
Shepperton Marina, Felix Lane, Shepperton, Middlesex TW17 8NS
☎ 01932 243722. Boat sales, brokers and insurance. (Also at Harleyford Marina.) (TBTA)

Twickenham & White Water Canoe Centre
Shepperton Marina, Felix Lane, Shepperton, Middlesex TW17 8NS
☎ 01932 247978/225988. Canoes, all accessories and equipment, coaching, mail order.

Lindon Lewis Marine
Shepperton Marina, Felix Lane, Shepperton, Middlesex TW17 8NS

☎ 01932 247427. Marine engineers, repairs, battery charging, chandlery, spares, Volvo Penta dealer.

J A Pleace (Riverworks) Ltd
Rosewell's Boathouse, Walton Bridge, Walton-on-Thames KT12 1QW
☎ 01932 226266. Piling and dredging. (TBTA)

Walton Marine Sales Ltd
Rosewell's Boathouse, Walton Marina, Walton Bridge, Walton-on-Thames, Surrey KT12 1QW ☎ 01932 226266. Boat sales, finance and insurance, repairs, marine engineers, diesel fuel, *Calor Gas*, chandlery, restaurant, club, permanent and visitors' moorings, crane, slipway, water points, mains electricity, telephone, refuse and sewage disposal, toilets, car park. (TBTA)

Bridge Marine Ltd
Thames Meadow, Shepperton, Middlesex TW17 8LU ☎ 01932 245126. Boat builders and repairers, slipway, crane, electric boat recharging, water. (TBTA)

JGF Passenger Boats
Walton Bridge, Cowey Sale, Walton-on-Thames, Surrey KT12 1QY ☎ 01932 253374. Passenger trips, party hire – day or evening, weddings, parties, discos. (Office: 6, Montague Close, Walton-on-Thames, Surrey, KT12 2NF.) (PBA)

Penton Hook Marina

Britain's largest inland marina, Penton Hook is situated on one of the prettiest reaches of the River Thames. It provides a safe haven for a wide range of craft, including narrow boats.

- 610 berths
- Petrol and diesel
- Boat lifting and hard standing area
- Electricity and water available on all berths
- Pump out
- Engineering and repair services
- Brokerage
- Chandlery
- Yacht club
- Launderette
- Visitor moorings
- 24 hour manned security and CCTV

Penton Hook Marina
Staines Road, Chertsey,
Surrey KT16 8PY
Tel: 01932 568681
Fax: 01932 567423
Email: pentonhook@mdlmarinas.co.uk

For further information, please contact the Marina Manager quoting ref. RTB.

Gibbs (Marine Sales)
Sandhills, Russell Road, Shepperton, Middlesex TW17 9HY ☎ 01932 242977. Boatbuilders, sales, repairs, marine engineers, chandlery, outboard sales and service, permanent moorings, crane, slipway, hardstanding, water point, power points, refuse disposal, toilets, car park, telephone. (TBTA)

Transatlantic Marine Ltd
The Boathouse, Sandhills, Russell Road, Shepperton, Middlesex TW17 9HY ☎ 01932 228998. Boats and small craft.

Eyot House Ltd
D'Oyly Carte Island, Weybridge, Surrey KT13 8LX ☎ 01932 848586. Boat brokerage, chandlery, marine engineers, repairs, slipway, *Calor Gas*, private moorings, winter storage, sewage and refuse disposal, water, toilets, telephone, car and trailer park. (TBTA)

Weybridge Marine Ltd
91, Thames Street, Weybridge, Surrey KT13 8LP ☎ 01932 847453. Permanent moorings, hardstanding, winter storage, slipway.

Nauticalia Ltd
Ferry Works, Ferry Lane, Shepperton, Middlesex TW17 9LQ ☎ 01932 244396. Boat sales, inflatables, sports boats, inboard and outboard engine sales and service, finance, chandlery, gifts, *Calor Gas*, DIY boatbuilding, permanent moorings, day-boat hire, water point, slipway. Ferry service to Weybridge. (TBTA)

Chertsey Meads Marine Ltd
The Meads, Chertsey, Surrey, KT16 8LN ☎ 01932 564699. Boat builders, repairers, marine engineers, diesel fuel, *Calor Gas*, cruiser hire, day-boat hire, permanent moorings, winter storage, hardstanding, crane and slipway, water point. (TBTA)

W Bates & Son (Boatbuilders) Ltd (Star Marina)
Bridge Wharf, Chertsey, Surrey KT16 8LG ☎ 01932 562255/565535. Chandlery, permanent moorings, winter storage, hardstanding, crane, water point, refuse and sewage disposal, toilets, mains electricity, car park. (TBTA)

Bates Wharf Marine Sales Ltd
Bridge Wharf, Chertsey, Surrey KT16 8LG ☎ 01932 571141. Boat sales, brokerage. (TBTA)

Kings Marine Ltd
Bridge Wharf, Chertsey, Surrey KT16 8LG ☎ 01932 564830. Boat sales, outboard sales and service, marine engineers, chandlery, permanent moorings.

4 All Marine
Harris Estate, Laleham Reach, Chertsey, Surrey KT16 8RP ☎ 01932 567744. Marine engineers, welding, repairs, call-out service, fitting out, diesel, *Calor Gas*, pump-out, water point, refuse disposal, slipway. (TBTA)

M Dennett
Laleham Boatyard, Laleham Reach, Chertsey, Surrey KT16 8RR ☎ 01932 563448. Boatbuilder, repairer and restorer of traditional craft, boat sales, slipway.

Penton Hook Marina (MDL)
Staines Road, Chertsey, Surrey KT16 8PY ☎ 01932 568681. Permanent and visitors' moorings, diesel fuel, petrol, winter storage, hardstanding, slipway, telephone, water points, refuse and sewage disposal, sewage pump-out, toilets, mains electricity, car parks. (TBTA)

Penton Service Centre Ltd
Penton Hook Marina, Staines Road, Chertsey, Surrey KT16 8PY ☎ 01932 568772. Repairs, craning, engineering.

Chertsey Marine
Penton Hook Marina, Staines Road, Chertsey, Surrey KT16 8PY ☎ 01932 565195. Chandlery, *Calor Gas*, clothing.

Marine Trimming Service
Penton Hook Marina, Staines Road, Chertsey, Surrey KT16 8PY ☎ 01932 563779. Marine hoods, trimming and upholstery, repairs.

Penton Hook Marine Sales
Penton Hook Marina, Staines Road, Chertsey, Surrey KT16 8PY ☎ 01932 570055. Boat sales (new and second-hand), finance, insurance. (TBTA)

Donzi Powerboats (UK) Ltd
Penton Hook Marina, Staines Road, Chertsey, Surrey KT16 8PY ☎ 01932 566300. Boat sales, etc.

Tideway Marine
Penton Hook Marina, Staines Road, Chertsey, Surrey KT16 8PY ☎ 01932 568879/568870. Marine engineers.

River Rescue Ltd
Penton Hook Marina, Staines Road, Chertsey, Surrey KT16 8PY ☎ 01932 571500. Marine engineers, boat repairs, mechanical repairs. Mobile breakdown service with membership facilities.

Aqua Marine
Units 14 & 15, Penton Hook Marina, Staines Road, Chertsey, Surrey KT16 8PY ☎ 01932 570202. Marine engineers. (TBTA)

Genet Marine Ltd
Chertsey Lane, Staines, Middlesex TW18 3NG ☎ 01784 458372. Marine engineers.

J Tims and Sons
Tims Boatyard, Timsway, Staines, Middlesex TW18 3JY ☎ 01784 452093. Permanent moorings only.

A C Marine
Tims Boatyard, Timsway, Staines, Middlesex TW18 3JY ☎ 01784 466700. Boat building, fitting out, engineering, surveys. Steel, g.r.p. wood. Dutch barge specialist.

H Chambers Ltd
Ferry Lane, Wraysbury, Staines, Middlesex TW19 6HG ☎ 01784 482051. Moorings, winter storage, slipway, boat hire.

River Services Ltd
Yard Mead, Windsor Road, Egham, Surrey TW20 0AA ☎ 01784 473300. Boat repairs, marine engineers, day boat hire, permanent and visitors' moorings, hardstanding, water point, toilets, refuse disposal, car park.

EMERGENCY FUEL SUPPLIES
See note under this heading on page 24
Shepperton Service Station
Petrol, diesel. Shop
Walton Bridge Road, Shepperton TW17 ☎ 01932 254201 (600 yards from Walton Bridge on Middlesex bank at roundabout).

Chertsey Service Station
Petrol, diesel. Shop
Bridge Road, Chertsey KT16 ☎ 01932 562702 (100yds off Chertsey Bridge, Surrey side.)

Swan Uppers in Boulters Lock

Elf Service Station
Petrol, diesel. Shop
Chertsey Lane, Staines TW18 ☎ 01784 463572 (Opposite Truss's Island moorings. Surrey bank.)

Jet Filling Station
Petrol, diesel
Laleham Road, Staines, Middlesex TW18. (Downstream of rail bridge on Middlesex bank.)

Sainsbury's Service Station
Petrol, diesel
The Causeway, Staines, Middlesex TW18. (Upstream of Staines Bridge, 100yds from Surrey bank.)

ROWING, SAILING AND CRUISING CLUBS AND TUITION

Middle Thames Yacht Club
Sunburylock Ait, Walton-on-Thames, Surrey KT12 2JE (ATYC, RYA)

Walton Rowing Club
Sunbury Lane, Walton-on-Thames, Surrey KT12 2JA ☎ 01932 224557 (ARA)

St George's College Boat Club
Sunbury Lane, Walton-on-Thames, Surrey KT12 2JA (ARA)

Thames Valley Skiff Club
The Pavilion, Dudley Road, Walton-on-Thames, Surrey KT12 2JY ☎ 01932 224215 (ARA)

Walton Bridge Cruiser Club
Walton Marina, Walton Bridge, Walton-on-Thames, Surrey KT12 1QW (ATYC, RYA)

Desborough Sailing Club
Ferry Lane, Shepperton, Middlesex TW17 9LQ (RYA)

Weybridge Sailing Club
Walton Lane, Weybridge, Surrey KT13 8LU (RYA)

Elmbridge Canoe & Kayak Club
Walton Lane, Weybridge, Surrey KT13 8LT

Weybridge Ladies' Amateur Rowing Club
Walton Lane, Weybridge, Surrey KT13 8LU (ARA)

Weybridge Rowing Club
Thames Lock, Jessamy Road, Weybridge, Surrey KT13 8LG ☎ 01932 842993 (ARA)

Weybridge Mariners Club
Lock Island, Shepperton, Middlesex TW17 9LW ☎ 01932 244787 (ATYC, RYA)

Paxmead Riverside Base
Dockett Eddy Lane, Shepperton, Middlesex TW17 9LL ☎ 01932 244214

Abbey Barge Club
Abbey Chase, Chertsey, Surrey KT16 8JW ☎ 01932 560672

Laleham Sailing Club
Laleham Burway, Chertsey, Surrey KT16 8RW (RYA)

Burway Rowing Club
Laleham Park, Laleham, Staines, Middlesex TW18 1SS (ARA)

Penton Hook Yacht Club
Penton Hook Marina, Staines Road, Chertsey, Surrey KT16 8PY (ATYC, RYA)

Staines Sailing Club
105, Chertsey Lane, Staines, Middlesex TW18 3LQ ☎ 01784 455887 (RYA)

Dreadnought Scullers
The Boathouse, Tim's Way, Staines, Middlesex TW18 3JY ☎ 01784 463900 (ARA)

Strodes Boat Club
Coopers Close, Chertsey Lane, Staines Middlesex TW18 3JX ☎ 01784 469140 (ARA)

Staines Boat Club
28, Riverside Drive, Staines, Middlesex TW18 3JN ☎ 01784 453595 (ARA)

Staines and Egham Unit Sea Cadet Corps
The Car Park, Staines Bridge, Staines, Middlesex TW18 4TG ☎ 01784 469064

Wraysbury Skiff and Punting Club
Runnymede Pleasure Ground, Riverside, Egham, Surrey TW20 0AA ☎ 01784 437206 (ARA)

PUBLIC LAUNCHING SITES

- **Sunbury village**
  Lower Hampton Road (B375). Below tail of Rivermead Ait. Light shallow draught vessels only
  Lower Hampton Road (B375). Opposite *Flower Pot Hotel*. Small craft only. Limited parking
- **Walton-on-Thames**
  Upstream of *Anglers Hotel* below *Swan Inn* off Manor Road. Limited parking. Small craft only
  Slipway 300 yards upstream of Walton Bridge at Cowey Sale. Car park. Small craft only
- **Weybridge**
  Downstream of Weybridge Marine at junction of Walton Lane and Thames Street. Small craft only
- **Shepperton**
  Shepperton Village Wharf. Off Ferry Square from Church Road, opposite Desborough SC
- **Laleham**
  Off Thames Side, 200 yards downstream of junction with Ferry Lane
- **Staines**
  Chertsey Lane. At Truss's Island. Small craft only over steep concrete slip. Car and trailer park
  Laleham Road (B376). Immediately under rail bridge opposite Tims' Yard. Access restricted by traffic

FISHING TACKLE SHOPS
Fishing below Staines Bridge is free, from a boat, the towing path, or where allowed by the riparian owner.

Tackle Exchange
97 Terrace Road, Walton-on-Thames, Surrey KT12 2SG ☎ 01932 242377/247224

Chertsey Angling Centre
40 Guildford Street, Chertsey, Surrey KT16 9BE ☎ 01932 562701

Ashford Angling Centre
357 Staines Road West, Ashford Common, Ashford, Middlesex TW15 1RP ☎ 01784 240013

Davies Angling
47/49 Church Street, Staines, Middlesex TW18 4EN ☎ 01784 461831

HOTELS, INNS AND RESTAURANTS
Phoenix Inn Thames Street, Lower Sunbury.

Magpie Hotel Thames Street, Lower Sunbury ☎ 01932 782024. Restaurant and bistro bar. Hotel rooms. Moorings adjacent.

The Flower Pot Hotel Thames Street, Lower Sunbury. Bar snacks.

Weir Hotel The Towing path, Sunbury Lane, Walton. Bar meals only at lunchtimes. Family room for children. Moorings.

Swan Inn Manor Road, Walton. Bar meals only. Children welcome. Moorings close by.

Anglers Tavern Manor Road, Riverside, Walton ☎ 01932 227423. Bar meals and dining. Moorings.

Shepperton Moat House Hotel Felix Lane, Shepperton ☎ 01932 241404. Restaurant.

Red Lion Russell Road, Shepperton ☎ 01932 220042/244526. Bar meals midday and evening. Restaurant lunch only (not Sundays). Moorings.

The Ship Hotel Russell Road, Shepperton ☎ 01932 227320. Bar meals, restaurant, B&B. Two mooring spaces outside.

Anchor Hotel Church Square, Shepperton ☎ 01932 221618. Egon Ronay recommended restaurant. Accommodation.

King's Head Inn Church Square, Shepperton. Real ale, lunchtime food.

Warren Lodge Hotel Church Square, Shepperton ☎ 01932 242972. Restaurant. Own moorings.

The Old Crown Inn Thames Street, Weybridge. Moor at NRA mooring below Shepperton Lock, 5 minutes' walk.

Lincoln Arms Thames Street, Weybridge ☎ 01932 842109/844620. Bar meals and dining, noon and evening. Use EA mooring below Shepperton Lock or in River Wey.

Thames Court Hotel Towing Path, Shepperton ☎ 01932 221957. Bar meals, dining (11am_9pm). Moorings by towing path.

The Kingfisher Chertsey Bridge Road. Mooring on left bank below Chertsey Bridge.

The Boathouse Inn Chertsey Bridge Road ☎ 01932 565644. Mooring by pub above Chertsey Bridge on right bank.

Three Horseshoes Inn Shepperton Road, Laleham ☎ 01784 452617. Dining, snacks, sandwiches. Moor opposite Harris's yard on towing path, taking care as shore is shallow, 2 minutes' walk.

Thames Lodge Hotel and Pack Horse Bar Thames Street, Staines ☎ 01784 464433 (*Forte*). Full hotel facilities, bars, restaurant. Moorings for guests outside hotel (150′).

Swan Hotel The Hythe, Staines. Bar meals, restaurant. All-day moorings outside with further public mooring downstream.

McDonald's High Street, Staines.

Pizza Express Clarence Street, Staines.

Runnymede Hotel Bell Weir Lock, Windsor Road, Egham ☎ 01784 436171. High-class hotel-restaurant. Moorings for guests below lock.

TAXIS

Walton ☎ 01932 221484
Weybridge ☎ 01932 858585
Shepperton ☎ 01932 244044
Chertsey ☎ 01932 571111
Staines ☎ 01784 442491

RAIL STATIONS AND TRAIN SERVICES

See note under this heading on page 26

Travel information (Surrey CC) ☎ 01784 442893. *South West Trains* Enquiries: ☎ 08457 484950.

Sunbury *South West Trains* Station Approach, Sunbury, Middlesex. 1900yds from the river. Trains to Upper Halliford and Shepperton; Teddington, Hampton Wick, Kingston and Waterloo via Wimbledon. Peak service (Monday–Friday only) to and from Strawberry Hill, Twickenham, Richmond and Waterloo.

Walton-on-Thames *South West Trains* Station Avenue, Walton, Surrey. 1½ miles from river. Trains to Weybridge and Woking; Surbiton and Waterloo. Also to Guildford (change at Woking for Guildford on Sundays).

Weybridge *South West Trains* Station Approach, Off Brooklands Road, Weybridge, Surrey. 1½ miles from river. Trains to Woking; Walton, Surbiton and Waterloo. Also to Guildford (change at Woking for Guildford on Sundays).

Shepperton *South West Trains* Station Approach, Off Green Lane, Shepperton, Middlesex. 1½ miles from river. Trains to Sunbury and Hampton; Teddington, Hampton Wick, Kingston and Waterloo via Wimbledon. Peak service (Monday–Friday only) to and from Strawberry Hill, Twickenham, Richmond and Waterloo.

Chertsey *South West Trains* Guildford Street, Chertsey, Surrey. 1¼ miles from river. Trains to Weybridge, Egham, Staines, Hounslow, Putney and Waterloo (change at Staines for Windsor, Richmond, and Reading lines).

Staines *South West Trains* Station Approach, Off Kingston Road, Staines, Middlesex. 500yds from river. Trains to Waterloo, Twickenham, Richmond and Putney; Egham; Reading; Wraysbury, Datchet and Windsor; Chertsey and Weybridge.

Egham *South West Trains* Station Road, Egham, Surrey. 1400 yards from river. Trains to Reading; Staines, Twickenham, Richmond and Waterloo. Also Chertsey and Weybridge.

BUS AND COACH SERVICES

Sunbury to Staines

Most major towns along the river in this section are connected by regular (at least hourly) bus services. Hampton Court, Walton-on-Thames and Staines are the main collecting points and routes run between Hampton Court and Staines via Sunbury or Walton; also to Weybridge, Chertsey, Windsor and, in the London direction, to Kingston and Richmond via main roads on either side of the river. Limited-stop coach services run through the area between Victoria and Guildford; and Heathrow and Dartford via Hampton and Kingston hourly. There are also night buses from Trafalgar Square to Sunbury.

Bus operators:
- First Beeline ☎ 01753 524144
- London United ☎ 020 8400 6665
- London Buslines ☎ 020 8571 2233
- Arriva Surrey and W Sussex ☎ 01737 242411
- Tellings Golden Miller ☎ 01932 340617
- Central London routes ☎ 020 7222 1234

4. Runnymede to Maidenhead

Distance

14.55 miles (Staines Bridge to Boulters Lock)

Maximum dimensions of craft from Runnymede to Maidenhead

Headroom 13´2˝ (4.01m) at Windsor Bridge
Length 134´4˝ (40.94m) at Bray Lock
Beam 17´10˝ (5.43m) at Boveney Lock
Draught 5´6˝ (1.7m) to Romney Lock
4´6˝ (1.3m) above Romney Lock to Reading.

Upstream of Staines the river has finally left suburbia and ahead lies a changing pattern of more spacious living with tracts of parkland and open countryside where, as yet, development has not been allowed to take place on the river's flood plain. The time will no doubt come when man's defiance of nature in the pursuit of his insatiable desire to control it will cause him to sweep the rules aside and rue the day he did. Even now you have probably noticed the newly erected tenements of 'court' and 'reach' where brick has replaced a reeded bank and computer-printed plaques forbid the passing sailor to linger.

Just before French Brothers' quay at Runnymede it is possible to moor opposite Pat's Croft Eyot and make for the National Trust teashop or climb Coopers Hill and visit the Magna Carta Memorial on the way, or attempt all three. The next stretch, wooded on both sides, opens out shortly to reveal more bungalows on the left bank while, on the right (to your left, remember), comes a short mooring in front of the present building which bears the famous name of the *Bells of Ouzeley*, transformed from an olde worlde bargees' resting place into a pseudo-Tudor 1930s roadhouse, later converted for the present purpose of a *Harvester* restaurant. Passing on by the former Crevald's Boat Services, which operates no more but whose present landlords still misleadingly call their building 'The Boathouse', one passes private moorings. From this point one can also reach the nearby Altwood BMW garage, or the shops further up if in need of stores. Then comes the tail of the Old Windsor weir stream on your right which circuits Ham Island ahead, and Old Windsor Lock on your left, tucked in behind Friday Island which sits in front of

Ham Island between the two streams, weir and navigation.

The lock cut above Old Windsor, known as the 'New Cut' is straight for half a mile, shortening the original river distance by nearly a mile. Ham Island, the island thus formed by the cutting, has been put to civic utility in the form of a sewage works. Above the main weir, which runs strongly in flood, one should keep to the towing path side, on the right bank (left hand side going upstream) and just short of the Albert Bridge it may be possible to moor for a visit to the *The British Raj* on the Datchet Road or the Royal Farms Windsor Farm Shop opposite.

The next reach past Datchet touches the Home Park of Windsor Castle and, in view of the strict security surrounding the monarch and her favoured home landing on, or approaching, the royal bank is forbidden. On this bank was the original towing path and it is still designated as such on many maps which show the legend alongside 'Prince Albert's Walk', which is no doubt the name given to it by Queen Victoria. Breakdowns have been known to occur on the Home Park side and the unknowing have even been seen landing; security, however, is so well ordered that matters are quickly and firmly sorted out. On the right-hand side beyond the Albert Bridge is the intake for the Datchet and Wraysbury reservoirs which dominate the horizon to the east. Next is Kris Cruisers boatyard at Datchet which offers a full boating service from day boats to holiday hire craft as well as engineering services,

---

Old Windsor Lock Daytime only
Old Windsor, Berkshire SL4 2JZ
☎ 01753 861822
179'0" (54·55m) long × 24'2" (7·36m) wide
Rise (fall) 5'9" (1·74m)
Max. draught 8'2" (2·48m)
Facilities Water point for can filling only.
Electric launch recharging point.

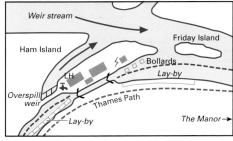

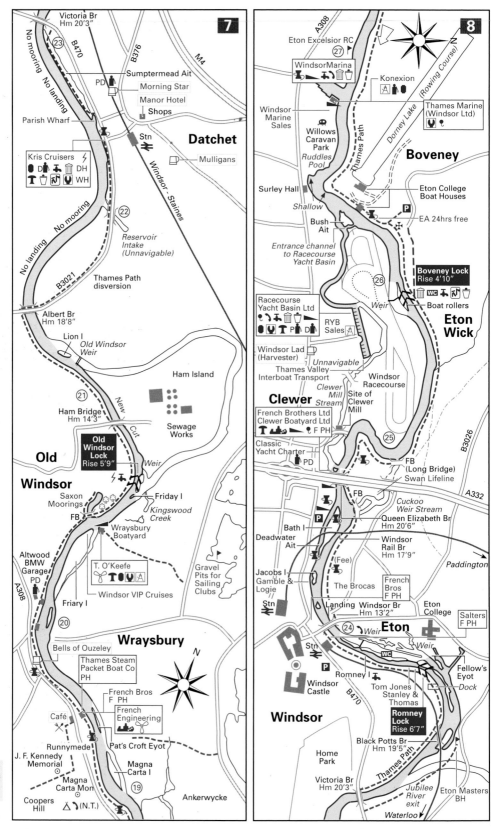

7

Victoria Br
Hm 20'3"

B470

B376

M4

Sumptermead Ait

PD

Morning Star

Manor Hotel

Shops

Parish Wharf

Stn

Datchet

Windsor – Staines

Mulligans

Kris Cruisers

DH
WH

Reservoir
Intake
(Unnavigable)

B3021

Thames Path
disversion

Albert Br
Hm 18'8"

Lion I

Old Windsor
Weir

Ham Island

Ham Bridge
Hm 14'3"

New Cut

Sewage
Works

Old

Windsor

Old
Windsor
Lock
Rise 5'9"

Weir

Saxon
Moorings

Friday I

FB

Kingswood
Creek

Wraysbury
Boatyard

Altwood
BMW
Garage
PD

T. O'Keefe

A308

Friary I

Windsor VIP Cruises

Wraysbury

N

Bells of Ouzeley

Thames Steam
Packet Boat Co
PH

French Bros
F PH

French
Engineering

Café

Runnymede

J. F. Kennedy
Memorial

Pat's Croft Eyot

Magna
Carta I

Magna
Carta Mon

Coopers
Hill

(N.T.)

Ankerwycke

Gravel
Pits for
Sailing
Clubs

8

N

A308

Eton Excelsior RC

WindsorMarina

Konexion

Windsor
Marine
Sales

Thames Marine
(Windsor Ltd)

Thames Path

Dorney Lake (Rowing Course)

Boveney

Willows
Caravan
Park

Ruddles
Pool

Surley Hall

Eton College
Boat Houses

Shallow

P

Bush
Ait

EA 24hrs free

Entrance channel
to Racecourse
Yacht Basin

Boveney Lock
Rise 4'10"

WC

Weir

Boat rollers

**Eton
Wick**

Racecourse
Yacht Basin Ltd

P

RYB
Sales

Windsor Lad
(Harvester)

Unnavigable

Windsor
Racecourse

Thames Valley
Interboat Transport

Clewer
Mill
Stream

Site of
Clewer
Mill

Clewer

French Brothers Ltd
Clewer Boatyard Ltd

F PH

Classic
Yacht Charter

PD

FB
(Long Bridge)
Swan Lifeline

B3026

A332

FB

Cuckoo
Weir Stream

P

Queen Elizabeth Br
Hm 20'6"

Bath I

Deadwater
Ait

Windsor
Rail Br
Hm 17'9"

Paddington

Jacobs I
Gamble &
Logie

(Fee)

The Brocas

French
Bros
F PH

Eton
College

Stn

Landing

Windsor Br
Hm 13'2"

Salters
F PH

Weir

Eton

Stn

P

WC

Weir

Romney I

Fellow's
Eyot
Dock

Windsor
Castle

Tom Jones
Stanley &
Thomas

Romney
Lock
Rise 6'7"

B470

Windsor

Home
Park

Black Potts Br
Hm 19'5"

Thames Path

Victoria Br
Hm 20'3"

Jubilee
River
exit

Eton Masters
BH

Waterloo

temporary and permanent moorings, electric hook-up, pump-out, water and diesel facilities for most of the year. Above the yard's pontoons is Datchet Wharf where there are public moorings, close to the site of the original Datchet bridges, of which over the years there have been five. At the new, Victoria Bridge, the landing prohibition in the Windsor Castle grounds ceases since the open space here is the Home Park on which the Royal Windsor Horse Show is held each year. Next on the left bank comes the downstream end of the Jubilee River or Maidenhead, Windsor and Eton Flood Alleviation Scheme Channel. Private moorings range along the left bank of the channel – right as viewed upstream – leading up to a new rail viaduct. At present the channel is not navigable and if it ever becomes so only very light craft will be able to use it along the several isolated sections.

The main river curves to your left and at Black Potts rail bridge which carries the South West Trains line from Staines across the Thames into Windsor and Eton Riverside Station it is advisable to use the channel against the towing path, now again on the right (Berkshire) bank – on your left as you proceed upstream – unless you draw more than 4 feet as the channel here is shallower than that through the right hand. The channel through the right-hand arch may be used with care and it may even be assumed by traffic coming downstream that you *will* use it, since on the river you drive on the right! If you have any doubts, though, about your draught, you should wait until the downstream traffic is clear before using the left-hand arch. Remember that upstream traffic should always give way to that running downstream since the latter has less steerage way at the normal cruising speed. This is a point that some of the navigational bureaucrats seemed to overlook when the byelaws were redrafted.

The rail bridge takes its strange name from the small Black Potts Ait below it and above is the tail of Romney Island, a point formerly known as 'The Needles' where the weir stream sweeps past Eton College on the Eton side and the Romney lock cut turns towards Windsor on your left. Fishing, as usual, is forbidden in the lock cut which is tightly curved and one reaches the lock with little warning. Romney Island gives its name to the lock whose chamber is as near in size to that at Bell Weir as Thames Water (a previous authority who undertook to rebuild it) could get it. The present lock was

Eton College Chapel and Romney Lock overspill

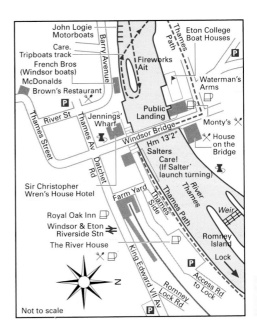

Windsor Bridge from Jennings' Wharf

reconstructed and opened in 1981 and has underwater sluices, like those at Bell Weir, as well as the conventional hydraulic gate paddles. For fast locking in the large chamber if few craft are passing up, it is wise to keep well back from the top gates to allow the gate paddles to be raised as quickly as possible. With a lockful of craft the keeper will have to run a slower fill to avoid any damage. However, the underwater sluices are designed to avoid the turbulence caused by gate paddles and the new chamber at Hambleden, 20 miles upstream, opened in 1994 has dispensed with gate paddles altogether.

Two small weirs take water from the lock cut into the weir stream which starts in earnest above the main weir opposite the head of Tangier Island, or Cutler's Ait as it was originally known. On your left as you leave the lock cut are Salters' moorings beyond the *River House* restaurant and ahead is the busy pool below Windsor Bridge. To your right is Eton with a new

riverside residential development and then two restaurants, one below and one above the bridge. Salters' launches arrive and leave from their Thames Side quay immediately below the bridge on the Windsor shore so be prepared to take avoiding action if they appear to be turning to depart. At the time of writing (2005), their usual schedules from Windsor include return trips to Staines on Mondays, Thursdays and Fridays and Maidenhead on Tuesdays and Wednesdays. On Monday and Friday afternoons there is also a service to Marlow.

Shoot Windsor Bridge through the centre arch and note that on this section this bridge has the lowest headroom of just 13´2´´ (4.01m) and that's the measurement in the middle! The river is up to 30ft (9.14m) deep below the bridge and in flood conditions turbulence can cause a helmsman some anxious moments. If coming downstream, heed the warning notice on the soffit of the bridge to keep right as you emerge to avoid the strong pull of Romney Weir. If going upstream it is most important here to remember that you must give way to downstream traffic. Immediately above Windsor Bridge on the Eton shore is a public landing, marking the site of the original bridge. On the Windsor side it is possible to moor at Jennings' Wharf, presented to the town by the successors to the brewery which was originally sited there. This meant that the walkway could be constructed from the bridge steps along to River Street. Pressure of traffic here and along Barry Avenue and the pedestrian crossing at this point means that the public slip at the corner by *Brown's* restaurant has had to be closed, but a slipping facility is available by the Queen Elizabeth Bridge.

From Barry Avenue, where French Brothers have now constructed a new gift shop and booking office, they run short and longer passenger trips lasting from 35 minutes to view Boveney Weir, 2-hour return trips up to Bray and all-day return excursions from Runnymede on Wednesday, Friday, Saturday and Sunday. There is also an inward service from Maidenhead and return every day except Sunday and Monday. These operate during the main summer season only. On race days at the course nearby there are special boat services to a landing stage at the racecourse upstream. Large passenger boats operate from short stages mounted inside the island on your left known as Fireworks Ait. Coming downstream, as they do, returning from Boveney Lock or the racecourse, they will swing out across the river above the bridge but below the tail of the ait and fetch up inside it. When level with the head of the ait going upstream, always make sure that a launch is not heading on a collision course with yours from behind it! Further along are the self-drive motor boats and rowing skiffs for hire from John Logie Motorboats Ltd and above the islands on the Windsor side and all along the Eton bank, known as the Brocas, are plentiful, but not free, moorings.

Further moorings may be found upstream and inside of Deadwater Ait on the Windsor side of the rail bridge – the last train rumbles across at 11.45pm but the first might not be popular at 5.40am! Many visitors to the river at Windsor complain of the lack of useful shops close to their moorings since, admittedly, much of the town close to the castle concentrates on the retail trade for the tourist. From Barry Avenue, however, easily reached by way of Windsor Bridge if you are moored on the Brocas at Eton, walk down

Approaching Romney Lock, Windsor

Romney Lock Daytime only
Romney Island, Datchet Road, Windsor, Berkshire SL4 6HU ☎ 01753 860296
257'7" (78·50m) long x 24'5" (7·45m) wide
Rise (fall) 6'7" (2·01m)
Max. draught 8'7" (2·62m)
Facilities Water point for can filling only, toilets upstream of lock house

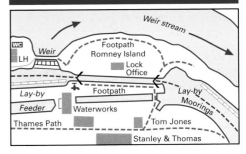

Goswell Road and under the narrow rail bridge. Turn left into Goswell Hill and almost immediately on your right you will find a flight of steps which takes you up into a new shopping precinct, King Edward

Court. Here you will find a Waitrose supermarket, shoe shops, two department stores, Boots, Mothercare and others. The precinct connects with Peascod Street in which will be found, among other well-known High Street names, Marks and Spencer, Woolworths and the Post Office. Turning left up Peascod Street takes you to the High Street where the four major UK clearing banks have their premises.

A leisure centre and local boat clubs occupy the right bank above the rail bridge before you approach the Queen Elizabeth Bridge which carries the Eton and Windsor relief road (A332) over the river and the side stream, known as the Cuckoo Weir Stream coming in on the left bank just below the bridge. A mooring can be made on the leisure centre side just below the new slipway. Payment for either facility should be made at the centre reception desk. Above the bridge on your left comes the Clewer Millstream wherein lie the yards of French Brothers and Clewer Mill Boatyard. A short walk from Stovell Road by footpath under the relief road will bring you to Pride's Garage which sells *BP* petrol, diesel and a range of groceries. The main channel now sweeps round in a wide arc to starboard. Do not approach the starboard bank too closely as it tends to silt up unless regularly scoured by passing craft. Then comes another change of direction around the parade ring of the racecourse before we follow a leisurely route beside the course up to Boveney Lock. A word of warning here – the trip boats tend to disappear into the weirpool to turn (as shown in the lock diagram) and come

Boveney Lock Daytime only
Lock Path, Dorney, Windsor, Berkshire SL4
6QQ ☎ 01753 862764
149'7'' (45·59m) long × 17'10'' (5·43m) wide
Rise (fall) 4'10'' (1·47m)
Max. draught 7'0'' (2·13m)
Facilities Sewage disposal and pump-out.
 Refuse disposal, toilets, water supplies
 for cans and hose filling. Boat rollers for
 light craft. Overnight moorings.

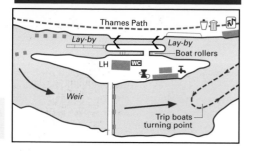

shooting out again to frighten the unwary. As you approach the lock, keep well over to the right-hand side of the river, making for the lay-by on the north, Buckinghamshire, bank – the county boundary here lying down the centre of the river.

Above Boveney the towing path on your right affords a stretch of free overnight 24-hour moorings just below the new hangar-like Eton College boathouse whence may come practising rowing college singles, pairs, fours or even eights, to upset the tyro helmsman. Behind the boathouse will be seen the imposing headquarters of the college's Dorney Rowing Lake, recently constructed and opened in 1999. Over on your left, the right bank as you come downstream, is the channel behind Bush Ait which leads into the Clewer Mill Stream, useful at its upper course as the approach to the Racecourse Yacht Basin where there are both permanent and visitors' moorings and all services including a restaurant. The channel is narrow, and navigating the twists and turns (shown on Chart No. 8) to this comprehensive marina should be treated with care. Ahead lies Ruddles Pool, a trap for anyone turning right too soon when going upstream. Often a marker buoy is placed here by the EA and should be observed carefully as it marks a nasty shoal on which the author once slithered one early spring when the buoy had been removed for repainting! Around this nasty bend we come into the straight that leads past the Willows Caravan Park against which are moored many houseboats. Please watch your wash! These are the only homes that many people who own them have and household chores in a suddenly disorientated chamber are unwelcome and evidence of damage can lead to the master of a vessel causing it to be taken to court.

Then comes Windsor Marina, in the same organization as Penton Hook lower down and Bray Marina which is a short cruise upriver within this reach. Unlike many of the marinas on the Thames, Windsor Marina was purposely dug out and is not a flooded ex-gravel pit. It started as a paddock alongside the river with the boats hauled out into the grass during the winter and the original sheds still lie within the curtilage of the chandlery and office buildings atop the slipway. Meakes of Marlow, a well known river name for many years, took on the job of 'marina-izing' the site and then sold out to the predecessors of the present owners. Next to it is the new boathouse of the Eton Excelsior Rowing Club.

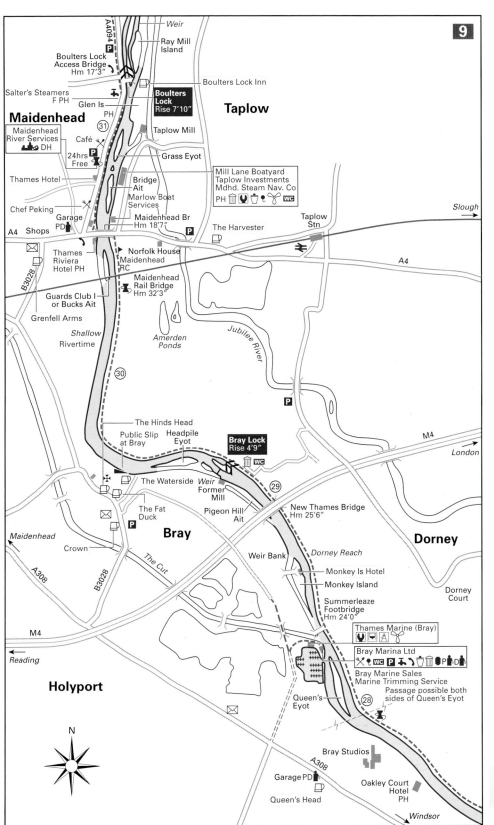

9

Weir

Ray Mill Island

Boulters Lock Access Bridge Hm 17'3"

Boulters Lock Inn

Salter's Steamers F PH

Boulters Lock Rise 7'10"

Taplow

Glen Is

PH

Maidenhead

③①

Café

Maidenhead River Services ⚓ DH

Taplow Mill

24hrs Free P

Grass Eyot

Thames Hotel

Bridge Ait

Mill Lane Boatyard Taplow Investments Mdhd. Steam Nav. Co

PH 🗑 ⚓ 🛒 ● ↻ ⚙ WC

Marlow Boat Services

Chef Peking

Maidenhead Br Hm 18'7"

The Harvester

Taplow Stn

Slough →

Garage PD

A4   Shops

Norfolk House Maidenhead RC

A4

Thames Riviera Hotel PH

Maidenhead Rail Bridge Hm 32'3"

B3028

Guards Club I or Bucks Ait

Jubilee River

Grenfell Arms

Shallow Rivertime

Amerden Ponds

③⓪

M4

London →

The Hinds Head

Public Slip at Bray

Headpile Eyot

Bray Lock Rise 4'9"

WC

P

The Waterside

Weir Former Mill

②⑨

New Thames Bridge Hm 25'6"

Dorney

The Fat Duck

Pigeon Hill Ait

Bray

Weir Bank

Dorney Reach

Crown

Maidenhead →

A308

The Cut

B3028

Monkey Is Hotel

Monkey Island

Dorney Court

M4

Summerleaze Footbridge Hm 24'0"

Thames Marine (Bray)

← Reading

⚓ 🍽 A ⚙

Holyport

Bray Marina Ltd

✕ WC P ⚓ ↻ 🗑 ● P ⛽ D ⚓

Bray Marine Sales Marine Trimming Service
Passage possible both sides of Queen's Eyot

Queen's Eyot

②⑧

N

Bray Studios

A308

Garage PD

Oakley Court Hotel PH

53

Queen's Head

Windsor →

Above: Jetty at *The Waterside*, Bray

Below: Brunel's Sounding Arch, Maidenhead

The Thames Path runs along the Buckinghamshire bank, to starboard as you cruise upstream while on your left, to port, comes the *Oakley Court Hotel*, scenario for many a Hammer House of Horror film, several of which were made at Bray Film Studios almost next door. This is followed by Queen's Eyot, which should be left to port unless you intend visiting Bray Marina which is on the Berkshire bank, level with the head of the eyot. Here one can obtain both petrol and diesel and all services as shown in the *Directory* section which follows. Above the marina is the outlet of the old Maidenhead flood relief channel and almost immediately a brand new footbridge, named Summerleaze Bridge after the gravel company which constructed it, with a built-in gravel conveyor slung beneath the walkway. This was designed to convey the spoil, much of which was naturally gravel, from the new flood relief channel which runs from above Boulters Lock ahead to Black Potts below Romney. Next comes the intriguingly named Monkey Island on which stands the *Monkey Island Hotel*. If you wish to stop here it is advisable to book well in advance as moorings need to be reserved. Avoid the backwater as it is generally shallow, particularly in summer.

Ahead, the river is spanned by the New Thames Bridge, constructed a few years before the M4 – which it now carries – when the early version of the motorway finished at the Maidenhead Thicket roundabout on the Bath Road not four miles away to the west. Under the bridge on the right bank, left facing upstream, a millstream runs back into the river from the former Bray Mill sited at the top of Pigeon Hill Ait. An overspill weir runs from the millstream just below the main weir at Bray, above which the two streams are divided by Headpile Eyot, a not uncommon name on the river. The main weir spans the stream between Headpile Eyot and Lock Island and against the left bank will be seen the diminutive Bray Lock. For many years this lock had the distinction of being the holder of the trophy for the annual lock gardens competition under the watchful care of its famous keeper, Alec Baldwin.

After Bray Lock comes the village whose church (St Michael's) was presided over by the accommodating Vicar of Bray, whose denomination changed with the monarchs'. However, history recalls two such gentlemen, Simon Aleyn in Tudor times and Francis Carswell during the reign of the Stuarts – 100 years apart. Before the church, and just

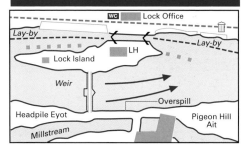

Bray Lock Daytime only
Amerden Lane, Taplow, Maidenhead, Berks
SL4 0EE ☎ 01628 621650
134'4'' (40·94m) long × 17'11'' (5·46m) wide
Rise (fall) 4'9'' (1·46m)
Max. draught 7'0'' (2·13m)
Facilities Refuse disposal, toilets

visible beyond the head of Headpile Eyot, is the Bray Parish slip beside the Waterside Inn, formerly The George. Here the Roux brothers cater extensively and expensively for a clientèle which appears to favour the motor limousine rather than the cruiser but, rest assured, there is parking here for the keeled as well as wheeled mode of transport. It is advisable to book in advance.

Upstream, the river curves to the right with a range of expensive properties on your left forming an area known as 'The Fisheries', though little fishing is indulged in on that particular bank since its householders come from the world of showbiz and seem to prefer cricket or golf! During the season, however, there will probably be an abundance of anglers on the towing path bank to your right – so beware! As the curve straightens out, you will see ahead of you one of the most impressive engineering feats of Isambard Kingdom Brunel, who managed to design his crossing of the Thames by the Great Western Railway without setting a single pier of the viaduct in the river. This structure, known as 'The Sounding Arch' in view of the echo effect one gets while calling across a span when underneath, holds the distinction of having the widest, flattest brick-spans in the world. Each is 123' wide and rises from the water level a mere 32', although the actual arches spring from abutments well above the river level to give soft elliptical curves to the soffits. The viaduct carries the main line from Paddington to the West Country and was widened early this century, conforming with

Brunel's design to accommodate the four tracks it now supports.

It is possible to moor on the Buckinghamshire bank to your right, below the viaduct, where River Road is separated from the river by a grass strip. Take care as certain sections under the stone wall here are shallow. The channel upstream and down is through the railway arch on the left bank, to your right going upstream, since the left hand channel is blocked above the railway bridge by a low footbridge onto Bucks Eyot, or Guards Club Island as it has become known. The footbridge itself is an adaptation of the old eel bucks which were positioned here and gave their name to the island. Next on the left bank comes the clubhouse of the Maidenhead Rowing Club, and on the right is the *Thames Riviera Hotel*. Across the road is a Star Service Station (*Texaco*) for petrol, diesel and groceries.

Maidenhead Bridge carries the original Bath Road – its threatened replacement fortunately pre-empted by the opening of the M4, since it owes its present design to Sir Robert Taylor and was opened in 1777. Six arches of the bridge now span the river. Reading from the left facing upstream, the navigation arches are nos 3 and 4 – no. 4 being the centre arch. Just inside no. 6 arch is Mike Free's boatyard, Marlow Boat Services, immediately followed by the rather spoiled façade of *Skindle's Hotel*. At the time of this revision, Skindle's is still due for redevelopment, but would-be developers are hamstrung by certain planning requirements. It is a regrettable but sad fact of life that alcohol seems to be more popular than the waters of Old Father Thames.

Once above Maidenhead Bridge steer for the *Thames Hotel* on the right bank, left as you pass upstream, leaving Bridge Eyot and Grass Eyot to starboard. It is, of course, possible to proceed up the Taplow channel behind Bridge Eyot but it is narrow and full of moored craft as well as the 5 passenger vessels of the Maidenhead Steam Navigation Company. If you elect to navigate on this side of the islands please proceed very slowly. Andrews' and Bushnell's sheds have disappeared below the *Thames Hotel* and the whole of the upper section of the site has been turned into riverside flats, known as Chandler's Quay. Just above the *Thames Hotel* comes the day-boat hire and contracting firm of Maidenhead River Services, run by Alan Thompson. French Brothers, runs its passenger boats and the Windsor service from above here in the summer season. Against Ray Mead Road are free moorings below the Riverside Gardens, a pleasure park which has car park and toilets as well as an excellent open-air and wood cabin café which has been run by the Jenner family for more than thirty years.

Behind Grass Eyot and Bridge Eyot, however, on the Taplow side of the river there has been a good deal of development of mooring and boatyard facilities in recent years – a list of these is given in the *Directory* at the end of this section. Above Grass Eyot on the Maidenhead side of the river against Ray Mead Road there is a steamer point, used by Salters Steamers Ltd and a little way downstream is the boarding point for the service and charter trips operated by Maidenhead Steam. On the Taplow bank can be seen the outlet of the Taplow Mill Stream below Glen Island. Taplow Mill is a paper mill and still uses electric power provided by turbines located in the millstream. There is no mooring on this side of the river which eventually takes you into the weir stream coming down from Boulters, or 'Maidenhead', Weir. In the centre of the river now rise Boulters and Ray Mill Islands with the *Boulters Lock Inn* and its café terrace facing you, while to the left on the roadside above the elegant stone bridge to the island is the world famous Boulters Lock. You can come alongside the concrete apron on the left but you may be safer at the new lay-by on the right – or even stem the current somewhere out in the middle of the very wide pool below the lock island. But on no account should you jump the queue of other craft waiting at either lay-by or get in the way of craft coming out of the lock downstream.

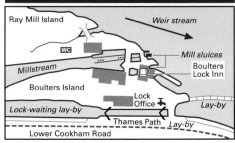

Boulters Lock Daytime only
Boulters Island, Maidenhead, Berks SL6 9PE
☎ 01628 624205
199'6'' (60·80m) long × 21'3'' (6·47m) wide
Rise (fall) 7'10'' (2·39m)
Max. draught 7'0'' (2·13m)
Facilities Water for can filling only, public telephone close to lock, car park opposite.

At this lock don't be too eager for the top gates to open. The lock may appear to be full but the lock-keeper hasn't gone to sleep. The extra length of the lock cut causes a surge to set up in it each time the lock is filled and the last few inches of difference take varying times to level off before the gates can be fully opened.

The Thames Path

On this section, the Path starts at Riverside, alongside Bell Weir Lock and continues upstream and around the Runnymede Pleasure Ground at Egham, staying with the National Trust land alongside the main A308 as far as Old Windsor. Here the path follows the river away from the road at the *Bells of Ouzeley* and takes the walker up to Old Windsor Lock. Keeping to the right bank (left as one proceeds upstream) you pass the accommodation bridge onto Ham Island across the lock cut and then rejoin the main river opposite Old Windsor weir. At the Albert Bridge you will have to join the road and cross the river for, as explained above, the old towing path is no longer available for security reasons as the land belongs to the Crown and was closed to the general public as long ago as 1848.

The present route has to follow the B3021 road, Southlea Road, into Datchet. Walkers are advised to stay on the right-hand pavement as the path on the left is not continuous and the road is busy and has a number of bad sightlines for oncoming traffic. At Datchet Wharf the river can again be seen where the B470 Windsor Road meets Southlea Road. Here the path returns to the river by a new route along Sumptermead Ait downstream of the Victoria Bridge. Crossing the bridge, the path continues alongside the river on the Berkshire (right) bank under Black Potts rail bridge and right round to Tom Jones' boatyard below Romney Lock whence it diverts behind the water-works and rejoins the river just above the entrance to the water intake. One may visit the lockside and even explore Romney Island but all trace of the old towing path here has vanished. There appears to have been no ferry from the *Cobbler*, now removed, to either shore for Thacker relates a fund of anecdotes in his *Thames Highway Vol II* of horses swimming up to Windsor Bridge from there or the right bank and a winch being used to bring the barges up to it.

At Windsor Bridge, cross the river into Eton and take the first turning on the left

Waiting to ascend Boulters Lock

over the bridge into Brocas Street. In a few yards, passing the rear of the Eton College Boathouses, you come to the Brocas and the river. The path now remains on the left (Buckinghamshire) bank all the way up to Maidenhead Bridge, passing Boveney and Bray Locks en route. At Maidenhead Bridge, which you will have had to approach up River Road, turn left over the bridge and then right into Ray Mead Road opposite the Star Service Station. Ray Mead Road forms the Thames Path right up to Boulters Lock where the road changes its name to Lower Cookham Road. A little way beyond the lock, the path stays by the river as the road veers away to the left behind the riverside houses which start there.

Angling

Above Staines a certain amount of free coarse fishing may still be found but a number of club and private fisheries have laid claim to angling rights and care is needed before

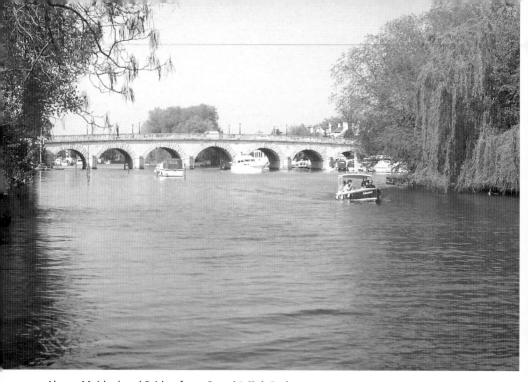

Above: Maidenhead Bridge from Guards' Club Park

Below: Ray Mill Island and Boulters Weir, Maidenhead

Longridge scouts in a mass locking down at Marlow

casting one's tackle in some quiet sheltered spot without reference to any notices on the bank or after extensive local enquiries. This book can only touch on the subject and the multiplicity of fishing interests and the transitoriness of some of them makes it difficult to be definitive.

There is free fishing on the towing path side from Bell Weir to Runnymede House, where the river meets the A308 at the bottom of Priest Hill. From Ham Bridge to the Albert Bridge the towing path fishing rights are held by the Old Windsor Angling Association who also have the rights to the stretch between Black Potts rail bridge and Romney Lock, including Romney Island. Between the Victoria and Black Potts bridges, however, fishing is free. There is no fishing in the lock cut, but above Windsor Bridge fishing is free on both sides of the river up to the rail bridge and also beyond it on the right bank up to the Queen Elizabeth (A332) Bridge.

On the towing path side, above the Queen Elizabeth Bridge, day tickets are available from the Salt Hill Angling Society or its agent, Windsor Angling Centre, up to a point a mile below Boveney Lock, after which the rights are controlled by the London Anglers' Association from whose bailiff tickets are available on the bank. Above Boveney Lock,

up to the start of the gardens at Dorney Reach, fishing is reserved by the Maidenhead and District Angling Association. Details of day-ticket arrangements should be available from tackle shops at Windsor and Maidenhead (see *Directory*.) There is free fishing from a boat or punt in the weir pool at Bray where trout may be had. Fishing is free above Bray Lock from the point where the towing path rejoins the river about 500 yards below the railway viaduct up to Ellington Road and also on the opposite bank to which the path crosses, from Maidenhead Bridge along Ray Mead Road up to Boulters Lock.

King's Tackle Shop in Ray Street is a short walk along Bridge Road from Maidenhead Bridge. Ray Street is the first turning to the right after the shopping parade.

Fishermen as well as boaters often notice when swans get into trouble with flotsam, discarded lines or where territory fights break out. There is an organisation dedicated to helping where this kind of incident occurs. Swan Lifeline can be contacted on ☎ 01753 859397.

Bray and Windsor Marinas

Bray Marina

Situated in a country park setting, Bray Marina provides berth holders with a delightfully tranquil mooring and its excellent facilities include a popular restaurant.

- 400 berths
- Petrol and diesel
- Boat lifting and hard standing area
- Electricity and water available on all berths (except bankside pontoons)
  - Engineering and repair services
  - New and used boat sales
  - Chandlery
  - Restaurant
- Visitor moorings
- 24 hour manned security and CCTV

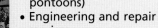

Bray Marina
Monkey Island Lane,
Bray, Berkshire SL6 2EB
Tel: 01628 623654
Fax: 01628 773485
Email: bray@mdlmarinas.co.uk

Windsor Marina

In a beautiful garden setting, Windsor Marina offers a wealth of attractions close by and its extensive facilities include a well stocked chandlery.

- 200 berths
- Petrol and diesel
- Boat lifting and hard standing area
- Electricity and water available on all berths
- Engineering and repair services
- Pump out
- Large chandlery
- Yacht club
- 24 hour manned security and CCTV

Windsor Marina
Maidenhead Road,
Windsor, Berkshire SL4 5TZ
Tel: 01753 853911
Fax: 01753 868195
Email: windsor@mdlmarinas.co.uk

For further information, please contact the Marina Manager quoting ref. RTB.

Directory

BOATYARDS, MARINAS, CHANDLERIES, TRIPPING AND HIRE

French Brothers Ltd
Runnymede Boat House, Windsor Road, Old Windsor, Berkshire SL4 2SG ☎ 01753 851900. Passenger trips, party hire, catering afloat. (PBA)

French Engineering
Runnymede Boat House, Windsor Road, Old Windsor, Berkshire SL4 2SG ☎ 01784 439626. Piling, dredging, riparian campshedding etc, towing and marine engineers.

Thames Steam Packet Boat Company
Runnymede Boat House, Windsor Road, Old Windsor, Berkshire SL4 2SG ☎ 01753 840909. Proprietors of the restored steamer *Nuneham*. Available for private hire with skipper and crew. Bar and catering aboard. (PBA)

Wraysbury Boathouse (T J O'Keefe)
28, Old Ferry Drive, Wraysbury, Staines, Middlesex TW19 5JT ☎ 01784 482569. Boatbuilder, repairer, chandlery, *Calor Gas*, engineering, permanent moorings, hardstanding, winter storage, slipway. (TBTA)

Saxon Moorings
The Priory, Church Road, Old Windsor, Berkshire SL4 2JW. Private moorings, refuse disposal, water point, toilets. Correspondence to: 'Sorbon', Aylesbury End, Beaconsfield, Buckinghamshire HP9 1LU ☎ 01494 671331.

European Waterways Ltd
35 Wharf Road, Wraysbury, Staines, Middlesex TW19 5JQ ☎ 01784 482439. Booking agents for luxury hotel boats *Magna Carta* and *Actief* plying between Shillingford and Greenwich.

Windsor VIP Cruises
Littlecote, Friary Island, Wraysbury, Staines, Middlesex, TW19 5JT ☎ 01784 481702. Private charter for small parties. (PBA)

Kris Cruisers
The Waterfront, Southlea Road, Datchet, Slough, Berkshire SL3 9BU ☎ 01753 543930. Day boats and weekly hire cruisers (*Blakes*), diesel fuel, engineering, *Calor Gas*, permanent and visitors' moorings, telephone, sewage pump-out, refuse disposal, water point. (TBTA, THCA)

Tom Jones (Boatbuilders) Ltd
Romney Lock Boathouse, Windsor, Berkshire SL4 6HU ☎ 01753 860699. Boatbuilders, traditional river craft specialists, marine engineers, moorings, hardstanding, crane, wet dock, chandlery, *Calor Gas*. (TBTA)

Stanley and Thomas Ltd
The Boatyard, Romney Lock, Windsor, Berkshire SL4 6HU ☎ 01753 833166. Restoration, refits, crane, anti-fouling. (TBTA)

Salter's Steamers Ltd
1 Thameside, Windsor, Berkshire SL4 1QN ☎ 01753 865832. Passenger trips, party hire. (TBTA, PBA)

French Brothers Ltd (formerly Windsor Boats)
The Promenade, Barry Avenue, Windsor, Berkshire SL4 5HZ ☎ 01753 851900/862933. Passenger trips, party hire. Boatyard at Clewer Boathouse, Clewer Court Road, Windsor, Berkshire, SL4 5JH. (PBA)

WINDSOR

Marina moorings Pontoon berths with water and electricity
Boat sales New and used, always 100 available
Chandlery Well stocked, also fuel, water pumpout
Club Bar and food
Service Engineering, shipwright, crane
Central location Easy access by road or river. All the services in a beautiful, secure, countryside setting to look after you and your boat
Security Staff on site 24 hours

RACECOURSE YACHT BASIN
(Windsor) Ltd, Maidenhead Road, Windsor, Berks, SL4 5HT
Telephone 01753 851501

www.ryb.co.uk

Thames Steam Packet Co
Details as for French Brothers Ltd
☎ 01753 840909

Bray Boats
Details as for French Brothers Ltd
☎ 01753 751900

John Logie Motorboats
The Promenade, Barry Avenue, Windsor, Berkshire SL4 5HZ ☎ Mobile 07774 983809. Day-boats for hire, motor, electric, and rowing boats, from Barry Avenue Promenade. Boatyard at Mill Lane, Clewer, SL4 5JH.

Clewer Boatyard Ltd
Clewer Court Road, Windsor, Berkshire SL4 5JH ☎ 01753 863478. Moorings, slipway, towing service, crane, boat repairs. (TBTA)

Classic Yacht-Charters
c/o Clewer Boatyard, Clewer Court Road, Windsor, Berkshire SL4 5JH ☎ Mobile 07768 456058. Three classic motor yachts, catering for up to 10 persons or minicruises for 4 between London and Oxford.

Racecourse Yacht Basin (Windsor) Ltd
Maidenhead Road, Windsor, Berkshire SL4 5HT ☎ 01753 851501. Permanent and visitors' moorings, repairs, marine engineer, diesel fuel, petrol, *Calor Gas*, chandlery, outboard sales and service, groceries, hardstanding, crane, slipway, telephone, water, refuse and chemical toilet disposal, toilets, car park, club and restaurant. (TBTA)

RYB (Marine Sales) Ltd
Racecourse Yacht Basin, Maidenhead Road, Windsor, Berkshire SL4 5HT ☎ 01753 851717. Boat sales, brokerage, finance and insurance.

RYB Sports Boats Ltd
Racecourse Yacht Basin, Maidenhead Road, Windsor, Berkshire SL4 5HT ☎ 01753 496999. Small craft.

Windsor Marina Ltd (MDL)
Maidenhead Road, Windsor, Berkshire SL4 5TZ ☎ 01753 853911. Permanent and visitors' moorings, hardstanding, chemical toilet and refuse disposal, diesel fuel, petrol, *Calor Gas*, chandlery, battery charging, mains electricity to some pontoons, telephone, water point, slipway, club. (TBTA)

Marine Tek
Windsor Marina, Maidenhead Road, Windsor, Berkshire SL4 5TZ ☎ 01753 864414. Steel boat repairs, outboard engine repair and servicing, electrical repairs and installation.

Windsor Marine Sales
Windsor Marina, Maidenhead Road, Windsor, Berkshire SL4 5TZ ☎ 01753 860303. Boat sales, brokerage, finance, insurance, crane.

Harris Marine Windsor
Windsor Marina, Maidenhead Road, Windsor, Berkshire SL4 5TZ ☎ 01753 850100. Marine engineers.

Konexion Ltd
Windsor Marina, Maidenhead Road, Windsor, Berkshire SL4 5TZ ☎ 01753 868300. Yacht chandlers. (TBTA)

Bray Marina Ltd (MDL)
Monkey Island Lane, Bray, Maidenhead, Berkshire SL6 2EB ☎ 01628 623654. Permanent and visitors' moorings, diesel fuel, petrol, hardstanding, small slipway, telephone, water points, showers, toilets, refuse and chemical toilet disposal, mains electricity to pontoons, car park, club. Other facilities as below. (PBA)

Bray Marine Sales
Bray Marina, Monkey Island Lane, Bray, Maidenhead, Berkshire SL6 2EB ☎ 01628 773177. Boat sales, brokerage, finance, insurance. (TBTA)

Thames Marine (Bray) Ltd
Bray Marina, Monkey Island Lane, Bray, Maidenhead, Berkshire SL6 2EB ☎ 01628 773472. Marine engineers, boat repairs, chandlery, craning. (TBTA)

Marine Trimming Service
Bray Marina, Monkey Island Lane, Bray, Maidenhead, Berkshire SL6 2EB ☎ 01932 563779. On-site trimming, upholstery and hood supplies and repairs.

Rivertime

Swan Upping, Fishery Road, Bray, Berkshire SL6 1UP ☎ 01628 786700. Electric launches for party hire for 8 to 10 persons. Corporate entertainment, lunches, suppers, etc. (PBA)

Marlow Boat Services Ltd

The Boathouse, Mill Lane, Taplow, Maidenhead, Berkshire SL6 0AA ☎ 01628 622965. Marine engineers, boat repairs, winter storage.

Dennis R Holtom

Brookwood Cottage, 82, Ray Mill Road East, Maidenhead, Berkshire SL6 8TD ☎ 01628 622791. Marine trimmers and upholsterers. Hoods, cushions, covers.

Taplow Marine Consultants

'Driftwood', Mill Lane, Taplow, Maidenhead, Berkshire SL6 0AA ☎ 01628 630249. Boat sales, brokerage, marine engineers, permanent and visitors' moorings, hardstanding, crane, refuse and chemical toilet disposal, toilets. (TBTA)

Mill Lane Boatyard

Taplow Boatyard, Mill Lane, Taplow, Maidenhead, Berkshire SL6 0AA ☎ 01628 636919. Boat sales, permanent moorings, hardstanding, storage.

Maidenhead Steam Navigation Co

Taplow Boatyard, Mill Lane, Taplow, Maidenhead, Berkshire SL6 0AA ☎ 01628 621770. Party hire of 5 passenger vessels for up to 140 guests, permanent moorings, hardstanding, crane, water point, refuse disposal, toilets, car parking. (PBA)

Fringilla

Taplow Boatyard, Mill Lane, Taplow, Maidenhead, Berkshire, SL6 0AA ☎ Mobile 07977 448117. Enquiries: PO Box 2036, Ascot, Berkshire SL5 9FZ. *Fax* 01344 638612. Luxury motor launch for up to 12 people with skipper and crew including catering. (PBA)

Maidenhead River Services

Lockbridge Boat House, Ray Mead Road, Maidenhead, Berkshire SL6 8NJ ☎ 01628 634247. Self-drive motor day-boats, towing service, tug and barge hire, riparian contracting.

EMERGENCY FUEL SUPPLIES

See note under this heading on page 24

Altwood BMW (Friary Garage)

Petrol, diesel, shop

95, Straight Road, Old Windsor, Berkshire ☎ 01753 855826 (upstream of *Bells of Ouzeley*).

SMC Windsor Service Station

Petrol, diesel

The Green, Slough Road, Datchet, Windsor, Berkshire ☎ 01753 543799 (300 yds from Datchet Wharf).

A A Clark Ltd

Petrol, diesel

72-74 Arthur Road, Windsor, Berkshire ☎ 01753 800600 (600 yds from Barry Avenue.)

BP Express Shopping Ltd

Petrol, diesel, shop

Maidenhead Road, Clewer, Windsor, Berkshire ☎ 01753 853164 (Close to Stovell Road moorings -500yds.)

Star Service Station

Petrol, diesel, shop, cash point

143, Bridge Road, Maidenhead, Berkshire ☎ 01628 503100 (Opposite Maidenhead Bridge, upstream Berkshire bank.)

ROWING, SAILING AND CRUISING CLUBS AND TUITION

Wraysbury Skiff and Punting Club

Runnymede Pleasure Ground, Riverside, Egham, Surrey TW20 0AA ☎ 01784 437206. Rowing. (ARA)

Brunel University Rowing Club

Runnymede Boathouse, Windsor Road, Egham, Surrey TW20 0AE. Rowing. (ARA)

Old Windsor Motor Boat School

3 Kingswood Creek, Wraysbury, Staines, Middlesex TW19 5EN ☎ 01784 481739. Motor cruising tuition. (RYA, TBTA)

Eton College Boat Club

Eton Masters' Boat House, Pocock's Lane, Eton, Windsor, Berkshire SL4 6HW ☎ 01753 537488. Rowing – college club. (ARA)

Eton College Boat House, Eton

Brocas Street, Eton, Windsor Berkshire SL4 6BW. Eton College BC.

The Windsor Boys' School BC

Barry Avenue, Windsor, Berkshire SL4 5HZ ☎ 01753 621112. Rowing. (ARA)

The Windsorian Rowing Club

Stovell Road, Windsor, Berkshire SL4 5JB. Rowing. (ARA)

Windsor Unit Sea Cadet Corps

(TS *Windsor Castle*) Stovell Road, Windsor, Berkshire SL4 5JB ☎ 01753 860022. Sea cadets.

Windsor & District Canoe Club

Stovell Road, Windsor, Berkshire SL4 5JB. Canoeing. (BCU)

Racecourse Yacht Basin Cruising Club
Racecourse Yacht Basin, Maidenhead Road, Windsor, Berkshire SL4 5HT. Motor cruising. (ATYC, RYA)

Eton College Boat House, Boveney
Lock Path, Dorney, Windsor, Berkshire SL4 6QQ. Eton College BC.

Dorney Lake Services
The Boat House, Dorney Lake, off Dorney Lane, Windsor, Berkshire SL4 6QQ. ☎ 01753 832756. Eton College BC.

Windsor Yacht Club
Windsor Marina, Maidenhead Road, Windsor, Berkshire SL4 5TZ. Motor cruising. (ATYC, RYA)

Eton Excelsior Rowing Club
Maidenhead Road, Windsor, Berkshire SL4 5TZ ☎ 01753 861099. Rowing. (ARA)

Bray Cruiser Club
Bray Marina, Monkey Island Lane, Bray, Maidenhead, Berkshire SL6 2EB. Motor cruising. (ATYC, RYA)

Maidenhead Rowing Club
Maidenhead Bridge, River Road, Maidenhead, Berkshire SL6 0AT ☎ 01628 622664. Rowing. (ARA)

Maidenhead Unit Sea Cadet Corps
(TS *Iron Duke*) Mill Lane, Taplow, Maidenhead, Berkshire SL6 0AA ☎ 01628 623089/631626. Sea Cadets.

PUBLIC LAUNCHING SITES
- **Windsor** Off Stovell Road, beside Windsor Leisure Centre. Details from Windsor Leisure Centre ☎ 01753 850004.
- **Bray** At the bottom of Ferry Lane next to the *Waterside Inn*.

FISHING TACKLE SHOPS
Windsor Angling Centre
153 St Leonards Road, Windsor, Berks ☎ 01753 867210

Kings Fishing Tackle
18 Ray Street, Maidenhead, Berks ☎ 01628 629283

HOTELS, INNS AND RESTAURANTS
Runnymede Hotel Bell Weir Lock, Windsor Road, Egham ☎ 01784 436171. High-class hotel-restaurant. Moorings for guests below lock.

Bells of Ouzeley Straight Road, Old Windsor ☎ 01753 861526. *Harvester* menu. Moorings across the road, to bank.

The British Raj Datchet Road, Old Windsor. Restaurant. Moor against towing path below Albert Bridge, 200yds west of Albert Bridge.

Mulligan's Restaurant 134, Horton Road, Datchet ☎ 01753 591173. Atmospheric restaurant – fish dishes a speciality. Small public mooring above boatyard and walk through village.

Morning Star Inn The Green, Datchet. Bar meals on weekday lunchtimes only. Small public mooring above boatyard and walk through village.

Manor Hotel The Green, Datchet ☎ 01753 543442. Bar meals (not Saturday pm) and restaurant midday and evenings. B&B. Special weekend rates. Small public mooring above boatyard and walk through village.

The River House Thames Side, Windsor, ☎ 01753 620010. Bar and restaurant. Formerly The Donkey House. A few mooring spaces against the quay leased to Salters Steamers Ltd (fee).

Royal Oak Inn Datchet Road, Windsor. (50yds from Thames Side). Bar meals all day.

House on the Bridge High Street, Eton ☎ Freephone 0500 860914. High class restaurant, booking advisable. Moorings for patrons below Windsor Bridge on Eton side.

Monty's Riverside Restaurant Windsor Bridge Court, Eton ☎ 01753 854479 or 858430. Restaurant associated with *House on the Bridge*. Landing adjacent at public stage. Moor on the Brocas (fee).

Waterman's Arms Brocas Street, Eton. Bar meals and dining, midday and evenings. Moor on the Brocas (fee).

Tiger Garden Restaurant High Street, Eton ☎ 01753 866310. Indian restaurant. Formerly 'The Cockpit'. Moor on The Brocas (fee).

Crown and Cushion Inn High Street, Eton. Bar meals, midday and evenings (last orders 2000). Moor on the Brocas (fee).

Sir Christopher Wren's House Hotel Thames Street, Windsor ☎ 01753 861354/859780. Full hotel facilities. Excellent restaurant. Moorings off Jennings' Wharf.

Castle Hotel High Street, Windsor ☎ 01753 851011. Excellent restaurant. Full hotel facilities. The Castle Restaurant.

Lloyd's No. 1 Restaurant Thames Street, Windsor ☎ 01753 851708. Pub and restaurant. (Wetherspoons)

Ye Harte & Garter Hotel High Street, Windsor ☎ 01753 863426. Hotel, restaurant and pub.

McDonald's Thames Street, Windsor.

Pizza Hut Thames Street, Windsor.

Pizzaland Thames Street, Windsor.

Brown's Barry Avenue, Windsor. Use moorings on Eton side.

Windsor Lad Maidenhead Road, Clewer, Windsor. ☎ 01753 864634. *Harvester* menu. Use visitors' moorings at Racecourse Yacht Basin, pub at head of yacht basin drive.

Oakley Court Hotel Windsor Road, Water Oakley ☎ 01753 609988. High-class hotel-restaurant. Moorings against hotel grounds.

Riverside Brasserie Bray Marina, Monkey Island Lane, Bray ☎ 01628 780553. Riverside restaurant.

Queen's Head Windsor Road, Water Oakley. Bar snacks, lunches. Visitors' moorings at Bray Marina below café (fee).

Monkey Island Hotel Monkey Island Lane, Bray ☎ 01628 623400. High-class hotel-restaurant. Bar snacks. Reserved moorings for patrons, please book (take care in backwater due to depth).

Crown Inn at Bray High Street, Bray. Bar food, restaurant. No local public moorings.

Waterside Inn Ferry Road, Bray ☎ 01628 620691. Chef proprietor: Michel Roux. High class restaurant. Lunches and dinners. Fully licensed. Moorings next to public slip.

Hind's Head Hotel High Street, Bray. Lunches, teas, dinners. No local public moorings.

The Fat Duck High Street, Bray ☎ 01628 580333. Restaurant. No local moorings.

Norfolk House Hotel Bath Road, Taplow ☎ 01628 784031/623687. Licensed restaurant. Hotel, B&B. Moorings on River Road below rail viaduct (fee), 300yds from Maidenhead Bridge.

Grenfell Arms Oldfield Road, Maidenhead. Bar food, barbecues in summer. Nearest mooring point at River Road, below rail viaduct (fee), 300yds from Maidenhead Bridge.

Thames Riviera Hotel Bridge Road, Maidenhead ☎ 01628 674057. Licensed restaurant and bar. Hotel accommodation. Mooring 50yds upstream alongside Ray Mead Road (free).

Chef Peking Restaurant Ray Mead Road, Maidenhead.☎ 01628 783809/783005. High quality licensed Chinese restaurant (booking advisable). Mooring further up Ray Mead Road above Thames Hotel.

Thames Hotel Ray Mead Road, Maidenhead ☎ 01628 628721/628060. Licensed restaurant and bar meals, midday and evening. Hotel accommodation. Mooring upstream above Bray Boats (free).

Jenner's Café Riverside Gardens, Ray Mead Road, Maidenhead ☎ 01628 621721. Hot meals, etc 0700–1600.

Boulters Lock Inn Boulters Lock Island, Maidenhead ☎ 01628 621291. Restaurant and bar meals from noon to 10pm. Own landing stage and moorings below Boulters Lock.

TAXI SERVICES
(Windsor to Marlow)

- Windsor (Five Star Cars) ☎ 01753 858888
- Windsor (Radio Cars) ☎ 01753 677677 Maidenhead (U-Want Taxis) ☎ 01628 622110/621449
- Maidenhead (Tartan Royale) ☎ 01628 673333
- Maidenhead (Station Taxis) ☎ 01628 771000
- Maidenhead (Star Cars) ☎ 01628 626263
- Cookham Cars ☎ 01628 850760
- Bourne End Private Hire ☎ 01628 525612
- Marlow Cars ☎ 01628 476395

RAIL STATIONS AND TRAIN SERVICES
Enquiries ☎ 08457 484950

See note under this heading on page 26

Wraysbury *South West Trains* Station Road, Wraysbury, Berks. 1½ miles from river. Trains to Sunnymeads, Datchet and Windsor; Staines, Twickenham, Richmond, Putney and Waterloo.

Sunnymeads *South West Trains* Acacia Avenue, Wraysbury, Berks. 1000yds from river. Trains to Datchet and Windsor; Wraysbury, Staines, Twickenham, Richmond, Putney and Waterloo.

Datchet *South West Trains* Manor House Lane, Datchet, Slough, Berks. 300yds from river. Trains to Windsor; Sunnymeads, Wraysbury, Staines, Twickenham, Richmond, Putney and Waterloo.

Windsor and Eton Riverside *South West Trains* Farm Yard, Windsor, Berks. (Nearest station for Salters quay). 100yds from river. Trains to Datchet, Sunnymeads, Wraysbury, Staines, Twickenham, Richmond, Putney and Waterloo. 400yd walk to Windsor and Eton Central Station.

Windsor and Eton Central *FGW Link*
Thames Street, Windsor, Berks. 200yds from river. Trains to Slough. Connecting services at Slough for stations between Paddington and Oxford including Taplow, Maidenhead, Reading, branch lines and all stations to Oxford. 400yd walk to Windsor and Eton Riverside Station.

Taplow *FGW Link* Approach Road, Taplow, Maidenhead, Berks. 1 mile from river. Trains to Slough (for Windsor) and Paddington; Maidenhead, Twyford (for Wargrave, Shiplake and Henley) and Reading. No Sunday service.

Maidenhead *FGW Link* Station Approach, Maidenhead, Berks. 1 mile from river. Trains to Twyford (for Wargrave, Shiplake and Henley) and Reading; Slough (for Windsor) and Paddington. Also Cookham, Bourne End and Marlow. Connections at Reading for stopping services to Oxford.

BUS AND COACH SERVICES
Runnymede to Maidenhead
Bus services along the river in this and later sections are not as numerous as in those closer to London. Main starting points for routes are Staines, Slough, Windsor and Maidenhead. There are regular services between Staines and Windsor via Old Windsor. Travel to points downstream means changing buses at Staines. There is a good service between Windsor and Maidenhead via Bray by Courtney Coaches (Borough Buses). To proceed beyond the section upstream by bus, start from Maidenhead from where buses ply to Cookham, Bourne End and High Wycombe (317) and Reading (127). There are also commuter coaches from Windsor or Maidenhead to London (Victoria or Aldgate).

Bus Operators:
- First Beeline ☎ 01753 524144
- Nightingale Coaches ☎ 01628 634040
- Reading Buses ☎ 0118 959 4000
- Arriva The Shires ☎ 0870 7288 188
- Armchair Passenger Transport (for Maidenhead–London commuter service) ☎ 020 8847 0561
- Courtney Coaches (Borough Buses) ☎ 01344 482200

Eton College from Romney Island

5. Maidenhead to Marlow

Distance

8.03 miles (Boulters Lock to Temple Lock)

Maximum dimensions of craft from Maidenhead to Marlow

Headroom 12´6˝ (3.81m) at Cookham Lock
         Cut Footbridge
Length   151´3˝ (46.10m) at Marlow Lock
Beam   19´11˝ (6.07m) at Marlow Lock
Draught 4´6˝ (1.7m) to Reading

Close behind Boulters Lock on Ray Mill Island is followed by a refreshment kiosk and a slipway and boathouse, ladies' and gents' toilets, while the rest of the island is given over to open spaces and gardens with an aviary at the centre. The entrance gates are locked overnight.

Boulters Lock Cut emerges going upstream right beside the weir having crossed the millstream down to Ray Mill, which now contains a number of private moorings looked after by Peter Freebody of Hurley who has a small yard and slip on Boulters Island. The Agency's boathouse is right at the end just before the mill sluices, which are now used to adjust water levels in conjunction with the main weir. Above the weir on the Buckinghamshire bank we come to Botany Bay and the grounds of Cliveden House which commence above the mouth of the Taplow Mill stream. From here the Jubilee River starts. This is the name for the Maidenhead, Windsor and Eton Flood Alleviation Scheme, which has been constructed over a lengthening period since the contracts were first let. The Buckinghamshire bank is now National Trust property right up to a point opposite the tail of Cookham Lock Cut and includes the group of islands in the river known as Bavin's Gulls or Sloe Grove Islands. Mooring is permitted both to the bank and the islands but a charge may be levied if the attendant feels like collecting it. Mooring on the towing path, Berkshire, side is also possible in a number of places once clear of the privately owned ones at the ends of the gardens. It is wise, though to test the depth against the bank first and if mooring overnight make sure that you have at least 2´ of water under your keel before retiring as river levels can fall as well as rise – even in flood conditions.

At the top of Cliveden Deep from which one can enjoy a magnificent view of the famous woods – a little spoiled perhaps following the notorious October gales in 1987 – the channel ahead is that known as the Hedsor Stream; the original course of the river whereon was sited a wharf under the control of landlord Lord Boston. This channel now runs though private property and is only navigable for a short stretch on the left going upstream where a few temporary moorings may be had for about 100 metres. Access overland is by way of a public footpath which runs behind the lock area up to the footbridge across the cut above the lock. However, access to the village is only possible during the hours of duty of the lock-keeper as there is no right of way across the main weir and the weir gate is normally locked out of hours. Payment for these and the other mooring sites around the lock area must be made on application to the lock-keeper. It is often wise to book in advance as they are popular in summer months.

The main weir stream runs in on the right bank (left as you go upstream) from Odney Common, 3 furlongs above the former My Lady Ferry which connected the Berkshire and Buckinghamshire shores. A narrower stream immediately above the ferry site, the Lulle Brook, completes the formation of what is known as Formosa Island. There are also temporary moorings to be had in the mouth of the Odney weir stream just behind the lock house and on the weirstream side of Sashes Island, but before venturing on to them please check with the lock-keeper.

On leaving Cookham Lock take care at the footbridge which is the lowest on this section at 12´6˝ (3.81m), lower even than Windsor, and again with a curved soffit so keep to the centre of the stream. At the end of the lock cut you will find on your left, going upstream, the entrances to the two weir streams, Odney and Lulle Brook, followed by a shingle slipway next to the *Ferry Inn*. The slipway is a public launching site but the moorings above it are reserved for customers of the restaurant. Over to your right is the entrance to the Hedsor weir stream and on the Buckinghamshire bank are the premises of DB Marine housing their sales, repair and services yard. Their day-

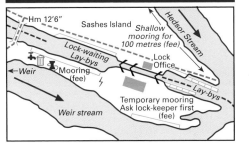

boat hire operation is on the Berkshire bank under Cookham Bridge which faces you.

Cookham Bridge replaces the old Upper Ferry and was first opened in 1840. The present structure dates from 1867 since the first bridge was badly constructed and fell into disrepair. Tolls were collected at the small hexagonal brick house beside the bridge on the Buckinghamshire bank until 1947 when Berkshire County Council bought the bridge from the proprietors for £30,000 and extinguished the tolls. Above what used to be Turk's Boathouse but is now run by David Barber, John Turk's successor (also as HM Swan Marker), is Salter's Steamer Point – the little white jetty running out from the towing path. Regrettably Salter's only ply a service through Cookham twice a week and the jetty is rarely used except for charter trips.

Above this point local council mooring is available in Bell Rope Meadow and also beyond the Cookham Reach Sailing Club. Our earlier remarks about navigating through sailing courses apply forcibly here, particularly as the Cookham club race below Bourne End rail bridge and the Upper Thames Sailing Club plot their race-track in Bourne End Reach a little way above the bridge at the head of the Bourne End Marina jetties. There is no mooring or landing on the Buckinghamshire bank until Bourne End

Marina (see *Directory*) and then comes the sailing club. Above is the site of the Spade Oak Ferry and the old wharf where mooring was possible against the Buckinghamshire bank until recently when it is alleged the London Anglers Association (who have the fishing rights here) had the mooring posts removed. The old *Ferry Hotel*, now the *Spade Oak*, which is a *Brewer's Fayre* house, stands over the level crossing from here on the towing path side, the river crossing from Cock Marsh on the Berkshire bank recently effected by a footbridge cantilevered out from the Bourne End rail bridge.

Most sailing dinghies will have turned before the lower of the Gibraltar Islands ahead, which going upstream should be left to port. The tranquil peace of the backwaters below Winter Hill can, however, be sampled if, perhaps, you are rowing a skiff or piloting a small day launch. Mooring to the lower island is also possible but the higher is private. Of interest is the railway line, never far from the towing path, on the left bank. It forms a spur from Bourne End into Marlow and carries a regular service to connect with the main line at Maidenhead. It is affectionately known as 'The Marlow Donkey' after an old tank engine which used to puff up and down in the days of steam and is also remembered in the name of the pub beside Marlow Station. The line has been kept open with the support of a local passengers' association and is used by commuters to London, among others, on a regular basis.

Past Woottens boatyard there are moorings on the opposite bank against the towing path and then comes the swift turn away from Winter Hill towards the Marlow Bypass bridge and the final run up to Marlow Lock. On the Berkshire bank is the Longridge boating base of the Scout Association. Take care as you pass for there may well be novice canoeists or dinghy sailors about between the turn and the weir stream. Below the lock there are further moorings provided by the Agency on the left, Buckinghamshire bank (right, if navigating upstream) as you approach the lock cut on the same side.

Those intending to visit the town will have to follow the Thames Path from this point to reach the High Street (see Thames Path section below). Salter's has another steamer point here which it uses when that at Higginson Park is not available. Overland the site is approached from Mill Road. The most satisfactory side of the downstream

Cookham Lock

lock cut to wait for Marlow Lock to open is on your right since a new lay-by has been installed in front of the millstream outfall. Make sure that your crew is aware of the high rise of level in the lock chamber – 7′1″ (2.16m). It is often wise to send a crew member on ahead, especially as the lock-keeper may not always be able to tend your lines. In any event he will only drop a loop of the one you hand him around a bollard which you might not be able to see from the bottom of the lock and hand it back to you. Once fast always remember to cut your engine, but make sure that you have forward and stern lines ashore and tended before doing so.

Marlow Lock's top sluice openings are above the water level when the lock is empty. It is wise, therefore, to keep well back from the top gates when locking up since there is a fierce flow into the chamber from the sluices even when opened by only two or three inches. If the lock-keeper asks you to move forward or even change the order of boats entering the lock you must obey his instructions. He is more than fully aware of the problem and will adjust the filling rate

accordingly. The sluices should never be wound fully open at the start of a fill unless there are no craft in the lock. A similar effect but less turbulent may be seen at Sonning, Caversham and Mapledurham further upstream.

Above the lock you come face to face with a famous view, recorded for over a hundred years by painters and engravers. Do not let the sight make you forget the dangers of the weir on your left, the shallows on your right and the bridge (at 12′8″/3.86m) ahead with the rowing club on the Berkshire bank above it and the canoe club on the Buckinghamshire bank just below it. Just below the church on your right (left coming downstream) is a public launching slip with a small staging beside it for landing or tying a skiff or canoe. Please do not moor blocking the slipway. The bridge is notable as being the only suspension bridge across the freshwater Thames – the one at Teddington only crosses the part-tidal section of the river – and was designed by William Tierney-Clark (spellings of the poor man's name vary even to the exclusion of the hyphen!). Rumour has it that it was a try-out of the

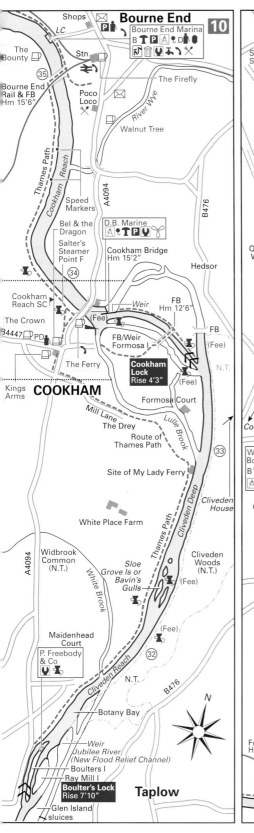
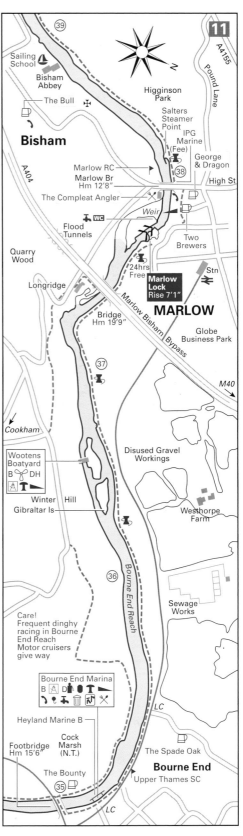

Cookham Bridge and Toll House

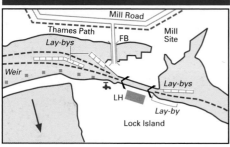

design for the larger and more important link between the principalities of Buda and Pest which form the Hungarian capital, for the bridge at Marlow appears to be a miniature version of one which crosses the Danube.

Above the bridge are private moorings on the town side of the river (left bank) and then Court Gardens and Higginson Park. Here there are good moorings controlled by Wycombe District Council as far as the towing path bridge. Beyond, the bankside is privately owned but you may moor free of charge for the first few boat-lengths where there is a timber waling. After the bush at the end of the timber, mooring is prohibited. Even further upstream is Marlow Sailing Club just below Temple where our next section starts.

Above: Temple Lock

Below: Marlow. Higginson Park moorings

The Thames Path

The Thames Path over this section has a few detours away from the river, some of which may never be resolved in view of the heavy cost of bridging the river where ferries once used to ply to carry the hauliers. It should be remembered that towing was not always carried out by horses, but men and boys often took up the lines and had to struggle along the muddy or dusty path to haul the barges upstream. From Boulters Lock, the Path follows the river to the top of Cliveden Reach where the former My Lady Ferry crossed to the Cliveden shore and the towing path continued thence alongside the old Hedsor stream. However the Thames Path now leaves the river westwards and follows into Mill Lane which joins Sutton Road. Turn right towards the village of Cookham and walk past the end of the High Street to follow the main road round past the lane to the church. From here you walk up Sutton Road towards the bridge and turn into the driveway which leads to DB Marine's day-boat letting point opposite the *Ferry at Cookham Inn*. Walk past the little boathouse and you come to the old steamer point and you have rejoined the river.

The Path runs past Cookham Reach Sailing Club into Bell Rope Meadow and towards Cock Marsh. Here was another ferry (now defunct), beyond the rail bridge, which ran across to Spade Oak. The official Thames Path now, however, uses a cantilevered footbridge running alongside the railway bridge to take the walker over onto the Buckinghamshire bank and through the Bourne End Marina, past the Upper Thames Sailing Club and on towards Marlow. The path beyond the rail bridge on the Berkshire bank will take you to *The Bounty* pub where there are moorings. Here the landlord always used to run a ferry to the footpath by the rail bridge on the opposite bank but, since the opening of the new footbridge, its use may have stopped.

It is still possible to continue your walk around through Cock Marsh to the former ferry cottage where you meet the houses and gardens and the path turns inland to join Winter Hill but then cuts its way between Winter Hill and Quarry Wood Road to come out onto the latter just before the Longridge Scouts' boating base. From here it is a short walk to Marlow Bridge to rejoin the main Path on the upstream Buckinghamshire side of the bridge.

The main Path having reached a point just short of Marlow Lock diverges away from

The Thames Path opposite Cliveden Wood

the river into Mill Road, which the walker must follow past the entrance to the lockside and round to the right until a small opening on the left turns into a narrow alleyway between high brick walls almost opposite Thamesfield Gardens. The Path comes out onto St Peter Street, at the end of which is the public slip. Beside the alley is the *Two Brewers Inn*. Opposite, a little way up the street on the left, we plunge again into a walled alley – even used of old by the bargemen and their horses! – to All Saints' churchyard from where we cross the road to join the Path beside the bridge by going down the footway opposite the war memorial. It is also possible to rejoin the Path opposite Court Garden by walking through Higginson Park which is opposite the *George and Dragon Hotel*. The Thames Path remains on the Buckinghamshire bank up from Marlow Bridge to Temple Lock which starts the next section.

Angling

The chances of free angling diminish as we go further upstream, although permits and day tickets may be available for some of the club waters. There is no weir fishing at Cookham and neither, unfortunately now, is there any at Marlow following legal advice on safety standards. Maidenhead and District AA has the stretch from the end of the gardens against the towing path up Cliveden Reach as far as My Lady Ferry. Permits should be available from their water bailiff on the bank. There is no fishing in the lock area, but along the towing path between Cookham Bridge and Bourne End rail bridge Cookham and District Angling Club tickets are available from King's of Maidenhead (see *Directory*).

Fishing for about a mile starting above the Upper Thames Sailing Club is for members of the London Anglers Association only and then, from opposite the top island by Woottens yard up to Riverswood Drive, fishing is reserved by Marlow Angling Club, although day tickets are again available from King's.

From Riverswood Drive up to Marlow Lock, or just short of it where the path diverts to Mill Road, fishing is free. Fishing is also available to patrons at *The Compleat Angler Hotel* above the weir. Apply at Reception.

Above Marlow Bridge up to a point on the towing path opposite Temple Island (below Temple Lock) fishing is again controlled by Marlow AC but day tickets are available from King's.

Directory

BOATYARDS, MARINAS, CHANDLERIES, TRIPPING AND HIRE

Peter Freebody and Co
Boulters Island, Lower Cookham Road, Maidenhead, Berkshire SL6 8JR
☎ 01628 824382. Permanent moorings, small boat repairs. (Main yard at Hurley)

DB Marine
Cookham Bridge, Cookham-on-Thames, Berkshire SL6 9SN ☎ 01628 526032
www.dbmarine.co.uk Volvo Penta and Perkins Main Dealer. Marine engineers, service, boat repairs, craning, antifouling, permanent moorings. Suppliers of new engines and parts - mail order service available.

Magna Carta Barge Cruising Holidays
Duffield Bank House, Duffield, Derbyshire DE56 4BG ☎ 01332 519136. Agents: European Waterways Ltd
☎ 01784 482439. Luxury hotel barge cruising the Thames between Cookham and Thames Barrier.

Bourne End Marina
Wharf Lane, Bourne End, Buckinghamshire SL8 5RR ☎ 01628 522813. Boat sales, diesel fuel, *Calor Gas*, chandlery, full engineering facilities, permanent and visitors' moorings, crane, telephone, water point, refuse disposal, pump-out, car park. Restaurant.

Heyland Marine
Bourne End Marina, Wharf Lane, Bourne End, Buckinghamshire, SL8 5RR
☎ 01628 528830. Family sailing and

rowing dinghies, yacht tenders, aluminium work punts, Canadian canoes, electric engines, marine accessories.

Dean Marine (Engineers)
Bourne End Marina, Wharf Lane, Bourne End, Buckinghamshire SL8 5RR ☎ 01628 525950. Marine engineers, breakdown service.

Thames Steamers
PO Box 46, Bourne End, Buckinghamshire SL8 5FP ☎ 01628 526346. Restored Victorian steam launch SL *Alaska* for private or corporate charter, catering, for parties up to 36. (PBA)

Westhorpe Leisure Ltd
Westhorpe Farm, Little Marlow, Marlow, Buckinghamshire SL7 3RQ ☎ 01628 484275. Temporary moorings on Buckinghamshire bank.

Woottens Boatyard
Gibraltar Lane, Winter Hill, Cookham Dean, Berkshire SL6 9TR ☎ 01628 484244. Boat builders, boat sales, marine engineers, chandlery, motor day launches for hire, permanent moorings, slipway, winter storage. Honda outboards. (TBTA)

Mac Hoods and Covers
Quarry Wood Boathouse, Gibraltar Lane, Cookham Dean, Berkshire SL6 9TR ☎ 01628 483411. Marine trimmers and upholsterers. Hoods, cushions, covers.

IPG Marine
Higginson Park, Marlow, Buckinghamshire SL7 2AE ☎ 01869 321002. Skiffs and punts for hire or charter.

EMERGENCY FUEL SUPPLIES
See note under this heading on page 24

Barnside Motors Ltd
Petrol and diesel
High Street, Cookham, Maidenhead, Berks ☎ 01628 522029/525555 200yds from Cookham Bridge, Berkshire side.

Bourne End Service Station
Petrol and diesel
The Parade, Bourne End, Buckinghamshire ☎ 01628 524747. 350yds from Bourne End Marina.

ROWING, SAILING AND CRUISING
CLUBS AND TUITION

Cookham Reach Sailing Club
Berries Road, Cookham, Berks SL6 9SD ☎ 01628 525569. Dinghy sailing (RYA)

Bourne End Cruiser & Yacht Club
Bourne End Marina, Wharf Lane, Bourne

The Bounty Riverside Inn

BOURNE END

Summer – open all day

Winter – weekends only

Food available 12 noon

till 8pm daily

Free moorings for customers

Patio and kiddies' playground

Phone Dave or Sue on

01628 520056

for directions

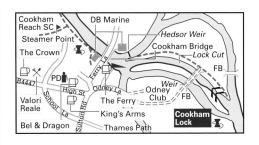

FISHING TACKLE SHOPS

Windsor Angling Centre
  153 St Leonards Road, Windsor,
  Berkshire ☎ 01753 867210
Kings Fishing Tackle
  18 Ray Street, Maidenhead, Berkshire
  ☎ 01628 629283
Maidenhead Bait & Tackle
  19 Station Hill Parade, Cookham Rise,
  Berkshire ☎ 01628 530500

HOTELS, INNS AND RESTAURANTS

Cliveden Hotel Cliveden Estate, Taplow
  ☎ 01628 668561. High-class hotel-
  restaurant, booking advisable. Moorings
  available in Cliveden Reach. Edwardian
  river launch, *Suzy-Ann*, also available for
  up to 10 passengers. (PBA)
Ferry-at-Cookham Sutton Road, Cookham
  ☎ 01628 525123. Moorings by river for
  patrons only, public slip alongside.
Bel and Dragon Inn High Street, Cookham
  ☎ 01628 521263. High-class restaurant
  and bar meals, midday and evening.
  Moorings above Cookham Sailing Club.
King's Arms High Street, Cookham
  ☎ 01628 530667. *Out & Out* menu and
  bar meals, midday and evening.
  Moorings above Cookham Sailing Club.
Valori Reale Restaurant High Street,
  Cookham. High-class restaurant.
  Moorings above Cookham Sailing Club.
Crown Inn The Moor, Cookham. Meals
  midday and evenings. Moorings above
  Cookham Sailing Club.
Two Roses Restaurant High Street,
  Cookham ☎ 01628 520875. Lunches,
  teas and dinner (English menu).
  Moorings above Cookham Sailing Club.
Cookham Tandoori Restaurant High Street,
  Cookham ☎ 01628 522584. Licensed.
  Booking advisable. Moorings above
  Cookham Sailing Club.
Bounty Inn Riverside, Bourne End
  ☎ 01628 520056. Restaurant, burger
  grill, lunches, teas, dinner. 240ft
  overnight moorings for customers, ferry
  available from Bucks bank on request.

End, Bucks SL8 5RR ☎ 01628 520157.
  Motor cruising (ATYC, RYA)
Upper Thames Sailing Club
  Wharf Lane, Bourne End, Bucks SL8 5RF
  ☎ 01628 520263. Sailing. (RYA)
Longridge Scout Boating Centre
  Quarry Wood Road, Marlow, Bucks SL7
  1RE ☎ 01628 483252. Scouts and
  Guides water-based activities, camping.
Marlow Canoe Club
  The Causeway, Marlow Bridge, Marlow,
  Bucks SL7 2AA. Canoeing. (BCU)
Marlow Rowing Club
  Marlow Bridge Lane, Marlow, Bucks SL7
  1RH ☎ 01628 482366. Rowing. (ARA)
**Bisham Abbey Sailing and Navigation
School Ltd**
  National Sports Centre, Bisham, Marlow,
  Bucks SL7 1RT ☎ 01628 474960.
  Sailing, shore based navigation and
  motor cruising tuition. (RYA recognised)
  (TBTA)
Marlow Sailing Club
  Temple Mill Island, Marlow, Bucks SL7
  1SA. Dinghy sailing.

PUBLIC LAUNCHING SITES

• **Cookham** Immediately downstream of
  the Ferry Inn. Shingle bottom. Approach
  via Odney Lane and Ferry Lane
• **Marlow** At the bottom of St Peter Street.
  Care! Parking restrictions

Poco Loco Mexican Restaurant 'The Old Red Lion', Hedsor Road, Bourne End ☎ 01628 530333. Licensed restaurant with a Mexican flavour. Mooring at Bourne End Marina (fee).

Walnut Tree Hedsor Road, Bourne End. Bar food and restaurant.

Kong's Peking Restaurant 78 The Parade, Bourne End ☎ 01628 522100. Chinese restaurant.

The Last Viceroy 74 The Parade, Bourne End ☎ 01628 531383. Indian restaurant.

Spade Oak Coldmoorholm Lane, Bourne End ☎ 01628 520090. Bar meals and dining all day. Mooring above Bourne End Marina, 300yds across rail line up lane.

Two Brewers St Peter Street, Marlow ☎ 01628 484140. Bar snacks and meals in *The Ferryman* restaurant, midday to midnight. Free mooring below Marlow Lock then Mill Road and footpath, public slip and landing nearby.

Compleat Angler Hotel Bisham Road, Marlow Bridge ☎ 01628 484444. Restaurant, English cuisine (expensive). Booking essential. Lunches, dinners, full hotel facilities. Mooring for patrons only.

George and Dragon The Causeway, Marlow ☎ 01628 483887. *Out & Out* menu. Bar meals, midday and evening. Moorings in Higginson Park, above Marlow Bridge (fee).

Wimpy High Street, Marlow.

Chequers Inn High Street, Marlow. Bar meals, limited seating for diners, midday and evening.

Bull at Bisham Inn Bisham Village ☎ 01628 484734/482675. Restaurant, bar meals, varied French menu. No closer moorings than Marlow (Higginson Park or Mill Road).

RAIL STATIONS AND TRAIN SERVICES
See note under this heading on page 26
Enquiries: ☎ 08457 484950

Maidenhead *FGW Link* Station Approach, Maidenhead, Berks. 1 mile from river. Trains to Twyford and Reading; Slough and Paddington. Also serving intermediate stops. Branch line to Cookham, Bourne End and Marlow.

Cookham *FGW Link* Station Hill, Cookham Rise, Berks. 1 mile from river. Trains to Bourne End and Marlow; Furze Platt and Maidenhead. Change at Maidenhead for main line.

Bourne End *FGW Link* Station Road, Bourne End, Bucks. 400yds from river. Trains to Marlow; Cookham, Furze Platt and Maidenhead. Change at Maidenhead for main line.

Marlow *FGW Link* Station Approach, Station Road, Marlow, Bucks. 800yds from river. Trains to Bourne End, Cookham, Furze Platt and Maidenhead. Change at Maidenhead for main line.

BUS AND COACH SERVICES
Maidenhead to Marlow
One bus route (Arriva 317) follows the river, more or less between Maidenhead and Bourne End, via Cookham. Marlow is served by buses between Reading and High Wycombe (Arriva 328, 329) but there is no bus connection between Bourne End and Marlow, except via High Wycombe where a change of buses is required. Use the train instead! A new local bus service now links Maidenhead with Henley and Marlow via Hurley, Monday to Saturday. Shortest journey time is about 40 minutes.

Bus Operators are:
- Arriva The Shires ☎ 0870 7288 188
- Reading Buses ☎ 0118 959 4000
- Borough Bus – Hurley Link ☎ 01628 796666

Passenger Boat Association (PBA)

The Passenger Boat Association was formed over 15 years ago by a few enthusiastic passenger boat operators in an endeavour to improve and co-ordinate the various services offered to the public and to create a close working relationship between the operators on the upper reaches of the river. The list below shows the names and locations of member firms in upstream order. Full details can be found in the Directory at the end of each section. Member firms are denoted by the legend (PBA) at the end of their entry.

One may cruise on any one of the passenger boats on the Thames knowing that all UTPBA members are very conscious of the comfort and safety of their passengers. A yearly certificate must be obtained from the Department of Transport which entails the most stringent checks and inspection of the vessels. Also all operators are subject to random checks to ensure that safety regulations are being observed. Crew members must also be trained in the various safety procedures on board.

Types of cruising vary from short round-trips from the popular venues such as Kingston, Henley, Windsor, Marlow and Reading to scheduled summer services between towns such as Oxford to Abingdon or Runnymede to Hampton Court. There are also boats for private charter for parties, weddings and conferences which offer a bar and refreshments and a number of purpose-built cruising restaurants in members' fleets. Further details can be obtained at the Tourist Information Centres listed in this book or from any of the member firms.

Richmond
Turk Launches Ltd
Teddington
Heritage Boat Charters
Kingston
Turk Launches Ltd
Hampton Court
Turk Launches Ltd
Chris Cruises Ltd
Walton-on-Thames
JGF Passenger Boats
Runnymede
French Brothers Ltd
Thames Steam Packet Boat Co
Wraysbury
Windsor VIP Cruises
Windsor
Salters Steamers Ltd
French Brothers Ltd
Thames Steam Packet Boat Co
Windsor Boats
Bray
Rivertime
Taplow
Cliveden Hotel (3D Marine)
Fringilla

Bourne End
Thames Steamers (Alaska)
Hambleden
Hambleden Sales and Charter Ltd
Henley-on-Thames
Hobbs & Sons Ltd
Great River Journeys Ltd (ss Streatley)
Wargrave
Windsor Belle Ltd
Reading and Caversham
Thames Rivercruise
Salters Steamers Ltd
(Kennet & Avon Canal)
Kennet Cruises
Wallingford
Great River Journeys Ltd
Oxford
Salters Steamers Ltd
Oxford River Cruises
Lechlade
Cotswold River Cruises
Godalming (River Wey)
Godalming Packetboat Company

6. Temple to Henley

·Distance

8.12 miles (Temple Lock to Harpsden Ferry)

Maximum dimensions of craft from Temple to Marsh Lock

Headroom 13´1˝ (3.98m) at Hurley Upper footbridge. **Note** Marlow Bridge is 12´8˝ (3.86m)
Length 130´8˝ (39.82m) at Hurley Lock
Beam 17´11˝ (5.46m) at Temple Lock
Draught 4´6˝ (1.37m) in main fairway up to Reading

Once upstream of Marlow – the navigator still taking care that rowers, canoeists and dinghy sailors from Bisham or Temple Mill Island are all avoided and not swamped – the river starts to become thickly wooded again on both banks. Ahead, over on the Buckinghamshire side, looms Temple Lock with the weir stream to your left as you proceed upstream. Below the weir on the site of Temple Mill is an expensive development of houses and maisonettes which appears to have lent nothing to the river, although perhaps it has the decency to nestle rather better into the background than its cousin further downstream on the site of the former Meakes boatyard opposite Higginson Park at Marlow.

Above Temple Lock is a short pound between locks standing at 1122 yards. But in this short distance there's a wealth of river activity, starting with the span of the new Thames Path footbridge which carries the towing path from the Buckinghamshire bank to Berkshire. Temple Estates Ltd recently formalised the mooring arrangements above the weir into Temple Marina (see *Directory*) and the Harleyford Estate on the Buckinghamshire bank above the footbridge houses a boating and caravanning leisure park of considerable size, where visiting craft can avail themselves of comprehensive services such as chandlery, engineering, bar and restaurant.

The Environment Agency has a campsite on one of the numerous islands between Hurley Lock and its weir; apply for a pitch to the lock-keeper. Opposite, off the old millstream, is the yard of Peter Freebody and Company where comprehensive boating services are available. Hurley Lock has sewage and refuse disposal, toilets and freshwater supplies, as well as angling facilities for weir permit holders around the island above the lock. On the Berkshire side of the river is the attractive village of Hurley with shop, post office and a number of hostelries as shown in the *Directory*. The village is best reached from above the lock by way of the track from the towing path. This is close to the upper footbridge before you come to Hurley Farm.

Avoid the weir above Hurley as you leave the lock area with its sanitary station followed by the overspills, for the pull of the

---

Temple Lock Daytime only
Temple, Marlow, Bucks SL7 1SA ☎ 01628 824333
134'7" (41·02m) long x 17'11" (5·46m) wide
Rise (fall) 4'1" (1·23m)
Max. draught 6'11" (2·10m)
Facilities Toilets, water tap for cans, moorings, tea-shop.

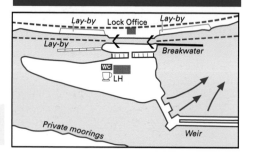

Hurley Lock Daytime only
Mill Lane, Hurley, Maidenhead, Berks SL6 5ND ☎ 01628 824334
130'8" (39·82m) long x 19'11" (6·07m) wide
Rise (fall) 3'5" (1·05m)
Max. draught 6'2" (1·88m)
Facilities Chemical toilet and refuse disposal, toilets, water for can and hose filling, campsite with 10 pitches.
Angling From camping island above Buck Weir.

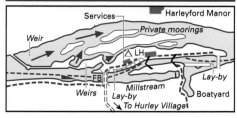

main weir is deceptive and it will be difficult to get a boat off if there is any stream running. On the Berkshire (right) bank, opposite the weir comes Hurley Farm and their caravan park which also has two boat slips for hand launching of craft; one for public use on payment of a fee and the other, higher up, for use by caravan park patrons only, ☎ 01628 823501.

On your right hand going upstream (left, Buckinghamshire bank) is Danesfield and here are both a rowing and a sailing club. On your left hand are the Frogmill private moorings, Hurley Farm's private slip, and fishing reserved by the London Anglers' Association, along the towing path. The river sweeps round after Danesfield and the main channel turns in among a group of islands, the first being Frog Mill Ait and its neighbour upstream known as Poisson Deux – a corruption of *Poisson d'eau*, or *douce* (freshwater fish) anglicized into Poison Ducks! – which should be left to port (starboard when coming downstream), while the smallest, against the Buckinghamshire bank should be left to starboard (port downstream). These are supposedly the site of the famous Hellfire Club founded by Sir Francis Dashwood who in the mid-eighteenth century lived at Medmenham Abbey which comes into view on your right, just below a launching slip which is really the site of the noted Medmenham Ferry. Reasonable moorings can be had just above the ferry site.

The towing path does not now cross the river as the ferry has fallen into disuse, but there is a footpath on both sides of the river for the walker. From the official Thames Path, on the right bank (Berkshire) which runs behind Frog Mill Ait, a footpath turns inland to connect to the main A4130 by the *Black Boys Inn,* while the path on the left bank, starting at Medmenham Ferry and continuing upstream, can be found at the end of the lane which leads down from Medmenham village and the noted *Dog & Badger Inn.* About halfway up the reach towards Magpie Island, opposite some moorings on the Buckinghamshire bank, you may find the path leading up to Lower Culham Farm where there is a farm shop.

Above Magpie Island, where the Thames Path has been obliged to divert away from the river as it is not the original towing path, Culham Court (not to be confused with Culham in Oxfordshire) looks down across the valley from Remenham Hill. Now comes the next disused ferry at Aston. Both sides of the ferry course can be used as launching

Above Hambleden Weir

slips for light craft. The one on the Buckinghamshire bank is approached from Ferry Lane leading to Hambleden Place from the Marlow-Henley road (A4155) at Mill End. The Berkshire slip slopes away from the end of Aston Lane which is signposted from the A4130 to Aston and passes the *Flower Pot Inn* on its way to the Thames. There are moorings along the towing path on the Berkshire bank but great care is needed, as we approach the recently reconstructed Hambleden Lock.

Hambleden Weirs and the stream below them offer a picturesque walk across the weir for ramblers, artists and photographers (Hambleden Mill is a famous calendar subject); and canoeists have a regular slalom course in the weir stream. Regrettably, for safety reasons brought to light by the possibility of litigation, anglers are no longer allowed to fish from the overfalls. Hambleden Mill itself now consists of some very upmarket dwellings inserted into the original mill-shaped structure, preserved no doubt by historical and timely writ – not timely enough, unfortunately, to preserve it as a mill! A trip back in time, though, is worth the walk into Hambleden Village proper, across the bottom lock gates from your Thames Path-side mooring – above or below the lock – over the weir and, on reaching the main road, cross it and walk the mile and a quarter to savour the sight of a true English village. Hambleden Lock is the latest to be enlarged – mainly lengthened and widened by almost half the size again of the old one – and provided with new-style chamber floor sluices, rather than gate paddles, as mentioned earlier when describing the new lock at Romney.

From Hambleden, we start on the long curve southwards and back towards the old Bath Road under which we passed at Maidenhead. Here the river meanders in a fine loop from Reading back into the Chilterns and out again. Ahead lies the famous Royal Regatta course which finishes near Henley Bridge below the Oxfordshire town of Henley-on-Thames, famed as the spiritual home of rowing. On this next reach you will have to bear in mind that steam yachts, motor cruisers, wherries, punts and even sailing dinghies have been reviled for the last 150 years or more by the rowing men who held their first regatta here in 1839 and had it accorded the title 'Royal' in 1851, the year of the Great Exhibition. It is over this course that we now follow that the first ever Oxford and Cambridge Boat Race was rowed, in 1829. No race was rowed after that until 1836 when the challenge was taken up again and the race rowed from Westminster to Putney – a wider river and a

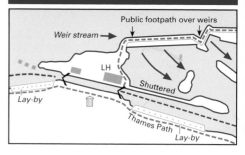

Hambleden Lock Daytime only
Mill End, Hambleden, Henley-on-Thames
RG9 3AZ ☎ 01491 571269
200'3'' (61·00m) long x 25'4'' (7·70m) wide
Rise (fall) 4'9'' (1·44m)
Max. draught 7'3'' (2·21m)
Facilities Refuse disposal.

bit of tide to boot if they slowed down, for they rowed it at the top of the flood.

The regatta course starts at the tail of Temple Island on the Buckinghamshire side and finishes 400 yards short of the bridge at Poplar Point at the head of Henley Reach. During the regattas – the Royal Regatta at

Hambleden Weir and Mill

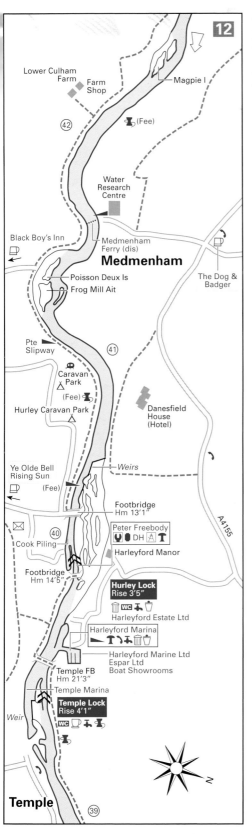

the end of June and into early July is now preceded by one for ladies and followed by one for veterans, with the Town Regatta following at the end of July – you will find the course laid out with booms and piling with directions as to which channel you may use when passing the course. Agency launches will be in attendance, with navigation staff to assist or annoy depending upon your temperament (and possibly theirs!).

It is all taken very seriously – still – and if ever the playing fields of Eton are built on you may rest assured that the seat of government may well be removed to Henley-on-Thames, where the Buckinghamshire bank has now become the Oxfordshire bank about 1500 yards below the bridge.

On this bank close to the county boundary is Fawley Court while opposite are the premises of the Remenham Club and the Upper Thames Rowing Club. Above Fawley Court as we approach the town is Phyllis Court Club and a residential development, sporting its own cruising club affiliated to the ATYC. The moorings here are all private. At the bridge, on the Berkshire bank, below is the Leander Club, the famous rowing establishment, and above is the recently constructed headquarters building of the Henley Royal Regatta. Beyond the Regatta building are a nursing home, boatyards, a boating club, a sea-cadet headquarters and Henley Rowing Club. This means that the river space here is busy for most of the year so keep a sharp lookout for every kind of craft – even swimmers. The main channel is up the eastern, Berkshire, side of the group of islands known as Rod and East Eyot, but inside the eyots on the Thames Path bank are pleasant moorings alongside Mill Meadows which is the home of the River and Rowing Museum, standing like a great boathouse behind the trees. Here is the story of the Thames, its boats and oarsmen, its geology and geography, its natural history and its trade and their impact on the town.

When not in the throes of regatta fever, Henley is a very pleasant town with good pubs and shops and there are plenty of moorings as well as a public slip. Negotiate the bridge with care, especially when coming downstream, for it spans the river at a deceptive angle and I remember a classic crunch some years ago when the river was up and my helmsman chickened out at the last moment, just short of the central arch. Hobbs' Yard is still to be found at the end of River Terrace and there are public moorings inside Rod and East Eyots, close to the rail

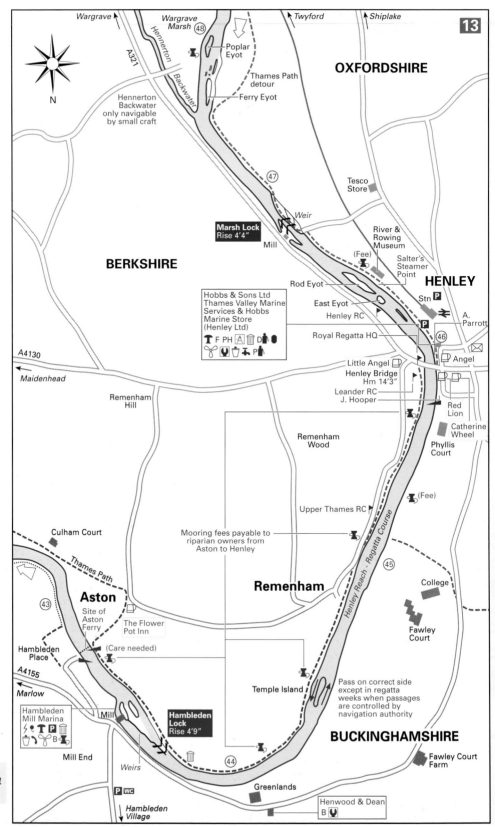

Wargrave ↗   *Wargrave Marsh* (48)   ↑ *Twyford*   ↑ *Shiplake*

Poplar Eyot

Thames Path detour

Ferry Eyot

OXFORDSHIRE

A321

Hennerton Backwater

Hennerton Backwater only navigable by small craft

N

Tesco Store

(47)

Weir

Marsh Lock Rise 4'4"

Mill

River & Rowing Museum

Salter's Steamer Point

(Fee)

BERKSHIRE

Rod Eyot

East Eyot

Henley RC

Royal Regatta HQ

HENLEY

Stn P

A. Parrott

(46)

Hobbs & Sons Ltd Thames Valley Marine Services & Hobbs Marine Store (Henley Ltd)

T F PH A ⌂ D

✂ ⚙ ♨ P

Angel

Little Angel

Henley Bridge Hm 14'3"

Leander RC

J. Hooper

A4130

← *Maidenhead*

Red Lion

Catherine Wheel

Remenham Hill

Remenham Wood

Phyllis Court

Upper Thames RC

(Fee)

Mooring fees payable to riparian owners from Aston to Henley

Culham Court

College

(45)

Thames Path

Remenham

Fawley Court

(43)

Aston

Site of Aston Ferry

The Flower Pot Inn

Henley Reach – Regatta Course

Hambleden Place

(Care needed)

A4155

← *Marlow*

Hambleden Mill Marina

⚡ ⛽ T P 🗑

🥤 ✂ ♨ B

Mill

Temple Island

Pass on correct side except in regatta weeks when passages are controlled by navigation authority

BUCKINGHAMSHIRE

Hambleden Lock Rise 4'9"

Mill End

Weirs

(44)

Fawley Court Farm

P wc

↓ *Hambleden Village*

Greenlands

Henwood & Dean B ⚓

Marsh Lock Daytime only
Wargrave Road, Henley-on-Thames RG9
3HY ☎ 01491 572992
135'2'' (41·19m) long x 21'1'' (6·42m) wide
Rise (fall) 4'4'' (1·33m)
Max. draught 7'2'' (2·18m)
Facilities None.
Angling From weir walkway on main weir.

Henley Bridge

station and car parks. A little way above the town comes Marsh Lock, on the site of two mills – one each side of the river, giving us a Mill Lane on the Henley side and a Mill Bank on the Wargrave Road side. The main weirs are on the Henley side, right as you go upstream, and should be avoided, especially if the stream is running strongly when you leave the lock coming down.

We are now heading more or less south upstream with wooded hills to the left and water-meadow to our right which stretches away to Harpsden Wood and Sonning Common, (not to be confused with Sonning-on-Thames which is five miles southeast of the common and which will be referred to in the next section). Turning into the trees at the end of the reach above Marsh, the outfall of Hennerton Backwater comes into the river on the Berkshire side. As noted on the chart this stream can be explored as a diversionary route but by small craft only – and ideally by canoe – since it leaves the river above us at Willow Lane, below Wargrave Manor in the next section.

At the mouth of the Hennerton Stream used to be the Beggar's Hole, or Bolney, now known as Harpsden Ferry, which gave its name to Ferry Eyot on the left, Oxfordshire bank but the new Thames Path, now with no ferry, here diverts away from the river towards the Henley-Twyford railway line. Next comes Poplar Eyot which may be passed on either side. Opposite, on the Berkshire bank, there is mooring alongside the old towing path. At this point Chart No. 13 and the present section finish, at Wargrave Marsh, just short of Henley Sailing Club and the village of Wargrave, which is covered in Section 7.

The Thames Path

The Thames Path starts this section along the old towing path which followed the Buckinghamshire bank from the town of Marlow and passed Temple Lock. Above this was a ferry, the operation of which, according to Thacker, was charged to the lock-keeper. Very close to what was the site of the ferry, which closed in 1953, a new footbridge was opened in 1989 to take walkers over to the Berkshire shore. Within a few yards, a footpath to the left takes you into Hurley Village, joining the High Street by *Ye Olde Bell Hotel*. In just under half a mile from the footbridge comes another, of older vintage, which allows you to cross onto the Hurley Lock Island, thus avoiding crossing the millstream although there is a track leading into Mill Lane which brings you into Hurley High Street and the village again. The Thames Path now goes in front of the lock-keeper's cottage, alongside the lock and the services block above and, by means of a further footbridge, you must return to the Berkshire bank just before Hurley Farm's land. Another track from the village rejoins the Path at this point.

Following the river closely now, you can keep to the water's edge past Medmenham Ferry, following a path with stiles and footbridges to a point just beyond the junction with the path to Lower Culham Farm downstream of Magpie Island. Here the Path branches off towards Culham Court, crossing in front of it, and approaches Aston Lane above the *Flower Pot Hotel*. Here, turn right and rejoin the river at Aston Ferry. Turn left over a stile and you will pass Hambleden Lock, Temple Island and the Henley Royal Regatta course to leave the riverside at Henley Bridge. A detour behind the Leander Club at Henley Bridge is posted during Regatta Week.

Cross the bridge and the Path now takes to the Oxfordshire bank along Thames Side

as far as Hobbs Boatyard. Continue past the boatyard on the river side until you reach Marsh weir when a picturesque wooden walkway takes you up to the lockside and back again into Bolney meadows. The original footbridges and lock, completed in 1773, were reputedly the work of portraitist Thomas Gainsborough's brother, Humphrey. A portrait of Humphrey by his brother Thomas now hangs in the River and Rowing Museum. At the time of writing Marsh Weir is being totally rebuilt and the footbridge section of the path has been closed. A signed diversion may still be in operation when this book is published. At the end of the meadow you will come to the site of Bolney Ferry, shown in some mileage tables as Harpsden Ferry, or Beggar's Hole, which took the hauling party across to Wargrave Marsh where the towing path continued up to Lashbrook Ferry, a distance of 1500 yards or so before returning the hauliers to the Oxfordshire bank. Here, however, the river must be left to follow a path and track, over the Henley railway track by the crossing near Shiplake Station, opposite the *Baskerville Arms*.

Angling

After fairly exhaustive enquiries, I can only give brief details of reserved fishing, notified from a mixture of sources. Readers are advised to consult the periodical volume *Where to Fish*, published annually and available for consultation in most public reference libraries, although be warned that out-of-date information is often contained therein because club and association secretaries do not always provide supplemental correcting information and old information, once included, tends to stick.

Above Temple Lock the London Anglers Association (LAA) has the fishing rights on the Berkshire bank from the Temple footbridge up to Hurley Lock. Permits are obtainable from the Association's bailiff on the bank. At Frog Mill Court, LAA has a stretch of fishing for members only, below Medmenham Ferry. The old towing path still exists on the Buckinghamshire bank above the ferry and runs almost up to Hambleden Place but I have no note of any fishing rights here. On the opposite bank from Aston Ferry, however, up to Hambleden Lock tail, Reading and District AA has water, also available to members of Tring Anglers. Three quarters of a mile above Hambleden Lock, on the towing path side almost to Henley

Bridge, is held by Remenham AS – apart from a reserved section signposted in the middle which is held by LAA. Day tickets are available on the bank for the Remenham AS sections. Fishing on the Oxfordshire and Buckinghamshire bank is reserved to Remenham AS members only. Above Henley Bridge, along Henley Promenade as far as Cold Bank Ditch on the towing path side, fishing is free.

Weir Permit holders may also fish from the banks of the camping island above Buck Weir upstream of Hurley Lock. Cars should be parked in the village car park which is reached from the High Street off the A4130 Maidenhead-Henley road. A footpath runs from the car park to the footbridge which carries the towing path onto the lock island. Report to the lock-keeper first and then cross Buck Weir onto the island. On occasion and without notice the site may not be available for individual days within the available period at this site, which is from 1 October to 31 March only.

Fishing is also available to Weir Permit holders from the walkway on the main weir structure at Marsh Lock. This is the weir next to the lock on the Oxfordshire side. There is a public car park in Mill Lane which is a turning off the A4155 Henley-Caversham road.

Directory

BOATYARDS, MARINAS, CHANDLERIES, TRIPPING AND HIRE

Temple Marina
Temple Mill Island, Temple, Marlow, Buckinghamshire SL7 1SA ☎ 01628 823410 or 01442 862850. Permanent moorings up to 15 metres, mains electricity, TV points, telephones, water.

Harleyford Estate Ltd
Harleyford Marina, Marlow, Buckinghamshire, SL7 2DX ☎ 01628 471361. Annual and visitors' moorings, hardstanding, slipway, telephone lines, water point, refuse and chemical toilet disposal, toilets, shop, car park, club. (TBTA)

Boat Showrooms Ltd
Harleyford Marina, Marlow, Buckinghamshire, SL7 2DX ☎ 01628 471361. Boat sales, brokerage, finance, insurance. (Also at Shepperton Marina.) (TBTA)

Peter Freebody & Co.

BOATBUILDERS, MILL LANE, HURLEY   **Est. over 300 years**

NEW BOATS DESIGNED & BUILT - PETROL, STEAM & ELECTRIC
SPECIAL ORDERS WELCOMED
REPAIRS & RESTORATIONS
ENGINEERING - SERVICE &REBUILDS
USED BOATS FOR SALE
MOORINGS & WINTER STORAGE
OPEN 7 DAYS A WEEK

TELEPHONE: (01628) 824382
www.boatbuilder.co.uk

Espar Ltd
Harleyford Marina, Marlow, Buckinghamshire, SL7 2DX ☎ 01628 471368. Marine engineers, boat repairs, craning service, chandlery.

Peter Freebody & Co
Thames Boat Houses, Hurley, Maidenhead, Berkshire, SL6 5ND ☎ 01628 824382/826691. Boatbuilders, sales, repairs and restorations, marine engineers, permanent moorings, winter storage.

Cook Piling
Ladye Place Boat House, Mill Lane, Hurley, Maidenhead, Berkshire, SL6 5ND ☎ 01628 822200. Bank protection, dredging, jetty construction, barge and plant hire.

Hambleden Mill Marina
Mill End, Henley-on-Thames, Oxon RG9 3AY ☎ 01491 571316/578870. Boat sales, brokerage, marine engineers, Edwardian launch for charter (12 passengers max.), permanent moorings, hardstanding, crane, telephone, refuse and chemical toilet disposal, electric launch recharging point, car park. (TBTA)

Henwood and Dean
Greenlands Farm, Dairy Lane, Hambleden, Henley-on-Thames, Oxon RG9 3AS ☎ 01491 571692. Boatbuilders, sales, repairs and restorations. Traditional Thames craft a speciality.

Actief Barge Cruising Holidays
The Mill House, Nettlebed, Henley-on-Thames, Oxon RG9 5RN ☎ 01491 641237 *Fax* 01491 641896. Agents: European Waterways Ltd ☎ 01784 482439. Thames cruising holidays in hotel boat *Actief*, plies between Windsor and Shillingford.

J Hooper
Thames Side, Henley-on-Thames, Oxon RG9 2LJ ☎ 01491 576867. Office: 54, Ancastle Green, Henley-on-Thames, Oxon RG9 1TS. Day-boat hire, double and single sculling skiffs and punts, motor launches.

A Parrott
The Boatyard, 15 Thames Side, Henley-on-Thames, Oxon RG9 1BH ☎ 01491 572380. *Calor Gas*, fishing tackle, chandlery, bait, moorings.

Hobbs' Boatyard
Wargrave Road, Remenham Hill, Henley-on-Thames, Oxon RG9 2LT ☎ 01491 572035. Boatbuilding, sales, repairs, permanent moorings and storage.

D A Brownjohn Boatbuilders
Hobbs' Boatyard, Wargrave Road, Remenham Hill, Henley-on- Thames, Oxon, RG9 2LT ☎ 01491 412580. Boatbuilder, repairs and restorations. Slipper launches built, engines fitted.

Hobbs and Sons Ltd
Station Road Boathouse, Henley-on-Thames, Oxon RG9 1AZ ☎ 01491 572035. Boatbuilding, sales, brokerage, finance and insurance, diesel fuel, petrol, water point, chandlery, outboard sales and service, day-launch hire, passenger trips, party hire, catering afloat, bank protection and piling contractors. (TBTA, THCA, UTPBA)

Hobbs Marine Store
Station Road Boathouse, Henley-on-Thames, Oxon RG9 1AZ ☎ 01491 574494. Boat sales, Hardy and Shetland agents, chandlery, yachting equipment, Evinrude outboard engine dealer.

Thames Valley Marine Services
Hobbs Boat House, Station Road, Henley-on-Thames, Oxon RG9 1AZ ☎ 01491 573121. Marine engineers, repairs.

EMERGENCY FUEL SUPPLIES
See note under this heading on page 24
Henley Service Station
Petrol, diesel
345, Reading Road, Henley-on-Thames, Oxon ☎ 01491 574149. At top of Mill Lane 300yds from Marsh Lock.

ROWING, SAILING AND CRUISING CLUBS AND TUITION
Harleyford Motor Yacht Club
Harleyford Marina, Harleyford, Marlow, Bucks SL7 2DX. Motor cruising. (ATYC, RYA)

Danesfield (Thames) Sailing Club
Medmenham, Marlow, Bucks SL7. Sailing.

Danesfield (Thames) Rowing Club
Medmenham, Marlow, Bucks SL7 ☎ 01491 571599. Rowing. (ARA)

Upper Thames Rowing Club
Remenham Lane, Henley-on-Thames, Oxon RG9 3DB ☎ 01491 575745. Rowing. (ARA)

Phyllis Court Club – Boat Owners' Association
Phyllis Court Club, Phyllis Court Drive, Marlow Road, Henley-on-Thames, Oxon RG9 2HT ☎ 01491 574366. Motor cruising. (ATYC, RYA)

Leander Club
Henley Bridge, Henley-on-Thames, Oxon RG9 2LP ☎ 01491 575782. Rowing. (ARA)

Henley Royal Regatta HQ
Henley Bridge, Henley-on-Thames, Oxon RG9 2LY ☎ 01491 572153. Regatta Admin. (ARA)

Henley Unit Sea Cadet Corps
TS *Guardian*, Wargrave Road, Remenham, Henley-on-Thames, Oxon RG9 3HY. Sea Cadets.

Eyot Boat Centre and Club
Lower Close, Wargrave Road, Henley-on-Thames, Oxon RG9 3JD ☎ 01491 574989. Canoeing. (BCU)

Henley Rowing Club
The Boathouse, Wargrave Road, Henley-on-Thames, Oxon RG9 3JD ☎ 01491 574950. Rowing. (ARA)

PUBLIC LAUNCHING SITES

- **Marlow** At the bottom of St Peter Street. Care! Parking restrictions
- **Medmenham** Next to former ferry site at end of Ferry Lane off A4155. Soft bottom, light craft only
- **Aston Ferry** At end of Aston Ferry Lane, continuation of Aston Lane off A4130. Shingle
- **Hambleden Place** At end of Ferry Lane off A4155 at Mill End on site of former Aston Ferry on Buckinghamshire bank. Shingle.
- **Henley-on-Thames** At corner of New Street and Thames Side by Wharfe Lane. Concrete slip. Keys from Town Hall or J Hooper alongside slipway.

FISHING TACKLE SHOPS

Kings Fishing Tackle
18 Ray Street, Maidenhead, Berks ☎ 01628 29283

Maidenhead Bait & Tackle
19 Station Hill Parade, Cookham Rise, Berks ☎ 01628 530500.

Alf Parrott
The Boatyard, 12 Thames Side, Henley-on-Thames, Oxon ☎ 01491 572380

Henley Sports
1 Grey's Road, Henley-on-Thames, Oxon ☎ 01491 573687

TOURIST INFORMATION OFFICES

Marlow 31, High Street, Marlow, Bucks ☎ 01628 483597.

HOTELS, INNS AND RESTAURANTS

Rising Sun Inn High Street, Hurley. Bar meals midday and evenings; dining evenings only.

Ye Olde Bell Hotel High Street, Hurley ☎ 01628 825881. High-class hotel-restaurant. Bar meals midday and evenings.

Black Boys Inn Henley Road, Hurley. B&B, bar meals and dining midday and evenings. Mooring usually available at Hurley Caravan Park (fee).

Danesfield House Hotel Henley Road, Medmenham ☎ 01628 891010. High-class, expensive, hotel-restaurant. Nearest mooring at Harleyford Marina visitors' moorings (fee).

Dog & Badger Inn Henley Road, Medmenham. Bar meals lunchtime and evenings; dining evenings only. Moorings free just above Medmenham Ferry.

Flower Pot Hotel Aston Ferry Lane, Aston. Bar meals and dining midday and evenings. Mooring to old ferry landing stage (300yds), or above Hambleden Lock.

Red Lion Inn Hart Street, Henley. ☎ 01491 562161. Riverside hotel-restaurant. Bar snacks. Moorings below Henley Bridge on Berks bank opposite hotel (fee).

Little Angel Inn Remenham Lane, Henley. Bar meals daily and seated dining (except Mondays) in high-class restaurant midday and evening. Moorings below Henley Bridge on Berks bank (fee) or by Rod Eyot.

Angel on the Bridge Thameside, Henley. Bar meals and seated dining midday and evenings. Bar open all day. Moorings outside.

Anchor Hotel Friday Street, Henley. Dining room, home made bar meals, midday and evenings.

Villa Marina Thameside, Henley ☎ 01491 575262/411394. Restaurant, Italian-style menu.

Wimpy Restaurant Duke Street, Henley.

Crispins Hart Street, Henley ☎ 01491 574232. Licensed restaurant.

Catherine Wheel Hotel Hart Street, Henley-on-Thames ☎ 01491 848484. Accommodation and Lloyds No 1 Restaurant. (Wetherspoons)

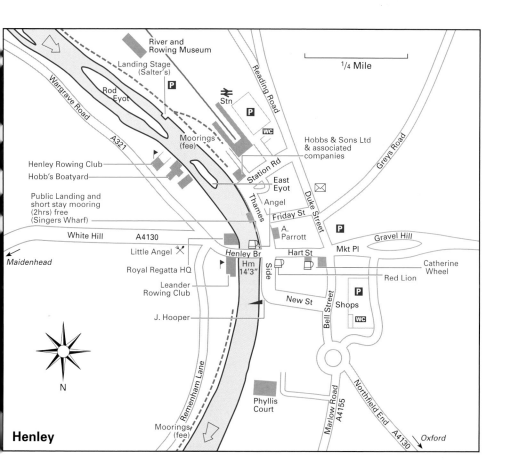

Henley

TAXIS
Marlow
- Bertran's ☎ 01628 485573
- APT Private Hire ☎ 01628 890808

Henley
- Chiltern Taxi Service ☎ 01491 578899
- County Car Hire ☎ 01491 579696

RAIL STATIONS AND TRAIN SERVICES
See note under this heading on page 26
Enquiries ☎ 08457 484950

Marlow *FGW Link* Station Approach,
Station Road, Marlow, Bucks. 800yds
from river. Trains to Bourne End,
Cookham and Maidenhead. Change at
Maidenhead for main line.

Henley-on-Thames *FGW Link* Station
Road, Henley-on-Thames, Oxon. 250yds
from river. Trains to Shiplake, Wargrave,
Twyford and Reading. Change at
Twyford for all stations to London and at
Reading for a fast service to London.

BUS AND COACH SERVICES
Temple to Henley
One bus route follows the river, more or less
between Marlow and Henley on the
Bucks/Oxon bank the jointly operated route
running between Reading and High
Wycombe. There is now a bus connection to
Maidenhead via Hurley from either Marlow
or Henley running Monday–Saturday.
Henley is also linked to Oxford via
Wallingford by Thames Travel.

Bus Operators are:
- Thames Travel ☎ 01491 837988
- Arriva The Shires ☎ 0870 728 8188
- Reading Buses ☎ 0118 959 4000
- Borough Bus – Hurley Link 01628
  796666

River Users' Groups (RUGs)

These groups were set up following recommendations in a *Leisure Policy Document* produced in 1980 by a riparian local planning authorities' working party, co-ordinated by the Thames Water Authority which was then the navigation authority for the river above Teddington. The aim was, and still is, for local monitoring of problems experienced by the various organisations who promote leisure activities along the Thames. The Association of Thames Yacht Clubs (ATYC) undertook the setting up and co-ordination of the groups under the chairmanship of E H (Harry) Fountain JP who was also deputy chairman of ATYC and its honorary secretary.

In the light of experience since 1980, by the exchange of views a greater understanding has developed between the clubs, firms, authorities and other organisations involved, all of whom are invited to send representatives to group meetings. This has led to a reduction of confrontation and conflict but it is incumbent upon all organisations to participate in local group meetings (approximately three a year) and make them an ongoing exercise.

Since the groups were first formed, adjustments and extensions have been developed – the Upper Tideway section from Teddington to Tower Bridge was added under the title of River Users' Amenity Group No. 9 and was established with the full co-operation of the Port of London Authority which supports the group equally with the Environment Agency.

The reaches of the river covered by the groups are as follows. Any enquiries for details of the groups' meetings or for information collated should be addressed in the first instance to the River Users' Groups' Co-ordinator, Environment Agency Thames Region, Kings Meadow House, Kings Meadow Road, Reading, RG1 8DQ ☎ 0118 953 5503.

River Users Group 1 Inglesham to Godstow
River Users Group 2 Godstow to Sandford
River Users Group 3 Sandford to Cleeve
River Users Group 4 Cleeve to Mapledurham
River Users Group 5 Mapledurham to Marsh Lock (Henley)
River Users Group 6 Marsh Lock to Boulters Lock (Maidenhead)
River Users Group 7 Boulters Lock to Bell Weir (Egham)
River Users Group 8 Bell Weir (Egham) to Teddington
River Users Amenity Group 9 Teddington to Tower Bridge.

Temple Lock from Temple footbridge

7. Reading – Wargrave to Mapledurham, including the River Kennet from its mouth to High Bridge

Distance

11.95 miles (Harpsden Ferry to Mapledurham Lock)

Maximum dimensions of craft from Marsh Lock to Mapledurham

Headroom 14´2´´ (4.41m) at Sonning Bridge, under tie plates
Length 131´4´´ (40.03m) at Caversham Lock
Beam 17´11´´ (5.46m) at Sonning and Caversham Locks
Draught 4´6´´ (1.37m) in main fairway up to Reading
4´0´´ (1.22m) in main fairway above Reading to Oxford

Maximum dimensions of craft from Kennet Mouth to High Bridge (EA/BW limit)

Headroom 9´6´´ (2.90m) at Watlington Bridge 7´0´´ (2.13m) beyond High Bridge
Length 122´8´´ (37.39m) at Blake's Lock 70´0´´ (21.34m) beyond High Bridge
Beam 18´11´´ (5.75m) at Blake's Lock 13´9´´ (4.20m) beyond High Bridge
Draught 3´3´´ (1.00m) to High Bridge 3´0´´ (0.91m) beyond High Bridge

Above Harpsden Ferry and Poplar Eyot the river winds between wooded banks and well-kept lawns with the odd vision of a sleek day-launch housed in idleness under a gabled boathouse. The river may well be busy with racing or practising by the stalwarts of the Henley Sailing Club beyond Handbuck Eyot which should be passed to starboard when proceeding upstream (port, coming down). The club's headquarters are just above Lashbrook Eyot beyond which, before the club house, is a 24-hour mooring. From here boatmen can walk along the old towing path into Willow Lane and up to the *St George and Dragon* pub and restaurant. Above the sailing club is Val Wyatt's Willow Marina.

On the left bank below the sailing club you are close to Lower Shiplake, where Shiplake rail station is sited, but mooring is not possible until the Thames Path rejoins the bank at the site of the former Lashbrook Ferry. Mooring against the bank opposite the *St George and Dragon* is possible but there is no access across the river. Just above the inn is Wargrave Slip at the end of Ferry Lane which is a turning off the High Street. The wide sweep of the river in front of Wargrave takes us round to Shiplake rail bridge. Below the bridge on the Wargrave side is the inlet which leads up to Bushnell's yard where the third generation of the Bushnell family still operates. Here, too, is now based the sumptuously refurbished steam launch *Windsor Belle*, built in 1901 by Arthur Jacobs of Windsor. Above the bridge on the same bank comes the mouth of the Loddon, into which runs St Patrick's Stream, and Shiplake weir stream, while over on the Oxfordshire bank is Shiplake Lock.

Shiplake Lock Daytime only
Mill Lane, Henley-on-Thames RG9 3NA
☎ 0118 940 3350
133'4'' (40·64m) long x 18'3'' (5·56m) wide
Rise (fall) 5'1'' (1·55m)
Max. draught 6'3'' (1·90m)
Facilities Chemical toilet and refuse disposal, water for can and tank filling, toilets, toilet pump-out unit, electric launch charging point.
Angling From weir walkway across westerly weir structure only. Also permitted from south bank of the camping island (1 November to 31 March).
Note The landing stages on the camping island are not built to Environment Agency safety standards and so cannot be relied upon. You should not use them.

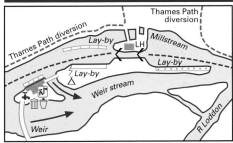

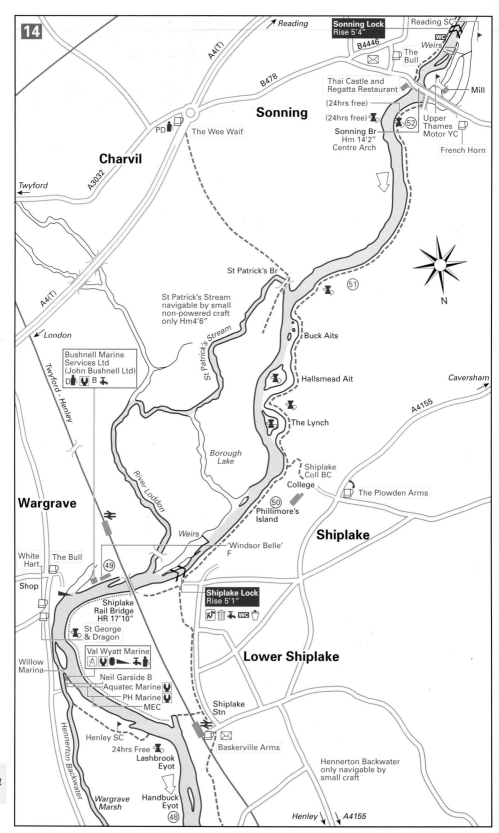

14

↗ *Reading*

Sonning Lock
Rise 5'4"

Reading SC

B4446

✉ The Bull

WC

Weirs

Thai Castle and
Regatta Restaurant

(24hrs free)

(24hrs free) 🍺

Mill

A4(T)

B478

Sonning

Upper
Thames
Motor YC

52

French Horn

PD 🚽

The Wee Waif

Sonning Br
Hm 14'2"
Centre Arch

Charvil

A3032

← *Twyford*

← *Twyford*

St Patrick's Br

St Patrick's Stream
navigable by small
non-powered craft
only Hm4'6"

51

A4(T)

← *London*

Buck Aits

Caversham

Twyford - Henley

Bushnell Marine
Services Ltd
(John Bushnell Ltd)
D 🚶 🚽 B 🔧

Hallsmead Ait

A4155

St Patrick's Stream

The Lynch

River Loddon

*Borough
Lake*

Shiplake
Coll BC

College

The Plowden Arms

50

Phillimore's
Island

Shiplake

Wargrave

White
Hart

The Bull

Weirs

'Windsor Belle'
F

Shop

49

Shiplake
Rail Bridge
HR 17'10"

Shiplake Lock
Rise 5'1"

St George
& Dragon

Val Wyatt Marine
🏕 🚽 🍴

Lower Shiplake

Willow
Marina

Neil Garside B
Aquatec Marine 🚽
PH Marine 🚽
MEC

Shiplake
Stn

Henley SC

24hrs Free 🍺
Lashbrook
Eyot

Baskerville Arms

Hennerton Backwater

Hennerton Backwater
only navigable by
small craft

*Wargrave
Marsh*

Handbuck
Eyot

48

Henley ↓ *A4155*

Leaving Shiplake Lock going upstream you will find the sanitary station and water point above the overspill weir on your port-hand side. Mooring here can be tricky, especially if the weirs are running strongly. Certainly, if coming downstream it would be very unwise to try and land facing downstream, necessary at the lock lay-bys we know, but in any other situation a recipe for disaster or embarrassment at best. Ahead lies a small eyot, Phillimore's Island, at the junction with the tail of the Borough Lake which leads from St Patrick's Stream – navigable by small craft, bearing in mind that there is a headroom at St Patrick's Bridge at the head of the stream, where it leaves the Thames, of only 4'6'' (1.37m).

Now 50 miles above Teddington, we pass Shiplake College on the Oxfordshire bank, along whose shore the Thames Path continues to run until a footpath winds off it into Church Lane and up to the *Plowden Arms* on the main A4155 Henley Road. Next the river meanders past two islands, an area which affords reasonable but secluded moorings, The Lynch and Hallsmead Ait, followed by Buck Aits and the entrance on the Berkshire side to the aforementioned St Patrick's Stream. There appears to be a conflict of opinion as to which side of the two larger aits one should pass. Maps show the channel running on the opposite side to the towing path which, if you are towing, could be a problem! Experience has shown, however, that the towpath side is shallow and one should take the wider route on the Berkshire or 'off' side. From St Patrick's Bridge, a footpath runs on the Berkshire bank to Sonning although the Thames Path remains on the Oxfordshire bank. From the Berkshire path at the bridge runs Milestone Avenue up to Charvil where a pub and a garage with a bank cash dispenser are located.

A mile and a half ahead comes the riverside village of Sonning and its quaint 18th-century bridge, the centre span being the only one that should be navigated. The river above the bridge turns sharply to your left and, as you approach upstream, take care that nothing is coming downstream towards the bridge since you will have to give way. Below the bridge there are good moorings where the towing path rounds into the millstream on the Oxfordshire side and one can moor for a fee on the Berkshire bank opposite – although the fee will be refunded if you make use of the facilities at the *Great House Hotel* or its associated *Thai Castle* or *Regatta* restaurants. The *Great House* also

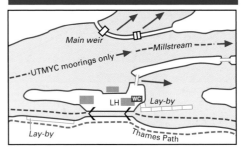

Sonning Lock Daytime only
Towing Path, Thames Street, Sonning,
Reading RG4 0UR ☎ 0118 969 3992
156'1'' (47·57m) long x 17'11'' (5·46m) wide
Rise (fall) 5'4'' (1·63m)
Max. draught 6'4'' (1·93m)
Facilities Refuse disposal, toilets.

owns the fishing rights along the Berkshire bank. Hotel guests may be able to fish free of charge.

Keep in the left-hand channel going upstream for Sonning Lock – those on the right lead from a mill-race and the weir. Do not moor below the lock, but wait until you are above it. The towing path below is elevated and the scrub and steep-sided banks do not make a comfortable resting place. The lock, similar in sluice arrangements to Marlow, fills with an early 'boil' so avoid the head of the lock when going up if you can.

Above Sonning on the Berkshire bank is Holme Park, grounds of the Reading Blue Coat School. Its rowing club boathouse will be seen on your left while, over on the right, the weir and mill streams lead to the Upper Thames Motor Yacht Club and Reading Sailing Club premises. These few pieces of gratuitous information should put the wary skipper on his guard for the sudden appearances of various forms of avoidable river traffic. From the wooded setting of Sonning Hill we rapidly come to the dreary expanses of Dreadnought Reach with its power lines and business-park architectural anarchy. The gravel pits to the right, however, have given way to the gradually assertive ambience of the Thames and Kennet Marina already being relocated within to allow the building of a 2000m rowing course.

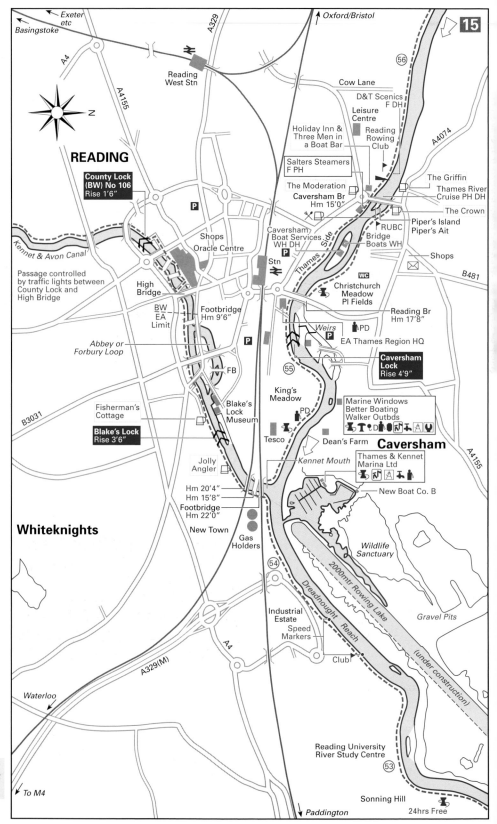

15

↖ Basingstoke

← Exeter etc

A4

A4155

A329

↑ Oxford/Bristol

Reading West Stn

Cow Lane

D&T Scenics F DH

Leisure Centre

Holiday Inn & Three Men in a Boat Bar

Reading Rowing Club

A4074

56

READING

Salters Steamers F PH

County Lock (BW) No 106 Rise 1'6"

The Moderation

Caversham Br Hm 15'0"

The Griffin

Thames River Cruise PH DH

The Crown

Piper's Island Piper's Ait

Kennet & Avon Canal

Shops Oracle Centre

Caversham Boat Services WH DH

RUBC

Bridge Boats WH

Shops

Thames Side

Passage controlled by traffic lights between County Lock and High Bridge

High Bridge

Stn

WC

B481

Christchurch Meadow Pl Fields

BW EA Limit

Footbridge Hm 9'6"

Reading Br Hm 17'8"

Abbey or Forbury Loop

Weirs

PD

EA Thames Region HQ

55

Caversham Lock Rise 4'9"

FB

King's Meadow

Fisherman's Cottage

Blake's Lock Museum

PD

Marine Windows Better Boating Walker Outbds

B3031

Blake's Lock Rise 3'6"

Tesco

Dean's Farm

Caversham

A4155

Jolly Angler

Whiteknights

Hm 20'4"

Hm 15'8"

Footbridge Hm 22'0"

New Town

Gas Holders

Kennet Mouth

Thames & Kennet Marina Ltd

New Boat Co. B

Wildlife Sanctuary

54

Gravel Pits

2000mtr Rowing Lake

Dreadnought Reach

(under construction)

Industrial Estate

Speed Markers

Club

A329(M)

A4

Waterloo

Reading University River Study Centre

53

Sonning Hill

24hrs Free

↙ To M4

↓ Paddington

High Bridge, Reading

The River Kennet

Gasholders and the rising crescendo of turbo-charged diesels and clickety-clacking electric commuter trains advertise the presence of Reading and its two railways, from below which the River Kennet enters, 54½ miles above Teddington on the right bank. A short detour will be made here to describe the portion of the Kennet that remains under the jurisdiction of the Thames Region of the Environment Agency, and a little beyond, although the river above a point just short of High Bridge was wrested from the ownership of the former Great Western Railway at the end of the Second World War and handed over to the Docks and Inland Waterways Board, introduced by the first Labour Government, shortly afterwards. From this umbrella organisation was set up the British Waterways Board – now de-suffixed into British Waterways (BW).

The entrance to the Kennet is at present being redeveloped, an event long overdue, although it is hoped that the Thames towing path bridge known as Horseshoe Bridge will remain, to prevent Thames Path walkers having to swim across Kennet Mouth. The next bridge connects the gas-holders with the old gas-works and the third carries the original South Eastern and South Western Railways lines, later Southern Region, into the main Reading station from Reigate and Staines respectively. The former Southern Railway station, virtually adjacent to the GWR's Reading General was amalgamated with the latter many years ago.

Keep away from the towing path, Kennet Side, as you approach Blake's Lock since the river here is shallow at the sides. Visitor short

Blake's Lock Daytime only – not always manned. Manual operation only. See page 146
Kennet Side, Reading, Berks RG1 3DS
☎ 0118 957 2251
122'8" (37·39m) long × 18'11" (5·75m) wide
Rise (fall) 3'6" (1·07m)
Max. draught 5'5" (1·63m)
Facilities None

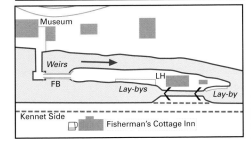

period registration for craft coming onto the Thames from the Kennet and Avon Canal is available from Blake's Lock, Sonning and Caversham Locks during lock-keepers' hours of duty. Boat crews may operate the lock when it is unattended by lock staff. Please leave the lock empty or emptying with all gates closed. Above the lock on your right as you proceed towards Reading is the Blake's Lock Museum which is operated by the local authority. Admission is free.

Above the lock cut and the weir is the quay at the museum over on your right. Here, the river divides but the main channel lies straight ahead on your port hand up to Kings Road Bridge. The channel to the north leads past Reading Marine's former boatyard, now relocated to Aldermaston, under Gas Works Road to the Abbey, or Forbury, Loop which is only navigable with care by small craft. There are shallows and the ground is rocky which, if contacted by rudder or propellers, can cause costly damage. First, after Gas Works Road, comes a footbridge, then Blake's Bridge, crossed by Forbury Road and then Kings Road before the loop rejoins the main line. The main line follows straight under Kings Road Bridge (9'6"/2.90m), Watlington Bridge (9'8"/2.95m) and Kennet Side Footbridge (9'6"/2.90m). Just above this last bridge there are adequate daytime moorings on both sides of the river for shopping and lunching, but all-night mooring is not recommended.

In front of High Bridge are mounted conventional traffic lights at the boundary between EA and BW water. They were set up at the instigation of Lionel Munk, a past Chairman of the Inland Waterways Association. The lights provide a means of safe passage through the tortuous and narrow section of the Kennet as it passes the new Oracle Centre which lines both banks of what was known as the Brewery Gut from County Lock to High Bridge. The brewery has gone but the name survives, the channel is still narrow and the current can be swift, particularly after heavy rain. Before negotiating High Bridge, or leaving the tail of County Lock where the upstream signal is positioned, a crew member should press the control button below the signal standard, and no attempt should be made to advance until the green light is shown. Meeting other craft, especially if the river is in flood, in this constricted channel through the 'Gut', could be disastrous. For details of the Kennet and Avon Navigation from County Lock to Great Bedwyn see Section 15 on page 199.

Assuming we have not ventured into the heart of Reading by way of the River Kennet, we continue upstream on the Thames to veer away from industry and the main town towards Heron Island on the outskirts of Reading's riparian twin, Caversham. On the Reading bank comes King's Meadow and an ideal mooring for the shopping expedition to the Tesco superstore, approached from the towing path. Upstream on the opposite bank – which temporarily, for the convenience of Caversham, also becomes the Berkshire bank as it loses Oxfordshire almost opposite the Tesco store but regains it between St Mary's Island and Scours Lane – comes the yard of Better Boating Co with mooring possible for a short stay as space is limited. Then after Heron Island which hides a weir stream comes a wider weir outfall and View Island which used to house a marina but is being redeveloped for leisure use by Reading Borough Council and the Environment Agency. Caversham Lock now appears against the end of Kings Meadow Playing Fields, almost under the watchful eye of Thames Region's headquarters and Middle Thames District Navigation Offices in Kings Meadow Road at the end of the open space. A handy mooring quay, for lock-waiting only, lies on your left-hand side as you approach upstream, out of the way of the weir.

At the end of the lock cut above Caversham Lock comes Reading Bridge – confusing but of historical interest. Reading Bridge is a very recent crossing compared with the original Caversham Bridge, which stood on the site occupied by the present 1926 concrete one as early as 1231. This ancient crossing of the river is some 900 yards further upstream. Reading Bridge dates

Caversham Lock Daytime only
Thames Side, Reading, Berks RG1 8BP
☎ 0118 957 5764
131'4" (40·03m) long x 17'11" (5·46m) wide
Rise (fall) 4'9" (1·44m)
Max. draught 6'0" (1·82m)
Facilities None.

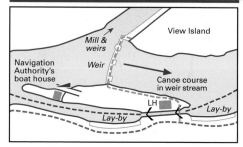

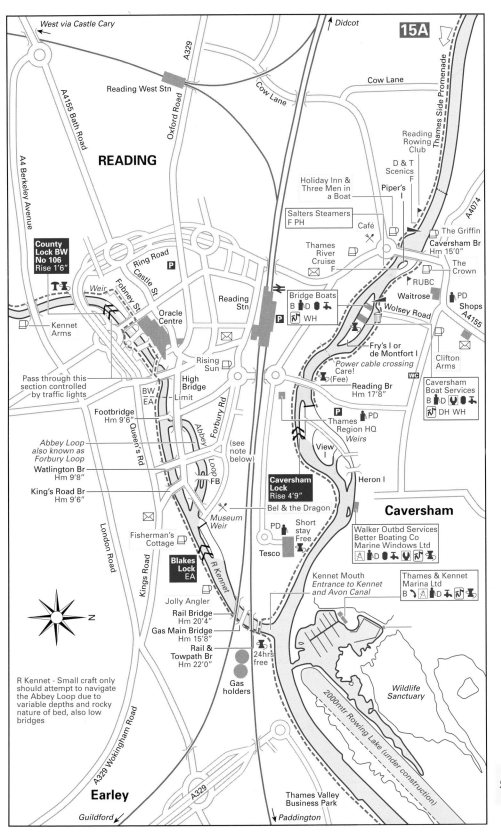

West via Castle Cary

Didcot

15A

Cow Lane

Cow Lane

A329

Reading West Stn

Oxford Road

A4155 Bath Road

Reading Rowing Club

D & T Scenics F

A4074

Piper's I

Holiday Inn & Three Men in a Boat

READING

Salters Steamers F PH

Café

The Griffin

Caversham Br Hm 15'0"

A4 Berkeley Avenue

Thames River Cruise F

The Crown

County Lock BW No 106 Rise 1'6"

Ring Road

P

Castle St

Reading Stn

P

RUBC

Waitrose

PD Shops

A4155

Weir

Fobney St

Bridge Boats B D
WH

Wolsey Road

Kennet Arms

Oracle Centre

Rising Sun

Fry's I or de Montfort I

Clifton Arms

WC

Caversham Boat Services B D
DH WH

Pass through this section controlled by traffic lights

High Bridge

BW
EA

Limit

Power cable crossing Care! (Fee)

Reading Br Hm 17'8"

Footbridge Hm 9'6"

Forbury Rd

(see note below)

P Thames Region HQ Weirs

PD

Queen's Rd

Abbey Loop also known as Forbury Loop

Abbey Loop

View I

Watlington Br Hm 9'8"

FB

Caversham Lock Rise 4'9"

Heron I

King's Road Br Hm 9'6"

Bel & the Dragon

Caversham

London Road

Fisherman's Cottage

Museum Weir

PD

Short stay Free

Walker Outbd Services Better Boating Co Marine Windows Ltd A D
N

Kings Road

Blakes Lock EA

Tesco

R Kennet

Jolly Angler

Kennet Mouth *Entrance to Kennet and Avon Canal*

Thames & Kennet Marina Ltd B A D N

Rail Bridge Hm 20'4"

Gas Main Bridge Hm 15'8"

Rail & Towpath Br Hm 22'0"

24hrs free

N

Gas holders

Wildlife Sanctuary

R Kennet - Small craft only should attempt to navigate the Abbey Loop due to variable depths and rocky nature of bed, also low bridges

2000mtr Rowing Lake (under construction)

Earley

A329 Wokingham Road

A329

Thames Valley Business Park

99

Guildford

Paddington

from 1923 and is notable for its early use of pre-stressed concrete, for the span is an elliptical curve of no less than 180′. On the lock island can be seen the boathouses for the inspection launches of the navigation authority. Above the bridge on the Caversham side are the Christchurch Playing Fields and ahead is Fry's or de Montfort Island, the latter name commemorating a duel which Simon de Montfort was supposed to have fought with Henry of Essex there in 1157. One may pass either side of the island, although it is easier to moor where there is a better depth of water against the Christchurch Playing Fields below the tail of the island. Besides the playing fields there is a children's play area which comes as a welcome break for young souls aboard who have exhausted the novelties of a small cabin cruiser.

The main channel runs on the wider, Reading, side and it is on this side of the island that you can find the premises of Caversham Boat Services and Bridge Boats, both offering weekly hire cruisers. Caversham Boat Services also offers rowing boats for hire from Christchurch Playing Fields. At the head of the island is the Island Bohemian Bowls and Social Club, members of which have to be ferried across from Brigham Road on the Reading bank. Almost opposite the head of the island on the Caversham side is Wolsey Road where a landing may be possible while, further up on the same footpath, you cross Reading University Boat Club's slip in front of its clubhouse.

Ahead stands Caversham Bridge, a complicated structure which still hints at St Anne's chapel, long gone, which stood in the centre of the old bridge. From the pier to your right facing upstream, a treacherous looking gangway appears to break away from the parapet of the bridge and descend to Piper's Island which houses a pub/restaurant and a thriving passenger tripping and day-boat hire operation. Patrons of the restaurant can moor alongside, but clear of the passenger boats, please. Immediately opposite, on the Reading side is the rather diminished branch office of Salter Steamers of Oxford, whose site now only offers passenger launches for party hire and a summer season of daily sailings to Henley and return (May to September).

Above the bridge on the Reading shore beyond the new Holiday Inn Hotel is Reading Rowing Club whose boathouse at No. 1 Thameside is curious in that the skiffs have to be manhandled out of the side of the building, but perhaps it makes life easier as they don't have to be turned from prow to the river to be dropped in. Opposite the rowing club is the Reading and Leighton Park Canoe Club, so Caversham Bridge is another busy area. There is also a passenger trip boat departure point from Thameside, D and T Scenics, running up to Mapledurham on a regular basis in season. Across the open space will be seen the Rivermead Leisure Complex. The children's playpark there is free of charge. However, there is normally no mooring along the Thameside Promenade.

With Reading's expanding business and leisure architecture receding along Richfield Avenue, the Thames escapes upstream, nudging the more upmarket properties of The Warren below Caversham Heights on the opposite bank, many sporting their own boathouses, or at least their own boats. Past Coombe Bank on your left you come to The Fisheries and the eerie stillness that surrounds St Mary's Island and yet another Bucks Eyot. The towing path side here is shallow so try not to moor until you reach Reading Marine Services at the bottom of Scours Lane. From here, you can reach Reading Retail Park and a Pizza Hut restaurant, a short walk up to the main road and across the roundabout.

Appletree Eyot and Poplar Island follow and may be passed on either side while the river becomes hemmed in by the closeness of the Reading–Didcot railway line in what are

Reading Bridge

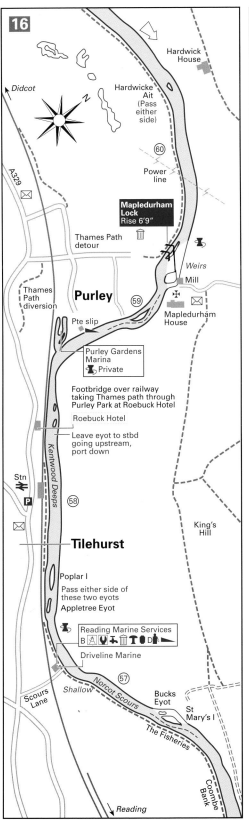

Didcot

Hardwick House

Hardwicke Ait (Pass either side)

60

Power line

Mapledurham Lock Rise 6'9"

Thames Path detour

A329

Weirs

Mill

Thames Path diversion

Purley

59

Pte slip

Mapledurham House

Purley Gardens Marina
Private

Footbridge over railway taking Thames path through Purley Park at Roebuck Hotel

Roebuck Hotel

Leave eyot to stbd going upstream, port down

Stn

P

58

King's Hill

Kentwood Deeps

Tilehurst

Poplar I

Pass either side of these two eyots

Appletree Eyot

Reading Marine Services
B A Y T T O D

Driveline Marine

57

Scours Lane

Shallow

Norcot Scours

Bucks Eyot

St Mary's I

The Fisheries

Coombe Bank

Reading

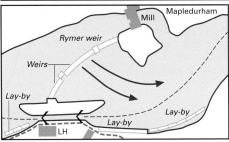

Mapledurham Lock Daytime only
Mapledurham Drive, Purley-on-Thames,
Reading RG8 8BE ☎ 0118 941 7776
202'5'' (61·69m) long × 21'1'' (6·42m) wide
Rise (fall) 6'9'' (2·05m)
Max. draught 7'0'' (2·13m)
Facilities Refuse disposal, shop.

Mapledurham

Mill

Rymer weir

Weirs

Lay-by

Lay-by

Lay-by

LH

known as Kentwood Deeps. Halfway along is Tilehurst Station and just beyond is a mooring for the *Roebuck Hotel*, which gives its name to the neglected ferry which plied here and a bus stop on the main road. At this point leave the eyots to starboard going upstream (port coming down) before turning below Purley Marina and the Purley estate but leave the eyot above the estate on your port hand (starboard coming down).

On the Oxfordshire bank stands Mapledurham House, noted as the home of the fictitious Forsytes but in reality the home of the Blount family. The house and grounds and the 15th-century mill which still grinds corn are open to the public on certain days only from Easter to September and frequent return boat trips from Caversham Bridge operate to the house. Passing the millstream we come to Mapledurham Weir, at the Oxfordshire end of which are old fashioned rymers – individual paddles which could be put in and taken out to control the water flow. On the Berkshire bank is the lock, the first to be mechanised in the improvement programme started in the 1950s.

Care is required in negotiating Mapledurham Lock when entering or leaving its tail. Note that the fall is 6′9″ which classifies the lock as a deep one and, with the long weir leading down to a restricted weir stream, the current below the lock can cause considerable helming problems. Coming upstream it is best to keep out of the weir current and sidle up to the lay-bys before entering the lock. Going downstream, once out of the lock it may be sensible to keep into the weir current so as not to be set too far over to the right bank which curves round to meet the unwary helmsman who doesn't

101

allow for the stream setting him to starboard. Again, like Marlow when proceeding into the lock to go upstream, the head sluices are above the empty water level so that the fill starts with a rush of 'white water'. Avoid going too close to the top gates when ascending.

Above the lock there is a piling lay-by, some posts and reasonable protection from the weir by the lock island. A footpath on the Berkshire bank brings the Thames Path back to the river, having left it at the Roebuck ferry. Intending visitors to Mapledurham House can only moor in the weir stream above the lock and walk forward to the mill and the church by prior arrangement. The village post office is away to the left and the main house is along the lane beside the church. The river now turns westwards again in a fine rural setting to pass Hardwicke Ait (which has almost disappeared) and Hardwick House, an Elizabethan manor house in which Queen Elizabeth I slept, nestles privately in the trees on the Oxfordshire bank.

The Thames Path

At the start of this section you may recall that the Thames Path had to leave the river at Harpsden Ferry on the Oxfordshire bank as the ferry lapsed many years ago. The route followed takes us to the Henley branch railway line at Lower Shiplake. By the station, go over the level crossing and walk down Mill Road to turn left into the driveway to Andrew Duncan House and follow the footpath beyond to Shiplake Lock. From here the Path goes along the Oxfordshire bank right up to Sonning, crossing the weir stream outfall by a footbridge onto the main B478 road which links Play Hatch with Sonning Eye, Sonning and Charvil. Turn left, cross Sonning Bridge and, immediately over the bridge, turn right onto a gravel track leading up to Sonning Lock.

From the lock the Thames Path stays on the Berkshire bank right through to Tilehurst, crossing the mouth of the River Kennet by the old Horseshoe Bridge, so called because of the slope and the long slatted sections which make it difficult to walk on. You pass beside Caversham Lock, shortly after which is King's Meadow Road to the left or a flight of steps onto Reading Bridge. Turning left off the bridge gives access to the town of Reading, or to the right across the river and down again takes you onto Christchurch playing fields. Caversham is more easily approached from a path up onto Caversham Bridge beside Salter Brothers' office half a mile ahead, since its shopping centre in Church Street and Prospect Street is much further west. Caversham Lock is probably now misnamed, since it inherited its title from a mill (now defunct) on the Caversham side of the river.

The Path now follows, above Caversham Bridge, the Thames Side Promenade and continues through Coombe Bank, The Fisheries and Norcot Scours to Scours Lane and Kentwood Deeps. A little way past Tilehurst Station, however, we must leave the river as the Roebuck Ferry no longer operates. Cross the railway and join the Oxford Road. Turn right along the footpath until you come to a bus stop where a flight of steps leads down into Skerrit Way in the Purley Park estate. This is a temporary route pending negotiations by the Countryside Commission. Keep to your left into Hazel Road and follow this road until the T-junction with New Hill where you turn right over the railway. At the next road junction, to your left you will see a track signposted Mapledurham Drive. Follow this through two gates and then fork right at the open field towards the weir and lock house which should be visible ahead. The Path joins the lockside at the tail of the lock and a gate at the head gives access to the open meadows along which the Path continues up to Pangbourne.

Angling

Holders of Weir Permits will find fishing available from the top, westerly, weir walkway structure at Shiplake. Between 1 November and 31 March fishing may also be permitted from the south bank of the camping island, facing into the weir pool, subject to the usual conditions. Note the warning on the lock details on page 93.

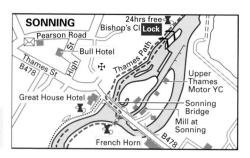

Above the lock on the towing path side up to Sonning Bridge, fishing is reserved for members of the Shiplake and Binfield Heath Fishing Club while, on the opposite bank, swims are reserved for the London Anglers. A riverside footpath starts above St Patrick's Bridge and for the last half mile, about halfway along up to Sonning Bridge, fishing is reserved for guests of the *Great House Hotel*, although permits may be granted to others on application there.

Between Sonning and Kennet Mouth are mainly private waters but on the Kennet, from the mouth to Blake's Lock, fishing is free to rod and line licence holders as it is from Kings Meadow up to Caversham Lock and from both banks between Reading and Caversham Bridges.

From a point opposite Caversham Court, along the Thames Side Promenade up to the sports ground next to Scours Lane, fishing is controlled by Reading Borough Council, although a number of sites in this stretch are free. Details from Reading Angling Centre (see *Directory* section) ☎ 0118 987 2216. From Scours Lane up to the site of the Roebuck Ferry, where the towing path ends on the Berkshire bank, fishing is free. From Purley to Mapledurham, access being by way of a footpath from Mapledurham Lock which does not form part of the newly designated Thames Path, fishing is reserved for London Anglers' Association members only. Opposite Purley on the off side between the former Roebuck Ferry and Purley Church, rights to fishing from the old towing path are held by the Elthorne Alliance and Reading and District Angling Association.

Directory

BOATYARDS, MARINAS, CHANDLERIES, TRIPPING AND HIRE

Val Wyatt Marine Sales Ltd
Willow Marina, Willow Lane, Wargrave, Reading, Berks RG10 8DY ☎ 0118 940 3211/940 3836. Boat sales and brokers, Freeman cruiser spares, hoods, boat repairs, diesel, petrol, *Calor Gas*, groceries, permanent and visitors' moorings, hardstanding, crane, slipway, winter storage, water point, toilets, car park. (TBTA)

PH Marine
(Peter Humphreys) Willow Marina, Willow Lane, Wargrave, Reading, Berks RG10 8DY ☎ 0118 940 4419. Marine engineer, BMW spares, Vetus, Lombardini, Morse, Bennett Trimtabs, Fischer Panda sales, service, parts and accessories, repairs.

Thames Valley Sterndrives
Willow Marina, Willow Lane, Wargrave, Reading, Berks RG10 8DY ☎ 0118 940 4419. Marine engineers, sales, service, parts and accessories, distributors for Mercruiser, Yamaha Sterndrives, BMW Marine, OMC Cobra.

Aquatec Marine
Willow Marina, Willow Lane, Wargrave, Reading, Berks RG10 8DY ☎ 0118 940 1422 ☎ Mobile 07831 196469. Marine engine service and repairs.

Marine Equipment and Components (MEC)
Willow Marina, Willow Lane, Wargrave, Reading, Berks RG10 8LH ☎ 0118 940 1141. Distributor of Vetus marine equipment, engines and spare parts, Morse Teleflex controls, Mastervolt electrics, Centa flexible couplings, Blakes paints and general chandlery. (TBTA)

Bluenine Marine
Willow Marina Willow Lane, Wargrave,

Nothing quite compares

Now under Tingdene ownership, the great location, unrivalled facilities, Cruiser & Narrow boat marinas & Dutch barge moorings at the delta between the River Thames & the Kennet Canal makes us special.

Explore the surroundings of the two marinas tucked away in a nature reserve & new facilities like a marine brokerage.

Maybe it's time to experience the difference

Thames & Kennet Marina Ltd
Caversham Lakes Henley Road
Reading Berkshire RG4 6LQ

Tel: 0118 948 2911 Fax: 0118 946 1541
Web: www.thameskennet.co.uk
Email: info@thameskennet.co.uk

Thames & Kennet
Marinas

Reading, Berks RG10 8LH ☎ 0118 940 6482. Outboard engines, sales, repairs and service.

Neil Garside
Willow Marina Willow Lane, Wargrave, Reading, Berks RG10 8DY ☎ 0118 940 6604. Launch and boat builder.

Bushnell Marine Services Ltd
Watermans Way, Station Road, Wargrave, Reading, Berks RG10 8HB ☎ 0118 940 2161. Boatbuilders, boat sales, brokerage, repairs and restorations, marine engineers, diesel fuel, permanent moorings, storage, crane, slipway, water point, toilets, car parking. (TBTA)

Windsor Belle Ltd
The Boatyard, Waterman's Way, Wargrave, Reading, Berks. Bookings and enquiries: Garden House, Bolney Road, Lower Shiplake, Reading, Berks RG9 3NR ☎ 0118 940 2393. Private charter of restored 1901 steamer *Windsor Belle* for up to 55 passengers. (PBA)

Thames & Kennet Marina Ltd
Caversham Lakes, Henley Road, Reading, Berks RG4 6LQ ☎ 0118 948 2911. Boat sales, brokerage, permanent and visitor's moorings, diesel fuel, Calor Gas, hardstanding, crane, telephones, water points, refuse disposal, toilet pump-out service, toilets, car park. Chandlery ☎ 0118 947 0944. (TYHA)

New Boat Co
Thames & Kennet Marina, Caversham Lakes, Henley Road, Reading, Berks, RG4 6LQ. ☎ 0118 947 9506. Boat sales for narrow and wide beam craft. Moorings.

Better Boating Company
The Boatyard, Mill Green, Caversham, Reading, Berks RG4 8EX ☎ 0118 947 9536. Permanent moorings, diesel fuel, hardstanding, crane, water point, toilet pump-out.

Mid-Thames Chandlery
The Boatyard, Mill Green, Caversham, Reading, Berks RG4 8EX ☎ 0118 947 9536. Chandlery, paints, *Calor Gas.*

Butcher Marine
The Boatyard, Mill Green, Caversham, Reading, Berks RG4 8EX ☎ *Mobile* 07860 191981. Office at 8 Sargood Close, Thatcham, Berks RG13 4FA ☎ 01635 867820. Boat repairs, antifouling, osmosis treatment, undercover storage.

S J Marine Engineering Services
The Boatyard, Mill Green, Caversham, Reading, Berks RG4 8EX ☎ 0118 947 6755. Marine engineers.

D Walker, Outboard Services
The Boatyard, Mill Green, Caversham, Reading, Berks RG4 8EX ☎ 0118 947 8641. Outboard motors sales and service. Mercruiser sterndrives and inboards,

Mercury outboards main dealer, all leading makes serviced. Sales, service, spares, propellers – spares by mail order.

Marine Windows Ltd
The Boatyard, Mill Green, Caversham, Reading, Berks RG4 8EX ☎ 0118 948 2664 Mobile 07836 250219. Manufacturers of boat windows, portholes and windscreens. Diving service available.

Caversham Boat Services
Fry's Island, De Montfort Road, Reading, Berks RG1 8DG ☎ 0118 957 4323. Marine engineers, boat repairs, engine servicing, holiday hire cruisers (*Blakes*), day-boats, permanent and visitors' moorings, diesel fuel, *Calor Gas*, telephone, water point, toilet pump-out, slipway. (TBTA, THCA)

Bridge Boats Ltd
Fry's Island, De Montfort Road, Reading, Berks RG1 8LD ☎ 0118 959 0346. Marine engineers, boat repairs, holiday hire cruisers (*Hoseasons*), diesel fuel, *Calor Gas*, permanent moorings, water, slipway, toilet pump-out. (TBTA, THCA)

Salter's Steamers Ltd
Waterman Place, Caversham Bridge, Reading, Berks RG1 8DS ☎ 0118 957 2388. Passenger launch proprietors, public trips, party hire. (TBTA, PBA)

Thames River Cruise
Pipers Island, Bridge Street, Caversham, Reading, Berks RG4 8AH ☎ 0118 948 1088. Party hire, corporate entertainment, weddings, centrally heated launches, day and evening charter, all year. (PBA)

D & T Scenics
Piper's Island, Bridge Street, Caversham, Reading, Berks RG4 8AH ☎ 0118 948 4574. Public passenger trips between Caversham Bridge and Mapledurham House, short trips during summer months. (PBA)

Reading Marine Services & Driveline Marine Ltd
Scours Lane, Tilehurst, Reading, Berks RG3 6AY ☎ 0118 942 3877. Boat sales, chandlery, *Calor Gas*, diesel, crane, slipway, moorings, repairs, marine engineers, outboards, refuse disposal, water, winter storage.

Thames Valley Boat Transport
Scours Lane, Tilehurst, Reading, Berks RG30 6AY ☎ 0118 941 2112. Boat delivery service.

Purley Gardens Marina
Thames Reach, Purley-on-Thames, Reading, Berks RG8 8BY ☎ 0118 942 8116. Permanent private moorings, club, slipway.

EMERGENCY FUEL SUPPLIES

See note under this heading on page 24

Henley ServiceStation

Petrol, diesel

345 Reading Road, Henley-on-Thames, Oxon ☎ 01491 579974. At top of Mill Lane, 300yds from Marsh Lock.

Star Service Station

Petrol, diesel, shop

New Bath Road, Charvil, Twyford, Berks ☎ 0118 969 5209. 1 mile from St Patrick's Bridge, up Milestone Avenue, off Berkshire bank.

Thames Valley Service Station

Petrol, diesel

George Street, Caversham, Reading, Berks ☎ 0118 946 1949. 300yds from Reading Bridge towards Caversham.

Caversham Bridge Service Station

Petrol, diesel

18 Church Street, Caversham, Reading, Berks ☎ 0118 947 9933. 100yds from Caversham Bridge in Caversham.

Shell Norcot Service Station

Petrol, diesel

856 Oxford Road, Tilehurst, Reading, Berks ☎ 0118 945 2975. 500yds up Scours Lane.

ROWING, SAILING AND CRUISING CLUBS AND TUITION

Henley Sailing Club

Willow Lane, Wargrave, Reading, Berks RG10 8LH

Shiplake College Boat Club

Shiplake College, Henley-on-Thames, Oxon RG9 4BW ☎ 0118 940 2455

Upper Thames Motor Yacht Club

The Club House, Mill Island, Sonning, Reading, Berks RG4 0TX ☎ 0118 969 2683. (ATYC)

Reading Sailing Club

Sonning Eye, Sonning-on-Thames, Reading, Berks RG4 0TX

Reading Blue Coat School Boat Club

Holme Park, Sonning-on-Thames, Reading, Berks RG4 0SU ☎ 0118 969 1925. (ARA)

Thames Valley Cruising Club

Fry's Island, Reading, Berks RG1 8DG (ATYC)

Reading University Boat Club

Caversham Bridge, Caversham, Reading, Berks RG4 8AG (ARA)

Reading Rowing Club

1 The Boathouse, Thameside Promenade, Caversham, Reading, Berks RG1 8EQ ☎ 0118 956 7091. (ARA)

Reading School

Thameside Promenade, Caversham, Reading, Berks RG1 8EQ ☎ 0118 926 1406 (school). (ARA)

Reading & Leighton Park Canoe Club

The Warren, Caversham, Reading, Berks (BCU)

Purley Cruiser Club

Purley Gardens Marina, Thames Reach, Purley, Reading, Berks RG8 8BY ☎ 0118 942 8116. (ATYC)

PUBLIC LAUNCHING SITES

- **Wargrave** End of Ferry Lane, off Church Street. Unsuitable for towed trailers. Contact Val Wyatt's or John Bushnell Marine Services for launching of larger craft
- **Reading/Caversham** Above Caversham Bridge next to Holiday Inn and below rowing club. Approach from Richfield Avenue

FISHING TACKLE SHOPS

Reading Angling Centre

9 Northumberland Avenue, Whitley, Reading, Berks ☎ 0118 987 2216

Thames Valley Angling

258 Kentwood Hill, Tilehurst, Reading, Berks ☎ 0118 942 8249

TOURIST INFORMATION OFFICES

Reading

Reading Visitor Centre, Church House, Chain Street, Reading RG1 2HX ☎ 0118 956 6226

HOTELS, INNS AND RESTAURANTS

Baskerville Arms Station Road, Lower Shiplake ☎ 0118 940 3332. Restaurant (closed Mondays and Sunday evenings). Moor against towing path, follow path into village opposite Henley Sailing Club.

St George & Dragon High Street, Wargrave ☎ 0118 940 3852. Own mooring at end of garden, free to patrons.

Bull Hotel High Street, Wargrave ☎ 0118 934 0140. Bar meals, midday and evenings; dining, evenings only. B&B. Book ahead.

Regatta Hotel High Street, Wargrave ☎ 0118 940 2590. Bar meals and dining, midday and evenings.

Plowden Arms Reading Road, Shiplake. Bar meals, midday and evenings. Moor above Shiplake Lock and use towing path to gain path to Reading Road.

Wee Waif Old Bath Road, Charvil ☎ 0118 944 0066. *Artist's Fare* menu, midday and evenings. Moor by St Patrick's Bridge and walk up Milestone Avenue.

Regatta Restaurant and Ferryman Bar Thames Street, Sonning

RIVER KENNET

Jolly Angler Kennet Side, Reading. Hot and cold meals and snacks. Mooring with care outside along Kennet Side.

Fisherman's Cottage Kennet Side, Reading. Hot and cold meals and bar snacks. Mooring with care outside along Kennet Side.

Bel and the Dragon Blake's Lock, Kenavon Drive, Reading ☎ 0118 951 5790

☎ 0118 969 2277. Sandwiches at the bar, midday only; dining, midday and evenings. Hotel accommodation. Moorings adjacent (fee refundable). Thai Castle and Regatta restaurants adjacent.

French Horn Hotel Sonning Eye ☎ 0118 969 2204/8677. Hotel-restaurant (booking advisable). Moorings against towing path just below Sonning Bridge.

Bull Hotel High Street, Sonning. Bar snacks, lunchtimes and evenings; restaurant. Moorings against towing path above Sonning Lock (free).

Mill at Sonning Theatre Playhatch Road, Sonning Eye ☎ 0118 969 8000. *Table d'hôte* menu in restaurant prior to show. Booking essential. Moorings against towing path just below Sonning Bridge.

Sonning Lock

McDonald's Friar Street, Reading.

Pizza Hut Oxford Road, Reading.

The Moderation Caversham Road, Reading. Bar snacks and hot meals, midday and evenings (except Sunday evenings). Mooring against Christ Church playing fields (fee), use Caversham Bridge.

TGI Friday's Caversham Road, Reading.

Holiday Inn Caversham Bridge ☎ 0118 939 1818. Carvery lunches, *table d'hôte* and *à la carte* daily in Bridges restaurant. *Three Men in a Boat Tavern* attached to hotel. Mooring above Caversham Bridge.

Millers Arms Paddock Road, Caversham ☎ 0118 947 2445. Bar food and meals, lunchtimes and evenings. Mooring (fee) when available _ at Better Boating Company's jetty below Caversham Lock.

The Clifton Arms Gosbrook Road, Caversham. Hot and cold bar snacks and meals.

Crown Inn Bridge Street, Caversham. Hot and cold bar snacks and meals, mooring against Christ Church playing fields (fee), use towpath to Caversham Bridge.

Griffin Hotel Church Street, Caversham.

Pizza Hut Reading Retail Park, Oxford Road, Tilehurst. Moor downstream of Scours Lane and walk up lane; retail park other side of roundabout.

Candlelit Cruises Marine Services, Scours Lane, Tilehurst, Reading, RG30 6AY ☎ 01495 240719 or 07790 742599. Restaurant cruises aboard passenger vessel *Candlelight*.

Roebuck Hotel Oxford Road, Tilehurst ☎ 0118 942 7517. Hotel-restaurant. Moor at Roebuck Ferry.

TAXIS

Henley
- Talbot Taxis ☎ 01491 574222
- Harris Taxis ☎ 01491 577036

Sonning
- Top Cars ☎ 0118 944 2222

Reading
- ABC Taxis ☎ 0118 939 3737
- 1st Royal ☎ 0118 956 0560

Caversham
- Haywards Hire Service ☎ 0118 947 4561

Tilehurst
- Calcot and Tilehurst Taxis ☎ 0118 945 1920

RAIL STATIONS AND TRAIN SERVICES

See note under this heading on page 26

Enquiries: ☎ 08457 484950

Henley-on-Thames *FGW Link* Station Road, Henley-on-Thames, Oxon. 250yds from river. Trains to Shiplake; Wargrave, Twyford and Reading. Change at Twyford for all stations to London at Reading for a fast service to London and other routes.

Shiplake *FGW Link* Station Road, Lower Shiplake, Henley-on-Thames, Oxon. 200yds from river. Trains to Henley; Wargrave, Twyford and Reading. Change at Twyford for all stations to London. Change at Reading for a fast train to London and other routes.

Wargrave *FGW Link* Station Road, Wargrave, Reading, Berks. 300yds from river. Trains to Henley and Shiplake, Twyford and Reading. Change at Twyford for all stations to London. Change at Reading for a fast train to London and other routes.

Reading *FGW Link* Station Hill, Reading. 500yds from Reading Bridge. Fast trains to London Paddington and Oxford only. Also to Twyford, Maidenhead, Taplow, Slough (for Windsor) and Paddington; Reading West and stations to Basingstoke. Trains to Wokingham, Egham, Staines, Richmond and Waterloo (*South West Trains*); Tilehurst, Pangbourne, Goring and Streatley, Cholsey, Didcot and Oxford; to Twyford, Wargrave, Shiplake, Henley-on-Thames; Wokingham, Guildford, Dorking, Redhill and Gatwick. Also Theale, Thatcham, Newbury, Kintbury, Hungerford, Bedwyn and Pewsey are served by one train an hour except Kintbury, Hungerford and Bedwyn have a very restricted Sunday service. On the Oxford line, Radley has an hourly Sunday service.

Reading West *FGW Link* Brunswick Hill, Off Tilehurst Road, Reading. 1¼ miles from Caversham Bridge. All stations to Basingstoke and to stations to Newbury and Pewsey (no Sunday service).

Tilehurst *FGW Link* Oxford Road, Tilehurst, Reading, Berks. 50yds from river. Trains to Pangbourne, Goring and Streatley, Cholsey, Didcot, Radley Oxford; to Reading and stations to London Paddington. Change at Reading for intermediate stations on Sundays.

BUS AND COACH SERVICES

Reading (Wargrave–Mapledurham)

Again one bus route follows the river between Henley and Reading on both banks (via Shiplake or Wargrave) but at alternate times. This is the jointly operated route running between Reading and High Wycombe. Other routes converging on Reading join at Sonning, including the one from Maidenhead. Upstream from Reading the main routes stop at Wallingford, where a change must be made to reach Oxford. There is a regular service as far as Pangbourne on the right (west) bank of the river. From Reading there are also services towards Newbury alongside the Kennet. London Line run express coaches to London from Reading and Newbury.

Bus Operators are:

- Arriva The Shires ☎ 0870 7288 188
- Reading Buses ☎ 0118 959 4000 or 0870 608 2 608
- London Line ☎ 0870 608 2 608
- Thames Travel ☎ 01491 837988
- Chiltern Buses ☎ 01491 680354

Distance
12.23 miles (Mapledurham Lock to Wallingford Bridge)

Maximum dimensions of craft from Mapledurham to Wallingford

Headroom	13´7˝ (4.14m) at Whitchurch Toll Bridge
Length	133´7˝ (40.71m) at Cleeve Lock
Beam	18´0˝ (5.48m) at Whitchurch Lock
Draught	4´0˝ (1.22m) in main fairway up to Oxford.

Upstream of Hardwick comes the Oratory School's boathouse on the left/Oxfordshire bank and ahead on the Berkshire bank lies Pangbourne Meadow to which it is possible to moor. There is no mooring immediately below Whitchurch Bridge which is still privately owned and collects a toll from all but pedestrians. On the Pangbourne side there are car park and toilets, next to a frequently active establishment for canoeists – the Dolphin County River Centre which is also home to the Pangbourne Canoe Club. Above the bridge the millstream comes in on your right as you proceed upstream and the weirpool, into which flows the River Pang, is to your left with the lock island for Whitchurch Lock dead ahead.

The lock lay-bys are on the left and have been recently reconstructed due to the shape of the bank. Access to the sanitary station, which is equipped for chemical toilet discharge only, is from the upstream end of the lay-by, below the lock.

> **Whitchurch Lock** Daytime only
> High Street, Whitchurch-on-Thames, Reading, Berks RG8 7DJ ☎ 0118 984 2448
> 135'3" (41·22m) long x 18'0" (5·48m) wide
> Rise (fall) 3'4" (1·01m)
> Max. draught 6'1" (1·85m)
> *Facilities* Chemical toilet disposal.

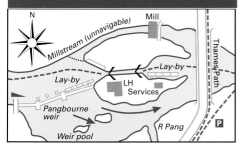

Coming downstream to Whitchurch Lock which lies at the end of the gangway for Pangbourne Weir, craft waiting for the lock may prefer to hold back in the stream off the Swan Inn, rather than go alongside the lay-by which runs along the top of the weir. This may be a wise move, particularly in flood conditions. The entrance to the millstream on the Oxfordshire bank is shallow and, where there is any deeper water on that side, there are private moorings. There is no access to either Pangbourne or Whitchurch villages from the lock.

The main shopping centre and the railway station are in Pangbourne, reached from the meadow below the lock, although the *Swan Inn* offers moorings to its customers at the head of the weir which is only just across the road from the station. The slipway off the *Swan*'s car park is not suitable for trailers, but small boats which can be manhandled can be launched, with the pub landlord's permission ☎ 0118 984 3199/4494.

Beyond the *Swan*, famed as the final resting place of the camping skiff abandoned by Jerome K Jerome's 'Three Men' in the pouring rain, are the boathouses of Pangbourne College and as evidence, the reach is often ruffled and the air disturbed with the echoing cries of 'Henry! You're not putting your back into it!' or some such other polite reminders to Henry's slovenly colleagues at their rowing practice. The rowers are not (usually) a problem . . . unlike the peculiar floating replacement for the towing-path cyclist, with his cap and megaphone, who has sadly disappeared in recent years to make way for a kind of Tannoy loudspeaker on floats with a 120hp Mercruiser on the back; something that a veteran rowing coach would never have countenanced. You will find others upstream at Radley and possibly Oxford itself. One wonders what the fair play of English rowing is coming to.

Railway, road and river almost join and then diverge, the river to follow its course away to Hartslock Wood and the site of Hart's Lock – fallen into disuse, according to Thacker, before any of the present pound locks were built, although it remained as a fish weir for some years afterwards. Close by is the Child Beale Wildlife Trust to which entry can be obtained from the river. Below the Trust are 24-hour moorings along the old

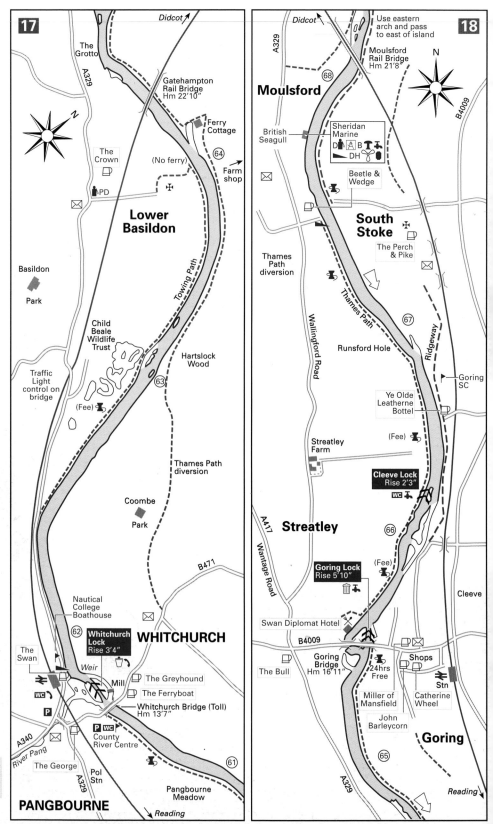

17

The Grotto

Didcot ↗

A329

Gatehampton
Rail Bridge
Hm 22'10"

Ferry
Cottage

The Crown

(No ferry)

(64)

Farm
shop

PD

**Lower
Basildon**

Basildon
Park

Towing Path

Child
Beale
Wildlife
Trust

Hartslock
Wood

Traffic
Light
control on
bridge

(Fee)

(63)

Thames Path
diversion

Coombe
Park

B471

Nautical
College
Boathouse

WHITCHURCH

(62)

**Whitchurch
Lock**
Rise 3'4"

The
Swan

Weir

Mill

The Greyhound

WC

The Ferryboat

P

Whitchurch Bridge (Toll)
Hm 13'7"

A340

P WC

River Pang

County
River Centre

The George

Pol
Stn

(61)

A329

Pangbourne
Meadow

PANGBOURNE

↘ *Reading*

112

18

Didcot ↗

A329

Use eastern
arch and pass
to east of island

Moulsford
Rail Bridge
Hm 21'8"

N

B4009

Moulsford

(68)

British
Seagull

Sheridan
Marine
D A B
DH

Beetle &
Wedge

**South
Stoke**

The Perch
& Pike

Thames
Path
diversion

Thames Path

(67)

Ridgeway

Runsford Hole

Wallingford Road

Goring
SC

Ye Olde
Leatherne
Bottel

(Fee)

Streatley
Farm

Cleeve Lock
Rise 2'3"
WC

A417

Streatley

(66)

Wantage Road

(Fee)

Goring Lock
Rise 5'10"

Cleeve

Swan Diplomat Hotel

B4009

The Bull

Goring
Bridge
Hm 16'11"

24hrs
Free

Shops

Stn

Miller of
Mansfield

Catherine
Wheel

John
Barleycorn

Goring

(65)

A329

↘ *Reading*

Above: Swan Inn and Pangbourne Weir

Below: Wallingford Bridge

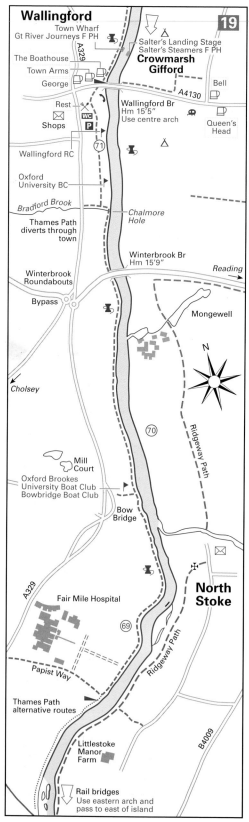

towing path which has had to be abandoned as the official Thames Path since the ferry at Gatehampton no longer runs, although this section is still usable up to Lower Basildon Church.

We now come to another of Brunel's fascinating railway bridges – this one set at such an angle that the bricklayers must have become giddy before they had finished turning the arches you see here. Yet again, when the rail tracks were doubled at the turn of the century, the original design was retained in the widened bridge. Known as Basildon or Gatehampton Bridge, the site of the old ferry is below it and the ferry cottage remains, as a private house.

From here the hills close in on both sides of the river, carrying rail and road through the Goring Gap, although the main road remains on the right bank (left as we proceed upstream) while the railway line has crossed onto the opposite bank, no doubt attracted by the potential custom of the larger of the two settlements of Goring and Streatley. There is ample free 24-hour mooring up on the right-hand side below the bridge (towing path side) and Ferry Lane leads into the village. Above the bridge and beneath it is the complicated weir system surrounding Goring Lock – another much photographed, easily enough from the curious trestle-style bridge which survives modern traffic.

On leaving Goring Lock note that this next reach, at 1100 yards, is the shortest on the river, 22 yards shorter than the distance between Temple and Hurley Locks at the top of the old Maidenhead District. Immediately to your left on leaving the head of the lock is the weir-stream leading to the moorings for the Swan Diplomat Hotel.

The setting is perhaps moderately more attractive since on the Oxfordshire bank lie the backwaters and streams of Cleeve and its mill, not overcome by the mass gathering of tax-losing motor craft as at Harleyford but perhaps enhanced by the manicured lawns and trees of the property of the tax-loopholed gentry. To the west lie water-meadows, as yet unsullied by rapacious developers, held off for the time being, no doubt, by the blessed conservationists. There are useful moorings along here on the towing path side which has crossed to the Berkshire bank by way of Goring Bridge. A short pull upstream and we enter Cleeve Lock.

Above Cleeve Lock you come to *Ye Olde Leatherne Bottle* inn, on the Oxfordshire side, which has a restaurant but only welcomes visitors to its moorings by prior

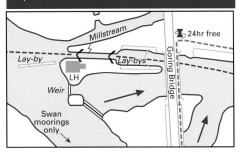

arrangement as accommodation is limited and depths are probably doubtful. Just above the inn are the sailing headquarters of Goring Sailing Club which means that the reach is often busy, and opposite, on the Thames Path side, there are mooring sites, below and above the club. From Cleeve Lock up to the sailing club on that side of the river one may follow the Ridgeway Path. Goring Bridge holds the unique distinction of carrying both the Ridgeway Path (from west to east) and the Thames Path (from east to west). From Cleeve Lock we have entered the longest reach of the river between locks at dead on 6½ miles up to Benson Lock.

Just above Runsford Hole, a little creek on the Oxfordshire bank at the 67-mile mark, we are confounded by the boundary

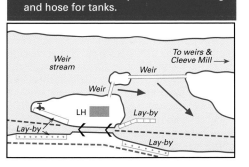

commission concerning the nomenclature of the banks. The Berks/Oxon boundary which has followed the river all the way (with the minor exception at Caversham) from Fawley Meadow below Henley, now strides away to the west and leaves the river totally within Oxfordshire as far as Kelmscot where it joins with Gloucestershire until it loses Oxfordshire and borders Wiltshire above St John's Lock and then loses it again to continue into Gloucestershire just above Lechlade.

Returning to Chart 18 and our progress upstream, we come to South Stoke on the left bank and Moulsford on the right, as viewed going downstream. South Stoke has moorings for which a fee is charged, opposite the famous *Beetle & Wedge* hotel while, at the bottom of Ferry Lane below the hotel at Moulsford, was a public launching site for small craft but developments at the hotel have rather restricted its use.

Beyond the *Beetle & Wedge* comes the boatyard of Sheridan Marine, which specialises in Freeman cruiser repairs and spares and then we curve northeastwards towards the second of the two curious railway viaducts on Brunel's Reading–Bristol line. This one, Moulsford Railway Bridge, requires care in passage since all craft are advised to use the eastern arch as the western is close to a group of islands which are a hazard to navigation. This means that, although upstream traffic may feel it has a right of way in keeping to starboard and using the right-hand arch, downstream traffic (to which it appears as the left-hand arch) has been advised to use it as well and upstream traffic should always give way.

Just below the Fair Mile Hospital on the west bank is another public launching slip at

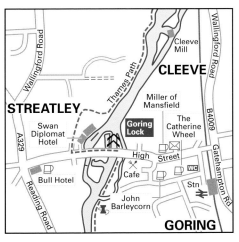

the site of the former Little Stoke Ferry. This can be found at the bottom of Papist Way which leads from Cholsey and the main A329 road from Pangbourne and Streatley to Wallingford. Standing back from the east bank is the village of North Stoke, opposite which there are isolated moorings on the towing path. A little further upstream, a footpath turns off the towing path and runs to the smoothed out S-bend of the A329 at Bow Bridge. From here you can walk into Cholsey, up Caps Lane, a distance of about a mile.

Ahead is the new Winterbrook Bridge which carries the Wallingford bypass linking the A4130 Wantage Road to the west of the town with the A329 and A4074 Reading roads, which run close to the right and left banks of the river respectively. On your left at the outfall of Bradford's Brook is Chalmore Hole, the site of an old ferry and also the legendary Wallingford Lock which was cleared away around 1883 although vestiges of it remained for some time afterwards – the source of Jerome's anecdote of an overlong evening's sculling in his *Three Men in a Boat*.

Wallingford Bridge crosses the top of the reach, bounded on the lefthand as one ascends by the edge of the town and on the right by the meadows below Crowmarsh. From opposite the Chalmore Ferry cottage, occupied by a navigation authority employee, the old towpath still runs up to the bridge. It is possible to moor to this bank with care but the better moorings are above the bridge at which there is a telephone. Motorists may care to note that the bridge itself is another crossing the Thames where traffic lights have been installed to prevent bumps and scrapes by ill-advised two-way traffic. Others are at Sonning, Clifton Hampden, and Lechlade, while there are right-of-way priorities on the suspension bridge at Marlow.

Since the restoration of the towing path on the west bank, the Thames Path now follows this bank up to Benson Lock at the head of this 6½ mile reach, from behind the *Boat House Hotel*. Opposite is a pleasure park for children, with swings, slides and a paddling pool, while there are convenient moorings against the towpath beyond the bridge on the town side.

The Thames Path

The Path approaches Pangbourne on that side of the river and then crosses the Whitchurch Toll Bridge since the closure of the Gatehampton Ferry two miles above the bridge. Passing up Whitchurch High Street, apart from the signposted section on the left through Whitchurch churchyard, with a choice of the *Ferryboat* or the *Greyhound* inns for refreshment, the Path has left the river to circumnavigate Coombe Park. Go up the hill (B471) until, at about half a mile from the toll bridge, you come to a junction with Hardwick Road on your right. Just beyond the junction on the left is the entry to a bridleway which leads down to Avoca Farm and Coombe Park Farm. Pass both and, at the point where the track turns down towards Hartslock Farm, take the footpath on the right which leads back to the river which it joins opposite the Child Beale Wildlife Trust.

The Path stays close to the river as far as Gatehampton Ferry Cottage, close to which there is a farm shop. Having veered away from the river, the walker can turn sharp left with the ferry cottage to his left and return to the river over the footbridge and turn right under the rail bridge. The Path now follows into Goring and, prior to the bridge, you bear right to join the High Street. Turn left here to cross Goring Bridge into Streatley and, in 100 yards, look for the lane on the right leading past Streatley parish church of St Mary's. From this lane, a footpath shows the route back to the river which is joined through a gate. A steep footbridge crosses a new marina entrance and then the Path follows the bank on the opposite side to the Ridgeway Path. You meet this path on Goring Bridge coming, as it does, from Avebury in Wiltshire and proceeding by the Thames to Mongewell Park it turns eastwards towards the Chilterns and arrives at Ivinghoe Beacon in Buckinghamshire.

At the *Beetle & Wedge* hotel the Path has to leave the river again because of the closure of South Stoke Ferry and you must turn left through the pub car park and up Ferry Lane to the main A329 Wallingford–Pangbourne road. Although it is intended to return the walker to the river at Moulsford Rail Bridge by means of a footpath from the main road opposite Offlands Farm, this new section may not be yet available and the walker must continue as far as Papist Way. This leaves the main road about a mile further north. Turn right here and descend the lane to the launching slip which is the former landing point of the Little Stoke Ferry (now closed).

The Thames Path now approaches Wallingford past the Fair Mile Hospital, under the new Winterbrook Bridge which carries the long awaited Wallingford bypass, up to Chalmore Hole – yet another suspended ferry. Here you can take a left turn on a footpath into the town alongside Bradford's Brook and then turn right at the A329, but this is not the proper route. The Thames Path follows a path between the fenced off gardens of the riverside properties as far as Chalmore Meadow, where Oxford University Rowing Clubs have taken over the old marina. From here you will have to leave the river either by way of St Lucian's Lane to the main road, or by the approved route of the Path, through a gap in the hedge into Lower Wharf. Another gap on your right between some red-brick cottages, with an archway adjoining them, leads into St Leonard's Lane past the old St Leonard's Church and on into Thames Street. Thames Street leads to the High Street and Wallingford Bridge but, to continue on the Thames Path, cross the High Street and follow Castle Lane for a few paces before turning right onto the footpath behind the *Boat House Hotel*.

Angling

There is free fishing for approximately 1½ miles above and below Whitchurch Bridge on the Thames but fishing in the tributary, the Pang, is private. Pangbourne Weir pool fishing is free but only by boat since there is no riparian access and the weir is private. London Anglers Association has reserved fishing at Gatehampton Farm and Hartslock Wood swims. Fishing is again free on the towing path sides above and below Goring Lock. There is now no weir permit fishing at Goring Lock owing to recent reconstruction of the weirs.

The towing path bank (right) between the *Beetle & Wedge* hotel and Cleeve Lock is reserved by the LAA, as is fishing from the opposite bank between the footbridge above Moulsford Rail Bridge down to South Stoke Ferry, and from the second meadow below the ferry down to Runsford Hole. Day tickets are available from the landlord of the *Leatherne Bottle Inn* at Cleeve for the latter stretch, for about a mile upstream.

Four stretches of water are reserved by the Jolly Anglers Club of Wallingford in the Wallingford area and the Oxford Alliance also has fishing rights in the area.

Directory

BOATYARDS, MARINAS, CHANDLERIES, TRIPPING AND HIRE

Walliscote Moorings
Walliscote Farm, High Street, Whitchurch-on-Thames, Reading, Berks RG8 7EP ☎ 0118 984 2962. Permanent moorings.

Thames Electric Launch Co
High Winds, The Bridle Way, Goring-on-Thames, Reading, Berks RG8 0HQ ☎ 01491 873126. Import and manufacture of electric launches 12–21′, agents for Kombi and Minn Kota electric outboards. (TBTA)

Sheridan Marine (John Freeman Sales Ltd)
Moulsford Boat House, Cholsey, Wallingford, Oxon OX10 9HU ☎ 01491 652085. Boat builder, broker, repairs and restoration – Freeman specialist, marine engineer, diesel, *Calor Gas*, chandlery, groceries, day-boat hire, permanent moorings, slipway, water point. Perkins, WaterMota and Thornycroft specialist (closed Fridays). (TBTA)

British Seagull
Moulsford Boat House, Cholsey, Wallingford, Oxon OX10 9HU ☎ 01491 652755. Outboard motors sales and service.

Great River Journeys Ltd
Town Wharf, Old Bridge, High Street, Wallingford, Oxon. Bookings and Enquiries to: Great River Journeys, PO Box 2468, Reading, Berkshire, RG2 9WW ☎ 0118 9761761. Passenger boat operator for private hire, public sailings and group travel between Dorchester and Henley-on-Thames, based at Wallingford Town Wharf. (PBA)

EMERGENCY FUEL SUPPLIES
See note under this heading on page 24

Pangbourne Service Station
Petrol, diesel, shop
Reading Road, Pangbourne, Reading, Berks ☎ 0118 984 2456. ¾ mile from mooring at Pangbourne Meadow, at George Hotel turn left along Reading Road.

Basildon Service Station
Petrol, diesel, shop
Reading Road, Lower Basildon, Reading, Berks ☎ 01491 671307. ¾ mile from end of old towpath below Basildon Church.

Betwin Motors
Petrol
Station Road, Goring-on-Thames, Reading, Berks ☎ 01491 872409. Behind *John Barleycorn Inn*.

Gibbs Garage
Petrol, diesel
Reading Road, Moulsford, Wallingford, Oxon ☎ 01491 652132. ½ mile from Moulsford Rail Bridge on west bank; use footpath under railway arch to reach A329.

Esso Service Station (On The Run)
Petrol, diesel, groceries etc.
Station Road, Wallingford, Oxon. 800 yards from Wallingford Bridge up High Street.

ROWING, SAILING AND CRUISING CLUBS AND TUITION

The Oratory School Boat Club
Sheepwash Lane, Whitchurch-on-Thames, Reading, Berks RG8 7HH. Rowing. (ARA)

Goring Gap Rowing Club
Oratory School Boathouse, Sheepwash Lane, RG8 7HH. Rowing (ARA)

Oxford Brookes University Boat Club and Bowbridge Boat Club
Bowbridge Boathouse, Reading Road, Cholsey, Wallingford, Oxon. OX10 9HG. Rowing (ARA)

County River Centre
Dolphin House, Whitchurch Road, Pangbourne, Reading, Berks RG8 7DA ☎ 0118 984 3162. Canoeing. (BCU)

Pangbourne College Boat Club
Pangbourne College Boathouse, Shooter's Hill, Pangbourne, Reading, Berks RG8 7DU ☎ 0118 984 2997. Rowing. (ARA)

Goring Sailing Club
Ridgeway Path, South Stoke, Reading, Berks RG8 0HZ Sailing. (RYA)

Oxford University Boat Club
Chalmore Meadow, Off St Lucian's Lane, Wallingford, Oxon OX10 9EP. Rowing. (ARA)

Wallingford Rowing Club
Thames Street, Wallingford, Oxon OX10 0HD. Rowing. (ARA)

PUBLIC LAUNCHING SITES

- **Pangbourne** Between Pangbourne Weir and the Swan Hotel. Launching by permission of the hotel manager. Light craft only (fee).
- **Moulsford** End of Ferry Lane, off *Beetle & Wedge* car park, opposite South Stoke
- **Cholsey** At end of Papist Way, site of Little Stoke Ferry. Approach from Reading Road south of Fair Mile Hospital
- **Wallingford** Above bridge on west bank beside *The Boat House Hotel*. Light craft only. Access restricted

TOURIST INFORMATION OFFICE
Wallingford
Town Hall, Market Place, Wallingford, Oxon ☎ 01491 826972.

HOTELS, INNS AND RESTAURANTS

Greyhound Inn High Street, Whitchurch. Bar meals, lunches and dinners, midday and evenings. Moorings in Pangbourne Meadow (NT) below toll bridge.

Ferryboat Inn High Street, Whitchurch. Bar meals, lunches and dinners, midday and evenings. Moorings in Pangbourne Meadow (NT) below toll bridge.

Copper Inn Church Road, Pangbourne ☎ 0118 984 2244. Restaurant for lunches, teas and dinners. Accommodation. Moorings in Pangbourne Meadow (NT).

George Hotel The Square, Pangbourne ☎ 0118 984 2237. Hot and cold bar snacks, carvery (daily). Lunch and dinner. Accommodation.

Cross Keys Church Road, Pangbourne. Bar meals, lunches and dinners, midday and evenings.

Swan Inn Shooters Hill, Pangbourne ☎ 0118 984 3199/4494. Bar meals, lunches and dinners, midday to 10pm. Moorings alongside, slipway for light craft.

Crown Inn Reading Road, Lower Basildon. Food available. Moor against end of old towing path at Lower Basildon Church and walk to main road.

Miller of Mansfield High Street, Goring ☎ 01491 872829. Restaurant and bar meals, midday and evenings. Accommodation. Mooring free below Goring Lock on towpath side (24 hours max.).

Catherine Wheel Station Road, Goring.

John Barleycorn Manor Road, Goring ☎ 01491 872509. Bar meals and dining, midday and evenings. Mooring below Goring Lock on towpath side.

Bull at Streatley Reading Road, Streatley. Bar meals and dining, midday and evenings. Mooring below Goring Lock on towpath side.

Swan Diplomat Hotel High Street, Streatley ☎ 01491 873737. High-class hotel-restaurant. Mooring for patrons alongside.

Leatherne Bottle Inn Bridle Way, Goring ☎ 01491 872667. Restaurant and bar snacks. Mooring alongside by prior arrangement only.

Perch & Pike High Street, South Stoke. Bar meals and dining, midday and evenings. Moor on east bank Ferry Lane (fee).

Beetle & Wedge Hotel Ferry Lane, Moulsford ☎ 01491 651381. Bar meals and restaurant, midday and evenings. Accommodation. Overnight mooring for patrons, slipway.

Queen's Head The Street, Crowmarsh. Bar meals and dining, midday and evenings. Free moorings below bridge on Crowmarsh side; on the town side, above, a fee is payable.

Bell Inn The Street, Crowmarsh. Bar meals and dining, midday and evenings.

The Boat House Old Bridge, High Street, Wallingford, Oxon. Bar meals and dining, midday and evenings. Mooring alongside hotel.

Town Arms High Street, Wallingford. Bar meals and dining, midday and evenings.

George Hotel High Street, Wallingford. Bar meals and dining, midday and evenings.

Dolphin Hotel St Mary's Street, Wallingford. Food available at lunchtimes. Breakfasts 10.15–11.30am.

TAXIS

- **Pangbourne**
  Pangbourne Taxi Service ☎ 0118 984 4953
- **Goring**
  Murdocks Taxis, Mountfield ☎ 01491 873963
- **Wallingford**
  Hills Taxis, Station Road ☎ 01491 837022/837497

RAIL STATIONS AND TRAIN SERVICES
See note under this heading on page 26
Network SouthEast
Enquiries: ☎ 08457 484950

Pangbourne *FGW Link* Station Road, Pangbourne, Reading, Berks. 100yds from river. Trains to Tilehurst and Reading; Goring and Streatley, Cholsey, Didcot, Radley, Oxford; and stations to London Paddington.

Goring & Streatley *FGW Link* Gatehampton Road, Goring, Reading, Berks. ½ mile from Goring Bridge. Trains to Pangbourne, Tilehurst and Reading; Cholsey, Didcot, Radley, Oxford; and stations to London Paddington.

Cholsey *FGW Link* Westfield Road, Cholsey, Oxon. 1½ miles from Little Stoke Ferry (Papist Way). Trains to Goring, Pangbourne, Tilehurst and Reading; Didcot, Radley, Oxford; and stations to London Paddington.

Wallingford The former Cholsey to Wallingford Branch line is still intact and a voluntary railway preservation society has been formed to operate steam services on the line in the summer season. Details from Cholsey and Wallingford Railway Preservation Society, PO Box 16, St John's Road, Wallingford, Oxon ☎ 01491 835067.

BUS AND COACH SERVICES
Whitchurch to Wallingford

Since the last edition there have been major alterations in bus services in this part of the Thames Valley. Pangbourne (and Whitchurch) are served by Reading Buses from Reading only. Other companies' buses run from Pangbourne to Goring and from Goring to Wallingford. There are sporadic services from Reading via Whitchurch Hill to Goring and then Wallingford. There are now no through services to Oxford except from Wallingford by Thames Travel's X39 or 105.

Bus operators:
- Chiltern Queens (Woodcote)
  ☎ 01491 680354
- Reading Buses (Reading)
  ☎ 0118 959 4000
- Thames Travel (Wallingford)
  ☎ 01491 837988

Leaving Whitchurch Lock

9. Wallingford and Abingdon

Distance

16.50 miles (Wallingford Bridge to Radley Ferry)

Maximum dimensions of craft from Wallingford to Abingdon Lock

Headroom 12´5´´ (3.78m) at Culham Lock Cut footbridge
Length 120´0´´ (36.57m) at Abingdon Lock
Beam 17´6´´ (5.33m) at Culham Lock
Draught 4´0´´ (1.22m) in main fairway up to Oxford

Upstream of Wallingford, on the west bank, are the ruins of Wallingford Castle while, on the east bank, is the modern Hydraulics Research Centre at Howbery Park. The Thames Path has been restored to its original bank on the west and a crossing by means of the lock gates and a weir walkway replaces the former Benson Ferry where it returns to the east. Proceeding upstream, Benson Lock is well over to your left thus avoiding the run-off from the weir above the island on your right or the millstream which discharges below it.

There are moorings above the lock under the care of the keeper and it is obviously possible to arrange overnight moorings at Benson Waterfront further up on your right. Although the boatyard no longer supplies petrol it just about covers everything else, and there is a BP service station operated by the local Vauxhall Main Dealer, Gurney's, at

the roundabout 300 yards north of the entrance to the boatyard.

The river here swings round to face west again and turns into a wooded reach headed by Shillingford Bridge. Moorings on the left between the caravan site and the bridge are private but I have moored on the opposite bank against the towing path (with care). There are better moorings above the bridge (the first 200 yards are reserved but you may moor beyond this point) and the hotel welcomes boaters as well as the fee for mooring against its bank, which this is. Navigation through the bridge should be via the centre arch as the other spans are deceptive in their height and curvature.

There now follow some genuine Thames meanders of the kind one studies in school geography lessons. They give rise to some convenient places to moor, although with no towing path an overnight stop will mean little chance of a foray to local hostelries. Eventually on the right, now the north bank, comes the attractive overbridge which signals the entrance of the River Thame – sometimes navigable for smaller cruisers (maximum of up to 1ft draught) to Dorchester Bridge. You can also moor just beyond the towpath bridge in the Thame and then use the footpath which leads into Wittenham Lane and out into the High Street. Dorchester-on-Thames is worth a visit, particularly now as a bypass has been built to relieve the village of the eternal stream of cars which wound their way through the historic twisted High Street. Here there are several inns, a post office and store, antiques shops, and Dorchester Abbey and museum.

Returning to our passage upstream on the main river, on our left are the Sinodun Hills and, standing close to the summit of Castle Hill, are the Wittenham Clumps. Here the river suddenly turns sharply to the right to face north again and, under Little Wittenham footbridge which spans two channels and the intervening island, we come to Day's Lock on our right and the weir over to our left. Below the footbridge, famed for an annual 'Poohsticks' competition in aid of the RNLI, on the island itself is the sanitary station. Do not use the landing stage here to wait for the lock but go to the pilings on the east bank to wait for the keeper's signals.

Above Day's Lock, when leaving or approaching, take care to avoid oncoming

Benson Lock Daytime only
Preston Crowmarsh, Wallingford, Oxon
OX10 6XJ ☎ 01491 835255
133'1" (40·56m) long x 17'11" (5·46m) wide
Rise (fall) 6'2" (1·87m)
Max. draught 7'0" (2·13m)
Facilities Water for cans only, moorings, electric launch charging point.
Angling From eastern side of breakwater only, downstream of the weir.

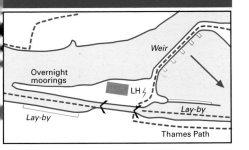

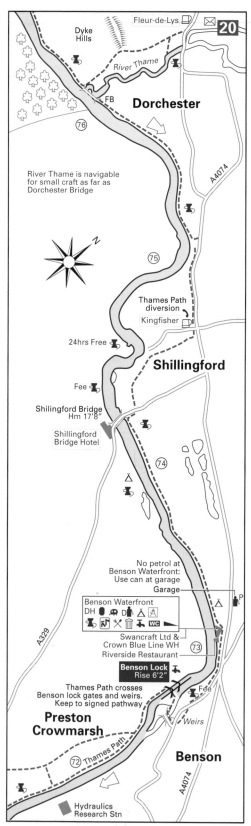

Dorchester

River Thame

Dyke Hills

Fleur-de-Lys

FB

River Thame is navigable
for small craft as far as
Dorchester Bridge

76

75

Thames Path
diversion

Kingfisher

24hrs Free

Shillingford

Fee

Shillingford Bridge
Hm 17'8"

Shillingford
Bridge Hotel

74

No petrol at
Benson Waterfront:
Use can at garage

Garage

P

Benson Waterfront
DH

Swancraft Ltd &
Crown Blue Line WH

Riverside Restaurant

73

Benson Lock Rise 6'2"

Thames Path crosses
Benson lock gates and weirs.
Keep to signed pathway

Fee

A329

Weirs

**Preston
Crowmarsh**

72 Thames Path

Benson

A4074

Hydraulics
Research Stn

122

Day's Lock Daytime only
Little Wittenham, Abingdon, Oxon OX14
4RB ☎ 01865 407768
154'10" (46·93m) long x 21'2" (6·45m) wide
Rise (fall) 5'2" (1·58m)
Max. draught 6'4" (1·93m)
Facilities Chemical toilet and refuse
  disposal, camping (five pitches on mid-
  river island).
Angling Downstream of the weir on the
  right bank 3 pitches.

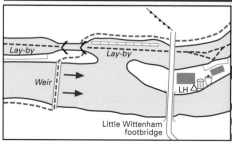

Lay-by

Lay-by

Weir

LH

Little Wittenham
footbridge

traffic. The right-hand bank when proceeding
upstream is shallow; downstream traffic may
not be able to see you and tends to force you
over to that side. Again, when proceeding
downstream, take care not to approach the
weir stream entrance too closely as the weir
draws strongly, especially if above normal level.

Chart 21, which takes us from Day's to
Appleford, has to occupy a full page for
obvious reasons, since the river here sweeps
in a great horseshoe through Clifton
Hampden and Long Wittenham, having
descended through a tighter shoe in the
opposite direction through Abingdon and
Culham, also depicted in Chart 22 as a full
page. Generally the river here is pressing
south from Oxford to which it reached
eastward, then north, then east, from its
source in Gloucestershire. A long left-hand
curve of 3 miles of river brings you through
Clifton Hampden Bridge, a graceful red-brick
structure credited to George Gilbert Scott as
its architect. The headroom is that stated for
the central arch although the two on either
side are equally easy to navigate.

Clifton Hampden village and church are
to your right as you proceed upstream; on the
same side as some suitable temporary
moorings which commence a short distance
above the bridge, against the towing path.
Over on the left is the famous *Barley Mow*
inn, opposite which is a convenient car park
for visiting motorists. Further along the lane
are a campsite, at Bridge House Caravan Site,
and The Lees, towards Long Wittenham,
where Paul Slack's moorings are available for
long-term rental. There is also a slip here. To
the right comes the entrance to Clifton Lock

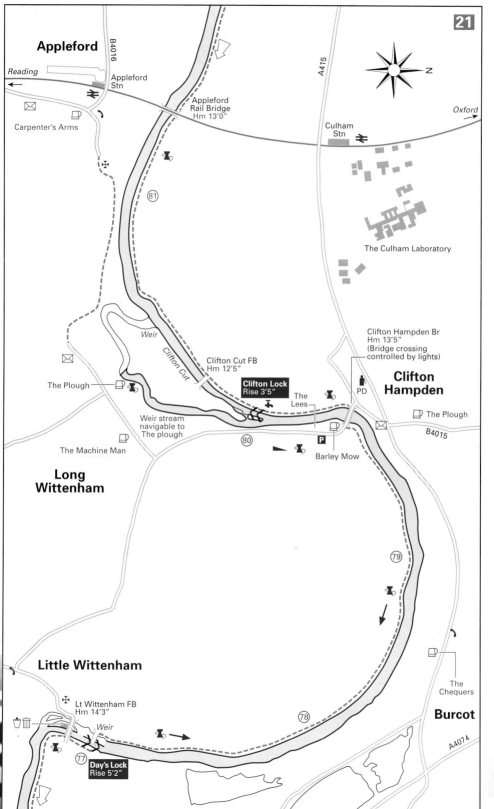

Appleford

Reading ←

B4016

Appleford Stn

Appleford Rail Bridge Hm 13'0"

Carpenter's Arms

A415

Oxford →

Culham Stn

(81)

The Culham Laboratory

Weir

Clifton Cut

Clifton Cut FB Hm 12'5"

Clifton Lock Rise 3'5"

The Plough

The Lees

Clifton Hampden Br Hm 13'5" (Bridge crossing controlled by lights)

Clifton Hampden

PD

The Plough

B4015

Weir stream navigable to The plough

The Machine Man

(80)

P

Barley Mow

Long Wittenham

(79)

Little Wittenham

The Chequers

Burcot

Lt Wittenham FB Hm 14'3"

Weir

(78)

A4074

(77)

Day's Lock Rise 5'2"

123

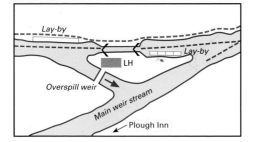

while to the left is the weir-stream which for its lower half is navigable, enabling the thirsty skipper to reach *The Plough* inn and the village of Long Wittenham.

From Clifton Lock Cut, which is crossed by the lowest footbridge on this section, you pass the weir on the left and a slow curve takes us past Appleford Church and the adjacent village for which there is a mooring just before the railway. Almost opposite, a little downstream, is a better mooring place against the towing path which is now following the north bank of the river. The hardly inspiring rail bridge carries the Didcot–Oxford Line across the river for the first time and we cannot now fail to notice the bulk of Didcot power station away to the south. In this reach we are reminded more forcibly of its presence with, on the south bank of the river, the unsightly structure of the power station's outfall and intake for cooling water and the resultant excessive weed which often grows in profusion in this reach because the water temperature has been artificially raised.

The navigation channel now approaches Sutton Bridge which precedes Culham Lock. Culham Bridge, with which it is sometimes understandably confused in name, does not span the present navigation channel but crosses the old Swift Ditch (See Chart 22) between the present main A415 and the Thames Path footbridge. Approach Sutton Bridge slowly, for any traffic coming downstream out of the lock has a job to manoeuvre in view of the closeness of the lock to the bridge and the immediate effect of

the weir stream which comes in over on your left – their right – below the bridge. There is a concrete lay-by with mooring bollards both above and below the bridge. Always tie up where you can see the lock-keeper's signals – if no other craft are above the bridge go there but be prepared to keep out of the way of anything coming down.

Along Culham Lock Cut there is a convenient mooring between the lock and the footbridge from which one may visit the enchanting Sutton Pools, fed by the weir stream which starts at the tail of Culham Reach. There is no mooring in this reach, which should be entered and left at its downstream end with extreme caution in view of the sharp turn into, and out of, the lock cut. A board in the centre of the main stream advises navigators 'Danger – Keep Away!' at the start of the weir stream, an instruction which should be rigidly followed although the first weir is some way down the stream.

Culham Reach is also the home of the Abbey Sailing Club, Abingdon Town Rowing Club and the Kingfisher Canoe Club, so the reach is well used by small craft. Over on your left are the new residential marina, followed by Wilsham Road where the above-mentioned clubs are all based. Abingdon Bridge carries the A415 into the town which stands on the west bank. The first available public moorings come up on the right (east) bank. These are close to the bridge alongside an attractive park through which the Thames Path runs. An indentation in the retaining wall above Wilsham Road denotes the old entrance to the Wilts and Berks Canal, while the wrought iron bridge at St Helen's Wharf by the *Old Anchor Inn* spans the mouth of

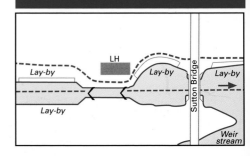

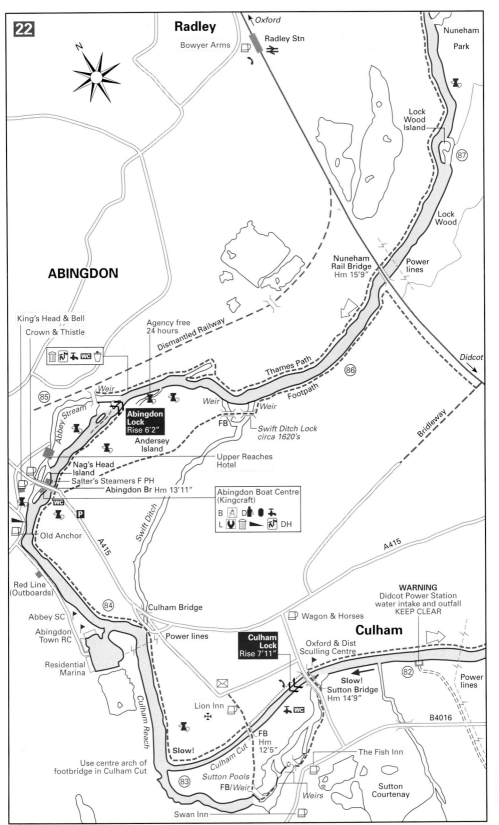

22

Radley

↑ *Oxford*

Bowyer Arms

Radley Stn

Nuneham Park

Lock Wood Island

Lock Wood

87

ABINGDON

Nuneham Rail Bridge Hm 15'9"

Power lines

Didcot →

King's Head & Bell
Crown & Thistle

Agency free 24 hours

Dismantled Railway

Thames Path

86

Footpath

Bridleway

85

Weir

Weir

Abingdon Lock Rise 6'2"

Abbey Stream

Andersey Island

Weir

FB

Swift Ditch Lock circa 1620's

Nag's Head Island

Upper Reaches Hotel

Salter's Steamers F PH

Abingdon Br Hm 13'11"

WC

P

Old Anchor

A415

Swift Ditch

Abingdon Boat Centre (Kingcraft)

B 🏕 D ⚓ 🚰
L 🚿 🗑 ⚓ DH

A415

Red Line (Outboards)

84

Abbey SC

Abingdon Town RC

Culham Bridge

Power lines

Wagon & Horses

WARNING
Didcot Power Station water intake and outfall KEEP CLEAR

Culham

Residential Marina

Culham Lock Rise 7'11"

Oxford & Dist Sculling Centre

82

Power lines

Slow!
Sutton Bridge Hm 14'9"

B4016

Culham Reach

Lion Inn

WC

FB Hm 12'5"

The Fish Inn

Use centre arch of footbridge in Culham Cut

Slow!

83

Sutton Pools FB/Weir

Culham Cut

Sutton Courtenay

Swan Inn

Weirs

125

the River Ock despite the legend which refers to the closed canal. Mooring at St Helen's Wharf, where there is a public slip, is difficult, although patrons of the *Old Anchor* manage to secure to the wall outside if there's room. The next boating base, which also incorporates private moorings around its island and a large chandlery as well as running day-boats and a diesel service, is Kingcraft at Abingdon Boat Centre, immediately below the bridge opposite the top of the public mooring area. Note that the main navigation channel keeps to the right of the island going upstream.

On the bridge itself, built on Nag's Head Island is the *Nag's Head*, the first of a number of inns and eating and drinking establishments in the town. Above the bridge Salters have a landing stage on the left. Behind Nags Head Island the tail of the Abbey Stream runs out with a backwater from the navigable channel under the western end of Abingdon Bridge. Above the island on the Abbey Stream was the Abbey Mill close to where the Upper Reaches Hotel now stands. The stream runs from above Abingdon weirs towards which we now move and, passing the swimming station and pleasure park, keeping well over to the right, we come to Abingdon Lock.

There are plenty of places to moor above Abingdon Lock although, if you wish to moor on the island facing the lock, then you should obtain the advice of the lock-keeper. Note, too, that you will be very unpopular if you obstruct the landing stage outside the sanitary station. Temporary mooring is also available on both sides of the river below the lock, all pitches being convenient for getting into the town by means of the Thames Path to the bridge and Bridge Street or the footpath into Abbey Close and the Market Place from the pleasure ground.

The river has now swung eastwards again in its second horseshoe after Day's Lock and a double bend takes us past two small weirs, almost hidden in the brushwood, which herald the head of the old navigation channel which bypassed Abingdon to join the present channel at Culham Bridge. This is the Swift Ditch, which was in use as the main channel until about 1790 when the new Abingdon Lock was opened at the same time as improvements had been made in the depths of the channel through Abingdon Bridge. There are adequate moorings between the two weirs and again before and after the rail bridge ahead. The towing path is on your left, although there is a recognised footpath on the right as far as the rail bridge which cuts across to the Swift Ditch weirs and the original 1620s lock – the oldest surviving pound lock in the UK – from Abingdon Bridge, virtually dissecting the land between the two channels which is known as Andersey Island. The river has now gradually turned north towards Oxford through Nuneham rail bridge, past Lock Wood and its curious backwater where there was once a flash lock and weir. In the eery silence as you pass Lock Wood Island, which you should leave to your right as you proceed upstream, you might imagine its popularity a hundred years ago when there was a rustic bridge and a lock cottage where one could have tea after a leisurely row down from Oxford. It may be possible to moor here to explore, but beware of the underwater piling and masonry in the backwater which is all that is left of a bygone tourist attraction.

Abingdon Lock Daytime only
Towing Path, Abingdon, Oxon OX14 3NW
☎ 01235 523044
120'0'' (36·57m) long × 18'9'' (5·71m) wide
Rise (fall) 6'2'' (1·89m)
Max. draught 5'0'' (1·52m)
Facilities Chemical toilet disposal and pump-out, refuse disposal, toilets, drinking water tap and hose for tank filling, overnight mooring with permission (fee).

The Thames Path

The Path now starts again from the western end of Wallingford Bridge, after extensive restoration work along the western bank up to Benson. Enter Castle Lane behind the *Boat House Hotel* and rejoin the river bank just above some private moorings beyond. The path now follows the old towing path which has recently been restored and continues above Benson Lock. Although the ferry no longer runs, provision has been made for walkers to cross the lock gates and the weir walkway to join the lane from Preston Crowmarsh and rejoin the river just before

Benson Waterfront at the head of the weir stream. Walk over the slipways and past the caravan site into fields which border the river up to Shillingford Bridge.

Another closed ferry ahead means that we can no longer cross the bridge and follow the footpath on the left-hand bank but have to cross the road and turn off to the left where a sign reads 'Private Road' (in fact, a public footpath). In 150 yards a swing gate takes us onto a path which borders Shillingford Court. Enter the village and turn up Wharf Road to the *Kingfisher* pub. From here, carry on along the main A4074 for about 700 yards and you will see a stile by a farm gate close to a point where the river nears the road. A path takes you back to the river bank which you can now follow, over the entrance to the Thame as far as Day's Lock. Two interesting diversions present themselves – to Dorchester by way of a path leaving the river after the Thame bridge, and to Wittenham Clumps by crossing Little Wittenham Bridge and climbing the hill from the path opposite Little Wittenham Church.

At Day's Lock the path changes banks by crossing the lock gates and the weir. Until comparatively recently you had to pay the lock-keeper at Day's the ferry fee for crossing his weir. Perhaps lock and ferry, which was sited above the lock were, by tradition, supervised by the same man? Unfortunately our historian, Thacker, does not enlighten us. Subsequently this arrangement fell into abeyance and walkers had a long trek by road from the Little Wittenham footbridge into Long Wittenham to rejoin the river at Clifton Hampden Bridge. However, under the Thames Path scheme, the old route has been restored and you can follow the river on its wide sweep round to Clifton Hampden Bridge where the path again changes sides to the north bank.

At Sutton Bridge just before Culham Lock, while the Thames Path and the navigation's towing path continues past the lock, a more interesting excursion can be made around the weir streams of the river proper, forming Sutton Pools. A footpath follows into Sutton Courtenay, joining the Appleford Road opposite *The Fish Inn*. Turn right here and, at the corner with Church Street, another path to your right sets off over the weir stream, turns upstream, crosses the top weir onto the lock island and then crosses the lock cut by a footbridge to meet the towing path halfway along the cut. Turn left off the bridge here and remain on this bank right through to Abingdon Lock where the next change of bank takes place.

Here again you must cross lock gates and weir as an alternative to the former ferry which used to ply just below the entrance to the Swift Ditch. Cross the lock gates, walk across the lock island to the weir and then follow round to the Abbey Stream footbridge. From here the Thames Path stays on the left-hand, western, bank as viewed when going upstream right up to Osney Bridge beyond the middle of Oxford.

Angling

Weir Permit holders can fish, subject to the following provisos, from lock sites at Benson, Day's and Clifton. At Benson, fishing is allowed from the weir-stream side of the breakwater below the lock. There is no car park at the lock and you will have to street park locally. Cross the millstream footbridge, now open as part of the Thames Path, and use the weir gangway to get to the lock and the site. Check with the lock-keeper before fishing. At Clifton, the site is along the Thames Path where it follows the lock cut above the lock. Signs are displayed along this stretch between which fishing is allowed but note that this is only between 1 November and 14 March in view of navigation traffic in the summer and autumn seasons. Fishing from the opposite bank is reserved by London Anglers for its members only. The nearest public car park is opposite the *Barley Mow* inn on the other side of the bridge at Clifton Hampden.

Benson Angling Society reserves coarse fishing at Benson, apart from the EA's fishery in the weir stream. Week and day tickets are available from the secretary or from Benson Waterfront. Sundays are reserved for matches in season. Wallingford Angling Association also has water in this area, upstream towards Shillingford, and the *Shillingford Bridge Hotel* has about 500 yards of fishing on both banks above the bridge reserved for guests and the High Wycombe Angling Club. Abingdon and Oxford AA and Tring Anglers have water at Clifton Hampden while London AA (members only) fishes both banks between the rail bridge at Appleford down to the Clifton Cut, at which point their water continues along the opposite bank to the towing path as far as the footbridge.

All water at Culham, except the weir pools (Sutton Pools), is controlled by Abingdon and District ARA while upstream, from a point 200 yards above Culham footbridge to Nuneham rail bridge, fishing is controlled by Abingdon Town Council. This is free to residents, but visitors can obtain tickets from the Town Clerk's office at Stratton Lodge, 52 Bath Street, Abingdon OX14 ☎ 01235 522642. Abingdon and Oxford AA has water at Radley.

Directory

BOATYARDS, MARINAS, CHANDLERIES, TRIPPING AND HIRE

Benson Waterfront Ltd
Benson Waterfront, Benson, Wallingford, Oxon OX10 6SJ ☎ 01491 838304. Permanent and visitors' moorings, all mooring services, restaurant and car parking, caravan park, adjacent shop.

Swancraft Ltd
Benson Waterfront, Benson, Wallingford, Oxon OX10 6SJ ☎ 01491 836700. Marine engineers, diesel fuel, *Calor Gas*, weekly cruiser hire (*Blakes*), water point, toilet pump-out, chemical toilet disposal, slipway. (TBTA, THCA)

Boat Breakdowns
The Boatworks, Benson Waterfront, Benson, Wallingford, Oxon OX10 6SJ ☎ 01491 833526/833120. On site and mobile breakdown service for engine, mechanical and emergency repairs in the upper Thames Valley.

Red Line Outboard Services
Ferry Boat House, Wilsham Road, Abingdon, Oxon OX14 5HP ☎ 01235 521562. Outboard sales and service, marine engineers, petrol, diesel fuel, chandlery.

Kingcraft Ltd
Abingdon Boat Centre, Nags Head Island, Abingdon, Oxon OX14 3HX ☎ 01235 521125. Small boat sales, repairs, engineers, diesel fuel, *Calor Gas*, large chandlery, books and maps, clothing, day-boat hire, permanent and visitors' moorings, slipway, water point, refuse disposal, pump-out service, car park. (TBTA, THCA)

EMERGENCY FUEL SUPPLIES
See note under this heading on page 24

Rectory Service Station
Petrol, diesel
Station Road, Wallingford, Oxon ☎ 01491 837329. 800yds up High Street from Wallingford Bridge.

Gurney's of Benson
Petrol, diesel
Gurney's Roundabout, Oxford Road, Benson, Oxon ☎ 01491 838308. Opposite Benson Waterfront – 300yds from river.

Turnpike Filling Station
Petrol, diesel
Abingdon Road, Clifton Hampden, Oxon ☎ 01865 407546

Halls Garage
Petrol
Sutton Courtenay, Abingdon, Oxon ☎ 01235 848236. ½ mile from Sutton Bridge in village.

Cross Roads Garage
Petrol, diesel
Drayton Road, Abingdon, Oxon ☎ 01235 528828/533403. ¾ mile from St Helen's Wharf.

ROWING, SAILING AND CRUISING CLUBS AND TUITION

Oxford University Boat Club
Chalmore Meadow, Off St Lucian's Lane, Wallingford, Oxon OX10 9EP. Rowing. (ARA)

Wallingford Rowing Club
Thames Street, Wallingford, Oxon OX10. (ARA)

Oxford & District Sculling Centre
Tollgate Road, Culham, Abingdon, Oxon (ARA)

Abingdon Town Rowing Club
Wilsham Road, Abingdon, Oxon OX14. (ARA)

Abbey Sailing Club
Wilsham Road, Abingdon, Oxon OX14. (RYA)

Kingfisher Canoe Club
Wilsham Road, Abingdon, Oxon OX14. (BCU)

PUBLIC LAUNCHING SITES
- **Wallingford** Above bridge on west bank beside *Boat House Hotel*. Light craft only. Access now restricted
- **Abingdon** St Helens Wharf. At end of Caldecott Road turn left towards church. Slipway is at bottom of West St Helen's Street

FISHING TACKLE SHOPS
The Right Angle
Wootton Road, Abingdon, Oxon
☎ 01235 524144

HOTELS, INNS AND RESTAURANTS
Riverside Restaurant Benson Waterfront. Food available all day, also takeaway and shop. Moorings outside – free to patrons, fee to visitors.

Crown Hotel High Street, Benson.

Shillingford Bridge Hotel Shillingford Road, Wallingford ☎ 01865 858567. High-class hotel-restaurant and bar meals. Mooring alongside.

Kingfisher Inn Henley Road, Shillingford. Buffet. It is possible to moor against the towing path just below Shillingford Bridge.

Cricketers Arms Thame Road, Warborough. Day fishing tickets available for Warboro & Shillingford AC.

Fleur-de-Lys Inn High Street, Dorchester. Bar food and hot meals midday and evenings. Mooring possible for small craft on River Thame below Dorchester Bridge.

George Hotel High Street, Dorchester. Bar food and restaurant midday and evenings.

White Hart Hotel High Street, Dorchester. Restaurant and snack bar, midday and evenings.

Abbey Tea Rooms High Street, Dorchester. Teas from 1500 until 1730 (approx).

Chequers Inn Burcot. Bar food midday and evenings. Boaters must walk from Clifton Hampden.

Barley Mow Clifton Hampden ☎ 01865 407847. Bar meals lunchtimes and evenings; dining evenings only. Moorings against towpath above the bridge. Cross bridge to pub.

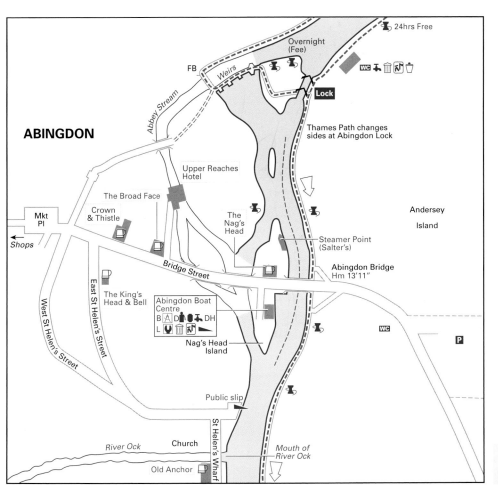

Plough Inn Abingdon Road, Clifton Hampden. Bar meals and dining all day. B&B. Moorings against towpath above the bridge, walk back into village.

Machine Man Inn Fieldside, Long Wittenham.

Plough Inn High Street, Long Wittenham. Bar meals and dining, midday and evenings. B&B. Mooring at end of garden in weir stream, below Clifton Lock.

Swan Inn The Green, Sutton Courtenay. Bar meals and dining midday and evenings. Moor downstream of Sutton Bridge on towing path side, cross bridge, take path into village.

Fish Inn Appleford Road, Sutton Courtenay. Bar meals at lunchtimes. Seated dining in the evenings, plus Sunday lunch.

Lion Inn High Street, Culham.

Waggon & Horses Abingdon Road, Culham. Bar food and separate restaurant, midday and evenings. Moor downstream of Sutton Bridge, at bridge turn right up to main A415, pub on right at crossroads.

Old Anchor Inn St Helen's Wharf, Abingdon. Room for up to six craft alongside road opposite, use fenders against stone wall.

Nag's Head Inn The Bridge, Abingdon. Buffet lunches. B&B accommodation. Public moorings below bridge on east bank (towing path side).

Broad Face Inn Bridge Street, Abingdon. Bar meals 1200–1430. Snacks and full dining in the evenings, plus Sunday lunch.

King's Head and Bell East St Helen's Street, Abingdon. Restaurant and lunchtime bar snacks.

Crown & Thistle Hotel Bridge Street, Abingdon ☎ 01235 522556/520087. Restaurant and bars.

Upper Reaches Hotel Thames Street, Abingdon ☎ 01235 522311. High-class hotel-restaurant. Mooring adjacent.

Bowyer Arms Foxborough Road, Radley. Bar meals and lunchtime snacks. Moor on towing path at footpath to Lower Radley, then cross railway and turn left.

TAXIS
Wallingford
- Hills Taxis, Station Road ☎ 01491 837022/837497

Benson
- Pontings ☎ 01491 826679

Sutton Courtenay

- 87 High Street, Sutton Courtenay ☎ 01235 847153

Abingdon
- Auto Taxis, Radley Road Industrial Estate ☎ 01235 527711/524780
- CB Taxis Abingdon, 2 Welford Gardens ☎ 0800 0835902

RAIL STATIONS AND TRAIN SERVICES
See note under this heading on page 26
Enquiries: ☎ 08457 484950
Appleford (closed Sundays) *FGW Link* Appleford Road, Appleford, Oxon. ½ mile from river. Sporadic service.
Culham (closed Sundays) *FGW Link* Station Road, Abingdon Road, Culham, Oxon. 1½ miles from Culham Lock. Sporadic service.
Radley *FGW Link* Foxborough Road, Radley, Oxon. 1 mile from Thames Path. Trains to Didcot, Cholsey, Goring, Pangbourne, Tilehurst, Reading; and Oxford.

BUS AND COACH SERVICES
Wallingford and Abingdon
Wallingford and Abingdon are served by Thames Travel of Wallingford. Direct links to Oxford are covered by Stagecoach Oxford and the Oxford Bus Company from Abingdon. Wallingford to Oxford is covered by Thames Travel.

Bus Operators are:
- Stagecoach Oxford ☎ 01865 772250
- Oxford Buses ☎ 01865 785400
- Thames Travel ☎ 01491 837988

10. Oxford – Radley to Binsey

Distance

6.77 miles (Radley Ferry to Medley Bridge)

Maximum dimensions of craft from Radley Ferry to Osney Bridge & Osney Bridge to Medley Bridge

Headroom	10′3″ (3.12m) at Folly Bridge
	7′6″ (2.28) at Osney Bridge
Length	113′8″ (34.64m) at Osney Lock
Beam	17′3″ (5.25m) at Osney Lock
Draught	4′0″ (1.22m) in main fairway up to Oxford. 3′0″ (0.90m) up to Lechlade

Again we are in rowing waters and are likely to remain so until well above Oxford, although our first encounter will probably be with the boys of Radley College which has a thriving rowing club. Practising takes place during term times between Radley Ferry, just below their boathouse, almost up to the tail of Sandford Lock. This is a slightly curving reach running almost due north to south towards us as we make our way upstream. Once past the boathouse which stands opposite Nuneham Park, the railway which has a station at Radley (but none now at Abingdon) starts to close with the river, being a mere 500 yards from it just below Sandford Lock.

The main weir stream for the lock comes out on the left-hand bank under the towing-path bridge. Navigators should note that fishing is allowed from this area, which is close to a car park at the end of Sandford Lane. It is not therefore advisable to moor here but to go up closer to the lock and use the rings on the left, below the lock.

Above Sandford Lock is the charming King's Arms inn, standing close to a new residential development on the site of Sandford Mill, which disappeared with its landmark chimney not so many years ago. Over on the right you may moor for the inn. Above the Four Pillars Hotel comes the tiny Kennington Island, also known as Rose Island, which should be left to starboard going upstream. The porthand bank juts out into the channel giving the sharpest corner on the river below Oxford and great care should be exercised in negotiating both this and the turn at the head of the island 150 yards further upstream. On the opposite bank there are free moorings above Kennington

rail bridge which carries a branch line, rarely used, leading into the motor works at Cowley. Above the bridge, on the towing path side the Hinksey Stream finally enters the Thames after its circuit through the meadows from North Hinksey and its confluence with the old mill stream which starts from a weir above Donnington Bridge.

The tree-lined approach to the Oxford bypass is more cheerful as we slide through a sylvan setting towards the picturesque reach below the Iffley weirs under the Isis Bridge which carries the A4074 across the river. Since the smaller weir close to the lock provides pedestrian access to the lock and overnight mooring is available on both the weir and lock islands, this and the footbridge at the bottom of the main weir stream are attractively roofed and blend well with the stone construction of the lock-keeper's house. On the right as you come downstream, do not be tempted to negotiate the attractive stone footbridge on your side as this merely carries the towing path across the entrance to the boat rollers which are, apparently, still usable. Before making use of the overnight moorings which are below the top weir on the downstream island, you must seek

Sandford Lock Daytime only
Sandford-on-Thames, Oxford OX4 4YD
☎ 01865 775889
174′0″ (53.03m) long x 21′9″ (6.62m) wide
Rise (fall) 8′10″ (2.69m) Deepest above Teddington
Max. draught 7′7″ (2.31m)
Facilities Drinking water tap, overnight mooring with permission, electric launch charging point.
Angling Fishing available from main weir gantry or both banks of weir stream near towpath footbridge.

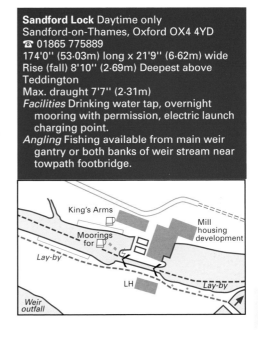

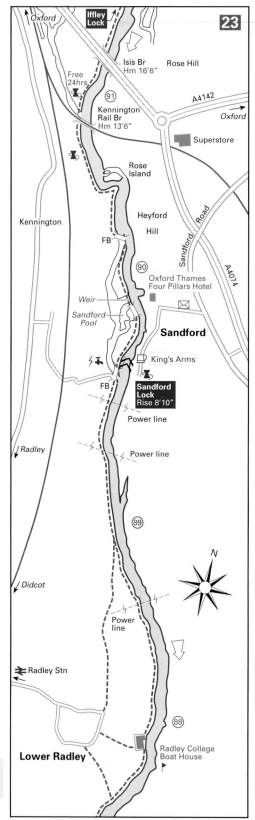

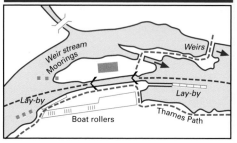

Iffley Lock Daytime only
Mill Lane, Iffley, Oxford OX4 4EJ
☎ 01865 777277
154'1'' (46· 96m) long x 21'3'' (6·47m) wide
Rise (fall) 2'9'' (0·81m)
Max. draught 7'5'' (2·26m)
Facilities Refuse disposal, boat rollers,
  overnight mooring with permission.

permission from the lock-keeper. Just above the lock on the towing path side is the famous old Isis Tavern, reputed to have had irregular drinking hours. Mooring is possible with extreme care if you wish to venture into this slice of Oxford history.

We now enter the long reach up to Folly Bridge which contains upwards of a dozen rowing clubhouses belonging to the Oxford University colleges, some boathouses being shared by more than two clubs. Many of the clubs used to operate from the famous college barges, but a number have disappeared and some commodious structures have appeared along the Christ Church bank between the two mouths of the River Cherwell. In addition, there are a number of non-university clubs, a riverside centre and a sea cadet centre at Donnington Bridge which also operate on this reach, often taking advantage of the lull in college activity when the undergraduates are on vacation.

Punting, for which Oxford undergraduates are renowned, is more properly confined to the Cherwell, the punting station being sited by Magdalen Bridge about a mile up the Cherwell, although there are also skiffs and small motor boats to be had from a pontoon in front of the *Head of the River* inn at Folly Bridge. Passage through the reach takes us past the busy rowing clubs and under the comparatively recently built Donnington Bridge, opened in 1962. Just below the bridge are the sheds and workshops of Salter Brothers, the famous firm of boatbuilders and operators of passenger launches which started in the 1850s. Close by, also on the

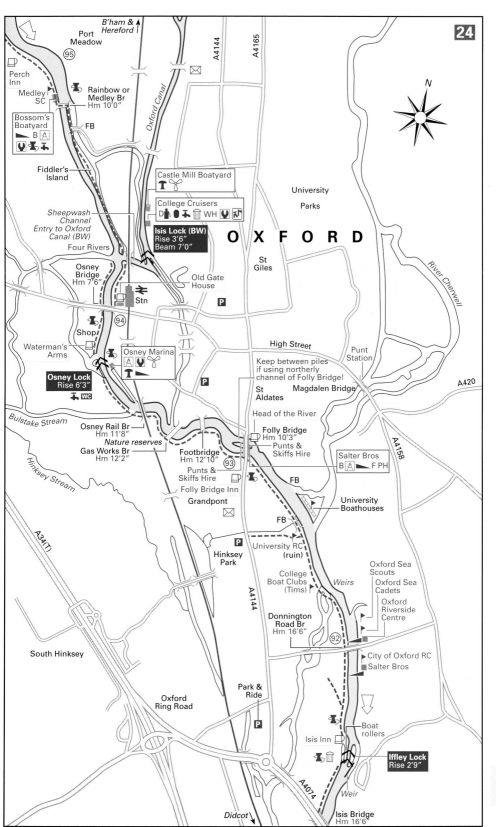

B'ham &
Hereford

Port
Meadow

Perch
Inn

Medley
SC

Rainbow or
Medley Br
Hm 10'0"

FB

Bossom's
Boatyard
■— B A

Fiddler's
Island

Oxford Canal

A4144

A4165

Castle Mill Boatyard

College Cruisers
D ■ ● ♨ 🗑 WH

University

Parks

Sheepwash
Channel
Entry to Oxford
Canal (BW)
Four Rivers

Isis Lock (BW)
Rise 3'6"
Beam 7'0"

O X F O R D

St
Giles

Osney
Bridge
Hm 7'6"

Old Gate
House

Stn

P

River Cherwell

Shop

Waterman's
Arms

Osney Marina
A

Osney Lock
Rise 6'3"
WC

High Street

Keep between piles
if using northerly
channel of Folly Bridge!

St
Aldates

Magdalen Bridge

Punt
Station

A420

Bulstake Stream

Hinksey Stream

Osney Rail Br
Hm 11'8"
Nature reserves
Gas Works Br
Hm 12'2"

Footbridge
Hm 12'10"

Punts &
Skiffs Hire

Folly Bridge Inn

Grandpont

Head of the River

Folly Bridge
Hm 10'3"
Punts &
Skiffs Hire

FB

Salter Bros
B A ■— F PH

University
Boathouses

A4158

A34(T)

Hinksey
Park

P

University RC
(ruin)

College
Boat Clubs
(Tims)

Donnington
Road Br
Hm 16'6"

FB

Weirs

Oxford Sea
Scouts

Oxford Sea
Cadets

Oxford
Riverside
Centre

South Hinksey

A4144

City of Oxford RC

Salter Bros

Oxford
Ring Road

Park &
Ride

P

Boat
rollers

Isis Inn

🗑

Iffley Lock
Rise 2'9"

Weir

A4074

Didcot

Isis Bridge
Hm 16'6"

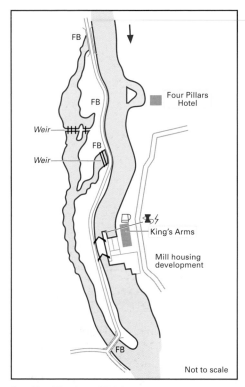

Sandford Lock and Weirs

be navigated on either side but be careful to note the instructions posted at the channel entrances, and keep between the marker posts when using the northerly channel (right-hand when proceeding upstream). It is advisable, on coming downstream, to take the southerly channel, although the width through the single arch may look restricted. Trying to turn into the northerly passage, though, is tricky since it involves a sharp left-hander and, once lined up for the arch, you may well find a punt or two or bigger traffic coming upstream blocking your way.

Above Folly Bridge the river narrows, and winds around gasworks and railway lands on the left bank which have subsequently been redeveloped for modern offices, flats and industrial purposes, while opposite lies the Grand Pont Nature Reserve.

Next is a disused rail bridge which has been imaginatively repainted and re-used as a footpath crossing. Just above, a small stream runs into the Thames on our right where it may be possible to moor for the town. This is the original stream which served Oxford until the thirteenth century, when it became so clogged that navigation was impossible so the Abbot of Oseney applied to Henry III to dig a cut for a new mill above what is now Osney Lock.

Take the left-hand arch of the bridge as you go upstream since the old channel, now clearer 750 years later, can still send down a hefty current, causing turbulence at the outfall just in the right-hand arch. The next bridge is the modern (only 96 years old!) rail bridge which was adapted and altered periodically up to 1958 as tracks were closed, or relaid into Oxford Station since Brunel first bridged the Thames here to reach Banbury in 1850. Eventually the bridge came to carry his main London—Worcester line, which it still does. On your left hand the combined Bulstake and Seacourt streams come back into the river under the towing path, the Bulstake having started above the next weir at Four Streams where the cut leads

eastern bank, are the City of Oxford Rowing Club, the Riverside Centre, Oxford Sea Cadets HQ and 22nd Oxford Sea Scouts campsite which is only available to scouts and youth groups. Salter Brothers also has a caravan and campsite nearby with 15 tent pitches with toilets, showers and its own slipway (see Boatyard and Club sections of the *Directory* at the end of this section for further details). There is a public slipway, on the right-hand, eastern, bank above the bridge which is available with permission from the Riverside Centre (☎ 01865 248673) or in advance from Oxford City Council (☎ 01865 249811).

Towards the head of the reach, above the site of the Oxford University Boat Club on the west bank, the river curves and widens to give a suitable stretch of moorings below Grand Pont Island. Here you will find Salter Brothers' main office, on the island below Folly Bridge which takes its name from a folly which stood on the site of the present peculiar building with its statuettes and wrought iron balconies. This area of Oxford is known as Grand Pont and is sufficiently close to the city centre to be a valuable stepping-off point to visit shops and colleges. The present bridge, built in the 1820's, can

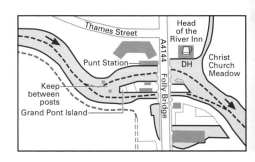

Above: Oxford. Rowing boats and punts at Folly Bridge, Oxford
Below: Oxford. *Head of the River Inn* at Folly Bridge

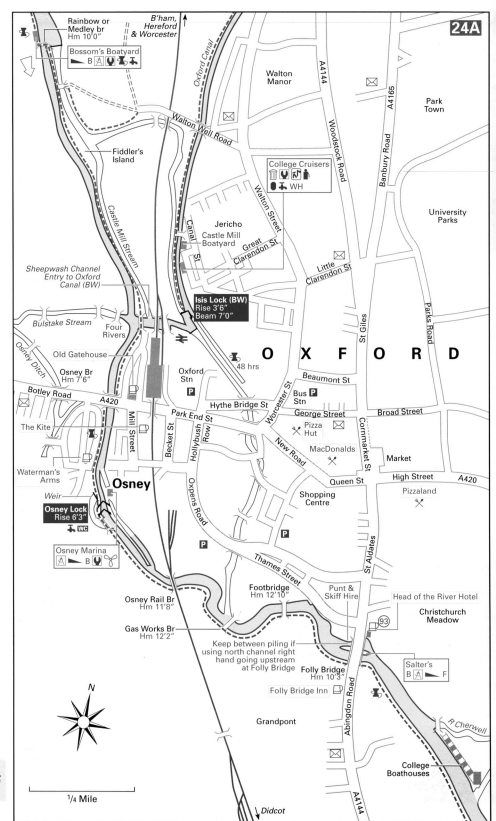

24A

B'ham, Hereford & Worcester

Rainbow or Medley br Hm 10'0"

Bossom's Boatyard B

Oxford Canal

Walton Manor

A4144

A4165

Park Town

Woodstock Road

Banbury Road

Fiddler's Island

Walton Well Road

Castle Mill Stream

College Cruisers WH

Walton Street

University Parks

Jericho

Canal St.

Castle Mill Boatyard

Great Clarendon St

Little Clarendon St

St Giles

Parks Road

Sheepwash Channel Entry to Oxford Canal (BW)

Bulstake Stream

Four Rivers

Isis Lock (BW) Rise 3'6" Beam 7'0"

Osney Ditch

Old Gatehouse

Osney Br Hm 7'6"

O X F O R D

48 hrs

Botley Road

A420

Oxford Stn P

The Kite

Mill Street

Becket St

Park End St

Hythe Bridge St

Beaumont St

Worcester St

Bus Stn P

George Street

Broad Street

Cornmarket St

Waterman's Arms

Weir

Osney

Hollybush Row

Pizza Hut

MacDonalds

Queen St

Market

High Street

A420

Pizzaland

Osney Lock Rise 6'3" WC

New Road

Shopping Centre

St Aldates

Osney Marina A B

Oxpens Road

P

P

Thames Street

Osney Rail Br Hm 11'8"

Footbridge Hm 12'10"

Punt & Skiff Hire

Head of the River Hotel

93

Christchurch Meadow

Gas Works Br Hm 12'2"

Keep between piling if using north channel right hand going upstream at Folly Bridge

Folly Bridge Hm 10'3"

Abingdon Road

R Cherwell

Salter's B A F

Folly Bridge Inn

N

Grandpont

College Boathouses

A4144

136

¼ Mile

Didcot

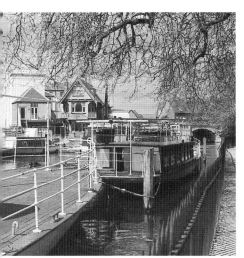

Salters' launches and offices at Folly Bridge, Oxford

off into the Oxford Canal and the Seacourt Stream at a weir above Hagley Pool which is about 600 yards above King's Lock. Neither is navigable except by small craft and canoes. On your right, so take care of emerging craft, is the lower entrance to Osney Marina and thence comes Osney Lock.

Above Osney Lock, adjacent to which is the Upper Thames District navigation office, come further useful moorings for walking into Oxford city centre and also for joining or leaving ship by rail, since Oxford Station is only a short walk up the towing path and across Osney Bridge. Just before the bridge is the upper entrance (or exit) to Osney Marina and Osney Marine Engineering's yard on the right-hand side proceeding upstream, so look out for emerging or turning craft.

Osney Lock Daytime only
East Street, Osney, Oxford OX2 0AX
☎ 01865 247050
113'8" (34·64m) long x 17'3" (5·25m) wide
Rise (fall) 6'3" (1·89m)
Max. draught 6'11" (2·10m)
Facilities Toilets, water tap for cans only.

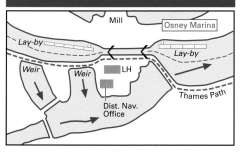

Here too, if your craft cannot be reduced to a height above the waterline of less than 7'6" (2.28m) you will have to turn and retrace your passage downstream, since the headroom of Osney Bridge will not let you through. Note also that the curvature of the bridge soffit means that even the recommended height is only available across the centre of the arch, hence the rubbing strakes on each side, and that to try and duck under anywhere but in the centre will probably cause severe damage to roof, lamps or windscreen, all casualties in past decades.

It is reputed that, in the heyday of Thames cruising in the 60s and 70s, small boys would line the bank offering to jump on board in threes and fours at a tanner a time each to sink one's cruiser a little further so that she would get through. One enterprising skipper, now a boatyard proprietor but then a keen amateur, dismantled the whole windscreen of his hire cruiser, carefully laid it on the bank, took the cruiser through the bridge and then sent his crew to carry the windscreen over the bridge and replace it on the upstream side! Coming downstream is even more difficult, especially if a current is running. The trick here, also executed by another customer of the same hire firm in the 70s, was to turn the cruiser round to face upstream and stem the flow until the cruiser made way very gently astern through the bridge – an approved method of maintaining control in a very sticky situation.

At Four Rivers, a little way above Osney, we come to a watery cross-roads – hence the name. On our left, to the west is the Bulstake Stream which eventually joins the Botley and Seacourt Streams which find their way back to the Thames, lower down; while to the east under the towing path bridge is the Sheepwash Channel, which now leads to the Castle Mill Stream and the Oxford Canal. This particular channel was the object of campaigning for a number of years by the Inland Waterways Association, who felt that too many boaters were being put off using this entrance to the canal by the presence of the railway's swing bridge just beyond the fixed bridge which carries the main line. The swing bridge is now left in the 'open to navigation' position since the old goods yards which it served are now the site of Berkeley homes.

Until the present main channel was improved with the construction of a proper weir and pound lock at King's in 1928 and the removal of Medley Weir at about the same date, many craft would use the canal to

The narrow (south) channel through Folly Bridge, Oxford

bypass the vagaries of the river between Godstow and Port Meadow, by entering the Sheepwash Channel and climbing the 7´0˝ rise by way of Isis and Wolvercote Locks and leaving the canal again through the ¾-mile long Duke's Cut, entered just above Duke's Bridge which carries the A40 over the canal. Duke's Lock, a stop lock which serves to accommodate any changes in level between river and canal at this point, is sited in the cut between the rail and road bridges and falls either way. The cut rejoins the Thames almost immediately above King's Weir and the channel runs round the back of the lock island to join the main line at a point less than 40 yards above the top gates of King's Lock. Users of the Oxford Canal must have registered their craft with British Waterways before proceeding. Details may be obtainable from College Cruisers Ltd at Combe Road Wharf on the canal in Oxford (see *Directory*).

The navigation continues northwards under Medley Bridge by Bossom's yard where the towing path changes sides to use the western bank away from the wide stretch of Port Meadow on the east. Here you may see cattle drinking from the river and wandering at will across this sudden expanse of green

after the confines of the urban riverscape. Also sharing the scene may well be the sailing dinghies of the Medley Sailing Club, whose premises are just upstream from Bossom's yard. The Oxford section ends with the village of Binsey set back from the towing path and a short stroll to the *Perch Inn* across the fields.

The Thames Path

The Thames Path starts its Oxford section on the western bank and crosses Radley School's slipway to continue on up to Sandford Lock. Cross the footbridges – one below the lock and three above – noting that the pools, although attractive, can be very dangerous, especially in wet weather when the river may be approaching flood conditions. The path crosses the Hinksey Stream outfall and stays on the western bank right up to Iffley Lock. Here it is possible to cross the lock and weirs into Iffley, but the Thames Path stays on the western side, past the boat rollers and the attractive stone bridge which leads to a lock-head mooring and past the *Isis Tavern*. Passing Donnington Bridge, further streams are crossed at Long Bridges where there are cruiser moorings and a pleasant walk takes you up to Folly Bridge. Here you must cross Abingdon Road and go down the path on the upstream side of the bridge to stay on the western bank.

Follow the river right round to Osney Lock and proceed alongside East Street which starts at the *Waterman's Arms* until you reach the A420 Botley Road and Osney Bridge. Go up onto the bridge and cross the road and the bridge, rejoining the path on the eastern bank above the bridge. The path now follows the river over the entrance to the Oxford Canal by means of a footbridge and finally, after crossing a spillway into Castle Millstream, takes a sharp left turn onto Medley, or Rainbow, Bridge which takes the towing path through Bossom's premises, past Medley Sailing Club and on to Binsey.

Angling

Weir Permit holders may fish at Sandford from the main weir gantry off the towing path above the lock and also from the banks on both sides of the weir stream outfall, including the short section of bank alongside the towing path below the bottom footbridge. If you intend to fish, please report to the lock-keeper first who will advise on the best location. There is a car park for fishermen and those visiting the lock at the bottom of Sandford Lane which is on the western bank of the river, reached from the southern end of The Avenue at Kennington.

Almost all other fishing in the area is reserved by local angling societies such as the Abingdon and Oxford Anglers Alliance, the Oxford District Anglers Association and the Abingdon and District Angling and Restocking Association. Oxford and District Angling Society holds the fishing rights to the river between Iffley Lock and Folly Bridge. Day tickets are not available. Tring Anglers also fishes Oxford Alliance waters. Salter Brothers permits fishing from its caravan and campsite at Donnington Bridge ☎ 01865 243421.

More precise details can be obtained from the tackle shops listed in the *Directory*, since our information comes from several published sources, all of which tend to be confusingly incomplete.

Directory

BOATYARDS, MARINAS, CHANDLERIES, TRIPPING AND HIRE

Salter Brothers Ltd & Salters' Steamers Ltd
Folly Bridge, Oxford OX1 4LA ☎ 01865 243421. Also at Donnington Bridge. Thames passenger launch proprietor, boatbuilder, sales, chandlery, party hire, public trips, catering afloat, moorings, slipway. (TBTA, PBA)

Riverside Boating Co Ltd
Folly Bridge, Oxford OX1 4LB ☎ 01865 722426. Day boats for hire.

Osney Marine Engineering Co
Osney Mill, Mill Street, Oxford OX2 0AN ☎ 01865 241348. Boat sales, repairs, engineers, permanent moorings, slipway.

Oxford River Cruises
7 Rogers Street, Oxford OX1 7JS ☎ 0845 266 9396. Passenger trips for up to 12 people.

College Cruisers Ltd
Combe Road Wharf, Combe Road, Oxford OX2 6BL ☎ 01865 554343. Boat repairs and breakdown service, marine engineer, diesel fuel, *Calor Gas*, weekly narrowboat hire on Oxford Canal and Thames (*Hoseasons*), permanent moorings on Oxford Canal, water point, refuse and chemical toilet disposal, pump-out service. (TBTA, THCA)

Bossoms Boat Yard Ltd
Near Binsey Village, Oxford OX2 0NL
☎ 01865 247780. Boat builders, repairs
and renovations, brokerage, recreational
moorings up to 70′, moorings, chandlery,
storage, slipway, water. (TBTA)

EMERGENCY FUEL SUPPLIES
See note under this heading on page 24
Cross Roads Garage
Petrol, diesel
Drayton Road, Abingdon, Oxon ☎
01235 528828/533403. ¾ mile from St
Helen's Wharf.
Kennington Service Station
Petrol, diesel
The Avenue, Kennington, Oxford
☎ 01865 735435. ¾ mile from Sandford
Lock, down Sandford Lane.
Oxpens Service Station
Petrol, diesel
Oxpens Road, Oxford ☎ 01865 721397.
Short walk from Gasworks Footbridge.

ROWING, SAILING AND CRUISING
CLUBS AND TUITION
Radley College Boat Club
Lower Radley, Abingdon, Oxon OX14
☎ 01235 521114. (ARA)
Falcon Rowing Club
Meadow Lane, Iffley Road, Oxford OX4
4BJ. (ARA)
City of Oxford Rowing Club
City Boathouse, Meadow Lane, Oxford
OX4 4BL ☎ 01865 242576. (ARA)
Oxford Unit Sea Cadets Corps
Meadow Lane, Donnington Bridge Road,
Oxford OX4 4BJ.
Oxford Riverside Centre
Donnington Bridge, Oxford OX4 4AZ
☎ 01865 248673. Youth sailing, tuition,
public slipway – see below.

22nd Oxford Sea Scouts
Meadow Lane, Donnington Bridge Road,
Oxford OX4 4BJ ☎ 01865 778459.
Campsite for scouts and youth groups.
Tim's Boathouse
Long Bridges, New Hinksey, Oxford.
Various university clubs.
Oxford University Rowing Clubs
University Boathouse, Towing Path,
Oxford OX1 4UN ☎ 01865 242975.
Rowing, base for 14 clubs, affiliated to
ARA.
Christchurch Meadows Boathouses
Christchurch Meadows, Oxford. 10
boathouses for 17 rowing clubs of the
University's colleges, affiliated to ARA.
Osney Marina Club – Boating Section
Osney Marina, Mill Lane, Oxford OX2
0AN. (ATYC)
Medley Sailing Club
Binsey, Oxford OX2 0NL. (RYA)

PUBLIC LAUNCHING SITES
Oxford Donnington Bridge on the upstream,
eastern side, by arrangement with the
Oxford City Riverside Centre (see text)

FISHING TACKLE SHOPS
The Right Angle
Wootton Road, Abingdon, Oxon
☎ 01235 524144
Dell's Fishing Tackle Ltd
136 Oxford Road, Cowley, Oxon
☎ 01865 711410
North Oxford Tackle
95 Islip Road, Summertown, Oxford
☎ 01865 556955
Fat Phil's Angling Centre
334-6 Abingdon Road, Oxford
☎ 01865 201020

TOURIST INFORMATION OFFICES
Abingdon 25, Bridge Street, Abingdon,
Oxon ☎ 01235 522711
Oxford The Old School, Gloucester Green,
Oxford ☎ 01865 726871

HOTELS, INNS AND RESTAURANTS
Bowyer Arms Foxborough Road, Radley.
Moor on towing path at footpath to
Lower Radley. Then cross railway and
turn left.
King's Arms Church Road, Sandford.
Mooring alongside opposite the pub or
below Sandford Lock, free.
Oxford Thames Four Pillars Hotel Henley
Road, Sandford-on-Thames
☎ 01865 334444. High-class hotel-
restaurant. Moorings.
Isis Tavern Riverside, Iffley Lock. Moorings
alongside outside the pub above Iffley
Lock.

Mediterranean Fish Bar 270 Abingdon Road, Oxford. ½ mile from Donnington Bridge.

Folly Bridge Inn Abingdon Road, Oxford. Mooring downstream of Folly Bridge (free).

Head of the River Inn Folly Bridge, Oxford. Mooring outside for two craft, otherwise use moorings below Folly Bridge, punts and rowing boats for hire nearby.

Waterman's Arms South Street, Osney. Mooring outside, above Osney Lock (free).

The Kite Mill Street, Osney.

Old Gatehouse 2 Botley Road, Osney,**Queen's Arms** 1 Park End Street, Oxford

Old Gatehouse 2 Botley Road, Osney, Oxford. Moorings between Osney Lock and Osney Bridge (free).

McDonald's Clarendon Centre, Cornmarket Street, Oxford

Pizza Hut George Street, Oxford.

Pizzaland High Street, Oxford.

Mick's Café Botley Road, Osney.

RAIL STATIONS AND TRAIN SERVICES

See note under this heading on page 26

Enquiries ☎ 08457 484950.

Radley *FGW Link* Foxborough Road, Radley, Oxon. 1 mile from Thames Path. Trains to Didcot, Cholsey, Goring, Pangbourne, Tilehurst, Reading; also to Oxford.

Oxford *FGW Link* Park End Street, Oxford. 300 yds from Osney Bridge. Trains to Radley, Didcot, Cholsey, Goring, Pangbourne, Tilehurst and Reading; also to Reading and London Paddington (fast). Other services to Bicester, Banbury, Birmingham, Worcester and Wolverhampton, also the south and southwest, etc.

BUS AND COACH SERVICES

Oxford (Radley to Binsey)

Abingdon and Oxford are served by Oxford Buses and Stagecoach Oxford bus companies. From Abingdon there are several services to Oxford, via Kennington and a service from Sandford which runs into Oxford. There are several direct coaches to London from Oxford which use the M40. Beyond Oxford there are fairly frequent buses towards Eynsham.

Bus Operators are:
- Oxford Buses ☎ 01865 785400
- Thames Travel ☎ 01491 837988
- Stagecoach Oxford ☎ 01865 772250

11. Binsey to Newbridge

Distance
12.63 miles (Medley Bridge to Newbridge –
The Rose Revived)

Maximum dimensions of craft from Medley Bridge to Newbridge

Headroom 8´5˝ (2.56m) at Godstow Bridge
   Note Osney Br. is 7´6˝ (2.28m)

Length	110´0˝ (33.52m) at Godstow Lock
Beam	15´1˝ (4.59m) at Northmoor Lock
Draught	3´0˝ (0.91m) in main fairway between Oxford and Lechlade

Where the river widened into Port Meadow, so it narrows to the confines of Godstow, its lock and its tiny bridge, away from the weir stream and the backwaters which run between Pixey Mead and Wolvercote from the Duke's Cut. There are sailing and rowing from these backwaters; St Edward's School in Oxford has its boathouse here just below the famous *Trout Inn*, where Colin Dexter's Inspector Morse used to soliloquise on the criminal mind over a beer or instruct his hungry side-kick Lewis on the niceties of the English language.

Mooring for the *Trout Inn*, or for any other purpose, while still reasonably close to civilisation is available in the reach between Godstow Bridge and the A34 Oxford western bypass crossing, known as Thames Bridge; not recommended for a night stop unless you are very hard of hearing! It is some time before you will arrive that you can

---

Godstow Lock Daytime only
Godstow Road, Lower Wolvercote, Oxford
OX2 8PJ ☎ 01865 554784
110'0'' (33.52m) long x 16'3'' (4.95m) wide
Rise (fall) 5'2'' (1.57m)
Max. draught 5'0'' (1.52m)
Facilities None.

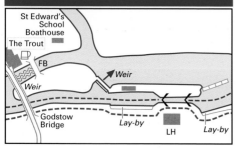

King's Lock Daytime only
Wolvercote, Oxford OX2 8PY ☎ 01865 553403
113'1'' (34.46m) long x 16'4'' (4.97m) wide
Rise (fall) 2'6'' (0.77m)
Max. draught 5'6'' (1.67m)
Manual operation only (see notes at end of section).
Facilities Water tap for cans, campsite.

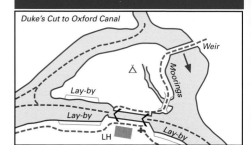

view the well-kept gardens of the keeper at King's Lock for the river winds in northerly, then easterly, then westerly meanders across the level flood plain below Wytham Hill away to your left.

There are plenty of mooring places on the right-hand bank, opposite the towing path and finally also, in the weir-stream outfall from King's Weir, there is mooring on the lock island, with the permission of the lock-keeper only and if space is available. There is also a campsite on the island with 10 pitches but facilities are restricted to a water tap point and gents' urinal.

Immediately clear of King's Lock going upstream, look out for craft emerging from the Duke's Cut into the Thames on your right. This is the easier entrance to the Oxford Canal but available only to craft already licensed with British Waterways and not exceeding the limiting dimensions of 6´10˝ (2.10m) beam, 7´0˝ (2.12m) headroom, 72´0˝ (21.95m) length, and 3´3˝ (1.00m) draught. The Duke's Cut has the distinction of being the most northerly stretch of the Thames, although the main fairway of the river to hold this record is half a mile upstream, where the current sweeps round in a double bend from east to south and then east again into Hagley Pool where the Seacourt Stream starts its journey. Our upstream course starts to press westwards again and in another half mile you may see the village and church of Cassington away to

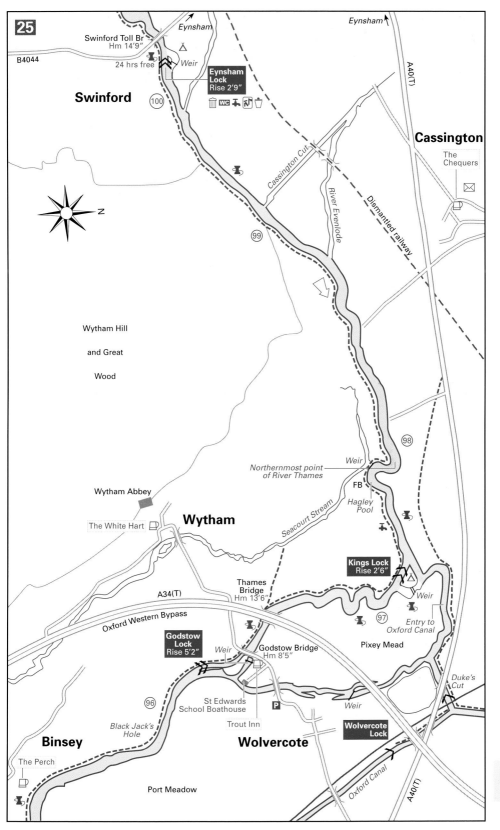

B4044

Eynsham ↗

Eynsham ↑

A40(T)

Swinford Toll Br
Hm 14'9"

24 hrs free

Weir

Eynsham Lock
Rise 2'9"

Swinford

100

🏛 WC ⚓ 🔌 🗑

Cassington

The Chequers

Cassington Cut

River Evenlode

Dismantled railway

99

Wytham Hill

and Great

Wood

Weir

Northernmost point
of River Thames

98

FB

*Hagley
Pool*

Wytham Abbey

Wytham

The White Hart

Seacourt Stream

Kings Lock
Rise 2'6"

A34(T)

Oxford Western Bypass

Thames
Bridge
Hm 13'6"

Weir

97

*Entry to
Oxford Canal*

Pixey Mead

Godstow Lock
Rise 5'2"

Weir

Godstow Bridge
Hm 8'5"

96

St Edwards
School Boathouse

P

Weir

Duke's
Cut

*Black Jack's
Hole*

Binsey

The Perch

Trout Inn

Wolvercote

Port Meadow

**Wolvercote
Lock**

Oxford Canal

A40(T)

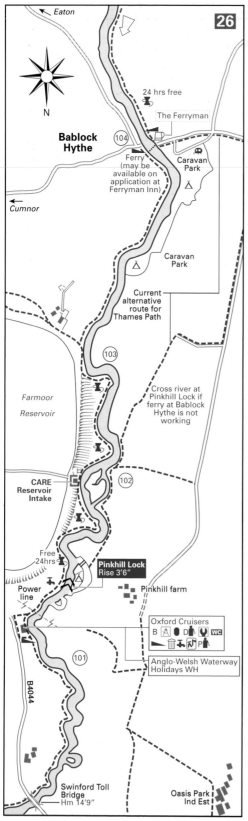

← Eaton

24 hrs free

The Ferryman

Bablock Hythe (104)

Ferry
(may be
available on
application at
Ferryman Inn)

Caravan
Park

← Cumnor

Caravan
Park

Current
alternative
route for
Thames Path

(103)

*Farmoor
Reservoir*

Cross river at
Pinkhill Lock if
ferry at Bablock
Hythe is not
working

CARE
Reservoir
Intake

(102)

Free
24hrs

Pinkhill Lock
Rise 3'6"

Power
line

Pinkhill farm

Oxford Cruisers
B A ⬤ D 💧 ⚡ WC
▬ 🗑 ♿ 🛒 P

(101)

Anglo-Welsh Waterway
Holidays WH

B4044

Swinford Toll
Bridge
Hm 14'9"

Oasis Park
Ind Est

---

your right, but there is no access to it from the river and even if there was you might be seriously injured attempting to cross the busy A40 trunk road which lies in between. However, there are some secluded moorings on this side and then the River Evenlode, a tributary which has lent its name to more than one navigation inspector's launch over the years, comes in on the right. Just above the 99-mile mark is the end of the short canal which allowed barges to be worked up to Cassington Mill. Hereabouts there are quiet moorings again before Eynsham Lock on the right and immediately below the lock on the left, although it is discourteous (and probably not very wise) to moor so as to obstruct the entrance to the sanitary station.

Above us now on the left is Beacon Hill on the edge of Wytham Great Wood. Across the valley lies the village of Eynsham from which the lock takes its name. First on the right is the old wharf stream which served the village and then the outfall of the weir, the gantry from which permit holders may fish. There are also camping facilities on the mid-river island formed by the lock and the weir stream.

Above Eynsham Lock there are further moorings below the ancient curves of Swinford Toll Bridge. Eynsham is the last village of a reasonable size close to the river

Eynsham Lock Daytime only
Swinford, Oxford OX8 1BX ☎ 01865 881324
113'3" (34·51m) long x 16'4" (4·97m) wide
Rise (fall) 2'9" (0·84m)
Max. draught 5'5" (1·65m)
Manual operation only (see notes at end of section).
Facilities Chemical toilet disposal and pump-out unit, refuse disposal, drinking water tap and hose for tanks, toilets, campsite on lock island. Free 24hr moorings upstream of head lay-by.
Angling Fishing available from walkway across weir structure only, use towing path from Swinford Bridge, no parking at lock, roadside parking where available on B4044.

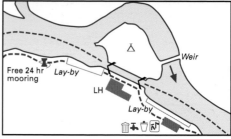

Free 24 hr
mooring   Lay-by

Weir

LH

Lay-by

🗑 🛒 ♿ 🛒

before Lechlade, which is 24 miles upstream. So here is an advisable place to moor for topping up one's store cupboard. Swinford Toll Bridge is the only other bridge besides Whitchurch which still collects a fee from every vehicle – pedestrians may pass free of charge – but which is in dire need of repair. Such necessity is hampered by an Act of Parliament with which bureaucracy refuses to tamper (and will no doubt continue to do nothing about until the bridge falls down and/or someone is killed by crumbling masonry). Navigate through the bridge with care – your passage is free – and enjoy the helming practice which now taxes you as the river winds towards and away from the Oxford Road in a series of five left- and five right-hand bends towards the Oxford Cruisers base at Farmoor.

Take note that this is the last major yard upstream on the Thames. There is a small yard at Lechlade but Oxford Cruisers is the final point for some 24 miles for things like marine diesel, petrol and the various little items that make a motor cruiser go phut-phut-phut or a narrow boat go thud-thud-thud . . . you have been warned! At the downstream end of the yard their drive will take you off to the main road or there is a path along the upstream end to it where you can turn right into the village of Farmoor for shops and post office.

Leaving Oxford Cruisers, in less than half a mile you will pass the ox-bow below Pinkhill Lock (on your right) and then the lock itself comes into view rather suddenly on the left with its weir stream discharging on your right. The lay-by for the lock is a short one on the left-hand side of the lock-cut, but be prepared to keep clear of the cut until the last minute as you will have difficulty seeing anything coming down out of the lock.

The river leaves Pinkhill Lock and continues to wander in and out of the curving bankside of the Farmoor Reservoir. There are several good moorings along the old towing path which runs on the reservoir side, but the Thames Path has had to divert to the opposite bank in view of the demise of the ferry at Bablock Hythe – one of the last to disappear and one that may well have been revived by the landlord of the newly named Ferryman Inn there. The keeper at Pinkhill Lock should be able to advise. Just below 102 miles is the reservoir's intake – it is advisable to keep clear – and at 103 miles we leave the Farmoor embankment and set course back southwards for Bablock Hythe

Pinkhill Lock Daytime only
Farmoor, Oxford OX8 1JH ☎ 01865 881452
113'6" (34·59m) long × 16'1" (4·90m) wide
Rise (fall) 3'6" (1·05m)
Max. draught 5'4" (1·62m)
Manual operation only (see notes at end of section).
Facilities Drinking water tap for cans only, campsite on mid-river island, toilets, shop.
Angling Fishing available to Weir Permit holders from the main weir which is crossed by the Thames Path.

and its vast caravan park which lies as a string along the west bank for more than half a mile. At the Ferryman Inn, the road from Stanton Harcourt to the west ends at a slip into the river and on the eastern bank the lane from Cumnor ends in the slip which was used by the ferry between the two. Nowadays the two slips are available free of charge for the public to launch light craft during daylight hours. Note that, before slipping or entering the Thames from other waterways, all craft must be registered with the Environment Agency at Reading, or by contacting the relevant District Navigation Office, which in the case of this, Upper Thames District, is located at Osney Lock (see page 14).

Equidistant between the villages of Northmoor and Appleton lies Northmoor Lock. There are footpaths to both villages in opposite directions on opposite sides of the river; the footpath to Northmoor leaving the towing path from a point opposite the Eaton Plantation and the path to Appleton running back from the bank a little way above the lock. The track from the lock into Appleton village is the private property of the farm owner.

There is a campsite just below the lock on the Thames Path, details ☎ 01865 862908. At this lock note the weir is made up of paddles and rymers, an early system of weir gates also used for flash locks.

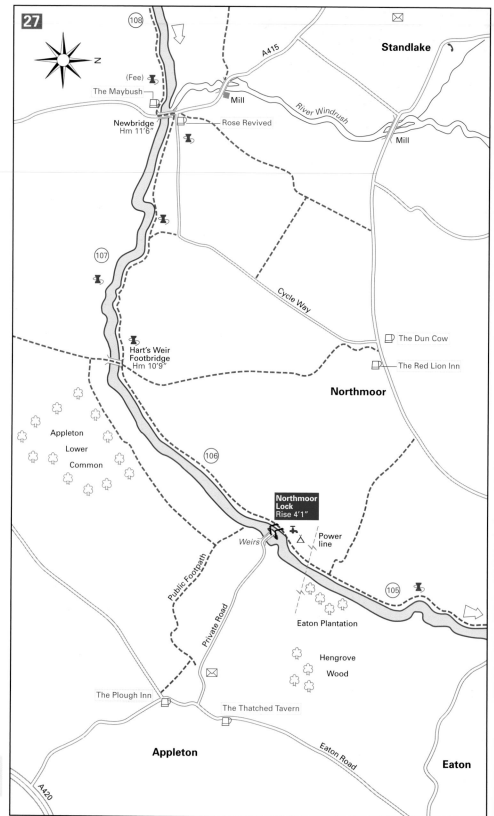

27

N

108

(Fee)

The Maybush

Newbridge
Hm 11'6"

Mill

Rose Revived

Standlake

A415

River Windrush

Mill

107

Cycle Way

Hart's Weir
Footbridge
Hm 10'9"

The Dun Cow

The Red Lion Inn

Northmoor

Appleton

Lower

Common

106

Northmoor
Lock
Rise 4'1"

Weirs

Power
line

105

Public Footpath

Private Road

Eaton Plantation

Hengrove

Wood

The Plough Inn

The Thatched Tavern

Appleton

Eaton Road

Eaton

A420

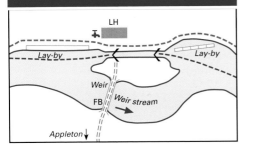

Further upstream we come to Hart's Weir Footbridge, site of an old flash weir which finally disappeared, according to Thacker, the historian, in about 1880. The weir was more often referred to as Ridge's, as was the subsequent footbridge, built at the time of the weir's demolition. Why it is now called Hart's remains a bit of a mystery, although our expert alleges that the name was given to more than one such weir but not this. Peter Chaplin's *The Thames from Source to Tideway* merely labels it 'FB'; I don't blame him! More importantly, from here, where there is a good mooring above the bridge on the right-hand side, a footpath takes one to Northmoor village – a little over a mile to the north. And another mile upstream will bring us to the end of our first truly rural section where *The Rose Revived* and *The Maybush* jockey for the privilege of quenching our thirst or feeding us. There should be adequate moorings for patrons at either inn but if coming upstream I have usually succumbed to the first, *The Rose Revived*, which stands on my side of the river and below the narrow bridge of Newbridge under which one must pass to land at *The Maybush*.

The Thames Path

Leaving Binsey, the Thames Path stays on the western bank past Godstow Lock and under the bridges, leaving the Oxford bypass bridge behind. In places, as the Thames meanders towards King's Lock, it is possible to take a short cut away from the river across the meadows to the lock which is clearly visible from Thames Bridge. Note, however, that these short cuts are not public rights of way. Beyond the lock it is safer to follow the towing path proper as you will have to cross the Seacourt Stream weir by the footbridge provided. The Path now follows the southern, left-hand bank to Eynsham Lock and beyond under Swinford Toll Bridge, negotiating all the meanders of the stream as far as Oxford Cruisers' base just off the B4044 Oxford Road which leads up to Farmoor village. Here you must use the boatyard's driveway to exit onto the road by turning left off the riverside just before the dock and walking about 250 yards up the road to a sign which points you back to the river. Cross a footbridge and turn south again towards Pinkhill Lock.

With no ferry running at Bablock Hythe you will have to cross the river here, but note that the right of way stays outside the hedge to the lock area and a stile allows you to retrace your steps to cross the top lock gates and follow the signed footpath over the weir. From here the path crosses a rough meadow to meet the river again at its next loop after the lock and then follows the main channel until it disappears again towards the Farmoor Reservoir Intake. At this point the footpath runs alongside a backwater which is a haven for wildlife and water plants, until the main channel returns for about another 250 yards. From here you must strike out south-westwards along a faintly visible path across fields away from the river to join Steady's Lane, a track you must follow which leads to your right up to Steady's Farm and Stanton Harcourt village. In a quarter of a mile you will come to a swing gate on your left leading to a bridleway which takes you for a mile before coming to a lane where you must turn left. At the lane's own turn to the right in about 500 yards, come off it by keeping straight on, on the track signposted to Bablock Hythe, and you will arrive at the river beside the *Ferryman Inn*. Here turn right and continue along the river bank on the original towing path, past the Lock Field Campsite and Northmoor Lock, (from where it may be possible to walk into Appleton along the private road), then around the end of Hart's Weir Footbridge, or Ridge's as it used to be known, until you reach the garden of *The Rose Revived* at Newbridge.

Angling

The only weir fishing permitted on this section to holders of the Weir Permit is at Eynsham and Pinkhill. At Eynsham fishing is available from the walkway across the weir structure only at the discretion of the lock-keeper. There are toilets below the lock and the weir is reached by crossing the bottom lock gates from the towing path. At Pinkhill the weir is crossed by the Thames Path so that fishing has to be conducted with a modicum of consideration for users of the path. The lock-keeper's permission should be obtained as always before fishing.

North Oxford AS has water at Godstow. Day tickets are available from Oxford Alliance agents. Oxford Angling and Preservation Society has water at Eynsham while the *Ferryman Inn* at Bablock Hythe issues day tickets for water 1½ miles downstream on the same bank as the inn (west). Upstream from here, fishing is reserved by Appleton and Tubney AS. At Newbridge both hotels, the *Rose Revived* with ¾ mile on the Thames and the tributary Windrush and the *Maybush* with ½ mile, have fishing tickets available. Other societies represented in the area are Witney AS, Newland AC (above Newbridge) and Stroud AA. More precise details should be available from tackle shops shown in the *Directory* or from the hotels and inns mentioned.

Directory

BOATYARDS, MARINAS, CHANDLERIES, TRIPPING AND HIRE

Bossom's Boat Yard Ltd
Near Binsey Village, Oxford OX2 0NL ☎ 01865 247780. Boat builders, repairs and renovations, brokerage, narrow boat hulls up to 70′, moorings, chandlery, storage, slipway, toilets, water. (TBTA)

Oxford Cruisers Ltd
Boat Hire Centre, Eynsham, Oxford OX8 1DA ☎ 01865 881698. Boat builders, sales, repairs, marine engineers, diesel fuel, petrol, *Calor Gas*, chandlery, groceries, permanent moorings, hardstanding, slipway, water point, refuse disposal, pump-out service, toilets, car park. (TBTA)

Anglo Welsh Waterway Holidays,
The Boat Hire Centre, Eynsham, Oxford, OX8 1DA. Booking is at Bristol: 2 The Hide Market, West Street, Bristol BS2 0BH ☎ 0117 3041122 or 0800 0186323

EMERGENCY FUEL SUPPLIES
See note under this heading on page 23
Farmoor Service Station
Petrol, diesel
Oxford Road, Farmoor, Oxon ☎ 01865 862922/864438. ¼ mile from Oxford Cruisers. **Note** Oxford Cruisers normally supplies both petrol and diesel.

ROWING, SAILING AND CRUISING CLUBS AND TUITION
Medley Sailing Club
Binsey, Oxford OX2 0NL Dinghy sailing. (RYA)

St Edward's School Boat Club
39 Godstow Road, Wolvercote, Oxford OX2 8AJ ☎ 01865 56140. Rowing. (ARA)

Oxford Sailing Club
Farmoor Reservoir, Cumnor Road, Farmoor, Oxon OX2 9NS ☎ 01865 863201. Not on the river. Dinghy sailing. (RYA)

Cokethorpe School Boat Club
The Rose Revived, Newbridge, Standlake, Witney, Oxon OX8 7QD. Rowing. (ARA)

PUBLIC LAUNCHING SITES
Bablock Hythe
- West bank at old ferry landing at end of Bablock Hythe Road via Eaton village
- East bank at old ferry landing beside Ferryman Inn, 2 miles from Stanton Harcourt

FISHING TACKLE SHOPS
Fat Phil's Angling Centre
334-6, Abingdon Road, Oxford ☎ 01865 201020

Dell's Fishing Tackle Ltd
136 Oxford Road, Cowley, Oxon ☎ 01865 711410

North Oxford Tackle
95 Islip Road, Summertown, Oxford ☎ 01865 556955

State Fishing Tackle
19 Fettiplace Road, Witney, Oxon ☎ 01993 702587

HOTELS, INNS AND RESTAURANTS
Perch Inn Binsey Lane, Binsey. Bar snacks and full meals, midday and evenings; barbecues at weekends. Moorings against towpath, short walk to pub across the meadows.

White Hart Inn Wytham ☎ 01865 244372. Real ale and excellent restaurant. Moor above Godstow Bridge and take lane to Wytham under western bypass.

Trout Inn Godstow Road, Wolvercote. Bar

Newbridge and *The Rose Revived*

snacks, lunches and dinners; riverside terrace. Moor above or below Godstow Bridge on west (towing path) bank and cross bridge.

Chequers Inn The Green, Cassington. Bar meals and snacks.

Talbot Inn Oxford Road, Eynsham. Bar meals, snacks, lunches and dinners; takeaway menu. Free moorings above Eynsham Lock, cross Swinford Bridge, pub 500yds.

Ferryman Inn Bablock Hythe, Northmoor ☎ 01865 880028. Bar meals, snacks and dining facilities; food served all day in summer. Free mooring above the old ferry slipway, caravan and residential park close by, fishing tickets available.

Thatched Tavern Eaton Road, Appleton ☎ 01865 864814. Bar snacks and dining facilities midday and evenings; book for Sunday lunch. Moor above Northmoor Lock on the off side where the footpath leads to Appleton.

Plough Inn Appleton.

Red Lion Northmoor.

Maybush Inn Newbridge ☎ 01865 300624. Bar meals and snacks, also full dining midday and evenings. Moorings outside are tricky, try below Newbridge on free public moorings. Fishing tickets available.

Rose Revived Inn Newbridge ☎ 01865 300221. Bar meals and snacks. Excellent restaurant for lunch and dinner. B&B. Fishing tickets available. 24-hr mooring alongside (free).

BUS AND COACH SERVICES
Binsey to Newbridge
Beyond Oxford there are fairly frequent buses (Stagecoach route 100) through Eynsham to Witney by way of Farmoor. A weekday service (Thames Travel route 18) runs every two hours between Oxford and Clanfield, calling at Eynsham, Northmoor and Bablock Hythe.

Bus Operators:
- Stagecoach Oxford ☎ 01865 772250
- Thames Travel ☎ 01491 837988

149

A discourse on the unique privilege of hand operating a hand-operated lock

It must have been around 1942 when I was first introduced to the Thames. I had been sent to a small boarding school near Woking and both parents, being stationed near London, could visit me from time to time. But what, in the middle of the Second World War, was there to entertain a seven-year-old boy at weekends? The school principal was helpful. The Aldershot and District Traction Company ran buses from Woking to Chertsey Bridge, Guildford or Bagshot. Guildford was interesting – your father could row a boat on the Wey from under the Town Bridge for half-a-crown an hour – but Chertsey Bridge was far more exciting. For here was the real Thames and above the bridge was, and still is, Chertsey Lock; in those days the paddle gear and the gate opening were all done by hand exactly as they are today from King's Lock and the locks upstream.

I must have caused the old gentleman who kept Chertsey Lock a number of anxious moments as I eagerly stepped forward to help work the sluices whenever a boat came in sight. But the ritual became so ingrained that I became blasé about red-tip-up-open, white-tip-up-closed for them, to the point where I decided that if the wheel wouldn't spin the way I wanted it to then it had to go the other way . . . I was finally levered away from the lock by the return of that epitome of the Edwardian Thames, the Salter's Steamer. *Cliveden* would go upstream to Windsor and *Hampton Court* would run down to Kingston. Our usual run was to Windsor and back from Chertsey aboard *Cliveden* but, if money was tight, I had to be content with Staines and return. The next time, many years later, that I went to look at the lock at Chertsey I was dismayed to see that those spinning wheels on top of the gates had disappeared. But childhood memories came flooding back when I came across them again at King's the first time I did the whole river from Teddington to 1¼ miles short of Hannington Bridge – in a motor-cruiser (sshh!)

So, from one who first spun the wheel over 50 years ago, remember, if the red tip is up the sluice is open and, if the white tip is up, it is closed. Also remember to close the sluice *after* you have opened the gate – sometimes the leakage from the other end can change the level before you can get to grips with the balance beams – but make sure you do, otherwise you will waste water and not get a change in level when the gates have been shut for the next locking.

Instructions for manual operation of powered lock mechanisms are displayed at the relevant positions. As a programme of improvements is carried out, such instructions will change. At some locks, boat crews may now be able to work locks out of duty hours with a low power-setting but, even at these, manual operation is possible in cases of total power failure.

Old Father Thames at St John's Lock

12. Newbridge to Lechlade and Cricklade

Distances

16.49 miles (Newbridge – *The Rose Revived* – to Lechlade Bridge)

11.08 miles (Lechlade Bridge to Cricklade High Bridge)

Maximum dimensions of craft from Newbridge to Round House, Inglesham (practical navigable limit)

Headroom 9'9" (2.97m) at Eaton Footbridge
Length 109'10" (33.52m) at Buscot Lock
Beam 14'8" (4.59m) at Buscot Lock
Draught 3'0" (0.91m) in main fairway between Oxford and Lechlade.

Above the winding point at Inglesham the river narrows and becomes fast flowing, making it unsuitable for anything but small dinghies and canoes, although there is a right of navigation from High Bridge at Cricklade and this portion of the river is patrolled by the River Authority at least once a year – usually by dinghy!

The new bridge at Newbridge is the most convenient stepping-off point for the final cruise up to Lechlade, 16½ miles of idyllic scenery rich with its own history of a very different river from that below Oxford or even again below Henley. One might take a whole day, or just a morning, to complete the trip through the last six locks, motoring or sculling between the reeds, through oak-lined avenues, or twisting through pastures of moody cattle. Traffic is normally light – few wish to venture beyond Oxford and many with their larger craft are physically unable to do so. Some perhaps regret the passing of those traditional Broads-built cruisers which came from Herbert Woods' yard, with fiendishly clever wheelhouses and screens which could disappear into the gunwales of one's cruiser with breathtaking speed and ease, all counterbalanced on runners in the style of the ubiquitous double-hung sash window of Georgian times. Designed to pass below Potter Heigham Bridge on the River Thurne, a number of these Broads-built cruisers appeared on the Thames – able to dodge Osney Bridge – as forerunners of the large fleets of GRP craft which the many hire cruiser firms of the 70s and 80s imported from Norfolk, a number of which still ply from the much lesser number of firms now operating.

Two miles above Newbridge, through level farmland and a number of sharp bends on the right, we come to the farm and hamlet of Shifford, followed on the same side of the river by the entry of the Great Brook, a tempting-looking channel to explorers but unfortunately unnavigable. Shifford Lock is just under ½ mile from this point and lies on your right as you approach from downstream. There's a side weir to the left and then, further over to the left, the main weir stream outfall which is navigable by small craft to Duxford Ford, still passable except in flood, by walkers (with boots) who wish to rejoin the towpath a good mile before Tenfoot Bridge, where the official Thames Path rejoins the river. Shifford is the last pound lock site established on the Thames in 1898.

The tree-lined lock cut finishes just short of the hamlet of Chimney opposite which is the main weir. Halfway along the cut is the footbridge which carries the path from Duxford over the river to connect with the original towpath which crossed at this point. Although there is a new footbridge from the footpath across to the south bank of the lock cut, there is no right of way at present above the lock on the north bank. There are suitable moorings above the weir on both

Shifford Lock Daytime only
Aston, Witney, Oxon OX18 2EJ ☎ 01367 870247
113'8" (34·64m) long x 15'1" (4·59m) wide
Rise (fall) 7'4" (2·23m)
Max. draught 5'3" (1·60m)
Manual operation only (see notes at end of previous section).
Facilities Water and hose for tank filling, moorings, electric launch charging point, shop.
Angling Fishing available at main weir and near house weir. Access from Chimney hamlet ¾ mile.

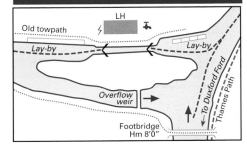

151

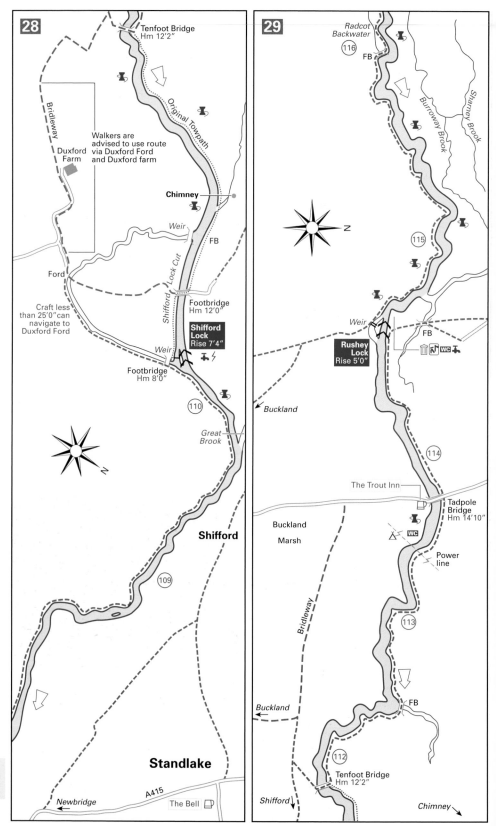

28

Tenfoot Bridge
Hm 12'2"

Original Towpath

Bridleway

Duxford Farm

Walkers are advised to use route via Duxford Ford and Duxford farm

Chimney

Weir

FB

Shifford Lock Cut

Ford

Footbridge
Hm 12'0"

Craft less than 25'0" can navigate to Duxford Ford

Shifford Lock
Rise 7'4"

Weir

Footbridge
Hm 8'0"

110

N

Great Brook

Shifford

109

Standlake

Newbridge

A415

The Bell

29

Radcot Backwater

116

FB

Burroway Brook

Sharney Brook

115

N

Weir

Rushey Lock
Rise 5'0"

FB

WC

Buckland

114

The Trout Inn

Tadpole Bridge
Hm 14'10"

WC

Power line

Buckland Marsh

Bridleway

113

Buckland

FB

112

Tenfoot Bridge
Hm 12'2"

Shifford

Chimney

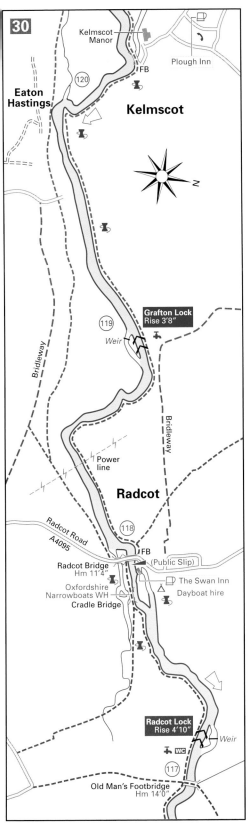

banks before we come to Tenfoot Bridge which brings the Thames Path walker back from the detour onto the towing path proper. From here on, the south bank paths lead to Buckland and Buckland Marsh as well as back to Duxford Farm and Hinton Waldrist. Around here, the river meanders through flat country while the view is restricted by levees for much of the route between Tenfoot and Tadpole Bridges.

At Tadpole Bridge is the well-known *Trout Inn*. Although we have already encountered others and will find another further upstream, this recently refurbished hostelry has a garden, camping facilities, moorings, food, ale, and fishing day tickets. A mile ahead stands Rushey Lock; with Shifford it makes two of the most isolated on the river. Access to the lock for walkers and fishermen is along the Thames Path which follows the track from Tadpole Bridge. Cars are not allowed to use the track but must be parked at the bridge.

Just above Rushey Lock, a couple of sharp bends to right and then left bring one to the mouth of Sharney Brook and the Burroway Brook, both running through part of the flat and perhaps rather boring water-meadows with not even a B-road in sight. The river wriggles as far as Old Man's Bridge for two miles from here – striking north, west, south and even southeast at times – but eventually progressing in a general westerly direction until, just above the last-named footbridge, we come to the approach to Radcot Lock,

Rushey Lock Daytime only
Tadpole Bridge, Buckland, nr Faringdon, Oxon SN7 8RF ☎ 01367 870218
113'6" (34·59m) long x 15'1" (4·59m) wide
Rise (fall) 6'0" (1·82m)
Max. draught 5'0" (1·52m)
Manual operation only (see notes at end of previous section).
Facilities Chemical toilet disposal, pump-out unit, drinking water for cans only, toilets, refuse disposal.
Angling Fishing available at main weir on downstream side and south bank only.

perhaps a misnomer, for the village and the bridge of the same name lie a mile upstream to the southwest. The lock, which is of fairly recent origin – a little over 100 years old (compared with Rushey which was 200 in 1990) – replaced Clarke's Weir which disappeared around 1870 at the same time as Harper's, now the site of the Old Man's Footbridge. This means that Clarke's and Harper's Weirs with their attendant flash-locks at 400 yards apart were closer even than Goring and Cleeve, which now have the distinction of having the shortest reach between them on the upper Thames.

In just under a mile the river comes out of its deserted countryside towards the bustling activity which surrounds the *Swan Inn* at Radcot Bridge, the first major road crossing since Newbridge. Here the navigation bears to the left away from the backwater leading to private moorings, originally known as Willmer's Moorings after their former proprietors, but now controlled by the Swan Inn. At the Swan there is a public launching site, although permission to use it must be obtained from the landlord first. There is limited parking and only light craft can be launched during daylight. The inn also has day tickets and information on fishing in the locality. Between Cradle Bridge, which carries the towing path over the re-entry of the original river course on your left, and the new Radcot Bridge which crosses the

artificial cut ahead, made in the eighteenth century, there are temporary moorings for visiting craft on the south bank.

Radcot Bridge is reckoned to be one of the trickiest to navigate on the river, particularly if coming downstream when you may easily be accompanied by a following wind! The approach consists of a double bend, avoiding what appears to be, and originally was, the obvious channel which ducks under the original Radcot Bridge. But the new cut, deemed necessary to accommodate a hoped-for increase in traffic from the new Thames and Severn Canal which was opened in 1789, turns north and then suddenly east to negotiate a newer bridge. Having a 'canal-ish' look about it, it is by that well-known canal engineer William Jessop and dates from 1790. The elder bridge is apparently the oldest on the river, having been established in the early thirteenth century under King John by the monastery and nunnery at Faringdon. It was largely reconstructed some time towards the end of the fourteenth century. New Bridge was only named such as it appears to be younger than Radcot, but probably only by about 50 years.

The problem for the navigator with Mr Jessop's bridge is that, having swung your cruiser to starboard in the downstream direction to shoot the bridge, there is little you can do if a cruiser is approaching upstream and is too close to the bridge (and your boat) to take avoiding action. Hopefully the current, the prevailing wind and her helmsman slamming her gear-lever into reverse will give you the room to which you are entitled (one of the reasons for low speed – certainly well below the speed limit).

Radcot also had a mill – known as Monk Mill – on the Thames, somewhere in the area of Cradle Bridge, but even Thacker has two shots at trying to locate it. Leaving Radcot and its claims to the civilised rural life with caravan park and 'modern amenities', we enter a fairly straight section after our double bend after the bridge in a southwesterly direction for half a mile; then comes a sharp turn to the northwest, known as Hell's Turn, next a few ripples and a final bend back westwards to the tail of Grafton Lock which is to the right; weir stream outfall to our left.

From Grafton Lock we have a reasonably straight course for a mile with occasional quiet moorings against the towing path as far as Eaton Hastings, on the left bank, where the river makes one of its fiendish U-turns – this one is right-handed – and then switches to the left towards the village of Kelmscot

Radcot Lock Daytime only
Clanfield, nr Faringdon, Oxon SN7 8JT
☎ 01367 240676
113'6'' (34·59m) long x 15'0'' (4·57m) wide
Rise (fall) 4'10'' (1·48m)
Max. draught 4'11'' (1·49m)
Manual operation only (see notes at end of previous section).
Facilities Toilets, drinking water for cans and hose for bulk supplies.
Angling Fishing available on south bank of weir stream on downstream side, space strictly limited on first-come-first-served basis.

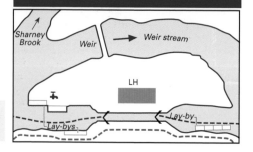

Grafton Lock Daytime only
Clanfield, nr. Faringdon, Oxon OX18 2RY
☎ 01367 810251
113'6'' (34·59m) long x 15'1'' (4·59m) wide
Rise (fall) 3'8'' (1·11m)
Max. draught 4'9'' (1·44m)
Manual operation only (see notes at end of
previous section).
Facilities Drinking water for cans and hose
for bulk supplies.
Angling Fishing available from walkway on
weir structure only, access by footpaths
from B4449.

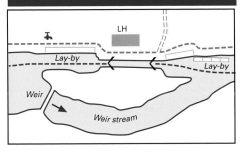

about which there is a confusion as to its spelling (one or two 'Ts'). I'll stick to one as that's the OS version. There are moorings on the right for a visit to the village and Kelmscot Manor (which is only open once a month) as it houses a museum and art collection relating to celebrated nineteenth-century artist, poet and socialist, William Morris. Also at Kelmscot are a telephone box and *The Plough Inn* for bar snacks and meals but there are no shops in the village.

Beyond Kelmscot where there are further moorings above the village we come to Eaton Footbridge which stands on the site of the last flash-lock on the Thames. The weir here, known as Hart's to that indefatigable pair Thacker and Taunt, historian and photographer of the Thames respectively, caused much anguish to the boatmen, especially in winter when there was barely headroom under the catwalk. It was not until 1938 that it was demolished, leaving clear passage between Buscot and Grafton, but the long forgotten mill for which it had doubtless been constructed had given way to an inn, *The Anchor*. This was burnt to the ground in 1979 and has never been rebuilt. Confusingly, the locals around Kelmscot often refer to the old pub as *The Weir*, possibly because the tenant of the pub was usually the weir-keeper. And, even more confusingly, a respected fishing annual still suggests that day and season tickets are available from it for 3 miles of fishing! The

footbridge is not a towing path crossing but links Kelmscot with the villages of Eaton Hastings or Buscot, to which the river now winds. The Oxfordshire/Gloucestershire boundary comes into the river a few hundred yards above Eaton Footbridge where a towing path footbridge crosses the entry of a small brook.

Now come twists and turns towards and away from Buscot village, the final sweep having on the right-hand bank an access bridge which crosses the outfall stream of the new weir. Do not try and approach it but follow the bend and then, curving back to the right, you will come to the lock with the old weir-pool on your left. This is now a National Trust area, beyond the weir-pool, with picnic site and car parking for river visitors. In the village beyond are a post office and stores only a short walk from the lock across the lower lock-gates, the side weir and the footbridge which crosses a backwater from the church. Curiously, the church is ½ mile from the village, well above the lock. Approaching Buscot Lock from above is difficult since there are weir streams leaving the channel virtually simultaneously on both banks. Sidling up to the lay-by on the left can be fraught, especially if the new weir is running strongly. Coming upstream you should have no problems if you keep clear of the outfall of the old weir. Do not get too close in on the lay-by or you may find it difficult to nose out and into the lock when signalled.

The 'wriggles' of the river prior to Buscot Lock could now be said to get worse as we make our way towards the highest lock on the Thames to meet 'Old Father Thames' himself. On the left a backwater sets off over a small weir by Buscot Church, built as part of Campbell Curtis' nineteenth-century scheme to bring industry to the area and establish a model village. However, the industry, started not unreasonably with a brick kiln whose products were loaded at Buscot Wharf about a quarter of a mile below the lock for shipment downstream, did not survive when Curtis attempted to sell brandy distilled from beet to the French. A sharp right-left-right bend sets us towards the main A417 Faringdon Road and as soon as the river almost touches it, separated by a cascade of willow trees, it takes a sharp right turn, to face away from the spire of Lechlade's parish church – as if to cheat the weary traveller of his hoped for destination. In fact you may only view your final quarry over your stern, not once but twice, for a

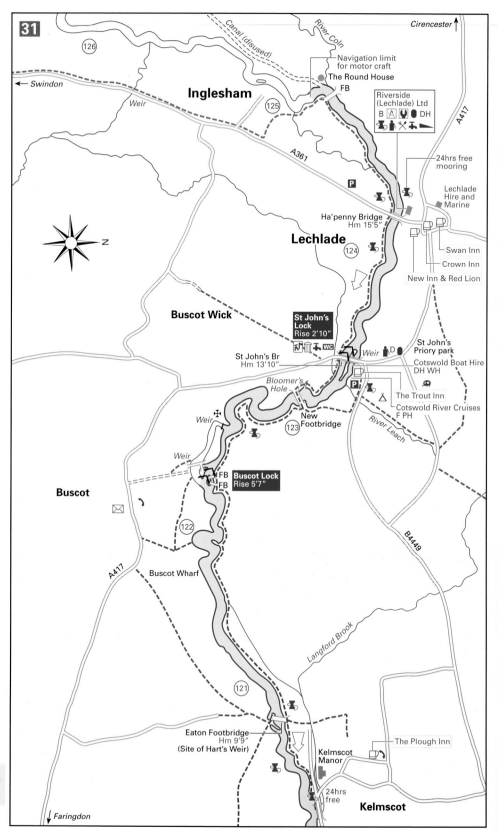

31

126

← Swindon

Canal (disused)

River Coln

Cirencester ↑

Navigation limit
for motor craft

The Round House
FB

Inglesham

Weir

125

A361

A417

Riverside
(Lechlade) Ltd
B 🏕 🚻 ● DH

24hrs free
mooring

Lechlade
Hire and
Marine

P

Ha'penny Bridge
Hm 15'5"

Lechlade

124

Swan Inn

Crown Inn

New Inn & Red Lion

Buscot Wick

St John's
Lock
Rise 2'10"

WC

St John's Br
Hm 13'10"

Weir

St John's
Priory park

Cotswold Boat Hire
DH WH

Bloomer's
Hole

The Trout Inn

Weir

New
Footbridge

123

P

River Leach

Cotswold River Cruises
F PH

Weir

Weir

FB
FB

Buscot Lock
Rise 5'7"

Buscot

122

B4449

A417

Buscot Wharf

Langford Brook

121

Eaton Footbridge
Hm 9'9"
(Site of Hart's Weir)

Kelmscot
Manor

The Plough Inn

24hrs
free

Kelmscot

↓ Faringdon

similar twist takes place some 400 yards further on at Bloomer's Hole, a basin where the Countryside Agency have installed the new footbridge to take the Thames Path up to the next lock by way of the river rather than the diversion described in our previous edition.

Out of the basin a left turn restores one's faith and sense of direction towards St John's Bridge and the lock. The lock cut is on the left and the weir stream on the right, although you may well be confused by the large number of craft moored in the weir stream on the *Trout Inn* moorings. A recent addition to the vessels here will be those of Cotswold Boat Hire who operate both day and weekly holiday craft. Just below the moorings the River Leach (which gives Lechlade its name) comes into the Thames on your right. Start preparing for St John's Lock as soon as you are in the lock cut. There is a pile and waling lay-by on the right before the bridge and then a basin between the bridge and the lock where there is a quayside lay-by over on the left. Here there is also a sanitary station and refuse point. On the opposite side of the basin a side weir discharges from the main weir stream which runs to the main weir on the downstream side of the bridge next to the *Trout Inn*. If the side weir is running strongly you may be well advised to await the lock below the bridge, although there is no means of landing from the lay-by here.

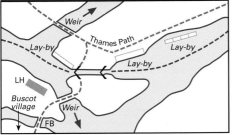

St John's Lock has an unrivalled view of the town of Lechlade across the water-meadows and while attractively laid out with the slumbering sculpture of 'Old Father Thames', facilities for waiting above the lock have always been rather spartan. The river turns sharply into the lock and a new convenient lay-by has been constructed on the right bank going downstream before the turn. There is another shorter lay-by on the same side just above the top gates round the corner but the prevailing wind in this open location has a habit of trying to blow you off.

Having left the last lock, we wind through the meadows towards the elusive tower of Lechlade Church, level with which are the town moorings along the towing path side for about 150 yards up to Ha'penny Bridge. The bridge is so called after the toll which used to be collected there from pedestrians (except church-goers and mourners). The tolls were extinguished in 1875 but the toll house remains perched on the townward end of the bridge. Traffic lights have been installed to allow traffic to cross in one direction at a time in view of the width and weakness in the span, the latter being rectified by Gloucester County Council in the mid-1970s.

There are further moorings above the bridge on the left, although to moor on the town side you may use the *New Inn*'s bankside if patronising the facilities or offering the fee, or again above the bridge on the town side Riverside (Lechlade) Ltd has moorings, water, chandlery and a café. You can still navigate officially for about another half mile to a point just beyond Inglesham Footbridge, where the Round House at the entrance to the Thames and Severn Canal still stands at 124.8 miles above Teddington. Here is a suitable winding point for anything

Above: St John's Lock, Lechlade
Below: Ha'penny Bridge, Lechlade

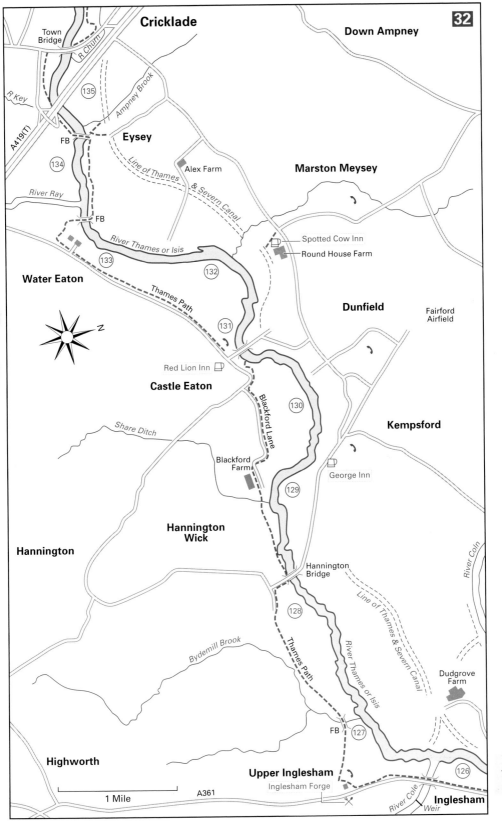

32

Town
Bridge

Cricklade

Down Ampney

R Churn

(135)

Ampney Brook

R Key

A419(T)

FB

Eysey

(134)

Line of Thames

Alex Farm

Marston Meysey

River Ray

& Severn Canal

FB

River Thames or Isis

Spotted Cow Inn

Round House Farm

(133)

(132)

Water Eaton

Thames Path

(131)

Dunfield

Fairford
Airfield

N

Red Lion Inn

Castle Eaton

Blackford Lane

(130)

Kempsford

Share Ditch

Blackford
Farm

George Inn

(129)

**Hannington
Wick**

Hannington

River Coln

Hannington
Bridge

(128)

Line of Thames & Severn Canal

Bydemill Brook

River Thames or Isis

Dudgrove
Farm

FB (127)

Highworth

(126)

1 Mile

A361

Upper Inglesham

Inglesham Forge

River Cole

Inglesham
Weir

St John's Lock Daytime only
Faringdon Road, Lechlade, Glos GL7 3HA
☎ 01367 252309
110'3" (33·60m) long x 14'10" (4·52m) wide
Rise (fall) 2'10" (0·85m)
Max. draught 4'4" (1·32m)
Manual operation only (see notes at end of previous section).
Facilities Chemical toilet disposal and pump-out unit, refuse, toilets, drinking water tap for cans, electric charging point.

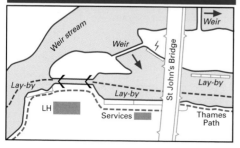

as long as a full-length narrow boat; with care in smaller craft it is sometimes possible to venture further, but you should consider this to be at the owner's risk. The author has managed to venture to about 127½ miles in a 28' Seamaster, only deciding (in a panic) that he and his companion, who was all for going on, should turn as the river looked as though it would soon be a lot narrower than 28 feet. Also it gets weedy and considerably overgrown in summer, with willow and other waterside saplings clogging water intakes and windscreens respectively.

As mentioned earlier, the legal head of navigation is at the Town Bridge at Cricklade, just over 135 miles above Teddington, but this very top section is fast flowing, unimproved and only suitable for canoeists who know how to deal with this kind of waterway. However, we have charted this part of the river in Chart 32, which shows the final section to Cricklade including the Thames Path which then continues to the source outside the jurisdiction of the Navigation Districts of the Environment Agency's Thames Region.

The Thames Path

The Thames Path leaves Newbridge on the same side as *The Maybush Inn*, having arrived at the bridge through the garden of *The Rose Revived*. Walk up the road past the front of the inn and then turn down beside it to join the river on the left-hand bank as you

go upstream. The path now follows the river until it flanks the weir stream which runs out below Shifford Lock. There is now a bridge at Shifford Lock but you must follow the bank until you come to Duxford Ford, which at average summer level is fordable. Not necessarily a right of way, you may join the river by crossing to the footbridge over the lock cut and then walking along the old towing path to Tenfoot Bridge. The Thames Path, however, leads away from the ford to Duxford Farm where you join a bridleway which takes you towards Tenfoot Bridge which you must cross and then turn left. Eventually the Thames Path will cross the new footbridge at Shifford Lock onto the lock island, where a newly created public footpath leads to the bridleway bridge that crosses the lock-cut referred to above. The Path will then remain on the right-hand bank all the way to Rushey Lock. Beyond Tenfoot Bridge follow the river round to Tadpole Bridge, where you may cross for refreshments at the *Trout Inn* but you will have to recross the bridge because the path remains on the right-hand bank up to Rushey Lock. Here it changes sides and remains on the left-hand bank again all the way up to Radcot Bridge.

At Radcot the path meets the A4095 between the old and new bridges. Here you must turn right and cross the new bridge and then cross the road down onto the river bank alongside the cut made in 1790 to accommodate the expected traffic following the opening of the Thames and Severn Canal. The path follows this bank via Grafton Lock all the way to Kelmscot and beyond by way of Eaton Weir up to Buscot. It crosses the new weir stream to the north of the lock and then back again across the weir itself to remain on the north bank. As you approach St John's Bridge and Lock you can now cross to the south bank by means of the new footbridge at Bloomer's Hole, avoiding the former detour which crossed the River Leach. This tributary enters the Thames just below the main weir outfall from St John's weir. Cross St John's Bridge and turn down onto the lockside by means of the steps through the gate on the bridge. Another gate at the end of the lock area leads onto the meadows through which path and river meander together up to Ha'penny Bridge at Lechlade and beyond.

The path continues under the bridge and remains on the left-hand bank, opposite the town of Lechlade, to a point where practical navigation for larger craft ceases in the pool at the entrance to the former Thames and Severn Canal. From this point it is planned that the path will leave the river to circuit Inglesham Church and then rejoin the river bank from the lane which leads down to Lower Inglesham Farm. However, at present the path veers away to the left from the river and joins the A361 Lechlade–Highworth road for just over a mile as far as Upper Inglesham. Here, turn into the village and follow the lane until it curves to the left back to the main road and, just after the last bungalow on your right, you will see a path leading off beside a farm gate. Go down the field to the stream at the bottom where there is a ford and a footbridge beside it to the left in a group of trees. The proposed new path along the river turns inland to join the old one at this point. A mile from Upper Inglesham brings you to Stert's Farm on your right. In another mile, path and bridleway take you forward through a gate into a lane which is joined by the driveway from a cottage. At the lane's end turn right for Hannington Bridge and the river again – but note that there are two watercourses under the bridge, one usually dry except in flood conditions. This is the one which the next footpath runs beside, with the main channel meandering some 100 yards away to the north. Follow this path, turning left to Blackford Farm in just over a mile and then join the lane which describes a dogleg, right and left, into Castle Eaton in another mile.

From Castle Eaton the planned route is to follow the south bank of the river from Castle Eaton Bridge right round to Water Eaton Footbridge. If it is not yet open, you will have to take to the road as far as Lower Part Farm, where a footpath takes you to the entrance to Water Eaton House, and then turn right towards the farm buildings. Circle away from the house to the west then north to the footbridge, on the north side of which turn left. Follow this fairly straight path to Eysey Footbridge which you must cross and turn right. Now you are approaching Cricklade, under the bypass. Bear right off the farm track after the access bridge and, crossing two stiles, you will find yourself in a lane which will lead you into the town. Turn right into Abingdon Court Lane and at the end turn right again down the High Street to High Bridge at the end which marks the limit of navigation.

Angling

Weir Permit holders will find a greater number of weirs on this section for fishing than hitherto. The following, counting upstream, have facilities: Shifford, Rushey, Radcot, Grafton, and Buscot.

At **Shifford Lock** there are two weirs, the main weir, from which fishing may be carried out from the walkway only, and the house weir, where fishing can be had on either bank of the overfall downstream. Access to the lock is by way of the Thames Path from Newbridge (about 3 miles) or from the hamlet of Chimney, about ¾ mile away. Chimney can be reached from Aston on the B4449. There is no parking at the lock so you will have to find a convenient place off the road but not so as to block gateways or access points.

Rushey Lock can be reached along the track from Tadpole Bridge about ¾ mile away where cars should be parked; there is no parking at the lock. Fishing is available from the downstream gangway across the weir structure, and a small length of bank on the south side of the weir. There is a permitted footpath across the weir gangway as part of the Thames Path (see above). Fishermen must ensure that passage for walkers is not obstructed.

At **Radcot Lock** fishing is available along a short stretch of the bank on the south side of the weir structure. Fishing is not permitted on the weir structure or the land on the far side of it. As space is strictly limited, fishing may have to be restricted by the lock-keeper to whom all anglers must report on arrival. Access to the site is from the A4095 at Radcot Bridge and then along the Thames Path for about half a mile. Cars may be parked in the meadow opposite the *Swan Inn* but only with the landlord's permission.

At **Grafton Lock** permit holders may fish from the walkway across the top of the weir structure only. To reach the lock one may use the Thames Path from either Kelmscot or Radcot – both around 1½ miles distant. There is also a footpath leading off the B4449 (Langley Lane) southwest of Grafton village, which is about two-thirds of a mile. At Radcot there is car-parking as described above. It may also be possible to park (neatly and causing no obstructions please) in Kelmscot or Grafton villages.

Buscot Lock has a comparatively new weir, the weir-stream of which is the fishing site. Anglers may fish from both banks of the weir channel between the new weir and the towing-path footbridge downstream. The weir gangway itself and the banks upstream are not available. The best approach is from the village of Buscot off the A417 Faringdon Road. There is a National Trust car park on the right at the end of the main street which continues as a public footpath to the lock for about a quarter of a mile. There are no facilities at the lock but the National Trust owns a picnic site by the old weir pool.

The *Maybush Inn* has half a mile of Thames fishing, as does the *Trout Inn* at Tadpole Bridge. For details of fishing available around Radcot, apply at the *Swan Inn* at Radcot Bridge. Rushey Lock to Old Man's Bridge on the right bank (off side, away from the Thames Path) is reserved by Clanfield AC. Permits for fishing from Grafton to Buscot Locks can be obtained from Turner's Tackle at Faringdon. Highworth AC has water from Buscot to Lechlade and Stroud AA has the stretch from the *Trout Inn* at St John's Lock up to Inglesham. Tickets can be obtained from the *Trout Inn*.

Other angling on this section is mainly private but a number of inns sell day tickets, either on behalf of owners of fishing rights or in respect of their own waters. For details of stretches not covered above, you are recommended to make enquiries at the fishing tackle dealers shown in the *Directory*.

Directory

BOATYARDS, MARINAS, CHANDLERIES, TRIPPING AND HIRE
Oxfordshire Narrowboats
Swan Inn Moorings, Radcot Bridge, Clanfield, Nr Faringdon Oxon. Holiday hire narrow boats only. Office at Lower Heyford on Oxford Canal ☎ 01869 340348. Email: enquiries @oxfordshire-narrowboats.co.uk.
Cotswold Boat Hire
Trout Inn Moorings, Lechlade-on-Thames, Glos GL7 3HA. Office: 19 Berton Close, Blunsdon, Swindon, Wilts SN26 7BE ☎ 01793 700241. Daily and weekly boat hire. (TBTA)
Lechlade Hire and Marine
Windermere House, Sherborne Street, Lechlade, Glos GL7 3AH ☎ 01367 252181. Dinghy and runabout sales, outboard engines, chandlery.
Riverside (Lechlade) Ltd
Park End Wharf, Thames Street, Lechlade, Glos GL7 3AQ ☎ 01367 252229. Boat repairs, engineers, diesel fuel, petrol, *Calor Gas*, chandlery, groceries, dayboat hire, permanent moorings, crane, water point, showers, toilets, restaurant, boat club.
Cotswold River Cruises
Trout Inn near St Johns Lock, Lechlade, GL7. Details from Cotswold River Cruises, 11 Hunt Street, Swindon, Wilts SN1 3HW ☎ 01793 574499. Passenger boat charter for local trips. (PBA)

CRUISING CLUBS
The Swan (Radcot) Cruiser Club
Radcot Bridge, Clanfield, Nr Faringdon, Oxon. (ATYC)
Anchor Boat Club
Eaton Hastings, Nr Faringdon, Oxon. (ATYC)
Riverside Marina Boat Club
Park End Wharf, Thames Street, Lechlade, Glos. (ATYC)

EMERGENCY FUEL SUPPLIES
See note under this heading on page 23
St John's Priory Caravans
Diesel, Calor Gas
Faringdon Road, Lechlade, Glos ☎ 01367 252360. A few yards from St John's Lock.
Lechlade Filling Station
Petrol, diesel
Burford Road, Lechlade, Glos ☎ 01367 252744 (¼ mile through the town from Ha'penny Bridge).

PUBLIC LAUNCHING SITE

Radcot Bridge
Public slip downstream of 'new' bridge, available free but with permission from landlord of the *Swan Inn* only.

FISHING TACKLE SHOPS

State Fishing Tackle
19 Fettiplace Road, Witney, Oxon ☎ 01993 702587

Turner's Tackle
4A Station Road, Faringdon, Oxon ☎ 01367 241044

HOTELS, INNS AND RESTAURANTS

Trout Inn Tadpole Bridge ☎ 01367 870382. Mooring above and below Tadpole Bridge, free for 24 hours (inn is south of bridge).

Swan Hotel Radcot Bridge ☎ 01367 810220. Moorings free below Radcot Bridge against hotel or on opposite bank. Also dayboats for hire.

Plough Inn Kelmscot. Moorings below Kelmscot Manor before FB on towing path side, walk from towing path into village.

Trout Inn St John's Lock ☎ 01367 252313. Bar meals daily and restaurant Thursday, Friday and Saturday evenings. Moorings side-on in weir stream beside inn.

New Inn Hotel Market Square, Lechlade ☎ 01367 252296. Accommodation. Moorings for hotel patrons at end of hotel garden.

Red Lion Hotel High Street, Lechlade. Moorings above and below Ha'penny Bridge on south/towing path bank (free).

Swan Inn Burford Street, Lechlade. Bar snacks, morning coffee, garden.

Rieunier's Restaurant Oak Street, Lechlade ☎ 01367 252587. High-class French cuisine (evenings).

Crown Inn High Street, Lechlade.

Colley's Supper Rooms High Street, Lechlade ☎ 01367 252218. Well-known chain of high-class restaurants (booking advisable).

Black Cat Restaurant High Street, Lechlade. Morning coffee, light lunches, afternoon tea.

Inglesham Forge Restaurant Upper Inglesham ☎ 01367 252298. Well-known high-class restaurant. Booking advisable, jeans out! River from here upstream is not navigable by large or motorised craft. Canoes should be hauled out.

George Inn Kempsford.

Red Lion Inn The Street, Castle Eaton.

Spotted Cow Inn Marston Meysey.

Red Lion Inn High Street, Cricklade.

White Hart Hotel High Street, Cricklade ☎ 01793 750206. Restaurant (not open Sunday evenings).

Vale Hotel High Street, Cricklade ☎ 01793 750223. Lunchtime snacks, evening dinners.

PUBLIC TRANSPORT

Nearest rail services are at Swindon, which can be reached by Thamesdown buses from Lechlade (Service 77) which plies between Swindon and Cirencester. For those walking beyond Cricklade to the source of the river there is also a rail station at Kemble, just over a mile from the *Thames Head Inn* on the A433. Trains run hourly during the day between Gloucester and Swindon. Buses also run between Swindon and Cirencester through Cricklade.

Bus services in the surroundings of the Upper Thames between Eynsham and Lechlade are irregular, some only running one day per week.

Bus operators:
- Stagecoach Swindon ☎ 01793 522243
- Thamesdown ☎ 01793 428428

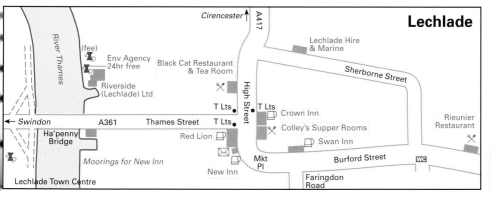

Rowing and canoeing on the Thames

Rowing has always been a major sport on the river, as is evidenced by the many clubs listed in the directories and traceable back to the early years of the nineteenth century. Besides rowing, many canoe clubs also use the river and these are all listed where the author has been able to establish contact with their officers or identify their locations. To enhance the value of this guide, it would be greatly appreciated if any omissions could be notified to the publisher so that amendments can be made in the next edition.

A number of firms specialise in supplying the rowing world and these are listed here in ascending order from Teddington upstream.

George Sims (Racing Boats) Eel Pie Island, Twickenham, Middlesex TW1 3DY ☎ 020 8892 8844. Rowing oars and sculls, ergometers, clothing suppliers.

Bill Colley 4, Bridge Boat Houses, Riverside, Richmond, TW9 1TH ☎ 0208 940 0504. Rowing boat builder, repairs.

Neaves Rowing Fittings 43a Dennis Road, East Molesey, Surrey KT8 9EE ☎ 020 8979 4086. Rowing boat fittings.

Aylings Ltd Riverside Works, Jessamy Road, Weybridge, Surrey KT13 8LN ☎ 01932 853020. Racing and training boats, sculls, equipment.

Janousek Racing Boats 1a Abbot Close, Byfleet, Weybridge, Surrey KT14 7JN ☎ 01932 353421. Composite racing shell builders.

J Sutton Laleham Reach, Chertsey, Surrey KT16 8RR ☎ 01932 560270. Oars and sculls maker.

Carl Douglas Racing Shells The Boat House, Timsway, Chertsey Lane, Staines, Middlesex TW18 3JZ ☎ 01784 456344. Office: 'Kanalia', Wildwood Close, Pyrford, Woking, Surrey GU22 8PL ☎ 01932 342315. Racing shell builders.

Len Neville The Boat House, Timsway, Chertsey Lane, Staines, Middlesex TW18 3JY ☎ 01784 463900. Rowing boat fittings.

Sutton Racing Blades Tom Jones Boatyard, Romney Lock, Windsor, Berks SL4 6HU. ☎ 01753 855540. Oars and sculls.

Eton Racing Boats Brocas Street, Eton, Windsor, Berks SL4 6BW ☎ 01753 671294 or 671296. Rowing boatbuilders, equipment, sales, coaching launches, racing oars and sculls, repairs etc.

Richard Way Booksellers 54b Friday Street, Henley-on-Thames, Oxon RG9 1AH ☎ 01491 576663. Booksellers specialising in rowing literature and the River Thames.

River and Rowing Museum at Henley Mill Meadows, Henley-on-Thames, Oxon RG9 1BF ☎ 01491 415600. Museum and library devoted to the history of rowing and the River Thames and connections with the town of Henley and its history.

Simon Johnson International Unit 14, Sheeplands Farm, High Street, Wargrave, Reading, Berks RG10 8DL ☎ 01734 404755. Oars and sculls, rowing fittings.

Collars Ltd 2 Queensford Farm, Dorchester-on-Thames, Wallingford, Oxon, OX10 7PH ☎ 01865 341277. Oars, sculls, rowing fittings, chandlery.

Glyn Locke Racing Shells Unit 20, Monument Industrial Estate, Chalgrove, Oxford OX44 7RW ☎ 01865 891330. High-performance rowing sculls, pairs and doubles builders.

George Harris Racing Boats Isis Boathouse, Iffley, Oxford ☎ 01865 243870. Racing shell builders.

Salter Brothers Ltd Folly Bridge, Oxford OX1 4LA ☎ 01865 243421. Rowing fittings, day-boats and tenders.

RIVER THAMES – RICHMOND TO CRICKLADE

Table of distances in miles

References to `left' and `right' banks in this table are as they appear to craft proceeding upstream

Miles above Teddington	Miles below Cricklade		Miles between places
[1]3·25	138·43	**Richmond Lock** and Sluices (max. rise 10´0´´)	3·01
[1]0·24	135·42	EA Thames boundary (with Port of London)	0·24
0·00	135·18	**Teddington Locks** (Maximum rise 8´10´´)	0·00
1·86	133·32	Kingston Railway Bridge	1·86
2·03	133·15	Kingston Bridge	0·17
2·91	132·27	Raven's Ait	0·88
3·70	131·48	Long Ditton Ferry	0·79
3·91	131·27	Thames Ditton Ferry	0·21
4·55	130·63	River Mole (left bank)	0·64
4·86	130·32	Hampton Court Bridge	0·31
5·05	130·13	**Molesey Lock** (rise 6´1´´)	0·19
5·86	129·32	Hampton Ferry	0·81
8·03	127·15	**Sunbury Locks** (rise 6´2´´)	2·17
9·60	125·58	Walton Bridge	1·57
10·96	124·22	Junction with River Wey Navigation (left bank)	1·36
10·98	124·20	**Shepperton Lock** (rise 6´8´´)	0·02
12·88	122·30	Chertsey Bridge	1·90
13·04	122·14	**Chertsey Lock** (rise 4´0´´)	0·16
13·26	121·92	M3 bridge	0·22
14·18	121·00	Laleham Ferry	0·92
14·99	120·19	**Penton Hook Lock** (rise 4´0´´)	0·81
16·51	118·67	Staines Railway Bridge	1·52
16·75	118·43	River Coln (right bank)	0·24
16·83	118·35	Staines Bridge	0·08
17·14	118·04	London Stone (site)	0·31
17·68	117·50	Runnymede bridges (A30 and M25)	0·54
17·71	117·47	Colne Brook (right bank)	0·03
17·83	117·35	**Bell Weir Lock** (rise 5´0´´)	0·12
19·90	115·28	*The Bells of Ouzeley*	2·07
20·75	114·43	**Old Windsor Lock** (rise 5´9´´)	0·85
21·51	113·67	Albert Bridge	0·76
23·00	112·18	Victoria Bridge	1·49
23·39	111·79	Black Potts Railway Bridge	0·39
23·75	111·43	**Romney Lock** (rise 6´7´´)	0·36
24·18	111·00	Windsor Bridge	0·43
24·60	110·58	Windsor Railway Viaduct	0·42
26·08	109·10	**Boveney Lock** (rise 4´10´´)	1·48
26·70	108·48	Surly Hall Point	0·62
27·69	107·49	Oakley Court	0·99
28·76	106·42	Monkey Island Hotel	1·07
29·00	106·18	New Thames Bridge (M4)	0·24
29·25	105·93	**Bray Lock** (rise 4´9´´)	0·25
30·51	104·67	Maidenhead Railway Bridge (`The Sounding Arch')	1·26
30·71	104·47	Maidenhead Bridge	0·20
31·38	103·80	**Boulters Lock** (rise 7´10´´)	0·67
33·00	102·18	My Lady Ferry	1·62
33·46	101·72	**Cookham Lock** (rise 4´3´´)	0·46
33·95	101·23	Cookham Bridge	0·49
34·65	100·53	River Wye (right bank)	0·70
35·00	100·18	Bourne End Railway Bridge	0·35
35·65	99·53	Spade Oak Ferry	0·65
37·74	97·44	**Marlow Lock** (rise 7´1´´)	2·09

1. Below Teddington

Miles above Teddington	Miles below Cricklade		Miles between places
37·90	97·28	Marlow suspension bridge	0·16
39·41	95·77	**Temple Lock** (rise 4´1´´)	1·51
40·05	95·13	**Hurley Lock** (rise 3´5´´)	0·64
41·63	93·55	Medmenham Abbey and Ferry	1·58
43·20	91·98	Aston Ferry (*Flower Pot Inn*, left bank)	1·57
43·71	91·47	**Hambleden Lock** (rise 4´9´´)	0·51
44·55	90·63	Temple Island	0·84
46·00	89·18	Henley Bridge	1·45
46·95	88·23	**Marsh Lock** (rise 4´4´´)	0·95
47·53	87·65	Bolney or Harpsden Ferry (Beggars' Hole)	0·58
48·43	86·75	Lashbrook Ferry	0·90
49·05	86·13	Wargrave Ferry (*St George & Dragon*)	0·62
49·33	85·85	Shiplake Railway Bridge	0·28
49·43	85·75	River Loddon (left bank)	0·10
49·54	85·64	**Shiplake Lock** (rise 5´1´´)	0·11
52·16	83·02	Sonning Bridge	2·62
52·45	82·73	**Sonning Lock** (rise 5´4´´)	0·29
54·33	80·85	River Kennet (Kennet & Avon Canal)/(left bank)	1·88
55·08	80·10	**Caversham Lock** (rise 4´9´´)	0·75
55·25	79·93	Reading Bridge	0·17
55·76	79·42	Caversham Bridge	0·51
58·24	76·94	Tilehurst Station wharf	2·48
58·63	76·55	Roebuck Ferry	0·39
58·96	76·22	Purley Ferry	0·33
59·48	75·70	**Mapledurham Lock** (rise 6´9´´)	0·52
61·64	73·54	Whitchurch Bridge	2·16
61·76	73·42	**Whitchurch Lock** (rise 3´4´´)	0·12
64·26	70·92	Gatehampton Ferry	2·50
64·54	70·64	Gatehampton or Basildon Railway Bridge	0·28
65·76	69·42	Goring or Streatley Bridge	1·22
65·83	69·35	**Goring Lock** (rise 5´10´´)	0·07
66·45	68·73	**Cleeve Lock** (rise 2´3´´)	0·62
67·73	67·45	South Stoke Ferry	1·28
68·41	66·77	Moulsford Railway Bridge	0·68
69·04	66·14	Little Stoke Ferry	0·63
71·23	63·95	Chalmore Hole (left bank)	2·19
71·71	63·47	Wallingford Bridge	0·48
72·95	62·23	**Benson Lock** (rise 6´2´´)	1·24
74·20	60·98	Shillingford Bridge	1·25
76·08	59·10	River Thame (right bank)	1·88
76·91	58·27	**Day's Lock** (rise 5´2´´)	0·83
79·44	55·74	Clifton Hampden Bridge	2·53
79·89	55·29	**Clifton Lock** (rise 3´5´´)	0·45
80·46	54·72	Clifton Weir	0·57
81·41	53·77	Appleford Railway Bridge	0·95
82·63	52·55	Sutton Bridge	1·22
82·70	52·48	**Culham Lock** (rise 7´11´´)	0·07
83·90	51·28	Swift Ditch (right bank)	1·20
84·55	51·63	River Ock (left bank)	0·65
84·80	50·38	Abingdon Bridge	0·25
85·28	49·90	**Abingdon Lock** (rise 6´2´´)	0·48
85·74	49·44	Horseferry	0·46
86·65	48·53	Nuneham Railway Bridge	0·91
88·21	46·97	Radley Ferry	1·56
89·86	45·32	**Sandford Lock** (rise 8´10´´)	1·65
90·96	44·22	Kennington Railway Bridge	1·10

Miles above Teddington	Miles below Cricklade		Miles between places
91·54	43·64	**Iffley Lock** (rise 2′9″)	0·58
92·54	42·64	River Cherwell, new mouth (right bank)	1·00
92·74	42·44	River Cherwell, old mouth (right bank)	0·20
92·99	42·19	Folly Bridge (Salter's Yard)	0·25
93·86	41·32	**Osney Lock** (rise 6′3″)	0·87
94·08	41·10	Osney Bridge	0·22
94·29	40·89	Sheepwash Channel to Oxford Canal (right bank)	0·21
96·26	38·92	**Godstow Lock** (rise 5′2″)	1·97
96·45	38·73	Godstow Bridge	0·19
97·39	37·79	King's Lock (rise 2′6″)	0·94
97·41	37·77	Channel to Duke's Cut and Oxford Canal (right bank)	0·02
97·91	37·27	Hagley Pool (outfall left bank)	0·50
98·89	36·29	River Evenlode (right bank)	0·98
100·10	35·08	**Eynsham Lock** (rise 2′9″)	1·21
100·20	34·98	Swinford Bridge	0·10
101·58	33·60	Pinkhill Lock (rise 3′6″)	1·38
103·90	31·28	Bablock Hythe Ferry (*Ferryman Inn*)	2·32
105·44	29·74	**Northmoor Lock** (rise 4′1″)	1·54
106·45	28·73	Hart's or Ridge's Weir Footbridge	1·01
107·61	27·57	New Bridge and River Windrush (right bank)	1·16
109·70	25·48	Old Shifford Farm	2·09
110·18	25·00	**Shifford Lock** (rise 7′4″)	0·48
110·74	24·44	Shifford Weir	0·56
111·94	23·24	Tenfoot Bridge	1·20
113·76	21·42	Tadpole Bridge	1·82
114·48	20·70	**Rushey Lock** (rise 6′0″)	0·72
116·89	19·29	Old Man's Footbridge	2·41
117·11	18·07	**Radcot Lock** (rise 4′10″)	0·22
117·76	17·32	Radcot Bridge	0·65
118·96	16·22	**Grafton Lock** (rise 3′8″)	1·20
120·96	14·22	Eaton Weir Footbridge	2·00
122·30	12·88	**Buscot Lock** (rise 5′7″)	1·34
123·23	11·95	Bloomer's Hole	0·93
123·35	11·83	River Cole (left bank)	0·12
123·45	11·73	**St John's Lock** (rise 2′10″)	0·10
124·10	11·08	Lechlade Bridge ('Ha'penny Bridge')	0·65
124·77	10·41	River Coln (right bank)	0·67
124·80	10·38	Entrance to Thames and Severn Canal (closed)	0·03
125·11	10·07	St John's Church, Inglesham	0·31
128·25	6·93	Hannington Bridge	3·14
129·46	5·72	St Mary's Church, Kempsford	1·21
130·95	4·23	Castle Eaton Bridge	1·49
133·49	1·69	Bridge to Water Eaton House	2·54
133·61	1·57	River Ray (left bank)	0·12
134·24	0·94	Footbridge to Eysey	0·63
135·10	0·08	River Churn (right bank)	0·86
135·18	0·00	Cricklade Bridge	0·08

ENVIRONMENT AGENCY

Environment Agency – Thames region

From 1 April 1996, the Environment Agency took over responsibility for navigation on the Thames together with responsibilities for waste disposal, pollution and sundry other matters relating to the water cycle. However, the Thames navigation above Teddington continued to be administered by those manning the offices, locks and patrol contact points before that date, so little change should have been noticed by river users.

Note In the text that follows I have highlighted in brackets certain differences in marking or procedure which relates to the river below Teddington, for which the navigation is supervised by the Port of London Authority.

The Agency's Thames Region encourages the pursuit of a variety of recreational activities along the 136 miles of the freshwater River Thames for which it is the navigation authority. In its *User's Guide*, available free of charge, the Agency claims that 'it must cater for: anglers, boating enthusiasts, canoeists, dinghy sailors and yachtsmen, holidaymakers in hired craft, naturalists, oarsmen, swimmers, sub-aqua divers and walkers'. The challenge 'is to ensure that everyone has an equal opportunity to enjoy their activity without impairing the enjoyment of others'. For ideas on a day out on the river, up-to-date information can be obtained from the Agency's website – www.visitthames.co.uk – and for details of lock closures and flood conditions you can phone 0845 988 1188. Other contact numbers will be found on page 14

Nine River User Groups, funded by the Agency, have also been set up to encourage a better understanding among organisations and groups who use the river for sport, enjoyment or trade; details of these and the contact points will be found on pages 92.

Publications

There are various regulations governing the use of the Thames and its banks for boaters of all sorts, anglers, riparian owners, towpath walkers and so on. The Agency has recently updated its byelaws and a new specification for boat safety has been published jointly with British Waterways. Both are now in effect. Details of various publications obtainable from Thames Region Headquarters at Reading, or in some cases from the District Offices, are given below. Unless a price is shown, booklets and leaflets are free of charge.

- *The Users' Guide to the River Thames* from Craft Registration at Reading, Navigation Offices, or Lock Offices
- *Thames Navigation Licensing and General Byelaws – 1993* These byelaws, in poster form, are also displayed at each lock
- *Thames Registration Byelaws – 1953* (incorporated in the above booklet). The *Thames Launch Byelaws, 1952* and The *Thames Navigation and General Byelaws, 1957* were replaced by the above new byelaws
- *Boat Safety* Plastic folder containing *Boat Safety Standards* booklet, check list and guidance notes
- *Navigation Levels of Service* Covers basic levels of service, vessel dimensions, hours of lock-staff, etc
- *Cruising on the River Thames – Boating Guide* List of boatyards offering boat-hire, moorings, passenger services, facilities at locks and boatyards. Fuller details are contained in this book under the *Directory* sections
- *Locks and Weirs on the River Thames – How do they work?* Cutaway view of a typical lock
- *Water Wisdom – Health and Safety* Advice on the risks of disease
- *Camping Beside The River Thames* Information on 30 campsites along the river with contact numbers (also contained in the text of this book)
- *Guide to River Thames Lock and Weir Fishing* Fuller details are contained in this book under the *Angling* heading at the end of each section
- *River Canoeists* Guidance notes for canoeists
- *Narrowboats on the Thames – Useful Hints and Tips*
- *A Boater's Guide to Navigation Signs*

The Port of London Authority also issues annual *Tide Tables* and the *Port of London*

River Byelaws – 1978 which are obtainable from the Chief Harbourmaster's Office, PLA, London River House, Royal Pier Road, Gravesend, Kent DA12 2BG ☎ 01474 562200. The free booklet *Pleasure Users Guide* and a *Leisure Guide* map are obtainable from PLA Public Relations, Baker's Hall, 7 Harp Lane, London EC3R 6LB ☎ 020 7743 7900 or on the PLA website – publicrelations@pola.co.uk)

Registration and licensing information

All pleasure craft must be currently registered with Thames Region. Registration certificates usually expire on 31 December although short period certificates may be obtained for craft entering the Thames from other waterways. There are also reduced charges available for craft only in use late in the year. Change of ownership during the registration period must be notified.

No craft with an engine may navigate without a licence. The licence is issued without charge to a registered launch, provided it is constructed and equipped in accordance with the current specification issued by Environment Agency and British Waterways (see *Boat Safety Scheme Guide*). The requirement for Boat Safety Certificates with licence renewal applications was phased in by Thames Region as from 1 January 1997, starting with craft built between 1960 and 1970. Licences are not transferable and the licence plate must be displayed in a prominent position (so that lock-keepers and Navigation Inspectors can see it.)

The *User's Guide* also details the conditions and method of marking the ship's name, and sets out the basic equipment which should be carried, such as fire extinguishers (numbers applicable are shown in the *Boat Safety Scheme Guide*), horn or whistle, anchors, bilge pump, mooring lines, life jackets, lifebelts and first aid equipment. Anchor weights based on those recommended for use in the tidal Thames for various sizes of craft are given in a table on page 173.

Rule of the River

Obey the 'Rule of the River'. Steer on the right-hand side of the fairway so that you pass oncoming vessels to your left, ie: 'Port to Port', *Byelaw 36*.

In the vicinity of bridges or sharp bends, a vessel going upstream (or against the tide if below Teddington) must give way, if necessary, to any vessel coming downstream or with the tide. Speeding is dangerous and illegal. Accidents occur more easily at high speeds, particularly from the wash that such speed creates. Cruising speed should not exceed walking pace and *Byelaw 27* governs the maximum speed at 8 kilometres per hour over the bed of the river which is equivalent to 4.97mph. This may be awkward if you are travelling downstream in flood conditions, especially through notorious narrow channels where the current can be strong. Check regularly the wash that your boat is making and if it causes a swell you are probably going too fast. (Below Teddington, and above Wandsworth the PLA speed limit is 8 knots through, on, or over the water. This works out at 9.2mph or 14.8 kilometres per hour. Also note, however, that the speed limit is expressed as 'through the water' and not 'over the bed' – a slight difference but, to the man trying to achieve steerage way in a fast running tide, '*quelle différence*'!)

You may overtake on either side of a vessel proceeding in the same direction but you should not exceed the speed limit, nor force the overtaken vessel to change course or stop (*Byelaws 35, 38, 39 and 42*). You should also signal your intention to overtake or signal permission to be overtaken when it is safe to do so. (There are prescribed signals for overtaking below Teddington in PLA waters since the *PLA Byelaws* have annexed *Rule 34* of the International Collision Regulations but not above, as the former NRA neglected to 'borrow' subsection C of *Rule 34* so presumably wished to discourage the practice!)

The official sound signals are taken from the *Thames Byelaws 18* to *21* and may be set out as follows.

(A 'short blast' is of 1 second's duration and a 'prolonged blast' is of 4 to 6 seconds' duration.)

- *One short blast*
  I am altering my course to starboard, ie: to my right
- *Two short blasts*
  I am altering my course to port, ie: to my left

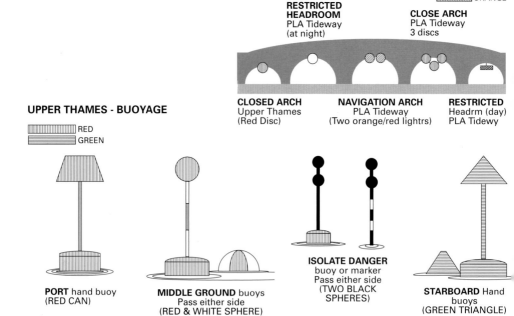

BRIDGE MARKS

▨▨▨▨▨ RED
▧▧▧▧▧ ORANGE

RESTRICTED HEADROOM
PLA Tideway
(at night)

CLOSE ARCH
PLA Tideway
3 discs

CLOSED ARCH
Upper Thames
(Red Disc)

NAVIGATION ARCH
PLA Tideway
(Two orange/red lightrs)

RESTRICTED
Headrm (day)
PLA Tidewy

UPPER THAMES - BUOYAGE

▨▨▨▨▨ RED
▤▤▤▤▤ GREEN

PORT hand buoy
(RED CAN)

MIDDLE GROUND buoys
Pass either side
(RED & WHITE SPHERE)

ISOLATE DANGER
buoy or marker
Pass either side
(TWO BLACK SPHERES)

STARBOARD Hand
buoys
(GREEN TRIANGLE)

- *Three short blasts*
  I am operating astern propulsion – this doesn't necessarily mean that I am making sternway but indicates that I am at least slowing or stopping
- *Five short and rapid blasts*
  You are taking insufficient action to avoid me or I have gone aground
- *One prolonged blast*
  To be sounded when the channel is obscured by bend or obstruction
- *Four short blasts followed by one short blast*
  I am about to turn fully round to starboard
- *Four short blasts followed by two short blasts*
  I am about to turn fully round to port
- *One prolonged blast followed by two short blasts*
  I am unable to manoeuvre

There are further sound signals prescribed in the *Byelaws* for craft in restricted visibility (22) and it is also allowable to supplement sound signals with lamp flashes of the same duration.

MARKING OF OBSTRUCTIONS

Thames Region has adopted the following shapes and colours for topmarks and buoys to be used for marking shoals and other obstructions in the river. Note that these shapes are adapted from, but not identical to, those used by the PLA in the tidal section since the upper Thames buoyage system has been modified from the IALA Maritime System for obvious reasons. The problems of shallows occur mostly in the early part of the year before reeds have grown through the surface to indicate an unnavigable state but you should remember that not all shallows are marked, especially those that lie outside the regular fairway. The diagram above gives a helmsman's eye view of the river when proceeding upstream. Remember that buoys and markers must be passed on the opposite hand when proceeding downstream.

The four main types of marker used are as follows.

- **Red can** ■

A red truncated cone-shaped buoy or a truncated cone at the top of a post. To be left on your port (left) hand when proceeding upstream.

- **Green triangle** ▲

A green triangle or full cone-shaped buoy or topmark. To be left on your starboard (right) hand when proceeding upstream.

- **Red and white sphere** ●
Either a red and white striped spherical buoy or a red sphere topmark on a red and white striped post. May be passed on either side as it marks the extent of shallows in mid-channel or at the extremity of an ait.

- **Two black spheres** ● ●
Mounted on a pillar or post, one above the other. May be passed on either side, but keep well clear as this marker indicates an isolated danger such as a wreck or sunken obstruction. If such obstructions are close to the bank then the appropriate port- or starboard-hand buoy or topmark will be used.

DREDGERS

Dredgers working in the river have their anchors marked by yellow buoys. Slow down and navigate on that side of the dredger from which two vertical WHITE diamond shapes (♦) are displayed. Two vertical RED balls (●) are displayed on that side on which chains and other obstructions may exist. If both sides have WHITE diamonds then adopt the rule of the river and pass with care on the appropriate side. At night, dredgers are lit with two vertical RED lights on the obstructed side and two vertical GREEN lights on that side which another vessel may pass.

OVERHEAD CABLES

In open reaches below Oxford, cables are usually at a minimum of 40′ (12m) above summer water level but you should allow a clearance of at least 13′ (4m) when passing beneath. If in doubt, lower masts or aerials. Above Oxford and also in locks, lock cuts and backwaters, cables may be lower. Main cable crossings are shown on the charts.

BRIDGES

On the freshwater Thames, bridges' navigation arches often have protective cutwaters at the piers on each side of the relevant arches. Bridges which have temporarily closed arches to navigation will usually display a large red disc at the crown of the arch. (Note that, below Teddington, navigation arches of bridges are denoted by the PLA with two orange-red lights displayed at the crown of the arch. Temporarily closed arches have three red discs in apex down formation, and restricted headroom is denoted by day by a 'bundle of straw' and, at night, by a single white light.)

ROWING, SAILING AND CANOEING

Rowing vessels, sailing boats, sailboards and canoes must all be currently registered with Thames Region before being used on the river. Registration certificates usually expire on 31 December, although short-period certificates may be obtained for craft entering the Thames from other waterways. There are also reduced charges available for craft only in use late in the year. The *River Users' Guide* details a lot of useful information for all who take part in these activities including notes on regattas, racing and coaching. Most rowing, sailing and canoeing clubs operating on the river are included in this book, in order to both advertise their facilities and to inform other users of the navigation as to where caution should be exercised.

LOCK WORKING

When arriving at a lock, form an orderly queue at the lay-by moorings. If there is no room, stand off well back from the gates. Queue jumping is bad manners. Move up to the position closest to the lock on the lay-by to allow craft behind you to moor to the lay-by to await their turn. Once secured in the lock, switch off your engine and any radio, TV or hi-fi (*Byelaw 51*) and make certain that you are held by a headrope and sternrope (*Byelaw 48*). Both lines should be tended while the lock is being filled or emptied to prevent the boat being caught on chains, projecting piles or rubbing strakes. Pay attention to the lock-keeper's instructions and do not restart your engine/s until the lock gates have been opened to allow craft to leave the lock chamber.

While in the lock you may not:
- strike matches or operate lighters
- open fuel tanks
- moor upstream of the top gates sill mark – a white line or plate

You may have to work the locks for yourself if the keeper is off duty but this is at your own risk. Instructions for hand operation of powered locks are posted on the operating pedestals. Do not open the sluices until the gates at the opposite end of the lock are properly closed and always leave the gates closed with the lock empty or emptying when you leave. Make sure that the top sluices have been shut if you are leaving in the upstream direction.

The lock measurements given in the main body of this book are those issued for guidance by the navigation authority which states that depths quoted may vary with water levels and for other reasons. The measurements given are the length of the lock between heel posts; the minimum width between walls or rubbing piles; and the rise (or fall) is taken from the standard head water level of the lock in question to that of the next lock below – no allowance having been made for the river gradient. The lock panels in the book also show the maximum draught which craft can have in order to traverse the shallower sill – usually the bottom sill with the lock empty.

LOCK STAFF: HOURS OF DUTY

It is anticipated that locks will be manned during the following hours, but river users are advised to check with the notices displayed at each lock.

Teddington Locks are manned 24 hours a day every day of the year. All others, except Blake's Lock, are open as follows.

January	0915 to 1600
February	0915 to 1600
March	0915 to 1600
Good Friday until Easter Monday	
inclusive	0900 to 1730
April	0900 to 1730
May	0900 to 1830
June, July, August	0900 to 1900
September	0900 to 1800
(until 1830 Saturdays and Sundays)	
October	0900 to 1700
November	0915 to 1600
December	0915 to 1600

Note Individual locks may be found closed to traffic for cleaning on weekday mornings between 0700 and 0900.

During the winter months, November to February, assisted lock passage may not be available as lock staff may be attending more than one site. Between April and October, additional summer relief staff are employed although, due to staff shortages, you may find a lock unattended during the duty lock-keeper's meal break. (Richmond Lock (PLA) is permanently manned when operable. The public are not permitted to operate it).

ANCHORING AND MOORING

In general, vessels have a right to anchor in the Thames for up to 24 hours in any one place. You may need permission to moor to the bank. Free and charged-for mooring places are indicated in this book. If there are no mooring rings or posts provided, place mooring stakes well back from the bank's edge and take care that they do not cause a hazard to passers-by. If stopping overnight or if you plan to leave the craft unattended for a length of time, do not moor in shallow water or with a tight rope or chain as water levels may fluctuate by as much as two or three feet in a few hours. Always ensure that there is at least two feet of water under your keel (your draught plus 2′) and at least 2′ of vertical play on any warp or chain.

CHARGING POWER POINTS FOR ELECTRIC BOATS

Electric charging points for the batteries of electric launches which have built-in chargers are sited at Molesey, Old Windsor, Cookham, Shiplake, Goring, Benson, Sandford, Shifford and St John's Locks. These consist of a 240volt outdoor weatherproof round 3-pin female connection. The fee for their use has now been revised (2005) into two parts; £5.50 for the mooring and £6.00 for the hook-up to the charging circuit making a total of £11.50 per night. Please contact the lock-keeper at the relevant lock before 4pm on the day you wish to use the facility to ensure a reserved mooring at the charging point for your boat.

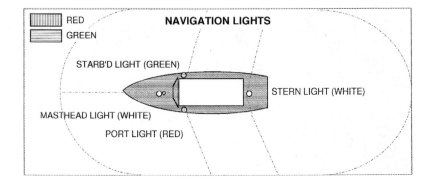

NAVIGATION LIGHTS

If you wish to navigate at night, your vessel must carry the prescribed lights. Details are given in the *Byelaws* but the diagram below gives a guide as to how the average motor launch of 20–30′ waterline length should be fitted. The masthead light, which may be mounted on a staff at the bow if there is no mast, must be exhibited at least 4′ (1.2m) above the hull.

RIVER SAFETY

When large red 'Caution Strong Stream' warning boards are displayed at locks, all craft are advised to moor up and await quieter conditions. These are usually indicated by large yellow 'Caution Stream Decreasing' warning boards when powered vessels may proceed with caution. When a yellow 'Stream Increasing' board is exhibited, powered vessels are advised to seek a safe mooring and all unpowered craft should moor up as soon as possible and not venture out until the red and yellow warning boards have been removed. In the event of a river accident you should telephone for the emergency services in the usual way by calling 999 or tell the nearest lock-keeper who can summon assistance. It is of benefit if you or a member of your party knows something about first aid, resuscitation, and how to help a person who is in difficulties in the water or is suffering from hypothermia. Children should always be accompanied by an adult when playing in or near the water.

SWIMMING

The Environment Agency supports the view of safety organisations which advise against swimming or diving in open watercourses such as the River Thames. However there are some notes on such activities in the authority's *Users' Guide to the River Thames* from which many of the notes in this section have been prompted.

SUB-AQUA DIVING

All diving activities must have prior approval in writing from the appropriate district navigation inspector. The diving area should, after consultation with the inspector, be marked with suitable surface marker buoys. Warn other river users that there are divers below the surface, either by flying the diving flag (International Code Flag A) or by displaying a similarly painted board visible to upstream and downstream traffic. Mark diving boats so that you and your club and activity can be easily identified. (*PLA Byelaws* require a red flag to be flown also, at the point where the diver enters the water).

ANGLERS, CAMPERS, WALKERS AND PICNICKERS

Before going fishing you must have a valid rod licence (if you are over 12 years of age). These are obtainable from post offices or from the Agency's Thames Region (see pages 14 and 21).

Fishing in lock cuts and lock approaches is not permitted between 15 March and 31 October and at no time over lock lay-bys where craft have to wait before using the locks. All craft have a right to navigate the full width of the river. Those in charge of craft are mostly reasonable people but their craft can inadvertently carry away fishing tackle as it is often difficult to see the line, particularly when anglers are hidden from view by bankside vegetation. If fishing at

Anchors and warps – weights and diameters

Craft	Anchors		Warps (diam)	
	COR (Plough/Delta)	Fisherman (conventional)	Chain	Nylon
20′ (7m) launch/narrow boat	4·5kg	7·0kg	6·3mm	10·0mm
30′ (9m) launch/narrow boat	9·0kg	14·0kg	8·0mm	14·0mm
35′ (11m) launch/cruiser	14·0kg	18·0kg	8·0mm	14·0mm
40′ (12m) narrow boat	11·0kg	16·0kg	8·0mm	14·0mm
40′ (12m) launch/cruiser	16·0kg	18·0kg	9·5mm	16·0mm
52′ (16m) narrow boat	16·0kg	18·0kg	10·5mm	18·0mm
70/72′ (22m) narrow boat	18·5kg	24·0kg	10·5mm	20·0mm

Note The metric equivalents for boat lengths quoted above are a rough guide only. Where a nylon warp is used, at least 3 fathoms (18′) of chain should be used between the anchor and the nylon warp, but it is recommended that as much chain as possible is incorporated between anchor and vessel – ideally all should be of chain. The length of chain supplied for the boat should be at least five times the depth in which the boat may operate, thus for the Thames an anchor chain of 80–100] long is recommended, since depths of as much as 20′ can be found in the middle reaches where gravel extraction deepened the river in the earlier years of this century.

vacant regular mooring places you must be prepared to move if a vessel wishes to moor.

When camping and/or picnicking please do not camp or light fires without permission. Don't throw rubbish into the river. Don't light fires near dried foliage or chop down trees for firewood. Everyone, including ramblers and towpath walkers, should follow the *Country Code* – shut gates, keep to footpaths, guard against fire, clean up your site before leaving, and take rubbish home with you unless you can put it in a litter bin nearby. Clear up any discarded tackle such as hooks or nylon line if you have been fishing. Walkers enjoy many miles of rights of way alongside the river but they should not allow youngsters to wander near the river's edge or let dogs annoy animals or wildlife or run loose at locksides. Boatmen attempting to moor in a lock are none too keen on being washed by a slobbery spaniel's tongue as their faces appear above the parapet!

ENVIRONMENTAL PROTECTION

Every year all regions of the Environment Agency investigate thousands of incidents which could endanger the state of our rivers, lakes and coastal waters. Every week, they follow up hundreds of reports of suspected pollution alone – many of them identified by vigilant members of the general public. In addition, their staff are constantly on the lookout for threats such as poaching, rubbish dumping, flooding and illegal water abstraction.

The Agency has a free emergency hotline for members of the public to report pollution, rubbish dumping, flooding and other environmental damage. The 24-hour Freephone number to call is 0800 807060. A leaflet is issued to interested parties, with a plastic credit card-sized plastic card bearing this number as a useful reminder.

While boating, walking or fishing along the river you are not only able to help in the campaign against these unwelcome incidents but you may even unthinkingly be causing them, so take care in how you use the river and, more particularly, in how you use your vessel. All motor craft have to conform to the specifications mentioned above. The only lavatories approved for use on launches on the freshwater Thames are the chemical types or those which discharge into holding tanks. Lavatories discharging overboard must be sealed by a navigation officer – or other steps must be taken to render them inoperable. Sealing is undertaken without charge by arrangement with any navigation office.

Avoid pollution – it is an offence to discharge sewage, oil, or any other matter likely to cause pollution into the river, or to leave rubbish on the banks. Take special care with petrol when refuelling. Oil contaminated bilge water is another potential source of pollution and must on no account be pumped into the river. Sewage pump-out stations and rubbish disposal sites at locks, boatyards and marinas are shown in the *Directory* sections and also, in most cases, on the charts. For pump-out stations look for the blue and white sign shown at most sites.

13. River Wey and Godalming Navigations

THE NATIONAL TRUST for Places of Historic Interest or Natural Beauty

Navigation authority

National Trust, River Wey and Godalming Navigations, Dapdune Wharf, Wharf Road, Guildford, Surrey GU1 4RR
☎ 01483 561389
Email swybeb@smtp.ntrust.org.uk

Distance

19.63 miles (River Thames to Godalming Town Bridge)

Maximum dimensions of craft

Headroom (average summer level)
Weybridge to Shalford 7´0˝ (2.15m) Shalford to Godalming 6´0˝ (1.85m)

Length	72´0˝ (21.90m)
Beam	13´10˝ (4.20m)
Draught	Weybridge to Guildford
(average	(3´0˝ 0.91m)
summer	Guildford to Godalming
level)	(2´6˝ 0.76m)

Opened in 1653, this waterway is one of the oldest in the country. Its 20-mile length runs from Godalming to Weybridge and is the southernmost part of the 2000-mile waterway network. Originally, the Wey Navigations were used for transporting barge loads of heavy goods via the Thames to London. Timber, coal, corn, flour, wood and even gunpowder were regularly moved up and down the waterway. Later, in 1796, the Basingstoke Canal was dug and connected to the Wey and, in 1816, the Wey and Arun Junction Canal was opened, connecting with the Wey at Stonebridge. The original navigation ran from Guildford to the Thames, the top 4½ miles to Godalming being opened in 1762 and remaining in separate ownership by a board of commissioners which represented local landowners.

The Wey, unlike many other less efficient waterways, survived the railway era and, under private ownership, continued to trade until well after the Second World War. The last owners, Stevens & Sons, donated their length of the Wey to the National Trust in 1964. The Godalming Navigation Commissioners handed over their 4½ miles to Guildford Corporation in 1968 who duly transferred it to the National Trust. Today it is one of the few financially self-supporting waterways, making no demands on the Trust's general finances or on public funds.

It is now managed and protected for its long-term preservation as a recreational asset and a living piece of industrial archaeology.

All craft entering the navigations, either from the Thames or the Basingstoke Canal, or by slipping at the sites mentioned in the following text, must be licensed before navigation is permitted. Scales of charges (which include lock tolls), information and licences are available on application to the above address or from Guildford Boat House, Millbrook, Guildford, Surrey GU1 3XJ ☎ 01483 504494; from the Lock Cottage at Thames Lock, Jessamy Road, Weybridge, Surrey ☎ 01932 843106 or Pyrford Basin ☎ 01932 340739. Short period licences are available; craft must comply with the requirements of the Boat Safety Sceme and adequate insurance cover must be held.

Powered inflatable boats are not permitted on the navigations.

Boat crews must be in possession of a windlass (lock handle) with a $1^{1}/_{16}$ in (27mm) square hole for working the unattended locks. Windlasses are available on loan from the National Trust offices or at Thames Lock on entry.

All craft should observe the maximum speed limit of 4mph or a brisk walking pace, to preserve the banks and wildlife habitat.

FROM THE THAMES

Access from the River Thames is from below Shepperton Lock from which you take the channel to starboard (right) if coming downstream and port (left) if coming upstream; passing two weir streams on your right and the exit of the River Wey proper to enter the Wey Navigation ahead. The channel, indicated by a notice board, winds to starboard and then round to port, past the stop-gate below the tail of Thames Lock. Here there is a mooring point for craft waiting to enter the Wey. Normally craft drawing more than 1´6˝ (0.46m) will need to use the lower pound to enter the lock. Moor

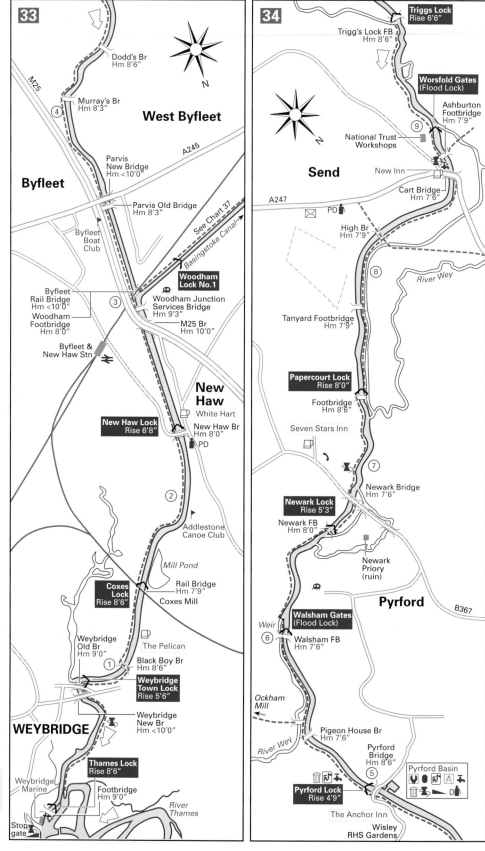

33

Dodd's Br
Hm 8'6"

M25

Murray's Br
Hm 8'3"

④

West Byfleet

A245

Parvis
New Bridge
Hm <10'0"

Byfleet

Parvis Old Bridge
Hm 8'3"

Byfleet Boat Club

See Chart 37

Basingstoke Canal →

Woodham Lock No.1

Byfleet
Rail Bridge
Hm <10'0"

Woodham Junction
Services Bridge
Hm 9'3"

③

Woodham
Footbridge
Hm 8'0"

M25 Br
Hm 10'0"

Byfleet &
New Haw Stn

New Haw

White Hart

New Haw Lock Rise 6'8"

New Haw Br
Hm 8'0"

PD

②

Addlestone
Canoe Club

Mill Pond

Coxes Lock Rise 8'6"

Rail Bridge
Hm 7'9"

Coxes Mill

Weybridge
Old Br
Hm 9'0"

The Pelican

①

Black Boy Br
Hm 8'6"

Weybridge Town Lock Rise 5'6"

Weybridge
New Br
Hm <10'0"

WEYBRIDGE

Thames Lock Rise 8'6"

Weybridge
Marine

Footbridge
Hm 9'0"

*River
Thames*

Stop
gate

176

34

Triggs Lock Rise 6'6"

Trigg's Lock FB
Hm 8'6"

Worsfold Gates (Flood Lock)

Ashburton
Footbridge
Hm 7'9"

National Trust
Workshops

⑨

Send

New Inn

A247

Cart Bridge
Hm 7'6"

PD

High Br
Hm 7'9"

River Wey

⑧

Tanyard Footbridge
Hm 7'9"

Papercourt Lock Rise 8'0"

Footbridge
Hm 8'6"

Seven Stars Inn

⑦

Newark Bridge
Hm 7'6"

Newark Lock Rise 5'3"

Newark FB
Hm 8'0"

Newark
Priory
(ruin)

Pyrford

B367

Walsham Gates (Flood Lock)

Weir

⑥

Walsham FB
Hm 7'6"

Ockham
Mill

River Wey

Pigeon House Br
Hm 7'6"

Pyrford
Bridge
Hm 8'6"

⑤

Pyrford Basin

Pyrford Lock Rise 4'9"

The Anchor Inn

Wisley
RHS Gardens

up inside the single gate and consult the lock-keeper who is normally available from 0900–1830 or until sunset. The stop-gate must be closed to raise the level of water over the bottom sill of the lock before craft having a draught in excess of 1´6˝ (0.46m) can clear the sill. The lock rises 8´6˝ (2.60m). From the lock there is a footpath into Weybridge for shops and restaurants. Licences, lock-handles and water are obtainable from the lock-keeper; 24-hour moorings are available on the towpath side above the lock.

Note Visiting craft should not be left unattended overnight without prior arrangement with the navigation offices at Guildford or most waterway staff.

Weybridge Town Lock 0.83 miles from the Thames, rises 5´6˝ (1.60m), is unattended and is approached through the rectangular arch on the starboard (right) hand of the old road bridge. Full shopping facilities can be reached within a few minutes' walk, either in Weybridge itself, back over the new bridge, or at Addlestone which is further along the towpath upstream. After the Town Lock the waterway is now a canal for the next 5½ miles up to Walsham Gates where it rejoins the river. This means that the channel will be shallow and the speed limit of 4mph must be adhered to. Lower speeds may well be necessary in all the canal sections, when passing other craft and when approaching a mooring.

Proceeding upstream, the *Pelican Inn* with a mooring stage for patrons will be seen to starboard, followed by the railway bridge at the tail of Coxes Lock (1.63 miles[1], 8´6˝/2.60m rise) which is also unattended. Helm with care below the lock as there is often turbulence from the millpond outfall from Coxes Mill; you may be set to port and then starboard in quick succession if the helmsman is not concentrating.

Byfleet and New Haw

New Haw Lock (2.33 miles[1]) has a 6´8˝ rise (2.05m), and above the lock it may be possible to moor temporarily for nearby services such as the *White Hart Inn*, telephone, garage and shops. Byfleet and New Haw Station (*South West Trains* from Waterloo) and a shopping centre are about 15 minutes' walk along the A318 on the opposite (eastern) side of the bridge. Beyond the M25 viaduct is the junction with the Basingstoke Canal, with which we deal in more detail in the next section. Under Woodham Footbridge, which carries the towing path over to the Basingstoke Canal and the adjacent rail bridge in about half a mile, you will find the Byfleet Boat Club from which rowing boats can be hired in summer.

A long curve to the left leads to the *Anchor Inn* at Pyrford, Pyrford Basin (on your right) and, above the bridge which carries Wisley Lane over the navigation, **Pyrford Lock** (4.83 miles[1]) which has a 4´9˝ rise (1.45m). The basin has mooring facilities for boat owners, water point, toilet pump-out, diesel fuel, *Calor Gas*, engineer's, repair shop, showers and a slipway. Electric boat charging can be arranged and there is a chandlery where Wey pattern lock handles and licences for the navigation are also obtainable ☎ 01932 340739. There are rubbish disposal facilities, a chemical toilet sluice and a water point at the lock.

Walsham Lock (5.83 miles[1]), also known as Walsham Flood Gates is normally left open to navigation except in times of flood. The lock cottage is occupied by an NT lengthsman who may be able to help or advise ☎ 01483 725180. Avoid the broad weir above the lock which is the point at which the river leaves the canalised section of the navigation to rejoin it back at Weybridge.

Newark Lock (6.53 miles[1]) which rises 5´3˝ (1.60m), should be approached with care since boats should avoid the Abbey Stream on the right and the Newark Millstream which enters a little higher up on the left. The *Seven Stars Inn* and a telephone box can be found down the road to the left at Newark Bridge.

Send

Following the winding course of the river for about ½ mile from Newark Bridge, one comes to another junction where the river comes in on the right to the next canalised section leading up to **Papercourt Lock** (7.33 miles[1]), a fairly deep unattended lock for the Wey at 8´0˝ (2.40m). Emergency assistance may be obtainable at the lock cottage ☎ 01483 224219. We now approach the village of Send which is to the left of the navigation. Access can be gained from High Bridge along a footpath or from the reasonable moorings above Cart Bridge at the back of the popular *New Inn*. At the wharf here there is a water point. Above Send is another flood lock **Worsfold Gates** (8.93 miles[1]), only operated in times of flood. The sluices, if in use, should

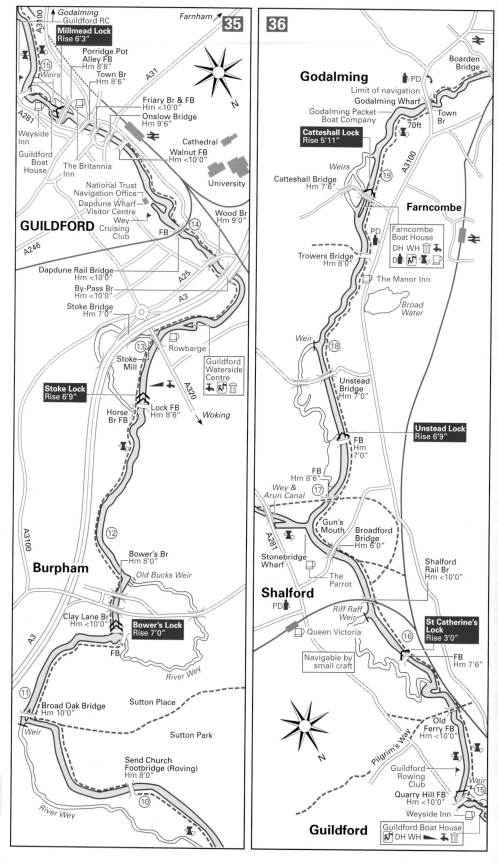

36

Map 35

Godalming / Guildford RC
Farnham

Millmead Lock
Rise 6'3"

Porridge Pot Alley FB
Hm 8'6"

Town Br
Hm 8'6"

A31

Weirs

Friary Br & FB
Hm <10'0"

Onslow Bridge
Hm 9'6"

Weyside Inn

A281

Guildford Boat House

The Britannia Inn

Cathedral

Walnut FB
Hm <10'0"

University

National Trust Navigation Office

Dapdune Wharf Visitor Centre

Wey Cruising Club

GUILDFORD

A246

Wood Br
Hm 9'0"

FB

14

Dapdune Rail Bridge
Hm <10'0"

By-Pass Br
Hm <10'0"

A25

A3

Stoke Bridge
Hm 7'0"

13

Rowbarge

Guildford Waterside Centre

Stoke Mill

Stoke Lock
Rise 6'9"

Lock FB
Hm 8'6"

A320

Woking

Horse Br FB

12

Bower's Br
Hm 8'0"

Old Bucks Weir

Burpham

A3100

Clay Lane Br
Hm <10'0"

Bower's Lock
Rise 7'0"

FB

A3

River Wey

11

Broad Oak Bridge
Hm 10'0"

Sutton Place

Weir

Sutton Park

Send Church Footbridge (Roving)
Hm 8'0"

10

River Wey

Map 36

Boarden Bridge

Godalming

PD

Limit of navigation

Godalming Wharf

Godalming Packet Boat Company

Town Br

70ft

Catteshall Lock
Rise 5'11"

A3100

Weirs

19

Catteshall Bridge
Hm 7'6"

Farncombe

PD

Farncombe Boat House
DH WH
D

Trowers Bridge
Hm 8'0"

The Manor Inn

Broad Water

Weir

18

Unstead Bridge
Hm 7'0"

Unstead Lock
Rise 6'9"

FB
Hm 7'0"

FB
Hm 8'6"

Wey & Arun Canal

17

Gun's Mouth

A281

Stonebridge Wharf

Broadford Bridge
Hm 6'0"

Shalford Rail Br
Hm <10'0"

The Parrot

Shalford

PD

Riff Raff Weir

St Catherine's Lock
Rise 3'0"

Queen Victoria

Navigable by small craft

16

FB
Hm 7'6"

N

Pilgrim's Way

Old Ferry FB
Hm <10'0"

Guildford Rowing Club

Quarry Hill FB
Hm <10'0"

Weir

15

Weyside Inn

Guildford Boat House
DH WH

Guildford

Above: Narrow boats moored by Cart Bridge, Send

Below: Guildford. St Nicola's Church and Debenham's store, Guildford

be treated with great care as they have unique hand-drawn paddles which are held open by means of pegs.

This is where we join the river again for a short spell up to **Trigg's Lock** (9.63 miles[1]) which rises 6′6″ (2.00m). The lock cottage here is occupied by another NT lengthman who may be available for help ☎ 01483 761549. In 1½ miles we rejoin the river just below Broad Oak Bridge by crossing above the weir which has tricked a few helmsmen in view of the sharp turn to port coming downstream; (starboard upstream). It is advisable to take the right-hand arch of Broad Oak Bridge (left-hand coming downstream), which is closer to the towing path.

Bower's Lock (11.73 miles[1]), unmanned, rises 7′0″ (2.10m) and necessitates a tight turn to port to gain entry. There are two lay-bys, one on either side of the channel, the tail of the weir stream being crossed by a footbridge. Above the lock there is a tight turn to port as we re-enter the river and it is advisable to sound the horn to warn downstream craft of your presence before turning. **Stoke Lock** (12.93 miles[1]) which rises 6′9″ (2.05m) is reputed to be the oldest pound lock in the county of Surrey, being first constructed in the middle of the seventeenth century to allow passage of craft from Guildford past the change in level at Stoke Mill.

At Guildford Waterside Centre, just past the *Row Barge Inn* opposite Stoke Mill, there are chemical toilet and rubbish disposal facilities, a free water point and a canoe access point.

Guildford

Underneath the redbrick railway bridge, Dapdune Bridge (14.44 miles[1]), about a mile above the *Row Barge*, Dapdune Wharf is situated on the left bank. The National Trust's Navigations Office is based at Dapdune Wharf, from where licences, lock handles and information can be obtained. There is also a slipway, water point, electric point, and 24-hour visitors' moorings. Dapdune Wharf has been refurbished as a visitor centre which is open to the public from April to October (Thursdays to Mondays). There is no charge for mooring, but if you wish to visit the exhibits an admission charge applies. The visitor centre has on display one of the last surviving Wey barges, which was rescued and restored by the National Trust, and interactive exhibitions that tell the story of the navigations. The National Trust run guided walks and special events at Dapdune Wharf and along the navigations; details can be obtained from the Navigations Office. From April to October the National Trust runs a trip boat from Dapdune Wharf to Millmead Lock.

Past Dapdune Wharf the river channel swings to the right towards the town centre. The original Wey Navigation ends at **Guildford Wharf** (15.19 miles above the Thames), halfway between Onslow Bridge and the original Guildford Town Bridge. During the summer season tripping boats operated by Guildford Boat House offer river cruises to the general public from the Town Wharf at Guildford upstream through Millmead Lock. Care should be taken when passing through this narrow section as tripping craft turn below Guildford Town Bridge. Moorings for shoppers in the town centre are provided above the Walnut Tree footbridge and again above Guildford Town Bridge where the towing path crosses the weir stream in front of the *Britannia* pub. It is unwise to moor directly in front of the new Odeon cinema just downstream of the footbridge as there are some underwater obstructions here.

Millmead Lock (15.33 miles[1]) is the lowest lock on the former Godalming Navigation and, like all locks apart from Thames Lock, is unmanned. Entry is just above the Debenham's store, behind the Yvonne Arnaud Theatre, leaving the weir stream ahead to the right and the mill outfall over on your left. The lock rises 6′3″ (1.90m) and takes craft up into a short cut which bypasses two separate weirs, both to starboard going upstream, and the millstream which runs off to port immediately above the lock. A short distance above the lock is Guildford Boat House, home of tripping boats *Harry Stevens*, a 56ft 60-seater river bus and the restaurant boat, *Alfred Leroy*, which operates day and evening cruises. The boatyard also lets some 16 narrow boats on short break or weekly hire, also licensed for the Thames and has a large collection of rowing boats and canoes available for hourly hire. Licences for the Basingstoke Canal which can be reached in less than a day cost extra. There is a covered slipway, water, toilets, pump-out and chemical toilet point. However service is restricted on Mondays Fridays and Saturdays which are the turnround days for the hire fleet. Since the yard specialises in short-breaks, cruises start on Mondays, Tuesdays or Fridays as well as

Saturdays. Books, postcards, ice-creams and mementoes, as well as licences for the Wey, are sold in the boatyard office where bookings and information are also obtainable ☎ 01483 504494/536186.

Just above the boat yard is *The Weyside Inn*. Further upstream after a sharp bend to starboard comes the Guildford Rowing Club on the opposite bank and then follows a fine stretch of river with good moorings on both banks as far as St Catherine's Hill. Beyond the St Catherine's Footbridge on the site of the old pilgrims' ferry comes a tight horseshoe bend, starting to port and then necessitating a careful sweep to starboard before approaching the entry of the old river below **St Catherine's Lock** (16.53 miles[1]) which rises 3′0″ (0.90m). Shalford rail bridge follows above the curiously named Riff-Raff Weir to port and should be navigated with care owing to the girder construction which supports the bridge soffit.

Broadford Bridge is the lowest on the navigation with an average summer level headroom of 6′4″ (1.90m). This may be a few inches less in wet weather, and a working guide is suggested as counting the headroom of 6′0″ to be on the safe side. Above the bridge on the left bank facing upstream is the *The Parrot* while beyond stands a new industrial estate on the site of an old fibre works, and an old gunpowder store can be seen standing on staddlestones. The entrance to the disused Wey and Arun Canal is on your left. The first few hundred yards of the old canal are used for Trust moorings but beyond lies the task of restoration of the canal down to Newbridge on the River Arun in Sussex, which is at last under way.

Unstead and Godalming

Following the river round to our right we come to **Unstead Lock** (17.73 miles from the Thames) having a rise of 6′9″ (2.05m). It is also along this part of the river that horse-drawn narrow boat trips in the NB *Iona* are conducted, so that special care should be taken to navigate on the correct side of the river – the 'off' side (away from the towing path) when passing or overtaking. Tripping information from ☎ 01483 414938. A shop and garage in Peasmarsh village, west of the river, can be visited better from the lock than from Unstead Bridge higher upstream. Beyond the bridge is Unstead Weir, although a smaller weir draws quite strongly at times close to the head of the lock. Just before the

quaint and not easily navigated Trowers Bridge (18.76 miles[1]), about a mile above Unstead Lock is the *Manor Inn* where moorings and refreshments are available.

We now approach Farncombe Boat House and Hectors-on-the-Wey tearoom, taking the cut to the right, the left-hand channels forming the weir stream from above Catteshall Lock. Farncombe Boat House ☎ 01483 421306, offers craft for hire, punts, skiffs and canoes. Water, diesel fuel, rubbish disposal and toilet discharge and pump-out are available. Refreshments are served in the Tearoom and there is access from the moorings here to the *Leathern Bottle Inn* in Farncombe village where there are garages, a launderette and a telephone.

Catteshall Bridge and **Catteshall Lock** (19.03 miles[1]) follow immediately beyond the boathouse. The lock rise is 5′11″ (1.80m) and although there is an access ladder in the lock chamber there is no footbridge, so you will have to use Catteshall Bridge to reach opposite sides of the lock. Craft longer than 40′0″ (12.20m) can now proceed above the entry to the weir stream (which used to act as the final winding hole for full-length narrow boats) since it is possible to wind at Godalming Wharf. After a sharp right-hand bend, Godalming Wharf is on the left and Godalming Bridge (19.63 miles from the Thames) ahead is the limit of navigation and the extent of the National Trust's property. Moorings are available on the towing path side below the bridge. There are also short-stay Trust visitors' moorings on the wharf frontage with an excellent freshwater point and sewage and refuse disposal facilities. Small craft may be able to venture further to the Boarden Bridge but, just beyond, passage is barred by a weir above the railway bridge.

1. Distances quoted after each lock name show miles above the junction with the R. Thames at Shepperton.

Towing path

There is a towing path throughout the Wey Navigation apart from a short section through Guildford town centre. The path starts at Thames Lock which can be reached from the *Old Crown* pub in Thames Street in Weybridge by following the path from the end of Church Walk which crosses the weir stream. The path leaves the lock on the left bank (right bank facing upstream) and, apart from a short diversion just below Weybridge, Town Lock continues to Black Boy Bridge

Guildford Boat House

below the *Pelican Inn*. Here it crosses to the right bank and remains on this side of the Navigation all the way up to Newark Lock, where it changes sides for a brief stretch, to Newark Bridge where it returns to the right bank.

At the next lock, Papercourt, the path changes sides again and follows the left bank round to Cart Bridge at Send. However it might be easier to walk into Send over Tanyard Bridge and rejoin the path beside the *New Inn* where the path leaves again on the right bank. The next crossing is virtually in Guildford itself at Wood Bridge where walkers should take care in view of the heavy traffic. A short diversion in the town, from Guildford Wharf where the original towing path ended, is now provided in the form of a riverside walk up to Guildford Town Bridge where the towing path for the Godalming Navigation starts. From Millmead, in front of the *Britannia* pub, a footway crosses to Millmead Lock island or one can join the towing path across Millmead Lock by using the alley from Millbrook beside the Yvonne Arnaud Theatre.

From Guildford to Godalming Town Bridge the towing path remains on the left bank (right as you proceed upstream).

Angling

Wey Navigation Angling Amalgamation have the fishing rights from Thames Lock to Walsham Gates and from Papercourt to the *New Inn* at Send. Byfleet Angling Association organise fishing in Coxes Mill Pond. Guildford Angling Society lease the fishing rights between Triggs Lock and Guildford Town Bridge. Godalming Angling Society cover the Godalming Navigation from Guildford Rowing Club to Godalming Wharf. The aforementioned associations issue day tickets which can also be obtained from the Navigations Office and some local shops (see *Directory*).

Directory

LOCKS, BOATYARDS, MARINAS, CHANDLERIES, TRIPPING AND HIRE

Weybridge Marine Ltd
91 Thames Street, Weybridge, Surrey KT13 8LP (Thames) ☎ 01932 847453. Permanent moorings, hardstanding, winter storage, slipway.

Thames Lock (National Trust)
Jessamy Road, Weybridge, Surrey KT13 8LG ☎ 01932 843106. Point of entry to River Wey, Wey licences, lock-handles, water point, telephone, information, National Trust weir- and lock-keeper.

Byfleet Boat Club Ltd
The Boathouse, 4 Old Parvis Road, West Byfleet, Surrey ☎ 01932 340828. Day-boats for hire.

Pyrford Marina Ltd
Pyrford Basin, Lock Lane, Pyrford, Woking, Surrey GU22 8XL ☎ 01932 340739. Boat brokers, insurance, licences, repairs, breakdown service, marine engineers, diesel fuel, *Calor Gas*, chandlery, outboard engine service, marine trimmer, slipway, water, sewage disposal and pump-out, toilets, electric boat charging (by arrangement), car park.

Pyrford Lock
Lock Lane, Wisley, Woking, Surrey GU23 6QW. Water point, rubbish disposal, chemical toilet disposal (unattended).

Walsham Lock
01483 725180. National Trust lengthsman.

Triggs Lock
☎ 01483 761549. National Trust lengthsman.

Dapdune Wharf
Wharf Road, Guildford, Surrey GU1 4RR ☎ 01483 561389. National Trust visitor centre and boatyard, Navigations office, slipway, moorings, water point, power point.

Guildford Boat House
Millbrook, Guildford, Surrey GU1 3XJ ☎ 01483 504494
Email: info@guildfordboats.co.uk River trips, rowing boat and canoe hire, narrow boat hire for short breaks or weeks, books, maps, licences, slipway, toilets, pump-out, water point.

Farncombe Boat House
Catteshall Lane, Godalming, Surrey GU7 1NH ☎ 01483 421306. Email: enquiries@farncombeboats.co.uk Narrow boat charter for the day, short break or

longer. Punt, rowing boat and canoe hire. Riverside bistro. Water point, diesel, sewage and rubbish disposal, pump-out. Recreational moorings, boat sales and bags of advice.

Godalming Packet Boat Co
The Wharf, Godalming, Surrey ☎ 01483 414938. Office: 57 Furze Lane, Farncombe, Godalming, Surrey GU7 3NP for further details. Horse-drawn narrow boat *Iona* for passenger trips and party bookings from Godalming Wharf, bar, refreshments and souvenirs aboard. (PBA)

EMERGENCY FUEL SUPPLIES
See note under this heading on page 24
Fillup Motor Co Ltd
Petrol, diesel
New Haw Road, Addlestone, Surrey ☎ 01932 847004/855499. By New Haw Bridge.

JB Motors
Petrol, diesel
Send Road, Send, Woking, Surrey ☎ 01483 222125. 400yds from Cart Bridge.

Warn's Garage
Petrol, diesel
7 King's Road, Shalford, Guildford, Surrey ☎ 01483 561630. Near Broadford Bridge.

Farncombe Service Station
Petrol, diesel
Meadrow, Godalming, Surrey ☎ 01483 421024. Near Catteshall Bridge.

ROWING, SAILING AND CRUISING CLUBS AND TUITION
Weybridge Rowing Club
Thames Lock, Jessamy Road, Weybridge, Surrey KT13 8LG ☎ 01932 842993. Rowing club. (ARA)

Addlestone Canoe Club
New Haw Road, Addlestone, Surrey KT15 3BN. Canoeing. (BCU)

Byfleet Boat Club (see under *Locks, Boat-yards, Marinas* etc., above).

Guildford Waterside Centre
Riverside, Woking Road, Guildford, Surrey GU1 1LW ☎ 01483 571996. Water point, chemical toilet and rubbish disposal, canoe access.

Wey Cruising Club
Dapdune Wharf, Woodbridge Road, Guildford, Surrey GU1 4RP. (ATYC)

Guildford Rowing Club
Shalford Road, Guildford, Surrey GU1 3XL ☎ 01483 565849. Rowing club. (ARA)

TRAIL-CRAFT LAUNCHING SITES
- **Pyrford** At Pyrford Basin by arrangement
- **Guildford** At Stoke Lock off Woking Road, Guildford. NT site, fee payable (arrange with lock-keeper on ☎ 01483 504939)

FISHING TACKLE SHOPS
Fishing Unltd
5 Worplesdon Road, Guildford, Surrey ☎ 01483 504106

Guildford Angling Centre
92 Haydon Place, Guildford, Surrey ☎ 01483 506333

TOURIST INFORMATION OFFICE
Guildford 14 Tunsgate, Guildford, Surrey GU1 3QT ☎ 01483 444333

HOTELS, INNS AND RESTAURANTS
Farnell Arms Thames Street, Weybridge. Moor above Thames Lock in the River Wey.

Pelican Inn Hamm Moor Lane, Addlestone. Moorings adjacent for patrons.

White Hart New Haw Road, Addlestone. Mooring may be possible just above New Haw Lock.

The Anchor Pyrford Lock. Moorings for patrons adjacent.

Seven Stars Newark Lane, Ripley. Moorings above Newark Bridge or below Papercourt Lock.

The Talbot Hotel High Street, Ripley ☎ 01483 225188. Moor at Walsham Gates or Newark Bridge (about a mile's walk).

New Inn Cart Bridge, Send. Moorings to towing path adjacent to inn.

Fox and Hounds Sutton Green. Mooring at Triggs Lock or Wareham's Footbridge.

The Row Barge Stoke Bridge, Guildford. Moorings adjacent.

Britannia Inn Millmead, Guildford. Moorings adjacent below or above Millmead Lock.

The Weyside Millbrook, Guildford. Moorings adjacent to pub frontage for patrons.

The Parrot Broadford Road, Shalford. Mooring above Broadford Bridge.

Manor Inn Meadrow, Farncombe ☎ 01483 427134. *Beefeater* menu. Moorings on towing path side behind the inn.

Leathern Bottle Meadrow, Farncombe. Moor at Farncombe Boathouse (fee).

'Hector's-on-the-Wey' Tea Room Farncombe Boathouse ☎ 01483 418769. Moorings at Farncombe Boathouse.

TAXIS

Weybridge
- ☎ 01932 858585

Byfleet
- ☎ 01932 351169

Woking
- ☎ 01483 776611/773661

Guildford
- ☎ 01483 560063

RAIL STATIONS AND TRAIN SERVICES
See note under this heading on page 26
Travel information ☎ 08457 484950.

Weybridge *South West Trains* Station Approach, off Brooklands Road, Weybridge, Surrey. 1 mile from Weybridge New Bridge. Trains to Walton, Surbiton and Waterloo; to Byfleet and New Haw, Woking, Worplesdon and Guildford. Also Addlestone, Chertsey, Egham, Staines, Hounslow, Brentford, and Waterloo. See also under River Thames.

Addlestone *South West Trains* Station Road, Addlestone, Surrey. Half a mile from river. Trains to Weybridge (change for Woking and Guildford; Surbiton, Wimbledon and Waterloo); or Chertsey, Egham, Staines, Brentford, Putney and Waterloo.

Byfleet & New Haw *South West Trains* Westfield Parade, Byfleet Road, Byfleet, Surrey. 1000yds from New Haw Bridge. Trains to Weybridge, Surbiton and Waterloo; to Woking, Worplesdon and Guildford. Change at Weybridge for trains to Addlestone, Chertsey and Staines. Change at Woking for Brookwood, Ash Vale and Aldershot.

Guildford *South West Trains* Walnut Tree Close, Guildford, Surrey. 300yds from river. Trains to Ash, North Camp, Wokingham and Reading; Effingham Junction. and Waterloo; Ash, Aldershot, Ash Vale, Ascot; Worplesdon, Woking, Byfleet, Weybridge, Walton, Surbiton and Waterloo. Also on *Thameslink* via Effingham Junction, West Croydon, *Citylink* to Luton. Farncombe and Godalming; also stations to Redhill and Gatwick. Fast trains between London and Portsmouth.

Shalford *South West Trains* Station Row, The Street, Shalford, Guildford, Surrey (Closed on Sundays). 700yds from Broadford Bridge. Trains to Guildford and all stations to Redhill. Change at Redhill for Gatwick.

Farncombe *South West Trains* Station Road, Farncombe, Godalming, Surrey. ¾ mile from Catteshall Bridge. Trains to Godalming or Guildford.

Godalming *South West Trains* Station Approach, Station Road, Godalming, Surrey. 1 mile from Town Bridge. Trains to Farncombe and Guildford. On main line from Waterloo to Portsmouth – other services may be available.

BUS AND COACH SERVICES
River Wey and Godalming Navigations
Most major towns along the river in this section are connected by regular (at least hourly) bus services. Limited-stop coach services run through the area between Victoria and Kingston and then to Guildford. For details in the Weybridge area, see Section 3. Most bus routes radiate from Guildford or in the mid-section of the waterway from Woking.

Bus operators:
- Arriva Guildford and West Surrey ☎ 0870 608 2 608
- Tillingbourne ☎ (01483) 276880
- Stagecoach, Hants and Surrey ☎ (01256) 464501
- or local bus information can be obtained by calling Traveline on ☎ 0870 608 2608.

DISTANCE TABLE

RIVER WEY – RIVER THAMES TO GODALMING TOWN BRIDGE

Table of distances in miles

Miles above Weybridge	Miles below Godalming		Miles between places
0·00	19·63	Junction with R Thames	0·00
0·13	19·50	**Thames Lock No. 16** (rise 8´6˝)	0·13
0·83	18·80	**Town Lock No. 15** (rise 5´6˝)	0·70
1·06	18·57	Black Boy Bridge	0·23
1·44	18·19	Coxes Rail Bridge	0·38
1·63	18·00	**Coxes Lock No. 14** (rise 8´6˝)	0·19
2·33	17·30	**New Haw Lock No. 13** (rise 6´8˝)	0·70
2·88	16·75	Junction with Basingstoke Canal	0·55
3·00	16·63	Byfleet Rail Bridge	0·12
3·50	16·13	Parvis Bridge (old)	0·50
4·31	15·32	Dodd's Bridge	0·81
4·83	14·80	**Pyrford Lock No. 12** (rise 4´9˝)	0·52
5·38	14·25	Pigeon House Bridge	0·55
5·83	13·80	**Walsham Gates No. 11** (rise in flood only)	0·45
6·53	13·10	**Newark Lock No. 10** (rise 5´3˝)	0·70
6·78	12·85	Newark Road Bridge	0·25
7·33	12·30	**Papercourt Lock No. 9** (rise 8´0˝)	0·55
7·69	11·94	Tanyard Bridge	0·36
8·13	11·50	High Bridge	0·44
8·63	11·00	Cart Bridge, Send (*The New Inn*)	0·50
8·93	10·70	**Worsfold Gates No. 8** (rise in flood only)	0·30
9·63	10·00	**Triggs Lock No. 7** (rise 6´6˝)	0·70
10·25	9·38	Send Church Bridge	0·62
11·06	8·57	Broad Oak Bridge	0·81
11·73	7·90	**Bowers Lock No. 6** (rise 7´0˝)	0·67
11·86	7·77	Bowers Bridge (old)	0·13
12·93	6·70	**Stoke Lock No. 5** (rise 6´9˝)	1·07
13·37	6·26	Stoke Bridge (*The Row Barge*)	0·44
14·19	5·44	Wood Bridge	0·82
14·44	5·19	Dapdune Rail and Footbridge	0·25
14·57	5·06	Dapdune Wharf (NT Navigation Office)	0·13
15·19	4·44	Guildford Wharf (start of Godalming Navigation)	0·62
15·33	4·30	**Millmead Lock No. 4** (rise 6´3˝)	0·14
15·56	4·07	Quarry Hill Footbridge	0·23
16·06	3·57	St Catherine's Footbridge	0·50
16·53	3·10	**St Catherine's Lock No. 3** (rise 3´0˝)	0·47
16·84	2·79	Shalford Rail Bridge	0·31
17·13	2·50	Broadford Bridge (headroom 6´4˝)	0·29
17·32	2·31	Gun's Mouth (Wey & Arun Canal)	0·19
17·54	2·09	Old Rail Bridge (NT Path)	0·22
17·73	1·90	**Unstead Lock No. 2** (rise 6´9˝)	0·19
18·06	1·57	Unstead Bridge	0·33
18·76	0·87	Trowers Bridge	0·70
19·03	0·60	**Catteshall Lock No. 1** (rise 5´11˝)	0·27
19·47	0·16	Godalming Wharf	0·44
19·63	0·00	Godalming Town Bridge (**limit of navigation**)	0·16

14. The Basingstoke Canal –
Byfleet to Greywell Tunnel

Navigation authority
Basingstoke Canal Authority, Canal Centre,
Mytchett Place Road, Mytchett, Surrey
GU16 6DD ☎ 01252 370073
Email info@basingstoke-canal.co.uk

Distance
31.13 statute land miles (Woodham
Junction, River Wey to Greywell Tunnel)

Maximum dimensions of craft
Woodham to Greywell

Headroom(at average summer level) 6´0´´
             (1·83m) Woodham to
             Farnborough Road Bridge
             5´10´´ (1·78m) Farnborough Road
             Bridge to Greywell
Length   72´0´´ (21·95m)
Beam   13´6´´ (4·11m)
Draught (at average summer level) 3´0´´
             (0·91m)

Author's note
The Basingstoke Canal might probably have
been dealt with first in this work if the
chronological order of the author's
acquaintance with the various waterways
connected with the Thames had dictated the
sequence. It was in 1941 that I was sent to
Cable House School, now in Horsell. In those
dark days of the war, Miss Blandford's noted
nursery school was on St John's Road just
below the *Rowbarge Inn*, backing onto Lock
No. 10. Not too many years ago the house in
which the school had been run and which
then belonged to Miss Blandford's brother-
in-law, Dr Brooke, was demolished to make
way for the present enclave of smart new
bijou residences which have been sandwiched
between Woodend Bridge and the pub. On
the other side of the canal were fields full of
kingcups and cowpats, part of Slocock's
Nursery – all now just a memory as I gazed
through my wing mirror down Lockfield
Drive on a recent return visit.

In the early 1940s the canal was still in the
ownership of the Harmsworths who had
bought it in 1923. It was also in water in
most places, certainly through St John's, held
back by a series of padlocked lock gates.
Somewhere near Arthur's Bridge we used to
navigate the canal on a raft constructed of
four oil drums and some suspect
matchboarding laid across the top. This was
my first acquaintance with a chain ferry, for
someone at Slococks had thoughtfully
stapled a chain across the canal so that those
wishing to get to the nursery headquarters,
which were on the north side of the canal
from Woking by this short cut, could do so.

LICENSING
All craft entering the navigation from the
River Wey, or by slipping at the sites
mentioned in the following text, must be
licensed before navigation is permitted.
Scales of charges (which include lock tolls),
information and licences are available by
post or in person from the address shown
above. A licence will also be issued to boaters
arriving at Lock No. 1 between 0900 and
0930 hours with their insurance and BSS
certificates, from the newly opened back-
pumping station and canal office. Boaters
should telephone the Basingstoke Canal
Authority at least a day in advance so that
the necessary arrangements can be made
☎ 01252 370073 *Fax* 01252 371758. A 72-
hour or 15-day short term licence is available
for visitors to the navigation. At least 7 days'
notice is required for a short term licence
which cannot be issued more than 28 days in
advance. Licence holders for the Basingstoke
Canal who wish to enter the Thames at
Weybridge or return from the Thames by
way of the River Wey Navigation must
obtain a Transit Licence, if not already in
possession of a full River Wey Licence.
Transit Licences are obtainable from the
National Trust's River Wey and Godalming
Navigation Office at Guildford or at Thames
Lock at Weybridge. Full addresses for these
are given on page 175. Craft wishing to moor
permanently on the canal must obtain a
mooring permit obtainable from the
Basingstoke Canal Authority as above.

Note All craft must observe the maximum
speed limit of 4mph.

HISTORY
The Basingstoke Canal was completed in
1794 as a means of transporting agricultural
produce from the Basingstoke area to
London via the Wey and Thames navigations
which were already in existence and well
used. The main contractor was John
Pinkerton, remembered in the name of the
Surrey and Hampshire Canal Society's

tripping boat. As was usual with many canals of the era, the final cost was nearly double the estimates and there were such small returns to the investors that it might well have disappeared altogether had it not been for early plans to extend the canal southwards; another to link it to the Kennet at Newbury; and, yet another in 1830, to use it for the transportation of materials for the former London and South Western Railway to Basingstoke and beyond. Then came the development of the military barracks at Aldershot in the 1850s and finally the establishment of a brickworks at Up Nately close to the terminus of the canal in the 1890s.

After several changes of ownership, occasioned by the decline to a limited amount of traffic, the canal came into the hands of Alexander Harmsworth, based at Ash Vale, who ran a cartage business as well as acting as bargee, barge builder and repairer. In 1949 the canal was auctioned and sold for £6000 and left to stagnate until 1966 when the Surrey and Hampshire Canal Society was formed to campaign for public ownership and restoration. Surrey and Hampshire County Councils joined forces to purchase their respective lengths of the canal and restoration of the canal started late in 1973 in partnership with volunteers organised by the Canal Society, with towing path clearance and dredging of the summit pound from Odiham eastwards by the end of 1974. The whole of this pound has been navigable since 1984. The 29 locks from Aldershot down to the River Wey were repaired, rebuilt or reconstructed – including the Deepcut Flight of 14 locks which raises the canal 100 feet in two miles – and the canal was finally re-opened by HRH the Duke of Kent in May 1991.

The summit pound in particular is a classic example of a contour canal, although the meandering starts from Deepcut Top Lock (No. 28), through loop and curve, to take in some fine scenery or avoid clashes with civilisation, which it manages to step up and away from at the topmost lock at Ash (No. 29). Galleon Marine at Odiham hires out narrow boats for holidays but suggests that, even for a week, its customers may not wish to descend from the 16 miles of lock-free sylvan waterway on which they are based, a challenge Thamesmen and women may care to consider!

From Byfleet

The Basingstoke Canal rises from Woodham Junction, near Byfleet, on the National Trust's Wey Navigation, three miles upstream from the Thames at Shepperton. A new footbridge links the Wey towing path on the opposite bank with the towing path of the Basingstoke which runs on the opposite bank to the Heathervale Caravan Park. The installation of back-pumping on the Woodham Flight in 2001 enables boats to lock up onto the Woking pound and cruise to the town, and return to the Wey, throughout the year even when other lock flights are temporarily closed to conserve water. After negotiating a number of moored houseboats above your first lock, Woodham Bottom lock (No.1), the Woodham flight of locks consists of a further five over a distance of a mile and a quarter and the lock house at No. 3 lock, now privately owned, is the only remaining lock-keeper's cottage on the canal. From Lock No. 6, just above Sheerwater Bridge there is a level pound of 3¾ miles as far as the first lock in the Goldsworth, or St John's, flight between Woking and neighbouring Horsell. Between Monument Bridge which carries the main road from Chertsey up to Maybury Hill and Chertsey Road Bridge, which is the main A320 road into Woking town centre, it may be possible to moor on the towing path side at the site of Spanton's Yard where timber used to be brought by canal from London. Monument Bridge Industrial Estate now lies alongside this stretch of the canal while, on the opposite bank, lies what is left of part of Horsell Common.

Woking

Above Chobham Road Bridge there are moorings for a visit to the *Wheatsheaf* which is about 50 yards to the north of the bridge; a new footbridge connects the site with the town centre across Victoria Way, the busy dual carriageway, to Woking's shopping centre including the Peacocks Arts and Entertainment Centre. Proceeding up the canal, it then ducks under Lockfield Drive (the A324) to set course for the village of St John's. Mooring and sustenance are again available at the *Bridge Barn* above Arthur's Bridge on the 'off' side before tackling the five locks in the ½-mile long Goldsworth, or St John's, flight. Goldsworth was the name of the nursery which was tended by the Slocock family, mentioned above. However, the

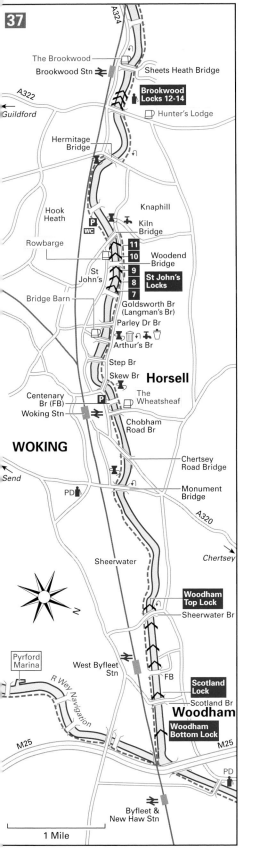

Goldsworth area itself seems to be that part of Woking around the railway sidings and junction of the Portsmouth and Alton lines which are crossed by the aptly named 'Twin' Bridges, two footbridges on a continuation south of the footpath which crosses Step Bridge over the canal, renowned in the author's youth for train-spotting! If a preference is required I suggest that 'St John's' is the more appropriate name for the flight of locks numbered 7 to 11.

At Kiln Bridge, originally St John's Bridge, at the top of Lock No. 11 is the village itself which gives its name to the common to the south, known as St John's Lye, along the western edge of which runs the canal, eventually meeting the Alton/West Country railway line on its embankment. At Hermitage Road Bridge the canal runs alongside the grounds of Brookwood Hospital, originally a 19th-century mental asylum. After the left-hand curve round to the Bagshot Road Bridge, which heralds the next lock-working session 1¾ miles from St John's Top Lock (No. 11), you might consider visiting the new retail park in front of Brookwood Hospital which can be reached up Bagshot Road to the north. Locks 12 to 14 at Brookwood are close to the petrol and diesel garage on the bridge and the *Hunter's Lodge* inn, shown in older guides as the *Nag's Head*. The next, Sheets Heath Bridge, leads southwards to Brookwood Station and a post office on the A324 Connaught Road, while ahead lies the almost hundred-foot rise of the canal through 14 locks in the next two miles – the Deepcut – leading up to the best and most glorious of the top 20-odd miles of the Basingstoke Canal and nearly all the reasons why it has been so energetically and lovingly restored.

Pirbright to Fleet

The Deepcut Flight starts at Lock 15, just above Pirbright Bridge which carries Brunswick Road from Connaught Road over into the military camps and Bisley Rifle Ranges away to one's right. On your left, beyond the towing path which crosses the canal from north to south at Pirbright Bridge, the railway follows the canal which slowly rises above it to cross it on the double-arched Frimley Rail Aqueduct just below the B3012 Guildford Road. The cutting, which is 1000 yards long, is as much as 70 feet deep in places, running between Lock 28 (Deepcut

189

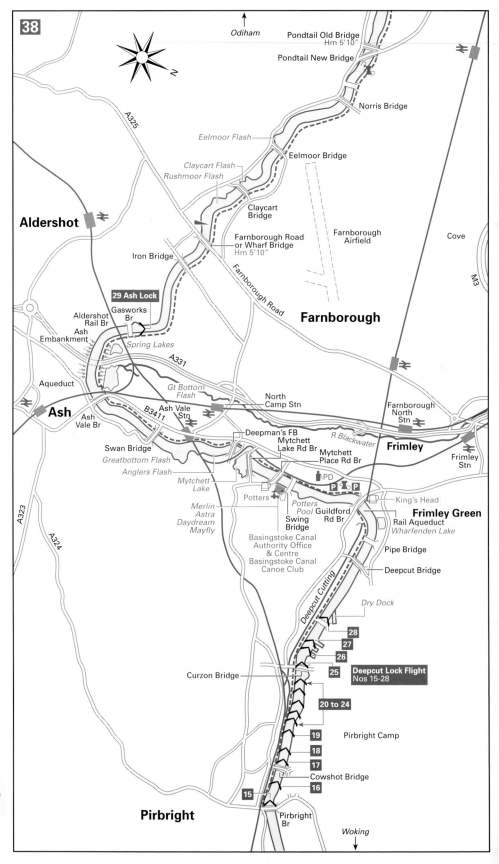

Odiham

Pondtail Old Bridge
Hm 5'10"
Pondtail New Bridge

Norris Bridge

N

Eelmoor Flash

Eelmoor Bridge

Claycart Flash
Rushmoor Flash

Claycart
Bridge

A325

Aldershot

Farnborough Road
or Wharf Bridge
Hm 5'10"

Farnborough
Airfield

Cove

M3

Iron Bridge

Farnborough Road

Farnborough

29 Ash Lock

Gasworks
Br

Aldershot
Rail Br
Ash
Embankment

Spring Lakes

A331

Aqueduct

Ash

Ash
Vale Br

Gt Bottom
Flash

North
Camp Stn

Farnborough
North
Stn

Farnborough
North
Stn

B3411

Ash Vale
Stn

R Blackwater

Frimley

Frimley
Stn

A323

Swan Bridge

Greatbottom Flash

Anglers Flash

Mytchett
Lake

Deepman's FB
Mytchett
Lake Rd Br

Mytchett
Place Rd Br

King's Head

Frimley Green

A324

Merlin
Astra
Daydream
Mayfly

Potters

Potters
Pool
Swing
Bridge

Guildford
Rd Br

PD

P   P

Rail Aqueduct
Wharfenden Lake

Basingstoke Canal
Authority Office
& Centre
Basingstoke Canal
Canoe Club

Pipe Bridge

Deepcut Bridge

Deepcut Cutting

Dry Dock

Curzon Bridge

28

27

26

25

Deepcut Lock Flight
Nos 15-28

20 to 24

19

Pirbright Camp

18

17

Cowshot Bridge

15

16

Pirbright

Pirbright
Br

Woking

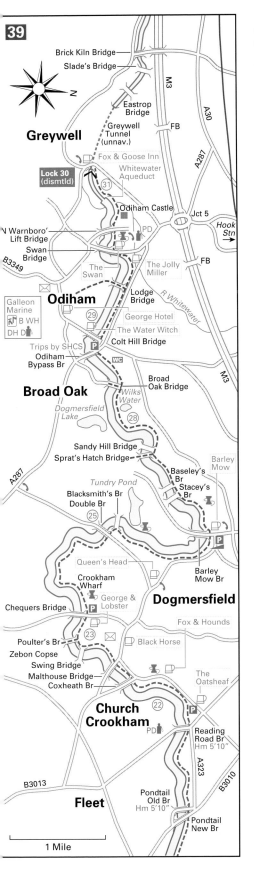

Top) where there is a restored dry dock, and Wharfenden Lake so that it has given its name to the nearby settlement on the B3015 opposite the Blackdown Barracks.

Wharfenden Lake is accessible for boats to visit the noted Lakeside Country Club at Frimley Green and the floating 'Wings Chinese Restaurant' while the canal turns southwards in a complete change of direction to cross the railway line to Basingstoke as already mentioned. Notice the recesses for the former stop gates on either side of the aqueduct to prevent the canal flooding the railway line in the event of a leakage or breach of the aqueduct, which was allegedly lead-lined when constructed. You may stop for refreshment almost immediately, for behind the house on the opposite bank to the towing path is the *King's Head*. It would be better, however, to negotiate Guildford Road Bridge, which acts as a roving bridge for the towing path, and take advantage of the moorings ahead at Frimley Lodge Park. Here there are toilets and a car park, only 500 yards ahead from the bridge – a short walk back to the pub.

The urban sprawl and yet another railway line (the Ascot, Bagshot, Camberley, Frimley and Ash Vale loop) approach the canal on the towing path side opposite a flash, one of a number with which the canal is endowed, known as Potter's Pool. Then with a caravan, camping and events field and the buildings of the Basingstoke Canal Centre on the left, you approach Mytchett Place Road Bridge and the *Potters Inn* beyond, with its 'off' side moorings and a slipway. A 45 seater passenger trip and charter boat, *Merlin*, is available for light lunches and cream teas, and two small day-trip narrow boats, *Daydream* and *Astra*, are also available for hire for self-drive or skippered trips, from the Canal Centre. *Mayfly*, a luxury 12 seater charter boat is also available for hire and details of these are listed in the Directory. Mytchett Lake is privately owned by the Ministry of Defence and appears to have been a hollow which was filled when the canal was constructed, as a reservoir. At the top end of the Mytchett Lake section is Mytchett Lake Rail Bridge which crosses at almost a right angle to Deepman's Footbridge which is private. Keep to the towing path side through Angler's Flash which follows and then, under Ash Vale Rail Bridge, comes the old Ash Vale Barge Yard on the left with Great Bottom Flash stretching away from it. Rowing boats are often available during the season from Ash Vale boathouse.

Swan Bridge follows, also named Heath Vale Bridge but the prior name is preferable as it reminds us that the *Swan Inn* is one of the few pubs right on the bank of the canal! Still travelling south, the canal is gradually closing, with the Blackwater River which comes under the canal and into the Spring Lakes below the famous Ash Embankment which takes the route westwards again. Ash Wharf makes a convenient mooring for shopping close by. Halfway across the 1000-yard long Ash Embankment, on the Surrey/Hampshire border, an aqueduct has been constructed to carry the canal over the new Blackwater Valley relief road. At the end of the embankment we come to the last (or first, depending which way you are cruising) rail bridge on the canal followed by Gasworks Bridge which is owned by the MoD and the Ash Lock Depot where water and refuse disposal facilities are available. Through the lock and you enter the last 15 miles of lock-free cruising, having climbed almost 196′ from the Wey at Byfleet.

Above Ash Lock the canal runs westwards between the regimented order of military precision, or what is left of it – being that part of Hampshire in which the author was incarcerated some 16 years after his childishly joyful towing path walks in Woking, when as a National Serviceman he took charge of an armoury not 1000 yards from Iron Bridge which carries Queens Avenue across the canal. The next, Wharf Bridge, or Farnborough Road Bridge, which carries the A325, is the first of the three very low bridges which give a headroom of only 5′10″ (1·78m). At Farnborough Road Wharf above the bridge there is a public slipway. Keys to unlock the barrier at this and a further slipway at Barley Mow Bridge at Winchfield must be obtained from the canal authority at the Mytchett Canal Centre, although a BW Yale-type key should fit.

Fleet to Greywell

On the south side of the canal there now follow three flashes, Rushmoor, Claycart and Eelmoor. The towing path runs opposite on the north bank and, at Eelmoor Flash, is in line with the end of the Farnborough Airfield runway. Eelmoor Flash was used, prior to the First World War, for military sea-plane trials. We are now approaching Fleet and must negotiate Pondtail New Bridge and Reading Road Bridge with care as they share Farnborough Road Bridge's low headroom. There is a car park and moorings at Reading

Road Bridge, close to town centre shops. From the latter bridge the canal continues past the *Fox and Hounds* canalside pub, meandering delightfully between villages and inns, under bridges, past copses, over embankments as though avoiding the bustle of the arteries of commerce which have usurped it – Crookham, Coxmoor Wood, Parsonage Copse, Tundry Pond, Dogmersfield, Winchfield and Barley Mow Bridge. Here there is another public slipway and a car park. Sprat's Hatch Bridge, Dogmersfield Lake, Wilks Water and Broad Oak, all pass in succession until just after Broad Oak Bridge we meet the Odiham Bypass Bridge bringing the A287 across the canal from Junction 5 of the M3 down to Farnham.

At Colt Hill is Galleon Marine on the south bank and *The Waterwitch Inn* just above it, right against Colt Hill Bridge, which leads to a car park. Here are a winding hole, telephone and tripping boat *John Pinkerton* which is operated by the Surrey and Hampshire Canal Society. Another mile towards Basingstoke, which alas you cannot reach by water, brings you to the *Swan Inn.* Then comes North Warnborough Lift Bridge, Odiham Castle and the Whitewater Aqueduct where you will have to turn for home. Ahead lie the ruins of Lock 30, which was built after the canal was opened, to add 12″ to the depth through the 1230-yard Greywell Tunnel at the eastern end of which it was sited. The footpath along the disused section takes the walker to view the eastern portal of the tunnel. In 1932 part of the tunnel roof collapsed and navigation was abandoned. In 1991 the Surrey and Hampshire Canal Society put forward a plan for restoration of a further 5 miles of the canal including the tunnel. The Society is now investigating the possibility of linking the western end of the canal to other waterways. You can view the restored entrance to the old tunnel, which is now the largest bat roost in Britain, and then walk across the road over the top to the *Fox and Goose* in Greywell Village for a pint.

The towing path

There is a towing path throughout the length of the canal, most of which has been designated as a Site of Special Scientific Interest in view of the abundance of aquatic wild life, the number and rarity of some species, and promoted by the fact that the canal has two distinct types of water: alkaline from the chalk aquifers at the western end and acidic where it passes through the heathlands to the east of Fleet.

A footbridge links the towing path of the River Wey Navigation with the Basingstoke once again at Woodham Junction, alongside the railway and motorway bridges. The path is on the south bank and proceeds by way of Scotland Bridge, from which it can be joined, past Lock No. 3 which is connected by Birchwood Drive, through to West Byfleet Station. Through Sheerwater the walker will eventually come to the site of Spanton's Yard, a former timber yard, where there are temporary moorings and Chertsey Road Bridge beyond. The canal is now level with Woking town centre to the south and the next bridge, Chobham Road Bridge, takes the path across to the north bank.

From Chobham Road the path climbs with the St John's Flight of locks to Kiln, or St John's, Bridge at the top of St John's Village. It is necessary to cross Kiln Bridge to reach the towpath now on the south bank as far as Brookwood Bridge. From Hermitage Road Bridge there is also a path on the north side along this reach up to Brookwood Bridge. From here the path stays on the north past the flight of three Brookwood Locks, passes Sheets Heath Bridge which gives access to Brookwood Rail Station, but then recrosses the canal on Pirbright Bridge to the south bank, below Lock 15 which starts the Deepcut Flight. This wooded section rises with the flight of locks between the canal and the railway and, just after the Pirbright rail junction, comes Curzon Bridge. The last three locks lead to the famous cutting beyond which is Deepcut Bridge and then the canal turns to cross the railway, the path following over the aqueduct but diverting onto Guildford Road Bridge, which takes the towing path onto what is now the western, former northern, bank. The towing path stays on this bank all the way to Greywell Tunnel. A public footpath is signposted on the north side of the *Fox and Goose* with a permissive footpath over Greywell Hill to the western end of the tunnel. The towpath has been restored for about a mile to the site of Penny Bridge at Up Nately.

Directory

BOATYARDS, MARINAS, CHANDLERIES, CLUBS, TRIPPING & HIRE

Basingstoke Canal Centre
Basingstoke Canal Centre, Mytchett Place Road, Mytchett, Surrey GU16 6DD ☎ 01252 370073. Information centre, exhibition, gift shop, club room, camping, playground, tea shop, boat trips, canal licences, mooring permits.

Mayfly
Luxury 54ft Victorian inspection launch available for lunch, dinner and buffet cruises from the Basingstoke Canal Centre. Contact John Cale Canal Cruises, Frimhurst Lodge, Guildford Road, Frimley Green, Camberley GU16 6NT ☎ 01252 837165

Merlin
Passenger trip and charter boat, light lunches and cream tea cruises, up to 45 people. Available at Basingstoke Canal Centre. Contact John Cale Cruises as above.

Daydream and Astra
Tripping narrow boats (also for hire by day or evening), skippered or self-drive cruises, party hire, picnic cruises. Available at Basingstoke Canal Centre. Contact John Cale Cruises as above.

Accessible Boating Association
6 Andrews Close, Church Crookham, Fleet, Hants GU13 0HF ☎ 01252 622520. Self-drive hire dayboat *Dawn* for the disabled, carrying 12 passengers, with wheelchair access. *Madam Butterfly*, 63′ 7-berth holiday hire boat equipped for disabled people and with wheelchair access. Based at Odiham.

Woking Recreational Boating for the Handicapped
Dalmahoy, Kettlewell Hill, Woking, Surrey GU21 4JJ ☎ 01483 714651. Free skippered short trips for up to 12 passengers with wheelchair access.

Surrey and Hampshire Canal Cruises
Mrs Marion Gough, St Catherines, Hurdle Way, Compton Down, Winchester, Hants SO21 2AN ☎ 01962 713564. Passenger tripping narrow boat *John Pinkerton* (bookings and information), operates from Colt Hill, Odiham. *Dragonfly*, 10 seater trip boat operating at rallies and canalside events at Woking and Odiham. For venues see website – www.s-h-c-c.co.uk

Galleon Marine
Colt Hill, Odiham, Basingstoke, Hants RG29 1AL ☎ 01256 703691. 2–8 berth narrow boat hire by week or short-break, motor day-boats, canoes, punts and rowing boats for hire, boat sales, outboard engines, bottled gas, chandlery, diesel fuel, pump-out, boat storage. (APCO, THCA, TBTA)

Basingstoke Canal Boating Club
Membership enquiries: Judith Morgan, 42 Woodlands Road, Farnborough, Hants GU14 9QS ☎ 01252 663674. Holds an annual rally early in September at the *Fox & Hounds*, Fleet.

Basingstoke Canal Canoe Club
Meets on Tuesday evenings in summer for training on the canal at the Basingstoke Canal Centre, Mytchett. Contact: ☎ 01252 622630.

NE Hants Water Activities Centre
Based at Courtmoor School, Fleet, Hants. Qualified canoeing instructors to teach children and adults. Special canoes for the disabled. Contact: ☎ 07967 988840.

Surrey and Hampshire Canal Society
Mrs Doreen Hornsey, 94a Aldershot Road, Fleet, Hants. GU51 3FT ☎ 01252 623591. Voluntary body concerned with the original restoration and continued maintenance of the canal, working parties, trip boat, fund raising and social activities. New members welcome.

EMERGENCY FUEL SUPPLIES
See note under this heading on page 24
Fillup Motor Co Ltd
Petrol, diesel, food
New Haw Road, Addlestone, Surrey ☎ 01932 847004/855499. By New Haw Bridge on River Wey.

College Filing Station
Petrol, diesel
College Road, Woking, Surrey ☎ 01483 723772. 500 yards from Monument Bridge under railway into Maybury Hill.

TCS Connaught Service Station
Petrol, diesel
Bagshot Road, Knaphill, Woking, Surrey ☎ 01483 798142. 20 yards north of Brookwood Bridge.

Jet Filling Station
Petrol, diesel, shop
257-9 Frimley Green Road, Frimley Green, Camberley, Surrey ☎ 01252 837325. 500 yards from Guildford Road Bridge (*King's Head*).

BP Mytchett Filling Station
Petrol, diesel, shop
150 Mytchett Road, Mytchett,

Camberley, Surrey ☎ 01252 744840. 500 yards from Basingstoke Canal Centre.

Glenland Service Station
Petrol, diesel
42 Reading Road South, Fleet, Hants ☎ 01252 626815. At Reading Road Bridge.

Swan Bridge Garage
Petrol, diesel
Hook Road, North Warnborough ☎ 01256 703778. By Swan Bridge.

PUBLIC LAUNCHING SITES
- **Mytchett** At Potter's by Mytchett Place Bridge. Further information from Basingstoke Canal Authority
- **Aldershot** Off Clubhouse Road near Wharf Bridge (Farnborough Road), south bank. BW pattern keys to barrier available from Basingstoke Canal Centre
- **Winchfield** By Barley Mow Bridge, north bank. BW pattern keys to barrier available from Basingstoke Canal Centre

FISHING TACKLE SHOPS
Goldsworth Angling Centre
73-5 Goldsworth Road, Woking, Surrey ☎ 01483 776667

Hampshire Tackle
342 High Street, Aldershot, Hants ☎ 01252 318937

The Creel
36 Station Road, Aldershot, Hants ☎ 01252 320871

Raison Brothers
2 Park Road, North Camp, Farnborough, Hants ☎ 01252 543470

Tackle Up
151 Fleet Road, Fleet, Hants ☎ 01252 614066.

HOTELS, INNS AND RESTAURANTS
The Wheatsheaf Chobham Road, Horsell, Woking ☎ 01483 773047. A *Porterhouse* restaurant. Moorings available at site of Spanton's Yard about ½ mile back along the towing path, north side of Chobham Road Bridge (50yds).

The Bridge Barn Bridge Barn Lane, Horsell, Woking ☎ 01483 763642. *Beefeater* menu. Moorings for patrons, canalside (south), opposite towing path.

Rowbarge Inn St John's Road, Woking. Moorings at Kiln Bridge, St John's, backing onto canal (south), approach from Woodend Bridge or Kiln Bridge via St John's Road.

Hunter's Lodge Bagshot Road, Knaphill, Woking. Mooring possible to towing path below Brookwood Bridge, 100yds from Brookwood Locks past 3H Motors garage.

The Brookwood Connaught Road, Brookwood, Woking.

King's Head Guildford Road, Frimley Green ☎ 01252 835431. *Harvester* menu. Moorings at Frimley Lodge Park 300yds along towing path, by Guildford Road Bridge and rail aqueduct.

Potters Mytchett Place Road, Mytchett. Mooring alongside, public slipway, cross Mytchett Place Road Bridge from towing path.

Swan Inn 2 Hutton Road, Ash Vale. At Heath Vale Bridge opposite the towing path.

Napier's 72 Vale Road, Ash. Former *Admiral Napier Inn*. Moor at Ash Wharf.

The Standard of England Ash Hill Road, Ash. 100yds from Ash Vale Bridge.

The Foresters Inn Aldershot Road, Church Crookham, Fleet. Restaurant. ¾ mile south from Norris Bridge.

The Oatsheaf Reading Road North, Fleet. 200yds northwest from Reading Road Bridge.

Fox and Hounds Crookham Road, Crookham. Mooring alongside; towing path side.

Black Horse The Street, Crookham Village. 300yds west of Malthouse Bridge opposite the village store.

George and Lobster Crondall Road, Crookham Village. 200yds north of Chequers Bridge.

Queen's Head Pilcot, Dogmersfield, Basingstoke. 600yds from towing path through Dogmersfield Village.

Barley Mow The Hurst, Winchfield, Basingstoke. Moorings at Barley Mow Bridge on towing path side.

The Water Witch Colt Hill Bridge, Odiham, Basingstoke. Moorings close by, at Colt Hill Bridge on south bank.

George Hotel High Street, Odiham, Basingstoke. ☎ 01256 702081. Half mile from Galleon Marine.

The Jolly Miller Bridge Road, Hook Road, North Warnborough, Basingstoke. Backs on to towing path on north bank in village.

The Swan Hook Road, North Warnborough, Basingstoke. Moorings. Last winding hole at Odiham Castle in ½ mile, at Swan Bridge, towing path side.

Anchor Inn North Warnborough. Moor near North Warnborough Lift Bridge and cross fields from south bank.

Fox and Goose Greywell Street, Greywell, Basingstoke. (For walkers only!) Across the road from Greywell Tunnel's eastern portal.

RAIL STATIONS AND TRAIN SERVICES

See note under this heading on page 26

South West Trains
Travel Information ☎ 08457 484950.

Byfleet & New Haw[2] *South West Trains* Westfield Parade, Byfleet Road, Byfleet, Surrey. ½ mile from Wey Towing Path. Weybridge, Surbiton and Waterloo; also Woking, Worplesdon and Guildford[2]; also to Brookwood, Ash Vale, Aldershot and Alton line. Farnborough, Fleet, Winchfield, Hook and Basingstoke.

West Byfleet *South West Trains* Station Approach, Madeira Road, West Byfleet, Surrey. 400yds south of Woodham Lock No. 3. Byfleet[2], Weybridge[2], Surbiton[2] and Waterloo; Woking, Worplesdon and Guildford[2]; also Brookwood, Ash Vale, Aldershot and Alton line. Farnborough, Fleet, Winchfield, Hook and Basingstoke.

Woking *South West Trains* Station Approach or High Street, Woking, Surrey. 650yds southwest of Chertsey Road Bridge. Waterloo (fast); Worplesdon (no Sunday service) and Guildford[2]; also Brookwood. Intermediate stations[1] to Waterloo; Ash Vale, Aldershot, Farnham and Alton; also to Farnborough, Fleet, Winchfield, Hook and Basingstoke.

Brookwood *South West Trains* Connaught Road, Brookwood, Woking, Surrey. 300yds south of Sheets Heath Bridge. Woking, Surbiton[2] and Waterloo; intermediate stations[1] to Waterloo; also to Ash Vale, Aldershot and Alton line; Farnborough, Fleet, Winchfield, Hook and Basingstoke.

Frimley *South West Trains* Bridgemead, Frimley High Street, Frimley, Camberley, Surrey. 1½ miles from Guildford Road Bridge. Camberley, Bagshot and Ascot. Change at Ascot for Staines[2], Richmond[2] and Waterloo. Ash Vale, Aldershot, Ash, Guildford[2].

Farnborough North *North Downs Line* Farnborough Street, Farnborough Green, Hants. 1 mile from Guildford Road Bridge. Blackwater, Wokingham and stations to Reading[2]; also North Camp, Ash, Guildford[2] and stations to Redhill and Gatwick.

Farnborough *South West Trains* Station Approach, Farnborough Road, Farnborough, Hants. 2 miles from Guildford Road Bridge. Fleet, Winchfield,

195

Hook and Basingstoke; also Brookwood, Woking and Waterloo. Change at Woking for intermediate stations[1] to Waterloo and stations on Aldershot and Guildford[2] lines.

North Camp *North Downs Line* Station Road West, Lysons Avenue, Farnborough, Hants. ½ mile from Mytchett Lake Road Bridge. Farnborough North, Blackwater, Wokingham and stations to Reading[2]; also Ash, Guildford[2] and stations to Redhill and Gatwick.

Ash Vale *South West Trains* Station Approach, Vale Road, Ash Vale, Aldershot, Hants. Against towing path north of Great Bottom Flash. Aldershot, Ash; also Frimley, Camberley, Bagshot and Ascot. Change for Staines[2] and London. Also to Guildford[2].

Ash *North Downs Line* Ash Church Road, Ash, Aldershot, Hants. A mile along Ash Hill Road from Ash Vale Bridge. North Camp, Farnborough North, Blackwater, Wokingham and stations to Reading[2]; also stations to Redhill and Gatwick; also to Aldershot, Ash Vale, Frimley, Camberley, Bagshot and Ascot. Change for Staines[2] and London line.

Aldershot *South West Trains* Station Road, Aldershot, Hants. 1¼ miles from Gasworks Bridge (southwest of canal) in town centre. Ash Vale, Brookwood, Woking and intermediate stations[1] to Waterloo; also Farnham, Bentley and Alton; also to Ash and Guildford[2]; also to Ash Vale, Frimley, Camberley, Bagshot and Ascot.

Fleet *South West Trains* Minley Road, Fleet, Hants. 1¼ miles from Reading Road Bridge up Fleet Road. Winchfield, Hook, Basingstoke and stations beyond; also Farnborough, Brookwood, Woking and intermediate stations[1] to Waterloo.

Winchfield *South West Trains* Winchfield, Basingstoke, Hants. 1½ miles from Barley Mow Bridge in Winchfield Village. Hook, Basingstoke and stations beyond; also Winchfield, Farnborough, Brookwood, Woking and intermediate stations[1] to Waterloo.

1. Intermediate stations between Woking and Waterloo are as follows.
Woking – West Byfleet – Byfleet and New Haw[2] – Weybridge[2] – Walton-on-Thames[2] – Hersham – Esher – Surbiton[2] – Wimbledon – Clapham Junction – Waterloo.
2. Stations marked [2] in the lists above and below are also on the Rivers Wey or Thames and are listed under their respective sections elsewhere in this guide.

BUS AND COACH SERVICES

Buses run frequently on a number of routes in the Byfleet and Woking areas of the canal but from Woking towards the canal summit, there are only two major routes – the no. 48 Countryliner service which operates hourly, Monday to Saturday, from Woking Station via Wych Hill, St John's, Hermitage Estate, Knaphill, Brookwood, Pirbright, Deepcut Post Office, Frimley Green, Mytchett and Farnborough and the Arriva route 35 which runs hourly Monday to Friday serving Camberley, Frimley, Deepcut, Lightwater, Bisley, Knaphill, Woking and Guildford.

Route 3 from Yateley to Aldershot passes through Frimley Green, Mytchett and Ash Vale. In the area of the summit level, route 200, between Camberley and Basingstoke, serves Odiham and North Warnborough.

Other services in the Aldershot, Farnborough and Fleet areas are served by Countrywide Travel services.

Further details of bus and coach services in the area can be obtained from Traveline on ☎ 0870 608 2608.

Bus operators are:
- Arriva Guildford and West Surrey ☎ 0870 608 2608
- Tellings Golden Miller ☎ 01932 340617
- Stagecoach Hants and Surrey ☎ 0845 121 0180
- Countywide Travel ☎ 01256 780079

Surrey and Hampshire Canal Society

Formed in 1966, the Surrey and Hampshire Canal Society was mainly responsible for the restoration of the Basingstoke Canal and now helps to maintain it as well as operating the John Pinkerton trip boat.

The Society issues a regular newsletter with news and pictures of the Basingstoke Canal, forthcoming events, working parties and fund-raising activities.

Details from:
Membership Secretary, Mrs Doreen Hornsey, 94a Aldershot Road, Fleet, Hants. GU51 3FT
☎ 01252 623591
Email:grador@totalise.co.uk
Website: www.basingstoke-canal.org.uk

DISTANCE TABLE

BASINGSTOKE CANAL – WOODHAM TO GREYWELL

Table of distances in miles

Miles above Woodham	Miles below Greywell	Locations	Miles between places
0·00	31·13	Woodham (junction with River Wey)	0·25
0·25	30·88	**Woodham Bottom Lock No. 1**	1·25
1·50	29·63	**Woodham Top Lock No. 6**	0·75
2·25	28·88	Sheerwater	0·75
3·00	28·13	Monument Bridge (Maybury Hill)	0·87
3·87	27·26	Woking, Wheatsheaf Bridge (Chobham Road)	1·37
5·25	25·88	**Goldsworth, Bottom Lock No. 7** (St John's Flight)	0·37
5·63	25·50	**Goldsworth, Top Lock No. 11** (*The Rowbarge*)	1·75
7·37	23·76	**Brookwood, Bottom Lock No. 12**	0·06
7·43	23·70	**Brookwood Lock No. 13**	0·07
7·50	23·63	**Brookwood, Top Lock No. 14**	1·13
8·63	22·50	**Deepcut (Frimley) Bottom Lock No. 15**	1·87
10·50	20·63	**Deepcut (Frimley) Top Lock No. 28**	1·37
11·87	19·26	Frimley Green (*The King's Head*)	1·37
13·25	17·88	Mytchett Lake	0·50
13·75	17·38	Ash Vale Station	2·25
16·00	15·13	**Ash Lock No. 29** (Canal Depot)	1·75
17·75	13·38	Wharf Bridge, Aldershot, Farnborough Road (A325)	2·88
20·63	10·50	Pondtail Bridges (A323)	1·00
21·63	9·50	Reading Road South Bridge, Fleet	2·00
23·63	7·50	Chequers Bridge, Crookham Wharf	1·50
25·13	6·00	Blacksmith's Bridge, Dogmersfield	1·12
26·25	4·88	Winchfield (*The Barley Mow*)	2·75
29·00	2·13	Colt Hill Bridge (*Waterwitch*, Galleon Marine)	1·13
30·13	1·00	North Warnborough (*The Swan*)	0·50
30·63	0·05	Whitewater Aqueduct (**limit for motor craft**)	0·50
31·13	0·00	**Greywell Lock No. 30** East end of Greywell Tunnel **Limit of navigation (canoes only)**	0·00

Brewery Gut passing the Oracle Centre at Reading, River Kennet

15. The Kennet & Avon Canal – Reading to Great Bedwyn

British Waterways

Navigation authority

British Waterways, The Locks, Bath Road, Devizes, Wiltshire SN10 1HB
☎ 01380 722859
Email
KandAenquiries@britishwaterways.co.uk

Distance

33.75 statute land miles (River Thames to Great Bedwyn, Church Lock)

Maximum dimensions of craft Reading to Bath

Headroom(at average summer level) 8´0´´ (2·41m)
Length[1] 70´0´´ (21·34m) at Burghfield Lock No. 103
Beam 13´2´´ (4·01m) at Guyer's Lock No. 84
Draught (at average summer level) 3´0´´ (0·91m)

1. Standard width 7´0´´ (2·12m) narrow boats can be accommodated up to 72´0´´ (21·95m) if set diagonally in the lock chambers.

It is possible to navigate the entire length of the Kennet & Avon Canal but, before exploring further than High Bridge, boat owners and hirers will need to ensure that they have the correct licence and also the necessary windlasses and keys to operate sluices and bridges. The keys also give access to British Waterways sanitary stations. All craft entering the navigation, either from the Thames or the Avon below Hanham Lock, or by slipping at the sites mentioned in the following text, must be licensed before navigation is permitted. Scales of charges (which include lock tolls), information and licences are available on application to the above address or from:

- British Waterways Customer Services, Willow Grange, Church Road, Watford WD1 3QA ☎ 01923 226422
- The Kennet and Avon Canal Trust, Canal Centre, Couch Lane, Devizes, Wiltshire, SN10 1EB ☎ 01380 721279
- authorised boatyards.

The lock-keepers at Blake's, Sonning and Caversham Locks are also able to issue visitor short-period licences and lock passes for the River Thames between the end of March and the end of October and at Blake's Lock for BW waterways, during normal hours between the end of March and the end of October.

To keep your craft on the canal you will need an approved permanent mooring. British Waterways moorings are available above County Lock, at Southcote, Tyle Mill, Kintbury and Hungerford in the area covered by this book. Application forms are available from the address above. Private mooring sites are listed in the *Directory* at the end of this section.

Details of any restrictions to navigation or unscheduled stoppages are available on Canalphone South ☎ 01923 201402, BW's own recorded message line; more general information can be obtained on ☎ 01380 722859 (Devizes office). An emergency helpline is available outside office hours by telephoning Freephone Canals ☎ 0800 479 9947.

Note All craft must observe the maximum speed limit of 4mph.

Further information on the canal may be obtained from The Kennet & Avon Canal Trust, The Canal Centre, Couch Lane, Devizes, Wiltshire, SN10 1EB ☎ 01380 721279.

INTRODUCTION

Those who navigate the Thames sometimes decide to venture onto other waterways that connect with it. As we note on pages 137, 175 and 187, the Oxford Canal, the River Wey and the Basingstoke Canal respectively still survive in navigable states, but the Oxford Canal can only accommodate narrow-beam (7´0´´) craft, the Wey is only 19 miles long, and the Basingstoke has a headroom problem. The River Kennet which joins the Thames at Reading, however, besides accommodating craft of slightly under 13´2´´ beam has a headroom of 8´0´´ and thus will take craft of reasonable size. The river itself leaves the canalised navigation at Newbury and follow the river to Hungerford where it then follows a tributary, the Dun, until it disappears near Picketfield Lock, from where the climb towards the canal summit begins in earnest. This section finishes at Great Bedwyn at the winding point just below Church Lock since it is not usual for craft wishing to return to

199

the Thames to proceed further. Although the waterway is now open throughout to Bath and Bristol, you need more than a week's cruising to venture so far. For details readers are referred to guides sold or published by the Kennet & Avon Canal Trust at Devizes or British Waterways.

The River Kennet is quite an old navigation. In 1723 it was possible to take a 120-ton barge to Newbury from the Thames. In 1794 a linking canal between Newbury and Bath was authorised and John Rennie was appointed engineer and architect, but it was not until 1810 that the linking canal between Newbury and Bath was opened, thus completing the through water route between London and Bristol. However, the canal suffered from severe competition from the Great Western Railway whose route it preceded and who eventually bought it. With declining traffic the canal was virtually unused by the end of the 1914-18 war. Traffic ceased altogether in the 1930s, although a final traverse of the route was accomplished in 1951 by the NB *Queen*.

In 1956 the government of the day introduced a Bill to abandon the waterway. However a petition to the Queen taken by canoe by the Kennet & Avon Canal Association resulted in the Bill being withdrawn.

Probably the most famous restoration story of the waterways of Great Britain started in 1962 when the Kennet and Avon Canal Trust was formed out of the original Canal Association which had been founded shortly after the Second World War. Derelict locks, rotting lock gates, leaking canal beds, decaying wharves, bridges and buildings needed to be restored. A partnership between British Waterways, the Kennet and Avon Canal Trust and the local authorities worked together until the first stage was completed and celebrated with a visit by Her Majesty the Queen in 1990. The remaining works securing the future of the canal were completed in 2003 following a substantial grant of £25 million from the Heritage Lottery Fund. From Reading to Hanham Lock No.1, Bristol, the official end of the canal where the tidal Avon starts, is 87½ miles and there are 104 locks not including Blake's Lock which is administered by the Thames Region of the Environment Agency.

From Reading

From the Thames you turn off into the Kennet about ¾ mile below Caversham Lock under the railway bridges. The scenery is urban around Blake's Lock which rises 3′6″(1.07m) and enables you to reach convenient moorings for shopping in the centre of Reading, since the Kennet upstream to High Bridge is under the jurisdiction of the Environment Agency and no further licence fee is payable from the Thames up to this point. Avoid taking the Abbey Loop, also known as the Forbury Loop, (on the right bank proceeding upstream) as the bridges are low and the water depth is only suitable for small craft.

The centre of Reading is close to the Kennet – much closer than the Thames which runs towards Caversham. Moorings can be found either above Blake's Lock Museum, below High Bridge, or at Chestnut Walk by the prison. Blake's Lock Museum was recently re-opened in what used to be a Victorian pumping station as a restaurant with ample mooring for patrons. Below High Bridge is the downstream end of the Brewery Gut one-way system between this point and County Lock. For more details see section 7.

Once past Blake's Lock you will require a windlass (lock-handle) to operate the locks. A Grand Union pattern one (1¼″) should be suitable but intending boaters are advised to purchase a Kennet & Avon pattern before proceeding. Most chandleries and the lock-keeper at Blake's Lock sell windlasses; Reading Marine will probably have them in stock at Padworth. If coming from the Thames you might enquire at Bridge Boats on Fry's Island which operates narrow boats for hire on the K & A.

In order to open some of the swing and lift bridges between Reading and Newbury, and to gain access to the various sanitary stations along the canal, you will also need to obtain a BW *Watermate* key. These are cylinder night-latch keys which will unlock doors or open special padlocks on swing and lift bridge mechanisms, provided to prevent the vandalism of canal property. These keys are available for sale at Blake's Lock and as above.

Under High Bridge and until the next lock, County Lock, care is needed with navigation owing to bends in the river through the Oracle Shopping Centre and note that no mooring is allowed in this area; which, after rain may give a swift current. Below the first lock as you approach the gates beware of a slight upstream current which comes round off the weir. Above County Lock Kennet Cruises may sometimes be operating its tripping boat *Lancing*, or its period hire boat *Rosina Emma* during the season – trips normally commence from *The Cunning Man* pub by Burghfield Bridge further upstream. Once at Fobney Lock, about 2 miles from Reading, there is a complete change of scenery and the often murky water may well have changed to a clear sparkling stream. If emptying Fobney Lock take care that all boats are securely moored to the landing stage below the lock before raising a paddle. Just before Southcote Lock is the rail bridge carrying the Basingstoke line across the navigation while the old Great Western line to Pewsey and Westbury, and eventually the West Country 'via Castle Cary', approaches the north bank and hugs our route all the way to Great Bedwyn. There is a slight detour away from the canal between Bull's Lock and Higgs' to the racecourse and main stations at Newbury. Note that there are some vicious bends in the river above Burghfield before you reach the M4 crossing near Theale. You will have to give way to downstream traffic approaching you since this section from Burghfield Cut up to Garston Lock, which was rebuilt in 1994, is very much a river navigation and the current may well be carrying oncoming craft faster than their helmsmen realise.

Thames-based craft will normally be carrying an anchor anyway but if your cruiser or narrow boat is not so equipped then you are advised to do something to rectify the situation. As I have already remarked, this section of the navigation is a canalised river which means that it can be subject to fierce currents after heavy or prolonged rainfall and, in the event of a breakdown, your anchor is probably your cruiser's only safe survival kit.

Theale and Tyle Mill Swing Bridges are now jacked electrically. Both these bridges require the BW *Watermate* key to operate them. Tyle Mill Lock just above the bridge has a sanitary station and a water point. There is also a slipway here but care should be exercised in its use. There are further swing bridges at Ufton, where the old Ufton Lock (No. 98) has been superseded by the rebuilding of the next lock upstream, Towney Lock which was re-opened in 1976, and Padworth. At Aldermaston there is a mechanically-operated lift bridge. Above Padworth Lock

(No. 96) on the towing path side is Reading Marine Company's new base on the old BW Maintenance Yard site, then comes the Aldermaston lift bridge just beyond Aldermaston Wharf which houses the Kennet & Avon Canal Visitor Centre, open from April to October. Boaters should take care to follow instructions concerning the operation of the lift bridge since there are certain restrictions as to times when the bridge may be opened to canal traffic. Some swing bridges along this part of the canal, and there are many, need to be unlocked with your windlass. Next is a winding hole below Aldermaston Lock (No. 95).

There is an approved method for negotiating Woolhampton Swing Bridge and Lock in view of their close proximity. Going upstream, boats should moor at the landing below the bridge. Your crew should then go and prepare the lock and open the bottom gates of the lock before opening the bridge. Once the bridge is open the boat goes straight through into the lock, the bridge is closed and the bottom gates closed for the lock to fill. Coming downstream you should empty the lock and open the swing bridge before leaving the lock.

By Woolhampton Swing Bridge is the *Rowbarge Inn* with the village, rail station – confusingly named Midgham, a village about 1¼ miles away – and post office on the off (north) side of the canal. At Oxlease Swing Bridge the towing path reverts to the north bank for a short stretch past Heale's Lock (No 93) and then crosses to the south bank on Cranwell's Swing Bridge. Meanwhile the Westbury line of the Great Western is running so close to the canal that a cruising holiday along this stretch might be a train-spotter's delight! At least you have the satisfaction of knowing that a sudden call to the office in the City can be acted upon speedily by making use of any of the stations between Reading and Great Bedwyn, or indeed returning to your boat from the City without the need for long walks or costly taxi journeys! Further rail information appears at the end of the *Directory*.

Just above Lock 92 (Midgham) is a winding hole (turning point) and again above Thatcham Bridge below Monkey Marsh Lock (No. 90), which is now a listed landmark as one of the original turf-sided locks, peculiar to the Kennet Navigation. In between, the canal passes what used to be Colthrop Board and Paper Mills, a reminder that the Kennet & Avon Canal was built to carry trade and did so from this site from

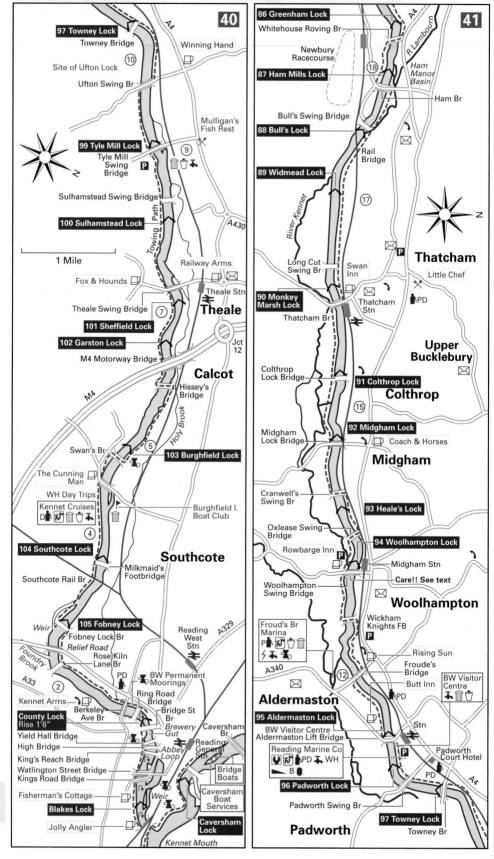

40

97 Towney Lock
Towney Bridge
Winning Hand
Site of Ufton Lock ⑩
Ufton Swing Br
Mulligan's Fish Rest
99 Tyle Mill Lock
Tyle Mill Swing Bridge
⑨
N
Sulhamstead Swing Bridge
Towing Path
A430
100 Sulhamstead Lock
Railway Arms
1 Mile
Fox & Hounds
Theale Stn
Theale Swing Bridge
Theale
⑦
101 Sheffield Lock
102 Garston Lock
Jct 12
M4 Motorway Bridge
Calcot
Hissey's Bridge
M4
Holy Brook
Swan's Br ⑤
103 Burghfield Lock
The Cunning Man
WH Day Trips
Kennet Cruises
Burghfield I. Boat Club
④
104 Southcote Lock
Southcote
Milkmaid's Footbridge
Southcote Rail Br
Weir
105 Fobney Lock
Reading West Stn
A329
Fobney Lock Br
Relief Road
Foundry Brook
Rose Kiln Lane Br
A33
PD
BW Permanent Moorings
②
Ring Road Bridge
Kennet Arms
Berkeley Ave Br
Bridge St Br
Brewery Gut
Caversham Br
Reading General Stn
County Lock Rise 1'6"
Yield Hall Bridge
High Bridge
Abbey Loop
King's Reach Bridge
Watlington Street Bridge
Kings Road Bridge
Bridge Boats
Fisherman's Cottage
Weir
Caversham Boat Services
Blakes Lock
Jolly Angler
Caversham Lock
202
Kennet Mouth

41

A4
R Lambourn
86 Greenham Lock
Whitehouse Roving Br
Newbury Racecourse
⑱
Ham Manor Basin
87 Ham Mills Lock
Ham Br
Bull's Swing Bridge
88 Bull's Lock
Rail Bridge
89 Widmead Lock
River Kennet
⑰
N
Thatcham
Little Chef
Long Cut Swing Br
Swan Inn
PD
90 Monkey Marsh Lock
Thatcham Stn
Thatcham Br
Upper Bucklebury
Colthrop Lock Bridge
91 Colthrop Lock
Colthrop
⑮
Midgham Lock Bridge
92 Midgham Lock
Coach & Horses
Midgham
Cranwell's Swing Br
93 Heale's Lock
Oxlease Swing Bridge
94 Woolhampton Lock
Rowbarge Inn
Midgham Stn
Care!! See text
Woolhampton Swing Bridge
Woolhampton
Froud's Br Marina
Wickham Knights FB
Rising Sun
Froude's Bridge
Butt Inn
PD
A340
⑫
BW Visitor Centre
Aldermaston
95 Aldermaston Lock
BW Visitor Centre
Aldermaston Lift Bridge
Stn
Padworth Court Hotel
Reading Marine Co
PD WH
B
PD
A4
96 Padworth Lock
Padworth Swing Br
97 Towney Lock
Towney Br
Padworth

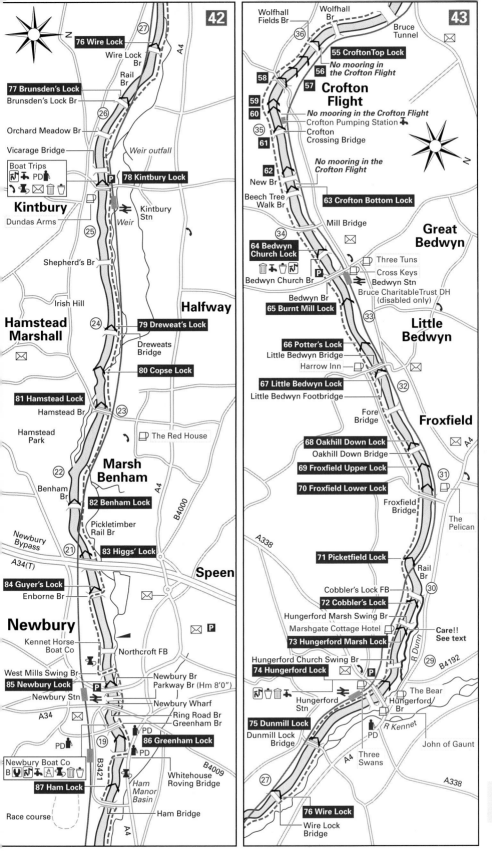

42

76 Wire Lock
Wire Lock Br
Rail Br
A4
27

77 Brunsden's Lock
Brunsden's Lock Br
26

Orchard Meadow Br

Vicarage Bridge

Weir outfall

Boat Trips
PD

Kintbury
Dundas Arms
25

78 Kintbury Lock
P
Kintbury Stn
Weir

Shepherd's Br

Irish Hill

Halfway

Hamstead Marshall
24

79 Dreweat's Lock
Dreweats Bridge

80 Copse Lock

81 Hamstead Lock
Hamstead Br
23

Hamstead Park

The Red House

Marsh Benham
A4
B4000

22

Benham Br

82 Benham Lock
Pickletimber Rail Br

83 Higgs' Lock

Speen

Newbury Bypass
21
A34(T)

84 Guyer's Lock
Enborne Br

Newbury
Kennet Horse Boat Co
Northcroft FB

West Mills Swing Br
85 Newbury Lock
P
Newbury Stn
A34
19

Newbury Br
Parkway Br (Hm 8'0")
Newbury Wharf
Ring Road Br
Greenham Br

86 Greenham Lock
PD
PD

Newbury Boat Co
B
PD

87 Ham Lock
Ham Manor Basin
Whitehouse Roving Bridge
Ham Bridge
Race course
A4

43

Wolfhall Fields Br
Wolfhall Br
Bruce Tunnel

36

55 CroftonTop Lock
56
No mooring in the Crofton Flight
58
57
59
60
Crofton Flight
35
No mooring in the Crofton Flight
Crofton Pumping Station
Crofton Crossing Bridge
61

62
New Br
No mooring in the Crofton Flight
Beech Tree Walk Br

63 Crofton Bottom Lock

Mill Bridge

Great Bedwyn

34
64 Bedwyn Church Lock
P
Bedwyn Church Br

Three Tuns
Cross Keys
Bedwyn Stn
Bruce CharitableTrust DH (disabled only)
Bedwyn Br
65 Burnt Mill Lock
33

66 Potter's Lock
Little Bedwyn Bridge
Harrow Inn

Little Bedwyn

67 Little Bedwyn Lock
Little Bedwyn Footbridge

Fore Bridge
32

Froxfield

68 Oakhill Down Lock
Oakhill Down Bridge
A4

69 Froxfield Upper Lock
70 Froxfield Lower Lock
Froxfield Bridge
31
The Pelican

A338

71 Picketfield Lock
Rail Br
30
Cobbler's Lock FB

72 Cobbler's Lock
Hungerford Marsh Swing Br
Marshgate Cottage Hotel
Care!! See text
73 Hungerford Marsh Lock

R Dunn

Hungerford Church Swing Br
74 Hungerford Lock
P
29
B4192

The Bear
Hungerford Br

Hungerford Stn

75 Dunmill Lock
Dunmill Lock Bridge
PD
R Kennet
John of Gaunt

A4
Three Swans

27

76 Wire Lock
Wire Lock Bridge

A338

203

1805 when the first paper mill was constructed here. Thatcham Bridge carries the towing path back to the north bank where the station and level crossing herald the start of Thatcham itself with the *Swan Inn*, post office, telephones, shops and the other attendant marks of civilisation. Thatcham is now a suburb, more or less, of Newbury which straddles the canalised river about an hour and a half's cruise (3½ miles and four locks) ahead. The four locks, Widmead, Bull's, Ham, and Greenham take you from cut to river and back to cut again, so always keep a lookout, particularly after rain, for the overspills and outfalls where the Kennet river leaves and rejoins the navigation. Just below Bull's Lock (No. 88) where the River Lambourn joins the Kennet we lose the railway temporarily as it crosses from the north to the south bank and heads past Newbury Racecourse for the main station in the town. Above Greenham Lock on the north bank, between the cut and the river, is the first site of the Newbury Boat Company at Greenham Lock Cottage while the next is on the opposite bank above Greenham Bridge on Greenham Island (see *Directory*).

Upstream of the ring road bridge (the A34) is Newbury Wharf with convenient moorings opposite, beside Victoria Park. The old crane has been reinstated here and the wharf building houses the Newbury Branch of the Kennet & Avon Canal Trust which has a shop and small display connected with waterborne trade on the Kennet from Newbury. Known also as the Town Wharf, this was the busy trans-shipment point for all the agricultural and raw materials carried on the river. Opposite the stone wharf building occupied by the Canal Trust, the building housing Newbury Museum is a former granary used in connection with the wharf. The Kennet Horse Boat Company run public boat trips during the season from the wharf. Upstream of the wharf is the new Park Way bridge, replacing the former temporary structure which had a restricted headroom. Beneath Newbury Bridge we come to the first lock on the canal proper, constructed in 1796, although the canal was not opened through to Bath until 1810. The original Kennet Navigation which we have just climbed was constructed between 1715 and 1724, thus linking Newbury to the Thames more than eighty years before the linking with the Avon at Bath.

Newbury to Great Bedwyn

Although the original navigation finished at Newbury, the new canal was cut using the course of the Kennet up to Kintbury so that the warnings about strong currents in times of heavy rain and the need to give way to downstream traffic still apply. However, above Kintbury Lock (No. 78) beyond Vicarage Bridge the last weir from the Kennet feeds the canal and although the line follows the Kennet valley to Hungerford, water for the forthcoming pounds will come from the Crofton Summit so that we have entered the canal section proper. Above Newbury Lock (No. 85) there is a winding point opposite West Mills Lane and above the swing bridge by the Weavers' Cottages is a mooring site, handy for shopping in Northbrook Street. Permanent linear moorings here are controlled by West Berkshire Council. Details on ☎ 01635 30267.

After Northcroft Footbridge on the north bank is another winding hole and river entry which leads to a slipway (use of which must be arranged with the Northcroft Centre on ☎ 01635 31199). This signals the return of another canal section through Guyer's and Higgs' Locks while, above Higgs', the Great Western line closes with the canal and crosses it on the curiously named Pickletimber Rail Bridge. Between Benham and Hamstead Locks the river returns for a brief spell below the wooded slopes of Hamstead Park and again above Hamstead to just below Copse Lock (No. 80). Once through Dreweat's Lock you have a mile and a half run to the next refreshment and service point at Kintbury whence tripping craft operate, railway trains run to Reading and London, and where the *Dundas Arms* dispenses hospitality beside the water. A winding hole above the bridge and lock island uses the backwater of the last river section of the Kennet and then beyond Vicarage Footbridge on the north bank is the Kennet outfall coming in under the towing path footbridge. After three more locks in three miles – just 90 minutes' cruise, not forgetting the speed limit of 4mph) – we come to the canalside town of Hungerford. Again most main services are available, including a passenger trip boat operated by the Kennet & Avon Canal Trust from Hungerford Wharf off Canal Walk below the lock. It should be noted that sewage pump-out facilities have been installed by British Waterways at Kintbury and Hungerford together with existing chemical toilet, rubbish disposal and water points, as shown on the charts.

Newbury Swing Bridge Cottages

Above Hungerford, the swing bridge crossing Hungerford Marsh Lock (No. 73) must be swung open for craft before using the lock. The necessity is probably obvious to craft locking down, but not immediately so to crews locking up! Be warned that you may well be viewed with amusement by the patrons of the *Marshgate Cottage Hotel* on the south bank below the lock. Just beyond Cobblers' Lock and the footbridge, the canal crosses the River Dun, a tributary of the Kennet, too low at this point to be of use as a water source for the canal. Below Picketfield Lock (No. 71) the railway crosses the canal yet again and hugs the north bank almost as closely as does the towing path on the south, right through to Great Bedwyn.

At Froxfield Bridge we leave Berkshire and enter Wiltshire and, between Froxfield Upper Lock and Oakhill Down (No. 68), there is a winding hole for full-length craft. Although this guide covers the canal as far as Bedwyn Church Lock (No. 64) the last winding point for craft wishing to return to the Thames is below the lock between the two bridges at Great Bedwyn. Do not enter the Crofton flight, locks 55–60, with the intention of mooring there. Mooring is prohibited at any time. Great Bedwyn has shops, a post office, railway station, garage, and boat services – a useful turning point on one's first cruise of the K & A. But, no doubt, the rest of this attractive waterway beckons. Further details can be found in guides which you may already have purchased in Reading or Newbury or, perhaps, you will indeed retrace your route to the Thames, determined to explore further on future occasions.

The towing path

The towing path starts at the Horseshoe Footbridge which carries the Thames Path over the mouth of the Kennet on the left-hand bank as one enters the navigation from the Thames. Two rail bridges and a service bridge between follow in quick succession and then one walks along a metalled path known as Kennet Side as far as the EA Thames Limit just below High Bridge, which carries Duke Street across the navigation. Now that the Oracle Shopping Centre is open, a riverside path from High Bridge to County Lock has been incorporated but you cannot call it a towing path as it is completely railed off from the Brewery Gut alongside which it runs. At High Bridge cross Duke Street/London Street, turning left and immediately right into Yield Hall Place which re-crosses the river towards Debenham's store. Or you can turn left here to walk on the Warner Cinema side without crossing Yield Hall Bridge. These riverside walks through the Oracle Centre bring you to Bridge Street and its bridge. Cross Bridge Street and take either the north route down Fobney Street, over to your right, or the southerly path, ahead, through the Anchorage Gardens past County Lock to the footbridge which climbs onto the Inner Distribution Road bridge. From here you descend the ramp to the northern bank of the river and double back under the flyover joining the northerly route from Fobney Street. The path now follows the west and north bank as far as the next lock (No. 105 Fobney Lock) from where it follows the south bank as far as Swan's Bridge, just below Burghfield Lock.

The following bridges act as roving bridges (where the towing path changes banks): Hissey's Bridge (north to south bank), Ufton Swing Bridge (south to north bank), Aldermaston Lift Bridge, by the rail station (north to south), Froude's Bridge (south to north), and Wickham Knights Footbridge (north to south). To reach Midgham Station at Woolhampton, the name having been overridden by the railway to avoid confusion with Wolverhampton, you can cross Woolhampton Swing Bridge. The next roving bridge is Oxlease Swing Bridge (south to north), then Cranwell's Swing Bridge (north to south), Thatcham Bridge

New Bridge, River Kennet, Newbury

(south to north) where there is a rail station alongside, then Ham Bridge (north to south) and, in a short stretch, Whitehouse Roving Bridge (south to north), below Greenham Lock.

The towing path now follows the north bank through Newbury to Newbury Lock and West Mills Swing Bridge above, where it returns to the south bank, passing Northcroft Footbridge which leads to the Northcroft Leisure Centre. Below Guyers Lock (No. 84) is Enborne Bridge which returns the towing path to the north bank where it runs for 7½ miles up to Dunmill Lock Bridge. Here it reverts to the south bank where it stays well beyond the end of our coverage – in fact as far as Pewsey.

Directory

BOATYARDS, MARINAS, CHANDLERIES, TRIPPING AND HIRE

The following firms may hire cruisers suitable for navigating the Kennet & Avon Canal at the eastern end from Reading although they are based on the Thames. Some firms will require an extra payment for the required British Waterways Licence since their boats will already be licensed by the National Rivers Authority to ply on the Thames.

Caversham Boat Services
Fry's Island, De Montfort Road, Reading, Berks RG1 8DG ☎ 0118 957 4323. Marine engineers, boat repairs, engine servicing, holiday hire cruisers (*Blakes*), day-boats, permanent and visitors' moorings, diesel fuel, *Calor Gas*, telephone, water point, sewage pump-out, slipway. (TBTA, THCA)

Bridge Boats Ltd
Fry's Island, De Montfort Road, Reading, Berks RG1 8LD ☎ 0118 959 0346. Marine engineers, boat repairs, holiday hire cruisers (*Hoseasons*), diesel fuel, *Calor Gas*, permanent moorings, water, slipway, pump-out. (TBTA, THCA)

The following are all based or have cruising points on the Kennet & Avon Navigation.
Kennet Cruises
14 Beech Lane, Earley, Reading, Berks RG6 2PT ☎ 0118 987 1115. Passenger trips from Burghfield Bridge aboard NB *Lancing*, also NB *Rosina Emma* available for day and period hire.

Burghfield Island Boat Club
Burghfield Island, Off Burghfield Road, Burghfield, Reading, Berks RG3 ☎ 0118 966 1668. Boat club, moorings for members only.

Reading Marine Co
Aldermaston Wharf, Padworth, Reading, Berks RG7 4JS ☎ 0118 971 3666. Narrow boat hire (*Hoseasons*), boat building, repairs, engineers, hull-blacking, boat sales, chandlery, *Calor Gas*, BW keys, windlasses, water, diesel, pump-out, refuse disposal. (TBTA, THCA)

Frouds Bridge Marina
Frouds Lane, Aldermaston, Berks RG7 4LH ☎ 0118 971 4508. Moorings, water, electricity. (TBTA)

Ham Manor Basin
Ham Lock, London Road, Newbury, Berks. Moorings; details from Newbury Boat Company (see below).

Newbury Boat Company
Greenham Lock Cottage, London Road, Newbury, Berks RG14 5SN ☎ 01635 42884. Canal services, boat sales, diesel, *Calor Gas*, narrow boat repairs, breakdown service, crane, dry dock, pump-out, refuse disposal, water, moorings. (TBTA)

Inland Waterways Holiday Cruises
Greenham Lock Cottage, London Road, Newbury, Berks RG14 5SN ☎ *Mobile* 07831 110811. Hotel narrow boats on Kennet and Avon and other canals and rivers of England and Wales. Full board. (TBTA)

Greenham Canal Services
Greenham Island, Newbury, Berks RG14 5SN ☎ 01635 31672. Day-boats for hire, narrowboat instruction, chandlery, slipway, moorings.

Kennet Horse Boat Co
32 West Mills, Newbury, Berks RG14 5HU ☎ 01635 44154. Passenger launch *Avon*, operating from Newbury Wharf and horse-drawn passenger barge *Kennet Valley*, operating from Kintbury Wharf for public trips and charter parties. Buffet catering aboard for maximum of 60 people.

Kennet & Avon Canal Trust
Hungerford Wharf, Canal Way, Hungerford, Berks RG17 0EQ. Bookings: ☎ 01488 683389. Office: Canal Centre, Couch Lane, Devizes, Wilts SN10 1EB ☎ 01380 721279. Wide beam passenger boat *Rose of Hungerford* for public trips in summer season (Sats, Suns and Weds pm), also private charter.

Bruce Charitable Trust
PO Box 21, Hungerford, Berks RG17 9YY ☎ 01672 515498. Narrow boat hire for the disabled. Day trips and period hire, operating from Great Bedwyn and Foxhanger (Devizes).

EMERGENCY FUEL SUPPLIES
See note under this heading on page 24.

Berkeley Service Station
Petrol, diesel
10 Berkeley Avenue, Reading ☎ 0118 957 3051. Near County Lock.

Elmgrade Ltd
Petrol, diesel
Bath Road, Lower Padworth, Reading ☎ 0118 971 3220. North of Aldermaston lift bridge.

Sun Garage (Watson Petroleum Ltd)
Petrol, diesel
Bath Road, Woolhampton, Reading ☎ 0118 971 3032. 500 yards north of Woolhampton Bridge.

Star Service Station
Petrol, diesel, shop
22 London Road, Thatcham, Newbury, Berks ☎ 01635 588300. 1 mile from Thatcham Bridge, north bank.

Swanbridge Service Station
Petrol, diesel, shop
256 London Road, Newbury, Berks ☎ 01635 47735. Within 400 yards of Whitehouse Roving Bridge.

Kintbury Service Station
Petrol, diesel
Newbury Street, Kintbury, Newbury, Berks ☎ 01488 658455. 400 yards south of Kintbury Bridge.

Star Service Station
Petrol, diesel
11 Charnham Street, Hungerford, Berks ☎ 01488 680100. 500 yards north of Hungerford Bridge.

LAUNCHING SITES AND ALTERNATIVES
- **Tyle Mill** Below the swing bridge on the north bank. Approach via Bath Road (A4) and turn down Sulhamstead Road. If not suitable, nearest launching point is at Padworth. Reading Marine Company has a crane at Padworth Lower Wharf (fee payable).
- **Newbury** In Kennet backwater off footpath at end of Moor Lane. Close to Northcroft Recreation Centre at end of Northcroft Lane ☎ 01635 31199. Slipway facility also at Newbury Boat Company (fee payable).

FISHING TACKLE SHOPS

Reading Angling Centre
   69 Northumberland Avenue, Whitley, Reading, Berks ☎ 0118 987 2216

Farlows-Sports Fish Ltd
   Haywards Farm, Station Road, Theale, Reading, Berks ☎ 0118 930 3860

Thatcham Angling Centre
   156 Sagecroft Road, Thatcham, Newbury, Berks ☎ 01635 871450

Field & Stream
   109 Bartholomew Street, Newbury, Berks ☎ 01635 43186

TOURIST INFORMATION OFFICES

Reading
   Town Hall, Blagrave Street, Reading, Berks ☎ 0118 956 6226

Aldermaston (open 1 April–31 October)
   Aldermaston Visitor Centre, Aldermaston Wharf, Padworth, Reading, Berks ☎ 0118 971 2868

Newbury
   The Wharf, Newbury, Berks ☎ 01635 30267
   Kennet & Avon Canal Trust, Stone Building, The Wharf, Newbury, Berks ☎ 01635 522609

HOTELS, INNS AND RESTAURANTS

Jolly Angler Kennet Side, Reading. Mooring outside along Kennet Side.

Fisherman's Cottage Kennet Side, Reading. Mooring outside along Kennet Side.

Bel and the Dragon Blake's Lock, Kenavon Drive, Reading Mooring above Blake's Weir.

Ship Hotel 4–8 Duke Street, Reading. Daytime mooring below High Bridge (overnight not recommended).

The Cunning Man Burghfield Bridge, Burghfield, Reading. Boat trips.

Fox & Hounds Sunnyside, Sulhamstead, Reading. 600yds south of Theale Swing Bridge.

Railway Arms 35 Station Road, Theale, Reading. On A4, 500yds north of Theale Swing Bridge, over railway.

The Winning Hand Bath Road, Beenham, nr. Theale, Reading. On A4 opposite Ufton Swing Bridge (north bank).

Padworth Court Hotel Bath Road, Padworth, nr Reading ☎ 0118 971 4411. On A4 Bath Road, 600 yards north of Padworth Swing Bridge or 600yds west of Towney Bridge.

Rising Sun Bath Road, Woolhampton, Reading. On A4, west of Froude's Bridge.

Butt Inn Station Road, Aldermaston, Reading. 250yds from Aldermaston Lock (south side).

Rowbarge Inn Station Road, Woolhampton, Reading. By Woolhampton Swing Bridge.

Coach & Horses Bath Road, Midgham, Reading. On A4, 500yds north of Midgham Lock (No. 92).

Berkshire Arms Bath Road, Midgham, nr. Reading ☎ 0118 971 4114. Premier Lodge and restaurant. 500yds north of Midgham Lock (No. 92).

Swan Hotel Station Road, Thatcham. Restaurant. 100yds over level crossing from Thatcham Bridge.

Old Waggon and Horses Market Place, Newbury.

McDonald's 63 Northbrook Street, Newbury.

Lock, Stock and Barrel Inn 104 Northbrook Street, Newbury. Beside Newbury Town Bridge and lock.

The Red House Marsh Benham ☎ 01635 582017

Dundas Arms Hotel Station Road, Kintbury, Newbury ☎ 01488 658263 or 658559. Canalside.

Blue Ball High Street, Kintbury, Newbury. 700yds down Station Road southwards and on into High Street from Kintbury Bridge.

John O' Gaunt Bridge Street, Hungerford. 100yds north of Hungerford Bridge.

Three Swans Hotel 117 High Street, Hungerford. 250yds south of Hungerford Bridge.

Bear Hotel Charnham Street, Hungerford ☎ 01488 682512. 200yds north of Hungerford Bridge.

Marshgate Cottage Hotel Marsh Lane, Hungerford ☎ 01488 682307. Below Hungerford Marsh Lock.

Pelican Inn London Road, Froxfield, Marlborough. West of Froxfield Bridge.

Harrow Inn High Street, Little Bedwyn. 300yds southeast of Little Bedwyn Lock.

Cross Keys High Street, Great Bedwyn. By Bedwyn Wharf Bridge on west bank.

Three Tuns High Street, Great Bedwyn. 400yds from Bedwyn Wharf Bridge on west bank.

RAIL STATIONS AND TRAIN SERVICES

See note under this heading on page 26
Enquiries: ☎ 08457 484950

- **Reading** *FGW Link* Station Hill, Reading. 500yds from Reading Bridge. Trains to London Paddington only and to Oxford only; also intermediately to Twyford, Maidenhead, Taplow (no Sunday service), Slough (for Windsor) and Paddington; Reading West and stations to

Basingstoke; also Tilehurst, Pangbourne, Goring & Streatley, Cholsey, Didcot, Radley and Oxford; also Twyford, Wargrave, Shiplake, Henley-on-Thames. Also Theale, Thatcham, Newbury, Kintbury, Hungerford, Bedwyn and Pewsey. *South West Trains* To Wokingham, Egham, Staines, Richmond and Waterloo. *North Downs Line*: Wokingham, Guildford, Dorking, Redhill and Gatwick.

- **Theale** *FGW Link* Station Road, Theale, Reading. 600yds from canal. Trains to Reading, plus Thatcham and Newbury line to Bedwyn.
- **Aldermaston** (closed on Sundays) *FGW Link* Basingstoke Road, Padworth, Reading. 100yds from canal. Reading to Newbury line.
- **Midgham** (closed on Sundays) *FGW Link* Station Road, Woolhampton, Reading. 100yds from Woolhampton Bridge. Reading to Newbury line.
- **Thatcham** *FGW Link* Pipers Lane, Station Road, Thatcham, Newbury, Berks. 20yds from canal. Reading to Newbury line.
- **Newbury Racecourse** *FGW Link* Newbury Racecourse, Hambridge Road, Newbury, Berks. ½ mile south, then west, from Ham Bridge. Trains at peak times only as for Newbury. Special service on race days. No normal Sunday service.
- **Newbury** *FGW Link* Station Road, Newbury, Berks. 500yds south of Newbury Lock. Trains to Thatcham, Theale and Reading; also Bedwyn. Peak time through trains to Paddington and the West of England.
- **Kintbury** *FGW Link* Station Road, Kintbury, Newbury, Berks. 40yds from Kintbury Bridge. Trains to Newbury and Reading; Hungerford.
- **Hungerford** *FGW Link* Station Road, Hungerford, Berks. 400yds from Hungerford Bridge. Trains to Kintbury, Newbury and Reading.
- **Bedwyn** *FGW Link* Great Bedwyn, Marlborough, Wilts. At Bedwyn Bridge. Trains to Hungerford, Kintbury, Newbury and Reading.

BUS AND COACH SERVICES

Two main bus routes run between Reading and Newbury, one via Bucklebury and a regular route along the A4 via Theale, Woolhampton and Thatcham. Burghfield is served from Reading by the buses to Tadley. Beyond Newbury, Hungerford and Bedwyn are served by routes to Marlborough. For details ☎ 08457 09 08 99.

Bus operators are:
- Newbury Buses ☎ 01635 567500
- Reading Buses ☎ 0118 959 4000

DISTANCE TABLE

KENNET & AVON CANAL READING TO GT BEDWYN
Table of distances in miles

Miles above River Thames	Miles below Great Bedwyn	Locks or locations	Rise of Lock	Miles between places
0·00	33·75	Horseshoe Bridge (junction with R. Thames)		0·00
0·32	33·43	Blake's (EA lock)	3´6˝	0·32
1·50	32·25	County (106)	1´6˝	1·18
2·50	31·25	Fobney (105)	7´8˝	1·00
3·50	30·25	Southcote (104)	5´3˝	1·00
5·00	28·75	Burghfield (103)	7´0˝	1·50
6·25	27·50	Garston (102)	7´7˝	1·25
7·00	26·75	Sheffield (101)	2´2˝	0·75
7·63	26·12	Sulhamstead (100)	4´1˝	0·63
9·00	24·75	Tyle Mill (99)	6´4˝	1·37
9·75	24·00	Ufton (98)	(degated)	0·75
10·37	23·38	Towney (97)	9´8˝	0·62
11·00	22·75	Padworth (96)	5´1˝	0·63
11·25	22·50	Aldermaston (95)	6´11˝	0·25
13·00	20·75	Woolhampton (94)	8´11˝	1·75
14·25	19·50	Heales (or Hales) (93)	8´11˝	1·25
14·75	19·00	Midgham (92)	7´9˝	0·50
15·50	18·25	Colthrop (91)	7´7˝	0·75
16·00	17·75	Monkey Marsh (90)	6´8˝	0·50
17·00	16·75	Widmead (89)	3´7˝	1·00
17·25	16·50	Bull's (88)	5´9˝	0·25
18·00	15·75	Ham Mills (87)	4´2˝	0·75
19·00	14·75	Greenham (86)	6´11˝	1·00
19·50	14·25	Newbury (85)	5´3˝	0·50
20·50	13·25	Guyer's (84)	7´0˝	1·00
21·00	12·75	Higg's (83)	5´10˝	0·50
21·63	12·12	Benham (82)	6´3˝	0·63
23·00	10·75	Hamstead (81)	6´5˝	1·37
23·37	10·38	Copse (80)	6´0˝	0·37
23·88	9·87	Dreweat's (79)	5´9˝	0·51
25·50	8·25	Kintbury (78)	5´9˝	1·62
26·13	7·62	Brunsden's (77)	4´11˝	0·63
26·87	5·88	Wire (76)	6´10˝	0·74
27·87	5·75	Dunmill (75)	5´8˝	1·00
28·50	5·25	Hungerford (74)	8´0˝	0·63
29·13	4·62	Hungerford Marsh (73)	8´1˝	0·63
29·50	4·25	Cobblers (72)	8´3˝	0·37
30·50	3·25	Picketfield (71)	7´0˝	1·00
31·00	2·75	Froxfield Lower (70)	7´0˝	0·50
31·19	2·56	Froxfield Upper (or Middle) (69)	6´11˝	0·19
31·38	2·37	Oakhill Down (68)	5´11˝	0·19
32·25	1·50	Little Bedwyn (67)	6´11˝	0·87
32·67	1·08	Potters (or Little Bedwyn Field) (66)	7´6˝	0·42
33·13	0·62	Burnt Mill (or Knight's Mill) (65)	7´9˝	0·46
33·75	0·00	Great Bedwyn Church (64)	7´11˝	0·62

Appendix

Useful addresses

Amateur Rowing Association The Priory, 6 Lower Mall, Hammersmith, London W6 9DJ.

Association of Pleasure Craft Operators Parkland House, Audley Avenue, Newport, Shropshire TF10 7BX

Blakes Holiday Boating Spring Mill, Earby, Barnoldswick, Lancashire BB94 0AA.

Boat Safety Scheme British Waterways, Willow Grange, Church Road, Watford, Herts WD17 4QA

British Canoe Union John Dudderidge House, Adbolton Lane, West Bridgford, Nottingham NG2 5AS.

British Marine Federation Meadlake Place, Thorpe Lea Road, Egham, Surrey TW20 8HE.

British Standards Institution (Sales Dept), Linford Wood, Milton Keynes, Bucks MK14 6LE.

Cruising Association CA House, 1 Northey Street, Limehouse Basin, London E14 8BT.

HM Coastguard The Coastguard Agency, Spring Place, 105 Commercial Road, Southampton SO15 1EG.

HM Customs & Excise New Kings Beam House, 22 Upper Ground, London SE1 9PJ

Hoseasons Holidays Sunway House, Lowestoft NR32 2LW.

Inland Waterways Association PO Box 114 Rickmansworth WD3 1ZY

Maritime and Coastguard Agency (MCA) Marine Office, Central Court, Knoll Rise, Orpington, Kent BR6 0JA

National Federation of Sea Schools Staddlestones, Fletchwood Lane, Totton, Southampton SO40 7DZ.

Register of British Shipping & Seamen Block 2, Government Building, St Agnes Road, Gabalfa, Cardiff CF4 4YA.

Residential Boat Owners Association PO Box 46, Grays, Essex RM18 8DZ

Royal National Lifeboat Institution West Quay Road, Poole, Dorset BH15 1HZ

Royal Yachting Association RYA House, Romsey Road, Eastleigh, Hants SO50 9YA.

Thames Traditional Boat Society 21 Landcross Drive, Abington Vale, Northampton NN3 3LR

The Yacht Harbour Association Evegate Park Barn, Smeeth, Ashford, Kent TN25 6SX

Yacht Designers & Surveyors Association Wheel House, Petersfield Road, Bordon, Hants GU35 9BU.

All other addresses relevant to the navigations described are shown in the preambles to sections or in the *Directory* sections within this book.

Thames Boating Trades Association (TBTA)

Like the Thames Hire Cruiser Association, the Thames Boating Trades Association is affiliated to the British Marine Federation (BMF) and represents a large number of firms in the boating industry which have business interests in the Thames Valley. Listed here are all those firms featured in the *Directory* sections of this book. Their locations can be discovered from the index. Members have the legend (TBTA) with their entries.

Further information about the Association is obtainable from the Hon. Secretary, Paul Wagstaffe Esq at 51 New Road, Bourne End Bucks SL8 5BT ☎ 01628 524376 or John Crevald Esq on ☎ 01344 886615.

MEMBERS WHO HAVE ENTRIES IN THE DIRECTORY SECTIONS OF THIS BOOK

4All Marine

Abingdon Boat Centre

TW Allen & Son (Yachts) Ltd

Aqua Marine Ltd

W Bates & Son (Boatbuilders) Ltd

Bisham Abbey Sailing and Navigation School
Boat Showrooms Limited
Bossom's Boatyard Ltd
Bourne End Marina
Bray Marine Sales Ltd
Bridge Boats Ltd
Bridge Marine
Bushnell Marine Services Ltd
Caversham Boat Services
Chertsey Meads Marine
Clewer Boatyard Ltd
Cotswold Boat Hire
Cotswold River Cruises
DBH Marine
Environment Agency, Thames Region
Eyot House Ltd
Farncombe Boat House
Frouds Bridge Marina (Kennet & Avon Canal)
Galleon Marine (Basingstoke Canal)
Gibbs (Marine Sales)
Guildford Boat House Ltd (River Wey)
Hambleden Mill Marina
Harts Boats
Heyland Marine
Hobbs & Sons Ltd
Inland Waterways Holiday Cruises (Kennet & Avon Canal)
Tom Jones Marina Ltd (Bourne End)
Kew Marine
Konexion Ltd
Kris Cruisers
London Tideway Harbour Company
M E C (Marine Equipment and Components)
Maritek Holdings Ltd (Taggs Boatyard)
Nauticalia Ltd
Newbury Boat Co (Kennet & Avon Canal)
Old Windsor Motor Boat School
Osney Marina (Osney Marine Engineering Co)
Oxford Cruisers
Penton Hook Marina
Penton Hook Marine Sales
J Pleace Riverworks Ltd
Racecourse Yacht Basin (Windsor)
Reading Marine Co (Kennet & Avon Canal)
Salter Brothers Ltd
Sheridan Marine
Stanley & Thomas
Swancraft Ltd
Taggs Boatyard Ltd
Taplow Marine Consultants
Thames (Ditton) Marina Ltd
Thames Electric Launch Co
Thames Marine (Bray) Ltd
Tough Brothers Ltd
Walton Marine Sales Ltd
Windsor Marina
Geo Wilson & Sons (Boatbuilders) Ltd
Woottens Boatyard
Wrayside Boathouse
Val Wyatt Marine Sales Ltd

ATYC

Association of Thames Yacht Clubs (ATYC)

The Association of Thames Yacht Clubs was founded in 1949 by the three motor cruising clubs now known as the Upper Thames Motor Yacht Club, based near Reading; the Thames Motor Yacht Club, based at Hampton Court; and the British Motor Yacht Club at Teddington. Originally entitled the Association of Thames Motor Boat Clubs (ATMBC), its aims were 'to promote and protect the interests of private boat owners on the Thames and to develop good fellowship between clubs and members'. To achieve its aims the ATMBC managed to get a representative appointed to the Board of the Thames Conservancy, then the navigation authority for the river above Teddington. The then Chairman, J R Pearce OBE, was duly elected and remained a member until the re-organisation in 1974 when Thames Water assumed responsibility for navigation. He was re-appointed to the Authority and, with other members of the Association, has served on various committees of regulatory and other bodies concerned with the river. It was due very much to the representations of the ATYC, as it had become known, that locks were enlarged and mechanised, 24-hour mooring sites were established, driftwood collection in the Tideway was instituted, and lay-bys and sanitary stations were installed. The number of clubs joining the Association has grown rapidly over the years and the sphere of influence has been extended seawards, thanks to the happy relationships which have been built up with the various Thames navigation authorities, the Port of London Authority and the Marine Unit (formerly Thames Division) of the Metropolitan Police.

An annual rally and boat handling competition is organised each year and a team event is run to compete for the *Motor Boat & Yachting* Jubilee Trophy. There are over 50 clubs in the Association and many inter-club competitions and rallies take place each year. Member clubs are shown in the Club section of the *Directories* with the (ATYC) legend at the end of the entry.

Further details are obtainable from the Chairman: Colin L Rennie JP, 75 Egremont Drive, Lower Earley Berkshire, RG6 3BS.

Index

Note: Plan numbers are shown in **bold** type preceded by **P**, with **T** indicating the Tideway plans on pages 4-5

A C Marine, 43
Abbey Barge Club, 44
Abbey (Forbury) Loop, 98, 200 **P15, P15A, P40**
Abbey SC, 124, 128 **P22**
Abbey Stream (Abingdon), 124 **P22**
Abbey Stream (Chertsey), 34 **P5**
Abbey Stream (Newark), 177 **P34**
Abingdon, 29, 124-6, 128, 129 **P22**
Abingdon Boat Centre (Kingcraft Ltd), 126, 128, 129 **P22**
Abingdon Bridge, 126, 129, **P22**
Abingdon Lock, 126, 129, **P22**
Abingdon Town RC, 124, 128, **P22**
Accessible Boating Association, 193
accommodation: listed at end of each section
Actief Barge Cruising Holidays, 88
Addlestone, 177
Addlestone Canoe Club, 184 **P33**
Albany Motor YC, 25 **P3**
Albany Park Canoe & SC, 25
Albany Reach, 18 **P3**
Albert Bridge (London) **T**
Albert Bridge (Old Windsor), 47 **P7**
Aldermaston, 201 **P41**
Aldermaston Lift Bridge, 201 **P41**
Aldermaston Lock, 201 **P41**
Aldershot, 188, 194 **P38**
Allen, T W, & Son (Yachts) Ltd, 19, 23 **P3**
Amateur Rowing Association, 211
Anchor BC, 162
anchoring, 172, 173
Andersey Island, 126 **P22**
Angler's Flash, 191 **P38**
angling and fishing tackle; information at end of each section
Anglo Welsh Waterway Holidays, 148 **P26**
Appleford, 124 **P21**
Appleton, 145 **P27**
Appletree Eyot, 100 **P16**
Aqua Marine, 43
Aquarius SC, 25 **P3**

Aquatec Marine, 103 **P14**
Ariel (BBC) SC, 25 **P2**
Arthur's Bridge, 188 **P37**
Ash, 192 **P38**
Ash Embankment, 192 **P38**
Ash Island, 19 **P3**
Ash Lock, 188, 192 **P38**
Ash Vale, 191 **P38**
Ash Vale Rail Bridge, 191 **P38**
Association of Pleasure Craft Operators, 211
Association of Thames Yacht Clubs (ATYC), 92, 212
Aston, 81, 90 **P13**
Astra, 191, 193 **P38**
Avon, River, 199, 200
Aylings Ltd, 164

Bablock Hythe, 145, 148 **P26**
Barber, David, 69
Barge Lock *see under* Teddington Locks
barges, fuel (Westminster Petroleum), 6 **T**
Barley Mow Bridge, 192 **P39**
Barnes Rail Bridge **T**
Barrier Gardens Pier **T**
Basildon (Gatehampton) Bridge, 114 **P17**
Basingstoke Canal, 29, 31, 175, 177, 180, 187-98 **P33 P37 P38 P39**
Basingstoke Canal BC, 194
Basingstoke Canal Canoe Club, 194 **P38**
Basingstoke Canal Centre, 191, 193 **P38**
Bates, W, & Son (Boatbuilders) Ltd (Star Marina), 43 **P5**
Bates Wharf Marine Sales Ltd, 43 **P5**
Battersea Bridge **T**
Bavin's Gulls (Sloe Grove Islands), 68 **P10**
BBC (Ariel) SC, 25 **P2**
Bedwyn Church Lock, 199, 205 **P43**
Belfast, HMS, 13 **T**
Bell, G S & E A, 21
Bell Rope Meadow, 69
Bell Weir, 36 **P6**
Bell Weir Lock, 36, 38 **P6**
Benham Lock, 204 **P42**
Benn's Island, 19 **P3**
Benson, 29, 121 **P20**
Benson Lock, 121 **P20**
Benson Waterfront Ltd, 128 **P20**
Better Boating Co, 98, 105 **P15A**
Binsey, 138 **P25**
Bisham **P11**
Bisham Abbey Sailing & Navigation School Ltd, 76, 77 **P11**

Black Potts Ait, 49, 55
Black Potts Rail Bridge, 49 **P8**
Blackfriars Bridge **T**
Blackwater River, 192 **P38**
Blake's Bridge, 98
Blakes Holiday Boating, 29, 29, 211
Blake's Lock, 97-8, 200 **P15 P15A P40**
Blake's Lock Museum, 98, 200 **P15**
Bloomer's Hole, 157 **P31**
Bluenine Marine, 103
Boarden Bridge, 181 **P36**
Boat Breakdowns (Benson Waterfront), 128 **P20**
boat hire and trips: listed at end of each section
Boat Safety Scheme, 211
Boat Shop, The, 6, 17, 23 **P1 P2**
Boat Showrooms Ltd (Harleyford), 87 **P12**
Boat Showrooms (Shepperton Marina), 40 **P4**
boatyards: listed at end of each section
Borough Lake, 95 **P14**
Bossom's Boat Yard Ltd, 138, 140, 148 **P24 P24A**
Botany Bay, 68 **P10**
Botley Stream, 137
Boulters Island, 56, 68 **P10**
Boulters Lock, 55, 56-7, 68 **P9 P10**
Boulters Lock Cut, 68
Boulters Weir (Maidenhead Weir), 56, 58
Bounty Riverside Inn, 77
Bourne, River, 34
Bourne End Cruiser & YC, 76
Bourne End Marina, 69, 75, 76 **P10 P11**
Bourne End Reach, 69 **P11**
Boveney Lock, 52 **P8**
Boveney Weir, 52 **P8**
Bow Bridge (North Stoke), 116 **P19**
Bow Creek, 3, 11, 12 **T**
Bow Lock, 3-6, 11, 12**T**
Bowbridge BC, 118 **P19**
Bower's Lock, 180 **P35**
Boyle Farm Island, 18 **P3**
BP YC, 25
Bradford's Brook, 116 **P19**
Bray, 54, 55, 65 **P9**
Bray Boats, 63
Bray Cruiser Club, 65
Bray Film Studios, 55 **P9**
Bray Lock, 55 **P9**
Bray Marina Ltd (MDL), i, 55, 60, 63 **P9**
Bray Marine Sales, 63 **P9**
Brentford, 3, 10, 11, 12 **T**

Brentford Dock Marina, 3, 6 T
Brentford Locks, 3, 10, 11 T
Brewery Gut, 98, 198, 200 **P40**
Bridge Boats Ltd, 100, 106, 200, 206 **P15 P15A P40**
Bridge Eyot, 56 **P9**
Bridge Marine Ltd, 40 **P4**
bridge marks, 170
bridges, 171
British Canoe Union, 211
British Marine Federation, 211
British Motor YC, 24 **P1 P2**
British Motor YC (Sailing Section), 25
British Seagull, 117
British Standards Institution, 211
British Waterways, 2, 3-6, 10, 13
  Canalphone South, 199
  emergency Freephone Canals, 199
  pre-booking of BW locks, 3-6
  visitor centre (Kennet & Avon Canal) 201, **P41**
  Watermate key, 3, 200
Broad Oak, **P39**
Broad Oak Bridge (Basingstoke Canal), 192 **P39**
Broad Oak Bridge (Wey & Godalming Navigation), 180 **P35**
Broadford Bridge, 181 **P36**
Brocas, The 51 **P8**
Brookwood Locks, 189 **P37**
Brownjohn, D A, Boatbuilders, 89
Bruce Charitable Trust, 207 **P43**
Brunel University RC, 64
Brunsden's Lock **P42**
Buck Aits, 95 **P14**
Bucks Eyot (Guards Club Island), 56 **P9**
Bucks Eyot (Reading), 100 **P16**
Bull's Lock, 201, 204 **P41**
Bulstake Stream, 134, 137 **P24, P24A**
buoyage, 170
Burcot **P21**
Burgan fuel barge, 6 T
Burghfield, 201 **P40**
Burghfield Bridge, 201 **P40**
Burghfield Cut, 201 **P40**
Burghfield Island BC, 207 **P40**
Burghfield Lock **P40**
Burnt Mill Lock **P43**
Burpham, **P35**
Burroway Brook, 153 **P29**
Burway RC, 44 **P5**
bus and coach services: listed at end of each section
Buscot, 155 **P31**
Buscot Lock, 155, 157 **P31**
Buscot Wick **P31**
Bush Ait, 52 **P8**
Bushnell Marine Services Ltd, 93, 105 **P14**
Butcher Marine, 105
Byfleet, 31, 177, 188 **P33**
Byfleet BC, 177, 183, 184 **P33**

Cadogan Pier, 6 T
Calcot, **P40**
Cale, John, Canal Cruises, 193
Canalboat Holidays Ltd, 29
Canary Wharf Pier T
canoeing, sailing and rowing on the Thames, 171
Cart Bridge, 177, 179 **P34**
Cassington, 142 **P25**
Cassington Mill, 144
Castle Eaton **P32**
Castle Mill Boatyard **P24 P24A**
Castle Mill Stream, 137 **P24A**
Catteshall Bridge, 181 **P36**
Catteshall Lock, 181 **P36**
Caversham, 98, 107 **P15 P15A**
Caversham Boat Services, 29, 100, 106, 206 **P15 P15A P40**
Caversham Bridge, 100 **P15 P15A P40**
Caversham Lock, 70, 98, 200 **P15 P15A P40**
Chalmore Hole, 116 **P19**
Chambers, H, Ltd, 43 **P6**
chandleries: listed at each section
Chaplin, T Harrison, 19, 24 **P3**
Charing Cross Rail & Footbridge T
Charvil, 95 **P14**
Chef King, 119
Chelsea T
Chelsea Bridge T
Chelsea Harbour, 3, 6 T
Chelsea Harbour and Pier T
Chelsea Yacht & Boat Company Ltd, 6 T
Cherry Garden Pier, 6 T
Chertsey, 34, 188 **P5**
Chertsey Bridge, 33, 34 **P5**
Chertsey Camping Club, 34
Chertsey Lock, 33, 34, 150 **P5**
Chertsey Marine, 43
Chertsey Mead, 34 **P5**
Chertsey Meads Marine Ltd, 34, 42 **P5**
Chertsey Road Bridge (Woking), 188 **P37**
Chertsey Weir, 34
Cherwell, River, 132 **P24 P24A**
Child Beale Wildlife Trust, 111 **P17**
Chillingworth Ait (Swan Island), 16 T
Chimney, 151 **P28**
Chiswick Pier, 6 T
Chiswick Quay, 3 T
Chiswick Quay Marina, 6
Chiswick Yacht & BC, 6
Chobham Road Bridge, 188 **P37**
Cholsey, 116, 118
Chris Cruises Ltd, 18, 23 **P3**
Christchurch Meadows Boathouses (Oxford), 132, 134, 140 **P24A**
Christchurch Playing Fields (Caversham), 100 **P15**
Church Crookham, **P39**
Church Island, 36 **P6**

City of Oxford RC, 134, 140 **P24**
Classic Yacht-Charters, 63 **P8**
Cleeve Lock, 114-15 **P18**
Clewer Boatyard Ltd, 52, 63 **P8**
Clewer Mill Stream, 52 **P8**
Clifton Hampden, 122 **P21**
Clifton Hampden Bridge, 122 **P21**
Clifton Lock, 122, 124 **P21**
Clifton Lock Cut, 124 **P21**
Cliveden Deep, 68 **P10**
Cliveden House, 68 **P10**
clubs: listed at end of each section
Cobblers' Lock, 205 **P43**
Coffin Lock *see under Teddington Locks*
Cokethorpe School BC, 148
Collars Ltd, 164
College Cruisers Ltd, 138, 139 **P24 P24A**
Colley, Bill, 164
Colliers Launches Ltd, 21
Colt Hill, 192
Colt Hill Bridge, 192 **P39**
Colthrop, 201 **P41**
Colthrop Lock **P41**
Cook Piling, 88 **P12**
Cookham, 68-9, 77 **P10**
Cookham Bridge, 68-9, 72 **P10**
Cookham Lock, 68, 69 **P10**
Cookham Reach SC, 69, 76 **P10**
Coopers Hill, 37, 47 **P7**
Copse Lock, 204 **P42**
Corporation Island (Richmond Ait), 16 T **P1**
Cotswold Boat Hire, 29, 157, 162 **P31**
Cotswold River Cruises, 162 **P31**
County Lock, 98, 199, 201 **P15 P15A P40**
County River Centre, 118 **P17**
Cowey Sale, 31 **P4**
Coxes Lock, 177 **P33**
Cradle Bridge, 154 **P30**
Cranwell's Swing Bridge, 201 **P41**
Cricklade, 151, 160 **P32**
Crofton Flight, 205 **P43**
Crofton Summit, 204 **P43**
Crowmarsh Gifford **P19**
Cruising Association, 6, 211 T
Cuckoo Weir Stream, 52 **P8**
Culham, **P22**
Culham Bridge, 124, 126 **P22**
Culham Lock, 124 **P22**
Culham Lock Cut, 124 **P22**
Culham Reach, 124 **P22**
Cutler's Ait (Tangier Island), 50

D & T Scenics, 100, 106 **P15 P15A**
Danesfield, 81
Danesfield (Thames) RC, 81, 89
Danesfield (Thames) SC, 81, 89
Dapdune Bridge, 180 **P35**
Dapdune Wharf, 180, 183 **P35**
Datchet, 29, 47-9 **P7**

Datchet Wharf, 49
Daydream, 191, 193 **P38**
Day's Lock, 121, 122 **P21**
DB Marine, 68, 75 **P10**
DBH Marine, 39 **P4**
De la Hunty Marine, 20, 24 **P3**
Deadwater Ait, 51 **P8**
Dean Marine (Engineers), 76
Deepcut Flight, 188, 189 **P38**
Deepman's Footbridge, 191 **P38**
Dennett, Mike, 35, 43 **P5**
Desborough Cut, 31 **P4**
Desborough SC, 44 **P4**
Didcot Power Station, 124 **P22**
distance tables
    Basingstoke Canal, 197
    Kennet & Avon Canal, 210
    River Thames, 165-7
    River Wey & Godalming
        Navigations, 186
Ditton Skiff & Punting Club, 25
    P3
Dogmersfield, **P39**
Dogmersfield Lake, 192 **P39**
Dolphin County River Centre,
    111
Donnington Bridge, 131, 132,
    140 **P24**
Donzi Powerboats (UK) Ltd, 43
Dorchester-on-Thames, 121 **P20**
Dorchester Bridge, 121 **P20**
Dorney Lake Services, 65
Dorney Rowing Lake, 52 **P8**
Douglas (Carl) Racing Shells,
    164
Dove Marina (London Tideway
    Harbour Co), 6
D'Oyly Carte Island, 31
Dreadnought Reach, 95 **P15**
Dreadnought Scullers, 45
dredgers, 171
Dreweat's Lock, 204 **P42**
Driveline Marine Ltd, 106 **P16**
Duck Ait, 19 **P3**
Duke's Bridge, 138 **P25**
Duke's Cut, 138, 142 **P25**
Duke's Lock, 138 **P25**
Dumsey Eyot, 34 **P5**
Dun, River, 199, 205 **P43**
Dunfield, **P32**
Duxford Ford, 151 **P28**

East Eyot, 83 **P13**
East Molesey **P3**
Eaton Footbridge, 155 **P31 P30**
Eaton Hastings, 154, 155
Edwards, F, Engineers Ltd, 21
Eel Pie Boatyard Ltd, 21 **P1**
Eel Pie Island, 16 **T P1**
Eel Pie Island Slipways Ltd, 21
    P1
Eelmoor Flash, 192 **P38**
Egham, **P6**
electric boats, 172
Elmbridge Borough Council, 19
Elmbridge Canoe & Kayak
    Club, 44

Embankment Pier, 9 **T**
emergencies, 8-9
*emergency fuel supplies: listed
    at end of each section*
Environment Agency, iii, 2, 14,
    168-74
    Craft Registration office, 14
    Lock & Weir Permit, 21
    publications, 168-9
    *registration and licensing
        information*, 169
    rule of the river, 169-70
Espar Ltd, 88 **P12**
Eton, 49, 50 **P8**
Eton College, 49, 67 **P8**
Eton College BC, 64
Eton College Boat House
    (Boveney), 52, 65 **P8**
Eton College Boat House
    (Eton), 64
Eton College, Dorney Rowing
    Lake, 52 **P8**
Eton Excelsior RC, 52, 65 **P8**
Eton Racing Boats, 164
European Waterways Ltd, 61
Evenlode, River, 144 **P25**
Eynsham, 144
Eynsham Lock, 144 **P25**
Eyot Boat Centre & Club, 90
Eyot House Ltd, 31, 42 **P4 P5**
Eysey, **P32**

Falcon RC, 140
Farmoor, 145
Farmoor Reservoir, 145 **P26**
Farnborough, **P38**
Farnborough Road Bridge, 192
    P38
Farncombe, 181 **P36**
Farncombe Boat House, 29,
    181, 183-4 **P36**
Fawley Court, 83 **P13**
Ferry Eyot, 86 **P13**
Festival Pier, 6 **T**
Fireworks Ait, 51
*fishing tackle shops and angling
    information: listed at end of
    each section*
Fleet, 192 **P39**
Fobney Lock, 201 **P40**
Folly Bridge, 132, 134, 135 **P24**
    P24A
Forbury (Abbey) Loop, 98, 200
    P15 P15A P40
Formosa Island, 68 **P10**
4 All Marine, 43 **P5**
Four Rivers/Streams, 134, 137
    P24 P24A
Four Streams, 134
Freddy fuel barge, 6
Freebody, Peter, & Co, 68, 75,
    80, 88 **P10 P12**
French Brothers Ltd, 47, 51, 52,
    56, 61 **P7 P8**
French Engineering, 61 **P7**
Friday Island, 47 **P7**
Frimley, **P38**
Frimley Green, 191 **P38**
Frimley Lodge Park, 191

Frimley Rail Aqueduct, 189 **P38**
Fringilla, 64
Frog Mill Ait, 81 **P12**
Frouds Bridge Marina, 207 **P41**
Froxfield Bridge, 205 **P43**
Froxfield Locks, 205 **P43**
Fry's Island (De Montfort
    Island), 99, 200 **P15A**
*fuel barges (Westminster
    Petroleum)*, 6
*fuel supplies: listed at end of
    each section*
Fulham Rail Bridge **T**

Galleon Marine, 29, 188, 192,
    194 **P39**
Garricks Ait, 19 **P3**
Garside, Neil, 105
Garston Lock, 201 **P40**
Gatehampton (Basildon) Bridge,
    114 **P17**
Genet Marine Ltd, 43 **P5**
Gibbs (Marine Sales), 42 **P4**
Gibraltar Islands, 69 **P11**
Glen Island, 56 **P9 P10**
Glover's Island (Petersham Ait),
    16 **T P1**
Godalming, 175 **P36**
Godalming Bridge, 181 **P36**
Godalming Packet Boat Co,
    184 **P36**
Godalming Wharf, 181 **P36**
Godstow, 138, 142
Godstow Lock, 142 **P25**
Goldsworth (St John's) Flight,
    188 **P37**
Goring, 114, 115 **P18**
Goring Bridge, 114, 115 **P18**
Goring Gap, 114
Goring Gap RC, 118
Goring Lock, 114, 115 **P18**
Goring SC, 115, 118 **P18**
Grafton Lock, 154, 155 **P30**
Grand Pont, 134 **P24**
Grand Union Canal, 7, 10, 29
    T
Grass Eyot, 56 **P9**
Great Bedwyn, 199, 205 **P43**
Great Bottom Flash, 191 **P38**
Great Brook, 151
Great Eastern Pier **T**
Great River Journeys Ltd, 89,
    117 **P19**
Greenham Bridge, 204 **P42**
Greenham Canal Services, 207
Greenham Lock, 204 **P41 P42**
Greenland Pier **T**
Greenwich, 11
Greenwich Pier, 9 **T**
Greenwich YC, 6 **T**
Greywell, 192 **P39**
Greywell Tunnel, 192 **P39**
Guards Club Island (Bucks
    Eyot), 56 **P9**
Guildford, 29, 175, 179, 180-
    81, 184 **P35 P36**
Guildford Boat House, 29, 175,
    180-81, 182, 183 **P35 P36**
Guildford RC, 181, 184

Guildford Road Bridge (Frimley Green), 191 **P38**
Guildford Town Bridge, 180
Guildford Waterside Centre, 180, 184 **P35**
Guyer's Lock, 204 **P42**

Hagley Pool, 137, 142 **P25**
Halfway, **P42**
Hallsmead Ait, 95 **P14**
Ham **P1**
Ham Dock, 16 **P1**
Ham Island, 47 **P7**
Ham Lock (Ham Mills), 204 **P41 P42**
Ham Manor Basin, 207 **P41 P42**
Hambleden Lock, 81, 82 **P13**
Hambleden Mill Marina, 88 **P13**
Hambleden Place, 90 **P13**
Hambleden Weirs, 81, 82 **P13**
Hamhaugh Island, 34 **P5**
Hammersmith Bridge, 7 **T**
Hammerton, W, & Co, 6, 21 **P1**
Hampton Court Bridge, 18 **P3**
Hampton Court Landing Stage, 18, 23 **P3**
Hampton Court Palace, 9, 18 **P3**
Hampton Court Park, 18 **P2**
Hampton Ferry Boat House Ltd, 19, 24 **P3**
Hampton SC, 19, 25 **P3**
Hampton Wick, 18
Hamstead, 204 **P42**
Hamstead Lock, 204 **P42**
Hamstead Marshall, **P42**
Handbuck Eyot, 93 **P14**
Hannington Wick **P32**
Ha'penny Bridge, 157, 158, 163 **P31**
Hardwick House, 102 **P16**
Hardwicke Ait, 102 **P16**
Harleyford Estate Ltd (Harleyford Marina), 80, 87 **P12**
Harleyford Motor YC, 89
Harpsden Ferry, 85-6
Harris (George) Racing Boats, 164
Harris Marine Windsor, 63
Harts Boats, 18, 23, 29 **P2**
Hart's Weir Footbridge, 147 **P27**
Headpile Eyot, 55 **P9**
Heale's Lock, 201 **P41**
Heath Vale Bridge (Swan Bridge), 192 **P38**
Hedsor Stream, 68
Hell's Turn, 154
Henley-on-Thames, 29, 82-5, 91 **P13**
Henley Bridge, 83, 85 **P13**
Henley RC, 83, 90 **P13**
Henley Reach, 82 **P13**
Henley Royal Regatta HQ, 83, 90 **P13**
Henley SC, 93, 107 **P14**

Henley Unit Sea Cadet Corps, 83, 90
Hennerton Backwater, 85 **P13 P14**
Henwood & Dean, 88 **P13**
Heritage Boat Charters Ltd, 23 **P1 P2**
Hermitage Bridge, 189 **P37**
Heron Island, 98 **P15A**
Heyland Marine, 75-6 **P11**
Higginson Park, 69, 72, 73 **P11**
Higgs' Lock, 201, 204 **P42**
High Bridge (Reading), 97, 98, 199, 200 **P15 P15A P40**
High Bridge (Send), 177 **P34**
Hinksey Stream, 131 **P24**
HM Coastguard (MCA), 2, 7, 211
HM Customs & Excise, 211
HMS Belfast, 13
Hobbs & Sons Ltd, 29, 89 **P13**
Hobbs' Boatyard, 83, 89 **P13**
Hobbs Marine Store, 89
Hollyhock Island, 36
Holm Island, 36 **P6**
Holme Park, 95
Holtom, Dennis R, 64
Hooper, J, 88 **P13**
Horsell, 188 **P37**
Horseshoe Bridge, 97 **P15 P15A**
Hoseasons Holidays, 29, 211
*hotels, inns and restaurants:
   listed at end of each section*
Howbery Park, 121
Hungerford, 199, 204 **P43**
Hungerford Lock **P43**
Hungerford Marsh Lock, 205 **P43**
Hungerford Wharf, 204
Hurley, 80
Hurley Farm, 80-81
Hurley Lock, 80 **P12**
Hurlingham YC, 6 **T**
Hydraulics Research Centre, 121 **P20**

Iffley Lock, 132 **P23 P24**
Iffley Weirs, 131 **P24**
Inglesham, 151, 157 **P31 P32**
Inglesham Footbridge, 157 **P31**
Inland Waterways Association, 98, 137, 211
Inland Waterways Holiday Cruises, 207
IPG Marine, 76 **P11**
Isis Bridge, 131 **P23 P24**
Isis Lock, 138 **P24 P24A**
Island Bohemian Bowls & Social Club, 100

Janousek Racing Boats, 164
Jennings' Wharf, 51
JGF Passenger Boats, 40 **P4**
John Cale Canal Cruises, 193
Johnson, Simon, International, 164
Jones, Tom, (Boatbuilders) Ltd, 61 **P8**
Jubilee River (Maidenhead,

Windsor & Eton Flood Alleviation Scheme Channel), 49, 68 **P8 P9 P10**

Kelmscot, 154-5 **P30 P31**
Kelmscot Manor, 155 **P30 P31**
Kempsford **P32**
Kennet, River, 14, 97-8, 108, 198, 199, 200 **P15 P15A P40-P43**
Kennet & Avon Canal, 29, 98, 199-210 **P15 P15A P40-P43**
Kennet & Avon Canal Trust, 199, 200, 203, 204, 207 **P41**
Kennet & Avon Canal Visitor Centre, 201
Kennet Cruises, 201, 206 **P40**
Kennet Horse Boat Co, 204, 207 **P42**
Kennet Side Footbridge, 98
Kennington Island (Rose Island), 131 **P23**
Kennington Rail Bridge, 131 **P23**
Kentwood Deeps, 101 **P16**
Kew Marina, 6
Kew Pier, 6, 9 **T**
Kiln Bridge, 189 **P37**
Kingcraft Ltd (Abingdon Boat Centre), 29, 126, 128 **P22**
Kingfisher Canoe Club, 124, 128
King's Lock, 137, 138, 142 **P25**
Kings Marine Ltd, 43 **P5**
Kings Road Bridge, 98 **P15A P40**
King's Weir, 138, 142 **P25**
Kingston, 18 **P2**
Kingston Bridge, 18 **P2**
Kingston Grammar School BC, 25
Kingston Rail Bridge, 18 **P2**
Kingston RC, 25 **P2**
Kingston Unit Sea Cadet Corps (TS *Steadfast*), 25
Kintbury, 199, 204 **P42**
Kintbury Lock, 204 **P42**
Konexion Ltd, 63 **P8**
Kris Cruisers, 29, 47-9, 61 **P7**

Laleham, 35, 45 **P5**
Laleham Camping Club, 35 **P5**
Laleham Reach, 35 **P5**
Laleham SC, 35, 44 **P5**
Lambeth Bridge **T**
Lambourn, River, 204 **P41**
Lashbrook Eyot, 93 **P14**
Launch Lock *see under Teddington Locks*
launching sites: listed at end of each section
Leach, River, 157
Leander Club, 83, 90 **P13**
Lechlade, 29, 151, 157, 158, 163 **P31**
Lechlade Hire & Marine, 162 **P31**
Lee, River (Lee Navigation), 3, 7, 10 **T**
Lensbury Motor CC, 25

Lensbury SC, 25
lifeboats, 2
lights, 172, 173
Limehouse Basin, 4, 6, 10-11 **T**
Limehouse Cut, 11 **T**
Limehouse Lock, 3-6, 10-11 **T**
Lindon Lewis Marine, 40
Lion Island **P7**
Lion Moorings, 21
Little Bedwyn Lock **P43**
Little Stoke Ferry, 116
Little Wittenham, 121 **P21**
Lock Island (Bray), 55 **P9**
lock working, 171-2
Locke (Glyn) Racing Shells, 164
Loddon, River, 93 **P14**
Logie (John) Motorboats Ltd, 51, 63 **P8**
London Bridge, 3 **T**
London Canals, Manager's Office, Paddington, 3, 11
London Coastguard, 2
London Docklands, 3
London Eye **T**
London Ring, 10, 11, 13
London River Services Ltd, 2
London River YC, 18, 25 **P2**
London Stone (site of), 36 **P6**
London Tideway Harbour Co (Dove Marina), 6
London Tourist Board, 2
London Waterway Office, 6
Long Wittenham, 122, 124 **P21**
Longridge Scout Boating Centre, 69, 77
Lower Basildon, **P17**
Lower Heyford, 29
Lower Shiplake, 93 **P14**
Lower Thames Navigation Office, 14 34 **P5**
Lulle Brook, 68 **P10**
Lynch, The, 95 **P14**

Mac Hoods & Covers, 76
Magdalen Bridge (River Cherwell), 132 **P24**
Magna Carta Barge Cruising Holidays, 75
Magna Carta Island, 37 **P7**
Magna Carta Memorial, 47 **P7**
Magpie Island, 81 **P12**
Maidenhead, 54, 58 **P9**
Maidenhead Bridge, 56, 58 **P9**
Maidenhead Rail Bridge (Sounding Arch), 54, 55-6 **P9**
Maidenhead RC, 56, 65 **P9**
Maidenhead River Services, 56, 64 **P9**
Maidenhead Steam Navigation Company, 56, 64 **P9**
Maidenhead Unit Sea Cadet Corps, 65
Maidenhead Weir (Boulters Weir), 56, 58
Maidenhead, Windsor & Eton Flood Alleviation Scheme Channel *see* Jubilee River
Mapledurham House, 101, 102 **P16**

Mapledurham Lock, 101-2 **P16**
Mapledurham Weir, 101 **P16**
marinas: listed at end of each section
Marine Equipment & Components (MEC), 103 **P14**
Marine Tek, 63
Marine Trimming Service, 43, 63 **P9**
Marine Windows Ltd, 106 **P15 P15A**
Maritime & Coastguard Agency (MCA), 2, 7, 211
Marlow, 69-73, 77, 90 **P11**
Marlow Boat Services Ltd, 56, 64 **P9**
Marlow Bridge, 70-72 **P11**
Marlow Bypass Bridge, 69 **P11**
Marlow Canoe Club, 70, 77
Marlow Lock, 70, 72 **P11**
Marlow RC, 70, 77 **P11**
Marlow SC, 72, 77
Marlow Weir, 70 **P11**
Marsh Benham, **P42**
Marsh Lock, 85 **P13**
Marston Meysey, **P32**
Martin, J, & Son, 18, 23 **P3**
Masthouse Terrace Pier **T**
Mayfly, 191, 193 **P38**
Medley Bridge, 138 **P24 P24A**
Medley SC, 138, 140, 148 **P24**
Medmenham, 81, 90 **P12**
Merlin, 191, 193 **P38**
Mid-Thames Chandlery, 105
Middle Thames Navigation Office, 14, 98
Middle Thames YC, 30, 44 **P4**
Midgham Lock, 201 **P41**
Mill Lane Boatyard, 64 **P9**
Mill Meadows, 83
Millennium Dome **T**
Millennium Footbridge **T**
Millmead Lock, 180 **P35**
Minima YC, 25 **P2**
Molesey BC, 25 **P3**
Molesey Lock, 18, 20, 21 **P3**
Monkey Island, 55 **P9**
Monkey Marsh Lock, 201 **P41**
Monument Bridge, 188 **P37**
mooring, 172
Moulsford, 115, 118 **P18**
Moulsford Railway Bridge, 115 **P18**
Mytchett, 194
Mytchett Canal Centre, 192
Mytchett Lake, 191 **P38**
Mytchett Lake Road Bridge, 191 **P38**
Mytchett Place Road Bridge, 191 **P38**

Nag's Head Island, 126 **P22**
National Federation of Sea Schools, 211
National Trust, 31, 37, 47, 68, 155, *see also* Wey & Godalming Navigation
Nauticalia Ltd, 31, 42 **P5**
Navigation & Recreation Offices, 14

navigation lights, 172, 173
navigation in the Tideway, 9-10
NE Hants Water Activities Centre, 194
Neal (Steve) Boats, 23 **P2**
Neaves Rowing Fittings, 164
Nelson Dock Pier **T**
Neville, Len, 164
New Boat Co, 105 **P15**
New Cut (Old Windsor), 47 **P7**
New Haw, 177 **P33**
New Haw Lock, 177 **P33**
New Thames Bridge, 55 **P9**
Newark Bridge, 177 **P34**
Newark Lock, 177 **P34**
Newark Millstream, 177
Newbridge, 147, 149, 151 **P27**
Newbury, 199, 200, 201, 204, 207 **P42**
Newbury Boat Company, 204, 207 **P42**
Newbury Bridge, 204 **P42**
Newbury Lock, 204 **P42**
Newbury Swing Bridge, 204-5 **P42**
Newbury Wharf, 204 **P42**
North Stoke, 116 **P19**
North Warnborough Lift Bridge, 192 **P39**
Northcroft Footbridge, 204 **P42**
Northcroft Recreation Centre, 204, 207
Northmoor, 145, 147 **P27**
Northmoor Lock, 145, 147 **P27**
Nuneham Park, 131 **P22**
Nuneham Rail Bridge, 126 **P22**

Oakhill Down Lock, 205 **P43**
Ock, River, 126
Odiham, 29, 188 **P39**
Odiham Bypass Bridge, 192 **P39**
Odiham Castle, 192 **P39**
Odney Weir Stream, 68
O'Keefe, T, 61 **P7**
Old Man's Footbridge, 153, 154 **P30**
Old Windsor Lock, 47 **P7**
Old Windsor Motor Boat School, 64
Oracle Centre, 98, 200 **P15 P15A**
Oratory School BC, 111, 118
Osney Bridge, 137 **P24 P24A**
Osney Lock, 134, 137 **P24 P24A**
Osney Marina, 137 **P24 P24A**
Osney Marina Club (Boating Section), 140
Osney Marine Engineering Co, 137, 139
Osney Rail Bridge, 134 **P24 P24A**
Otter Marine Services, 20, 24 **P3**
Oxford, 131-7, 140 **P24 P24A**
Oxford & District Sculling Centre, 128 **P22**
Oxford Brookes University BC, 118 **P19**

Oxford Canal, 14, 137, 138, 142, 199 **P24 P24A P25**
Oxford City Council, 134
Oxford City Riverside Centre, 134, 140 **P24**
Oxford Cruisers Ltd, 145, 148 **P26**
Oxford River Cruises, 139
Oxford SC, 148
Oxford Sea Scouts, 134, 140 **P24**
Oxford Unit Sea Cadet Corps, 134, 140 **P24**
Oxford University BC, 118, 128, 134 **P19 P24**
Oxford University RCs, 132, 140 **P24**
Oxfordshire Narrowboats, 29
Oxlease Swing Bridge, 201 **P41**

Paddington Arm, 10
Padworth, 29, 200, 201 **P41**
Padworth Lock, 201 **P41**
Pang, River, 111 **P17**
Pangbourne, 111, 118 **P17**
Pangbourne Canoe Club, 111
Pangbourne College BC, 111, 118
Pangbourne Meadow, 111 **P17**
Pangbourne Weir, 111, 113 **P17**
Papercourt Lock, 177 **P34**
Park Way Bridge, 204 **P42**
Parr Boat Hire, 23 **P2**
Parrott, A, 88 **P13**
Parvis Bridges (Byfleet) **P33**
Passenger Boat Association (PBA), 79
Pat's Croft Eyot, 47 **P7**
Paxmead Riverside Base, 34, 44 **P5**
Peasmarsh, 181
Penton Hook, 35 **P5**
Penton Hook Lock, 35-6 **P5 P6**
Penton Hook Marina (MDL), i, 35-6, 41, 43 **P5 P6**
Penton Hook Marine Sales, 43
Penton Hook YC, 45
Penton Service Centre Ltd, 43
Petersham Ait (Glover's Island), 16 **T P1**
Petersham Boat Services, 21 **P1**
PH Marine, 103 **P14**
Pharaoh's Island, 34 **P5**
Phillimore's Island, 95 **P14**
Phyllis Court Club (Boat Owners' Association), 83, 90 **P13**
Picketfield Lock, 199, 205
Pickletimber Rail Bridge, 204 **P42**
Pigeon Hill Ait, 55 **P9**
Pinkhill Lock, 145 **P26**
Piper's Island, 100 **P15 P15A**
Pirbright, 189 **P38**
Pirbright Bridge, 189 **P38**
Pixey Mead, 142 **P25**
Platt's Eyot, 20, 30 **P3**
Pleace, J A (Riverworks) Ltd, 40 **P4**

Poisson Deux (Poison Ducks), 81 **P12**
police, 2, 14
Pondtail New Bridge, 192 **P38 P39**
Poplar Dock Marina, 3, 6, 7
Poplar Eyot (Henley), 82, 86 **P13**
Poplar Island, 100 **P16**
Port Hampton Ltd, 20, 24 **P3**
Port of London Authority (PLA), 2, 7, 8, 9, 10
Port Meadow, 138 **P24 P25**
Potters Lock **P43**
Potter's Pool, 191 **P38**
Preston Crowmarsh **P20**
Prospect Pier **T**
public launching sites: listed at end of each section
publications, 7, 9, 168-9
Purley, 101 **P16**
Purley Cruiser Club, 107
Purley Gardens Marina, 101, 106 **P16**
Putney Bridge **T**
Pyrford, 177, 184 **P34**
Pyrford Basin, 175, 177, 184 **P34**
Pyrford Lock, 177, 183 **P34**
Pyrford Marina Ltd, 183 **P37**

Queen Elizabeth Bridge (Windsor), 51, 52 **P8**
Queen Elizabeth Pier (London) **T**
Queen Mary Reservoir, 35 **P5**
Queen's Eyot, 55 **P9**
Queen's Reach, 18 **P2**

Racecourse Yacht Basin CC, 65
Racecourse Yacht Basin (Windsor) Ltd, ii, 52, 62, 63 **P8**
Radcot, **P30**
Radcot Bridge, 154, 163 **P30**
Radcot Lock, 153-4 **P30**
Radley, **P22 P23**
Radley College BC, 131, 140 **P23**
rail stations and train services: listed at end of each section
Raven's Ait, 18 **P2**
Raven's Ait Conference & Watersport Centre, 18, 25 **P2**
Ray Mill Island, 56, 58, 68 **P9 P10**
Reading, 29, 97, 100, 107, 198, 200 **P15 P15A P40**
Reading & Leighton Park Canoe Club, 100, 107
Reading Blue Coat School BC, 95, 107
Reading Bridge (Caversham), 98-100 **P15 P15A**
Reading Marine Co, 29, 98, 200, 201, 207 **P41**
Reading Marine Services & Driveline Marine Ltd, 100, 106 **P16**

Reading RC, 100, 107 **P15 P15A**
Reading Road Bridge (Church Crookham), 192 **P39**
Reading SC, 95, 107 **P14**
Reading School, 107
Reading University BC, 100, 107 **P15 P15A**
Reading University River Study Centre **P15**
Red Line Outboard Services, 128 **P22**
Regent's Canal, 10 **T**
Register of British Shipping & Seamen, 211
Remenham, **P13**
Remenham Club, 83
Residential Boat Owners Association, 211
restaurants: listed at end of each section
Richmond, 9, 10, 14, 16 **P1**
Richmond Ait (Corporation Island), 16 **T P1**
Richmond Boat Hire, 21 **P1**
Richmond Bridge, 16 **T P1**
Richmond Canoe Club, 24 **P1**
Richmond Footbridge, 8, 10, 16 **P1**
Richmond Landing Stage, 6, 14, 21 **T P1**
Richmond Lock and Weir, 3, 8, 10, 12, 16, 17 **T P1**
Richmond Rail Bridge, 16 **T P1**
Richmond sluices, 11, 14 **T**
Richmond YC, 24 **P1**
Ridgeway Path, 115 **P18 P19**
Riff-Raff Weir, 181 **P36**
River & Rowing Museum (Henley), 83, 89, 164 **P13**
River Police, 2, 14
River Rescue Ltd, 43
River Services Ltd, 43 **P6**
River Thames Society, viii-1
River Users' Groups (RUGs), 92
Rivermead Island, 30 **P4**
Rivermead Leisure Complex, 100
Riverside Boating Co Ltd, 139
Riverside (Lechlade) Ltd, 157, 162 **P31**
Riverside Marina BC, 162
Rivertime, 64 **P9**
Rod Eyot, 83 **P13**
Romney Island, 49 **P8**
Romney Lock, 49-50, 51 **P8**
Romney Weir, 50 **P8**
Rose Island (Kennington Island), 131 **P23**
Round House, 157 **P31**
rowing, sailing and canoeing on the Thames, 171
Royal Canoe Club, 25 **P2**
Royal National Lifeboat Institution (RNLI), 2, 211 **P1**
Royal Regatta Course, 82-3 **P13**
Royal Yachting Association, 8, 211
Ruddles Pool, 52 **P8**

Rule of the River, 169-70
Runnymede Bridge, 36 **P6**
Runnymede Meadow, 37 **P6**
Runsford Hole, 115 **P18**
Rushey Lock, 153 **P29**
RYB (Marine Sales) Ltd, 63 **P8**
RYB Sports Boats Ltd, 63

safety, 7, 8, 13, 14, 173, 211
sailing, canoeing and rowing on the Thames, 171
St Catherine's Lock, 181 **P36**
St Edward's School BC, 142, 148 **P25**
St George's College BC, 44
St Helena Pier, 16 **T**
St Helen's Wharf (Abingdon), 124-6, 128
St John's Bridge, 157 **P31**
St John's (Goldsworth) Flight (Basingstoke Canal), 188-9 **P37**
St John's Lock (River Thames), 150, 157, 158, 160 **P31**
St John's (village), 188
St Katharine Haven and Pier, 3, 6 **T**
St Mary's Island, 98, 100 **P16**
St Patrick's Bridge, 95 **P14**
St Patrick's Stream, 93, 95 **P14**
Salter Brothers, 132, 134, 139, 164 **P24 P24A**
Salter's Steamers Ltd, 50, 56, 61, 69, 100, 106, 107, 139 **P6 P8 P10 P11 P13 P15 P15A P19 P22**
Sandford Lock, 131, 134 **P23**
Sashes Island, 68, 69
Saxon Moorings, 61 **P7**
Scotland Lock **P37**
Seacourt Stream, 134, 137, 142 **P25**
Send, 177, 179 **P34**
Shalford, **P36**
Shalford Rail Bridge, 181 **P36**
Sharney Brook, 153 **P29**
Sheepwash Channel, 137, 138 **P24 P24A**
Sheerwater Bridge, 188 **P37**
Sheets Heath Bridge, 189 **P37**
Sheffield Lock **P40**
Shepperton, 45 **P4**
Shepperton Lock, 31, 33, 34, 175 **P5**
Shepperton Marina Ltd, 30, 39 **P4**
Sheridan Marine (John Freeman Sales Ltd), 115, 117 **P18**
Shifford, 151 **P28**
Shifford Lock, 151 **P28**
Shillingford Bridge, 121 **P20**
Shiplake College, 95 **P14**
Shiplake College BC, 107 **P14**
Shiplake Lock, 93, 95 **P14**
Shiplake Rail Bridge, 93 **P14**
Sims (Geo.) Racing Boats, 21, 164 **P1**
SJ Marine Engineering Services, 105

Skiff Club, 25
Skiff Lock *see under* Teddington Locks
Slack, Paul, 122
Sloe Grove Islands (Bavins Gulls), 68 **P10**
Small Boat Club, 18, 25 **P2**
Sonning, 95, 102 **P14**
Sonning Bridge, 95, 102 **P14**
Sonning Lock, 95, 98, 102, 109 **P14**
Sounding Arch *see* Maidenhead Rail Bridge
South Dock Marina, 3, 6 **T**
South Stoke, 115 **P18**
Southcote, 199 **P40**
Southcote Lock, 201 **P40**
Southwark Bridge **T**
Sou'West SC, 25 **P3**
Spade Oak Brewers Fayre, 78 **P11**
Spanton's Yard, 188
Spelthorne, Borough of, 36
Sprat's Hatch Bridge, 192 **P39**
Spring Lakes, 192 **P38**
Staines, 36, 37, 45 **P6**
Staines & Egham Unit Sea Cadet Corps, 45
Staines BC, 45 **P6**
Staines Bridge, 36, 37 **P6**
Staines SC, 45 **P6**
Standlake, **P27 P28**
Stanley & Thomas Ltd, 61 **P8**
Star Marina, 43 **P5**
Steven's Eyot, 18 **P2**
Stoke Lock, 180, 184 **P35**
Stonebridge, 175 **P36**
Streatley, 114, 115 **P18**
Strodes BC, 45
sub-aqua diving, 173
Sulhampstead Lock **P40**
Summerleaze Bridge, 55 **P9**
Sumptermead Ait **P7**
Sunbury, 20, 30, 45 **P4**
Sunbury Court Island, 30 **P3 P4**
Sunburylock Ait, 30 **P4**
Sunbury Locks, 30 **P4**
Surbiton **P2**
Surrey & Hampshire Canal Cruises, 193 **P39**
Surrey & Hampshire Canal Society, 188, 192, 194, 197
Sutton, J, 164
Sutton Bridge, 124 **P22**
Sutton Pools, 124 **P22**
Sutton Racing Blades, 164
Swan Bridge (Heath Vale Bridge), 192 **P38**
Swan Island (Chillingworth Ait), 16 **T**
Swan Island Harbour, 6, 21 **P1**
Swan Lane Pier **T**
Swan (Radcot) Cruiser Club, 162 **P30**
Swancraft Ltd, 29, 128 **P20**
Swift Ditch, 124, 126 **P22**
Swinford Toll Bridge, 144-5 **P25 P26**

Tadpole Bridge, 153 **P29**
Tagg's Boatyard Ltd, 23, 29 **P3**
Taggs Island, 19 **P3**
Tamesis (Sailing) Club, 18, 25 **P2**
Tangier Island (Cutler's Ait), 50
Taplow, 56 **P9 P10**
Taplow Channel, 56
Taplow Investments
Taplow Marine Consultants, 64
Taplow Mill, 56 **P9**
taxi services: listed at end of each section
Teddington, 10-12, 18 **P1 P2**
Teddington Lock Island, 14
Teddington Locks 3, 10, 16-18, 19 **T P1 P2**
 Barge Lock, 16-17, 18
 Coffin (Skiff) Lock, 17, 18 **P2**
 Launch Lock, 16-17, 18 **P2**
Teddington Weir, 16 **P2**
Temple Island, 82 **P13**
Temple Lock, 73, 80 **P12**
Temple Marina, 80, 87 **P12**
Temple Pier (London) **T**
Tenfoot Bridge, 153 **P28 P29**
Thame, River, 121 **P20**
Thames & Kennet Marina Ltd, 95, 104, 105 **P15 P15A**
Thames & Severn Canal, 154, 157 **P31 P32**
Thames Barrier, 7, 9 **T**
Thames Barrier Navigation Centre (TBNC), 2, 8
Thames Boating Trades Association (TBTA), 29, 211-12
Thames Bridge (Oxford western bypass, Godstow), 142 **P25**
Thames Canoe Club, 25 **P3**
Thames Ditton, 29 **P3**
Thames Ditton Island, 18 **P3**
Thames Ditton Island CC, 25 **P3**
Thames Ditton Marina, 18, 22, 23 **P2**
Thames Electric Launch Co, 117
Thames Hire Cruiser Association (THCA), 28-9
Thames Lock (Weybridge), 33, 34, 175, 183 **P5 P33**
Thames Locks, 3-6, 10, 11 **T**
Thames Marine (Bray) Ltd, 63 **P9**
Thames Motor YC, 25 **P3**
Thames Navigation Service, 9
Thames Path: information at end of each section
Thames Refueller fuel barge, 6 **T**
Thames River Cruise, 106 **P15 P15A**
Thames SC, 18, 25 **P2**
Thames Steam Packet Boat Co, 61, 63 **P7**
Thames Steamers, 76
Thames Traditional Boat Society, 211

Thames Valley Boat Transport, 106 **P8**
Thames Valley CC, 107
Thames Valley Marine Services, 89 **P13**
Thames Valley Skiff Club, 44 **P4**
Thames Valley Sterndrives, 103
Thames Young Mariners' Project, 16, 24 **P1**
Thameside, 100
Thatcham, 204 **P41**
Thatcham Bridge, 204 **P41**
Theale, **P40**
Theale Swing Bridge, 201 **P40**
tides, 7-8
Tideway, 2-13
    landing, mooring & fuel points, 6
    navigation notes, 7
    transit details, 10-13
Tideway Marine, 43
Tideway YC, 24 **P1**
Tilehurst, 101 **P16**
Tim Barfield Marine, 24 **P3**
Tims, J, & Sons, 43 **P6**
Tim's Boathouse, 140 **P24**
TMP Marine Services Ltd, 20, 24 **P3**
Tough Brothers Ltd, 17, 21 **T P1 P2**
tourist information offices: listed at end of each section
Tower Bridge, 13 **T**
Tower Pier, 9 **T**
towing paths: information at end of each section
Towney Lock, 201 **P40 P41**
trail-craft launching sites: listing at end of each section
Transatlantic Marine Ltd, 42 **P42**
transport services: listed at end of each section
Trigg's Lock, 180, 183 **P34**
Trowers Bridge, 181 **P36**
Truss's Island, 36, 38 **P6**
Turk, R J, & Sons, 30, 39 **P4**
Turk Launches Ltd, 21, 23 **P2**
Twickenham, 16 **P1**
Twickenham & White Water Canoe Centre, 40
Twickenham Bridge, 16 **T P1**
Twickenham RC, 24 **P1**
Twickenham YC, 24 **P1**
Tyle Mill, 199, 207 **P40**
Tyle Mill Lock, 201 **P40**
Tyle Mill Swing Bridge, 201 **P40**

Ufton Swing Bridge, 201 **P40**
Unstead, 181 **P36**
Unstead Bridge, 181 **P36**
Unstead Lock, 181 **P36**
Unstead Weir, 181 **P14**
Upper Inglesham, **P32**
Upper Thames Motor YC, 95, 107
Upper Thames Navigation Office, 14, 137
Upper Thames RC, 83, 89 **P13**
Upper Thames SC, 69, 77 **P11**

Val Wyatt Marine Sales Ltd, 103 **P14**
Vauxhall Bridge, 12 **T**
VHF radio, 8
Vicarage Footbridge, 204 **P42**
Victoria Bridge (Windsor), 49 **P7 P8**
View Island, 98 **P15A**
Virginia Currer Marine Ltd, 63

Walbrook & Royal Canoe Club, 25 **P2**
Walker, D, Outboard Services, 105 **P15 P15A**
Wallingford, 116, 118, 121, 128 **P19**
Wallingford Bridge, 113, 116 **P19**
Wallingford RC, 118, 128 **P19**
Walliscote Moorings, 117
Walsham Lock (Walsham Flood Gates), 177, 183 **P34**
Walton, 31, 45 **P4**
Walton Bridge, 30 **P4**
Walton Bridge Cruiser Club, 44
Walton Marina, 30, 40 **P4**
Walton Marine Sales Ltd, 40
Walton RC, 44 **P4**
Walton Reach, 30 **P4**
Wandsworth Bridge **T**
Wapping Pier **T**
Wargrave, 93, 107 **P14**
Wargrave Marsh, 86 **P13 P14**
Wargrave Slip, 93
Water Eaton **P32**
Waterloo, 9 **T**
Waterloo Bridge **T**
Watlington Bridge, 98 **P15A P40**
Way, Richard (Booksellers), 164
Weedon, 29
weir permits, 21
West Berkshire Council, 204
West Byfleet, **P33**
West India Dock Entrance, 3-6, 7, 12 **T**
West Mills Swing Bridge, 204-5 **P42**
West Molesey, 30 **P3**
Westhorpe Leisure Ltd, 76
Westminster Bridge **T**
Westminster Petroleum fuel barges, 6 **T**
Westminster Pier, 9 **T**
Wey & Arun (Junction) Canal, 175, 181 **P36**
Wey CC, 184 **P35**
Wey, River, and Wey & Godalming Navigations, 14, 29, 30, 31, 34, 175-86, 188 **P33-P37**
Weybridge, 31, 34, 45, 175, 177 **P5 P33**
Weybridge Ladies' Amateur RC, 44
Weybridge Marine Ltd, 31, 42, 183 **P5 P33**
Weybridge Mariners' Club, 34, 44 **P5**
Weybridge RC, 44, 184 **P5**

Weybridge SC, 44
Weybridge Town Lock, 177 **P33**
Wharfenden Lake, 191 **P38**
Whatford, C, & Sons, 18, 23 **P3**
Wheatley's Ait, 30 **P4**
Whitchurch, 111 **P17**
Whitchurch Bridge, 111, 145 **P17**
Whitchurch Lock, 111, 120 **P17**
Whitewater Aqueduct, 192 **P39**
Widmead Lock, 204 **P41**
Wilks Water, 192 **P38**
Willmer's Moorings, 154
Willow Marina, 93, 103 **P14**
Wilson (Geo) & Sons (Boat Builders) Ltd, 30, 39 **P4**
Wilts & Berks Canal, 124
Winchfield, 192, 194
Windsor, 49-52, 65 **P8**
Windsor & District Canoe Club, 64
Windsor Belle Ltd, 93, 105 **P14**
Windsor Boys' School BC, 64
Windsor Bridge, 50-51 **P8**
Windsor Castle, 47, 49 **P8**
Windsor Marina Ltd (MDL), i, 52, 60, 63 **P8**
Windsor Marine Sales, 63 **P8**
Windsor Unit Sea Cadet Corps, 64
Windsor VIP Cruises, 61 **P7**
Windsor YC, 65
Windsorian RC, 64
Winterbrook Bridge, 116 **P19**
Wire Lock **P42 P43**
Wittenham Clumps, 121
Woking, 188, 188-9 **P37**
Woking Recreational Boating for the Handicapped, 193
Wolvercote, 142 **P25**
Wolvercote Lock, 138 **P25**
Woodham Flight, 188 **P33 P37**
Woodham Footbridge, 177 **P33**
Woodham Junction, 188 **P33 P37**
Woolhampton, **P41**
Woolhampton Swing Bridge and Lock, 201 **P41**
Woolwich, 9
Woottens Boatyard, 69, 76 **P11**
Worsfold Gates, 177-80 **P34**
Wraysbury Boathouse, 61 **P7**
Wraysbury Skiff & Punting Club, 36, 45, 64 **P6**
Wytham, 142 **P25**

Yacht Designers & Surveyors Association, 211
Yacht Harbour Association, 211